Another World is Possible

Another World Is Possible

Globalization & Anti-Capitalism

Arbeiter Ring Publishing
201E-121 Osborne Street
Winnipeg, Manitoba
Canada R3L 1Y4
www.arbeiterring.com
Cover design by Relish Design Studio
Printed in Canada by Trancontinental
Fourth printing October 2010

With assistance of the Manitoba Arts Council/Conseil des Arts du Manitoba.

We acknowledge the support of the Canada Council for our publishing program.

ARP acknowledges the financial support to our publishing activities of the Manitoba Arts Council/Conseil des Arts du Manitoba, Manitoba Culture, Heritage and Tourism, and the Government of Canada through the Canada Book Fund.

Arbeiter Ring Publishing acknowledges the support of the Province of Manitoba through the Book Publishing Tax Credit and the Book Publisher Marketing Assistance Program.

Printed on 100% recycled paper.

LIBRARY AND ARCHIVES CANADA CATALOGUING IN PUBLICATION

McNally, David
    Another world is possible : globalization and anti-capitalism / David McNally.--2nd ed.

Includes index.
ISBN 1-894037-27-8 (pbk.)

1. Protest movements. 2. Political activists. 3. Capitalism. 4. Globalization. 5. Internationalism. I. Title.

JZ1318.M32   2006   322.4   C2006-905450-9

Published in the UK by The Merlin Press
96 Monnow St.
Monmouth, Wales NP4 00A

ISBN 978 0 85036 585 6

CONTENTS

PREFACE TO THE SECOND EDITION

So much has changed since the first edition of *Another World is Possible: Globalization and Anti-Capitalism* appeared in early 2002, yet much remains the same. The first edition was filled with the optimism of the upsurge of global justice activism that began with the Zapatista rebellion of 1995 and ran through the great protests of 2001 in Quebec City and Genoa. Just as I was finishing that edition, the wave of repression and war unleashed by western governments in response to the events of September 11, 2001 was breaking. Since then, as a result of post 9/11 repression, global justice struggles have suffered in parts of the world, particularly in the North. But – and this is one of the key arguments of this book – such struggles have not ground to a halt. In fact, as I show below, they continue to surge forward in much of the Global South, most remarkably in Latin America. So, if this new edition is tempered by the aftermath of 9/11, it remains intransigent in its insistence that mass movements of the poor and the oppressed represent the one genuine source of hope in the world today.

It was my privilege to receive living proof of that during the Americas Social Forum in Caracas, Venezuela in early 2006. To join with tens of thousands of activists fighting for a world free of oppression, hunger and violence was truly inspiring. To meet activists in the *barrios* of Caracas who struggle day in and day out for freedom, justice and equality was all the reminder I needed that the fundamental message of this book – as much their message as mine – remains as timely as ever.

I owe thanks to many people, particularly to the many social justice groups that have invited me to conferences, workshops and gatherings to discuss the ideas presented here. Thanks to David Camfield for his detailed comments on the first edition, to Larry Patriquin for sharing with me his students' reactions to this book, and to Alan Sears who insisted on the importance of a new edition. Thanks too to Esyllt Jones, my editor at Arbeiter Ring Publishing, for her enduring encouragement and support throughout the course of work on each edition, and Tony Zurbrugg of Merlin Press, whose suggestions were most valuable as I set about working on this new edition. My research efforts were assisted by support from the Social Sciences and Humanities Research Council of Canada.

A book filled with hope for a better world is nurtured by many things: solidarity, friendship, laughter, comradeship in the struggle for a better world. It is also nurtured by love. Across the years in which I have worked on each edition, I have been sustained by the love of my partner, Sue Ferguson, and our three boys, Adam, Sam and Liam. All of them are constant reminders as to what life can be. In many ways, this is their book too. But once again, by way of dedication, this one is for Sam.

1. FROM THE MOUNTAINS OF CHIAPAS TO THE STREETS OF SEATTLE: THIS IS WHAT DEMOCRACY LOOKS LIKE

"A new lie is sold to us as history. The lie about the defeat of hope, the lie about the defeat of dignity, the lie about the defeat of humanity."

– *First Declaration for Humanity and Against Neoliberalism*, by the Zapatista Army of National Liberation, January 1996

When history moves – really moves, that is – it does so in great convulsive jolts. Suddenly, the glacial pace of everyday life is disrupted and world-shaking events occur. At such moments, the downtrodden may rise from their knees to claim some control over their lives and history moves onto a stage where the powerful no longer write all the lines. With such shifts in the tectonic plates of political life, an era of protest, resistance and change begins. At other times, the rich and powerful of the world gather their forces to clamp down on the oppressed of the world. Then begins an era of repression, empire and war.

Then there are moments of great tension when both trends are at work. Today, we find ourselves at precisely such a crossroads. In the mid-1990s, when the Zapatista rebellion in southern Mexico kick-started a wave of global justice movements, we entered an era of protest and resistance – one that continues today in countries like Bolivia. Then, in September 2001, another great historic shift occurred as the US government cynically manip-

1

ulated the terrible attacks on the Twin Towers in New York to launch war and occupation against Afghanistan and Iraq. We live at present at the complex intersection of these events – a growing revolt against global injustice, on the one hand, and an aggressive drive toward empire and war, on the other.

As a result, we also live at a moment filled both with hope and despair. Much of the time, particularly for those of us who live in the North, it is the latter sentiment that dominates public life. These are, after all, nasty and brutal times. War machines march across Iraq and Afghanistan. Haiti and Palestine are occupied by invading armies. Human rights are in retreat almost everywhere, most notably in Europe and North America, where governments systematically violate civil freedoms in the name of a "war on terror". Meanwhile, a variety of religious fundamentalisms – Christian, Hindu, Jewish and Muslim – promote bigotry and repression. It seems as if our world is utterly governed by intolerance and oppression.

Yet, there is something radically incomplete about such a picture. Like so many interpretations of the world in which we live, it forgets and conceals the real movements of resistance, the heroic struggles for global justice, which take place every day across this planet.

In the midst of poverty and violence, something else, something better and more hopeful, is also at work. The dream of a better world can regularly be found in the streets, marching, chanting, building blockades and challenging oppression. To be sure, we encounter it more in the Global South, particularly in Latin America, than anywhere else. But these movements, as they always do, stir hope around the globe.

Hope rises up with each revolt of the downtrodden: the 40,000 indigenous peoples who revolted against the government in Quito, Ecuador (January 15-22, 2000); the hundreds of thousands who joined the general strike against electricity privatization in Puerto Rico during the same month; the workers and indigenous peoples whose revolt overturned water privatization

2

in Cochabamba, Bolivia (April 2000); the one million South African workers who held a one-day strike against poverty (May 11, 2000); the Nigerian workers who have waged half a dozen mass strikes against fuel and transport hikes in the first five years of this century; the millions of Indian workers who struck against "globalization, privatization and liberalization" (April 2001); the thousands of students and poor people in Papua New Guinea who revolted against their government's capitulation to the International Monetary Fund (June 2001); the one million courageous workers who took strike action in Colombia during the same month to protest the "neoliberal model" imposed by the IMF; the 200,000 who stared down the riot police in Genoa, Italy (July 20-22, 2001); the millions of workers in South Africa who launched a three-day general strike against privatization (August-September 2001); the half million poor and indigenous people in Bolivia who seized control of the capitol city, La Paz, on two different occasions in 2005 and 2006 to demand public control of oil and natural gas; the million and a half students, workers and unemployed youth who successively shut down Paris and other French cities in early 2006 to force withdrawal of legislation that would have made it much easier for employers to fire young workers.

All these events, and others discussed throughout this book, are stirring evidence that, in the face of violence and brutality, oppressed people around the world are reemerging as makers of history. History, rather than merely something done to them – a nightmare from which they are trying to awake, to paraphrase James Joyce – is, at least during crucial moments, once again something made by ordinary people.

For the elites in North America and western Europe, the first great shock, the first recent recognition that they couldn't have everything their own way, came in late fall of 1999 when mass protests in Seattle shut down the Millennium Round meetings of the World Trade Organization (WTO). Having been lulled by the success of the neoliberal juggernaut and the claim, made triumphantly in 1989 by US State Department functionary Francis Fukayama, that we had arrived at the permanent victory of capitalism and "the end of history," global elites were thrown into a state of "shock and surprise" by the Seattle protests, to use the words of the Canadian Security Intelligence Service (CSIS). Despite acts of brutality by riot police wielding tear gas and pepper spray, despite mass arrests and the declaration of a state of emergency, protesters stared down the authorities. In the process they publicly humiliated the political leaders associated with the WTO and served notice that a militant new movement might be in the making.

That the ruling elites were seriously shaken was obvious from the response they created in the mainstream media. Many establishment publications immediately tried the time-worn trick of simply slandering and dismissing them. The *Wall Street Journal*, losing its upper-class cool, denounced the Seattle demonstrators as "global village idiots." Thomas Friedman of the *New York Times*, which apparently couldn't find any other news fit to print, disparaged them as "a Noah's ark of flat-earth advocates, protectionist trade unions, and yuppies looking for their 1960s fix." Not to be outdone by its heavyweight cousins, *Newsweek* rushed to condemn the Seattle protesters as losers who "have virtually no grasp of the issues."

These alarmed voices merely proved that the ruling class in the West was seriously rattled. In the face of a growing protest movement, the elite response became increasingly shrill. British Prime Minister Tony Blair exclaimed that the protesters threaten "nothing less than civilization," while Canada's Trade Minister called them "dinosaurs." Behind the knee-jerk attacks lurked deepening concerns: What if these people won't go away? What if their movement has real staying power? And what if they start to win the battle for public opinion?

At least until the terror attacks of September 11, 2001, the global justice movement was winning key battles for public opinion, even in the North. And in much of the South, it has continued to do so. The *Economist* magazine, one of Britain's major voices of ruling class opinion, suggested in early 2001 that "the anti-globalisation movement is unlikely to fade quickly. The demonstrators are ... succeeding better than might have been expected in the court of public opinion."[1] Similarly, writing about the 1999-2001 wave of global justice protests, a columnist for *Fortune* magazine bluntly opined: "the movement appears to have legs."[2] A detailed CSIS report with the intriguing title *Anti-Globalization – A Spreading Phenomenon* suggested the same.[3] And closer to the mainstream, a cover article in the Canadian weekly magazine *Maclean's* mused that we might be witnessing the emergence of a "new New Left."[4]

That's why the September 11, 2001 terror attacks in the US came as a godsend for ruling classes. Deliberately promoting fear and panic within the public, western governments introduced draconian legislation authorizing indefinite detention without charges, secret trials, random deportation, and gulag-style prisons. Dissent was criminalized, civil rights curtailed. I discuss many of the effects of these developments in chapter Five.

Without a doubt, these developments seriously damaged protest politics and ended talk of a new left, at least in the North, for the time being. But they did not stop struggles for global justice. Indeed, after something of a pause in many parts of the world, such struggles seem to be resurging today.

But before turning to latest developments, it will be helpful to return to the moment when the new wave of global justice protests first announced itself in dramatic style.

The Mountains Roared and the Zapatistas Launched a Movement

Although few realized it at the time, a new left of sorts was officially launched, in the form of the global justice movement, on January 1, 1994. That day saw two momentous events. First, the North American Free Trade Agreement (NAFTA) became law in Canada, Mexico, and the United States, inaugurating the globalization regime throughout the region.[5] Second, and more important, a hitherto-unknown guerrilla movement called the Zapatista Army of National Liberation (EZLN) occupied the town of San Cristobal de las Casas, the old colonial capital of the Mexican state of Chiapas, declaring that NAFTA was a "death sentence" for indigenous peoples and peasants throughout Mexico.

The Zapatista insurgents denounced Mexico's elites for their commitment to policies that benefit only the rich. "They don't care that we have nothing, absolutely nothing, not even a roof over our heads, no land, no work, no health care, no food or education, not the right to freely and democratically elect our political representatives, nor independence from foreigners," they exclaimed. "We declare that we will not stop fighting until the basic demands of our people have been met, by forming a government for our country that is free and democratic."

On the face of it, these were not particularly radical words – echoing, as they did, the rhetoric of the American Revolution of 1776, or the French Revolution of 1789. But in the context of the neoliberal offensive embodied in NAFTA, they were a virtual declaration of war. Rather than appeal to the elites to behave righteously, the Zapatistas called on all the oppressed – indigenous peoples, poor peasants, women, and rural and urban workers – to organize themselves for struggle. Proclaiming their solidarity with working class movements, for instance, the EZLN explained, "We, the insurgent combatants, use the colours of red and black in our uniform, symbols of the working people in their strike struggles."

And the independent workers' movements of Mexico responded in kind. On January 7, 1994, tens of thousands of urban workers demonstrated their opposition to the military siege against the EZLN in the Lacondan jungle. Five days later, workers and students marched in massive numbers to the center of Mexico City to demand an end to the government's offensive against indigenous peoples. Electrical workers, teachers, autoworkers, healthcare and transportation workers all held meetings to oppose the government's war in Chiapas, and to stop its privatization policies. By early 1995, a new independent workers' movement, the *Intersindical,* had been formed, uniting democratic unions, rank-and-file caucuses in the corrupt "official" unions, workers' cooperatives, parties of the left, and community organizations. Then, when 1,111 indigenous leaders arrived in Mexico City as part of a Zapatista march in September 1997, they were greeted by half a million cheering people, the vast majority militant workers. [6]

The Zapatistas did more than galvanize support in Mexico. Their inspiring communiqués resonated with activists around the world. To hundreds of thousands of people ground down by neoliberalism, the Zapatistas represented the renewal of hope. In the face of unbridled, triumphant, naked capitalism, the EZLN had raised up the banner of resistance. They had brazenly announced that it is the oppressed of the world who represent democracy – not the rich men (and a few women) shuttled to directors' meetings and global conferences in limousines.

At a time when capitalist globalization was declared the salvation of humankind, they dramatically challenged the orthodoxy promoted by press and politicians everywhere. They reclaimed words like freedom, democracy, and prosperity from the globalizers, and replaced them with words like crime and misery:

> During the last years, the power of money has presented a new mask over its criminal face ....

> A new world war is waged, but now against the entire humanity. As in all wars, what is being sought is a new distribution of the world.

> By the name of "globalization" they call this war which assassinates and forgets. The new distribution of the world consists in concentrating power in power and misery in misery...

> Instead of humanity, it offers us stock market indexes, instead of dignity it offers us globalization of misery.[7]

Of course, not everyone who took to the streets to protest globalizing capitalism had encountered the Zapatistas. But their spirit – the spirit of protest, resistance, freedom, and democracy – spread from one corner of the world to another. And so too did the conviction that, despite their pious phrases, what our rulers are offering us is little more than "globalization of misery."

Given the echoes of the French Revolution in Zapatista declarations, it is perhaps fitting that the next great explosion against globalization came in France. That nation, after all, is the land of European revolution, having given birth to the continent's most profound revolutionary experience of the eighteenth century, to another revolution in 1830, to two great revolutionary uprisings in February and June of 1848, to the first (short-lived) workers' government, the Paris Commune of 1871, and to the great modern revolt of students and workers in May of 1968 (which I discuss in chapter 7).

France 1995: "Take to the streets, before they throw us into them!"

While the French newspaper *Le Monde* may have exaggerated in describing the events of December 1995 as "the first revolt against globalization," it is probably fair to say that these were the first mass strikes against the globalization agenda.[8]

The wave of struggle that peaked in December 1995 had actually started with youth and student protests a year earlier. Only a matter of weeks after the Zapatistas occupied San Cristobal de las Casas, tens of thousands of young people throughout France – high school and university students, young workers and unemployed – launched school strikes and mass demonstrations against the government's plans to lower the minimum wage for those under twenty-five. Banners at demonstrations urged students to "Take to the streets, before they throw us into them!" These militant youth mobilizations forced the government to backtrack. But the most impressive actions were yet to come.

The heat began to rise in early October 1995 with an enormous strike by five million public sector workers against legislation to freeze their wages. This was followed by a nation-wide strike by university students protesting overcrowded classrooms and libraries, deteriorating facilities, and poor job prospects for graduates. The radically democratic culture of the student strikes was a clear sign that something was changing. Unlike bureaucratic mass actions where students or workers protest for a day or two and then go back to work and school when instructed to do so, the student strikes were highly participatory. More than sixty campuses were occupied by student protesters, some of whom took their university presidents hostage. Student strikers held regular general assemblies which democratically decided upon tactics; the assemblies also elected delegates to a national student strike coordinating committee. At the university in Toulouse as many as two thousand activists participated in daily meetings. Street demonstrations were held every day, sometimes on a rotating around-the-clock basis, alongside occasional bouts of street-fighting with police.[9]

In late November, the students were joined by workers – millions of them. This escalation of the protest movement owed much to the government's introduction of a major neoliberal reform program, known as the Juppé Plan, after the prime minister who introduced it, Alain Juppé. The prime minister's plan involved $12 billion in cuts to healthcare, family allowances, and pensions; privatization of France Telecom and the public railway company, SNCF; closure of whole sections of the rail system (and layoffs of thousands of workers); a two percent hike in the regressive value-added sales tax.

To protest the program, two major union federations called for twenty four-hour strikes on November 24 and 28. But when one million workers struck on the 24th, the railworkers decided to stay out on indefinite strike action. They also persuaded other workers to join them. Postal and transit workers soon took up their call. And the movement kept growing. Nurses, teachers, sanitation workers, telephone operators, airport maintenance staff, auto workers, and many others joined the action. Virtually the whole of the public sector was paralyzed.

Despite disruption of public services, the strikers received huge support: a remarkable two-thirds of people polled favoured a general strike to defeat the Juppé plan. Soon, students and workers began to organize together, planning common marches and protest actions. Things peaked in early December with two-and-a-half million workers on strike and an estimated two million people marching in three hundred demonstrations across the country. In a wonderful spirit of solidarity, a rally of 100,000 in Marseilles was led by unemployed workers.

At the mass demonstrations, students mixed with workers, and street performers turned out to add a festive air to the events. Homeless people and immigrant workers played central roles in the burgeoning movement. The very character of the working class was being transformed in the process. As one commentator put it:

> There were young and old workers, black workers, women workers, white and "grey" collar workers, university and college-educated workers, and so on. There they all were in the streets of every city, town, and village of France, headed up by the railworkers, chanting, "tous ensemble, tous ensemble!" ("everyone together, everyone together!").[10]

As the movement grew and the radicalization deepened, solidarity blossomed, transforming people's sense of themselves. At night, striking Paris bus drivers took out buses to drive homeless people to shelters, their vehicles adorned with banners exclaiming, "Bus drivers in solidarity with the most dispossessed layers of the population."

The women's movement too came back to life, mobilizing 40,000 people – its largest action in years – on November 25 in an action dedicated, among other things, to the defense of abortion rights.

The amazing outpouring of solidarity took even the participants by surprise. They began to experience themselves as social beings, members of a real human community, and not as simply atomized, passive consumers of the products of capitalism. As one sociologist observed: "people are surprised to find themselves expressing a spontaneous solidarity in the streets and are reminded that they belong to a social entity whose only objective is not the production and consumption of merchandise."[11]

Faced with such formidable opposition, Juppé blinked, reversing cuts to the rail system and pledging more funds for universities. At that moment, rather than push to complete victory by toppling the government and the whole of its program, the trade union officials and some student leaders agreed to a compromise and managed to de-escalate the struggle. While much more could have been achieved, the December 1995 events in France nonetheless indicated the tremendous power of grassroots working class struggle involving women, students, immigrant workers and homeless people. The French events also served notice that anti-globalization protests would not be confined to countries of the South. Instead, resistance would henceforth also occur at the very centers of global capitalism – indeed, as we shall see, the struggles in France were far from over. But few guessed that the United States would soon get a taste of the action.

Before the Shock of Seattle: Meltdown and Revolt in East Asia

Before the surprise of the Battle in Seattle, the planet's rulers had to absorb an equally great shock: a massive economic collapse in their favourite economies, the East Asian "tigers" and "dragons."[12] For years IMF and World Bank officials had been telling everyone who would listen that East Asia was living proof of their successful formula for economic growth: low wages (ably assisted by restrictions on union freedoms); high levels of foreign investment; low taxes; and minimal spending on public services.

So taken were the global elite by developments in countries like South Korea, Thailand, Indonesia, the Philippines, Malaysia and Taiwan that the World Bank issued a report in 1993 with the title *The Asian Miracle*. The economic model applied in East Asia was touted as the cure to all that ailed the world's poor.

The ostensible miracle soon stood exposed as a fraud. With a calamitous economic collapse sweeping through one East Asian economy after another in the course of 1997-98, the World Bank prepared a new report: *Rethinking Asia's Miracle*. And small wonder: the East Asian meltdown was one of the most devastating experienced anywhere since the Great Depression of the 1930s.

The crisis began in July 1997 when global investors – the very people the World Bank and IMF lauded as the keys to prosperity – pulled the plug on Thailand. Growing sour on the country's prospects, especially the foreign debt encouraged by the World Bank and IMF, banks and investment agencies began withdrawing their funds. Overnight the Thai currency, the baht, collapsed. Economists then rushed to reassure investors that Indonesia was not vulnerable to such a collapse. They should have saved their breath. So severe was the ensuing Indonesian meltdown that 260 of the 282 companies on the country's stock exchange disintegrated.

South Korea's collapse followed within weeks. At its peak, ten thousand Korean workers were laid off each day – 300,000 per month. As the crisis reverberated throughout the region, $600 billion (US) was wiped off the balance sheets of East Asia's stock markets.

In a matter of a few months, miracle had turned to nightmare. Like any addict, countries hooked on foreign investment learned the pain of forced withdrawal. Whereas Indonesia, Korea, Malaysia, Thailand and the Philippines had received an inflow of $95 billion in 1996, a year later they experienced a capital outflow of $20 billion – a reversal of $115 billion in the space of twelve months. Suddenly, the globalization model had been turned upside down. As easily as foreign capital flows could boost economies, so could it devastate them. And, as always in such situations, it was the poor who suffered the most.

In the course of five months, between August and December 1997, wages in South Korea were cut in half – for those lucky enough still to have jobs. In Thailand, the cost of rice and flour jumped by 47 per cent in a single month, signaling calamity for the poor. Meanwhile, Indonesia saw the annual per capita income collapse from $1,200 (US) to $300 (US). In Surabaya, the country's largest industrial city, the minimum wage fell from $2 a day to 30 cents. So severe was the ensuing poverty that many mothers, no longer able to buy milk, began feeding their babies with tea.

Alongside suffering and deprivation, however, grew anger and resistance. In Indonesia, it took fewer than six months for anger over economic hardship to push hatred for the dictatorship of Suharto to a point of no return. When the dictatorship shot and killed six student protesters on May 12, 1998, the student movement merely regrouped. Six days later, it took to the streets of Jakarta, spurring the city's poor and students around the country into action. Seizing the parliament building, students danced on the roof chanting "Bring Suharto down!"

The beleaguered dictator returned, but it was too late. With food riots sweeping the islands that make up Indonesia and students in open revolt, Suharto gave up power on May 21. A pro-western dictatorship that had come to power in 1965 by drowning half a million people in blood was knocked over like a bowling pin. The Asian crisis had brought global elites their first casualty. All eyes turned next to South Korea, the most industrialized of the East Asian economies, and one where workers had a decade-long experience of militant resistance.

In the late 1980s, a tremendous working class upheaval swept South Korea. Union membership doubled from one to two million in the course of a huge strike wave between 1986 and 1990. Sit-down strikes – where strikers occupy their places of work – became increasingly widespread. In the industrial cities of Masan and Changwon a full-fledged workers' revolt took place in 1987-88 when company assaults on a group of striking women provoked an outpouring of solidarity strikes. In the course of these strikes, thirty new independent unions joined together. So impressive was the solidarity and so powerful the militancy that radical workers at the time described Masan-Chawong as a "liberated zone." Following the formation of the (illegal) Korean Confederation of Trade Unions (KCTU) in November 1995, the largest-ever strikes erupted. The first round came in December 1996. That was followed, in January 1997, by a month of mass strikes involving 630,000 workers protesting new labor law restrictions and legislative changes that would allow for mass layoffs. In a mere decade, the South Korean working class had built one of the most combative union movements in the world.

This new workers' movement faced its biggest challenge with the economic meltdown of 1997-98. As a condition of its $57 billion aid package to "alleviate" the crisis, the IMF insisted that the South Korean government implement massive job cuts. Given that workers had recently fought a general strike against layoffs, the government tread softly, convening a tripartite commission of business, government and labour leaders to negotiate an agreement. Representatives of the KCTU were invited, along with those of the more moderate Federation of Korean Trade Unions. In early 1998, to the dismay of union activists, the leaders of the KCTU signed an accord which, in exchange for modest concessions, accepted mass layoffs and all the basic terms of the IMF bail-out. Within days, hundreds of angry KCTU delegates rebelled, voting down the agreement, removing the leaders who had signed the deal, and setting the date for a nation-wide general strike. A few days later, however, the strike call was reversed as militants realized they did not have adequate support for the action.

Nevertheless, resistance to the IMF conditions continued to mount. On May 27 and 28, 1998, about 120,000 workers took strike action against layoffs. On the heels of that mass strike, workers at Kia Motors forced concessions from management after waging a three-week series of strikes against wage cuts. Throughout 1999, 2000, and 2001, militant resistance to layoffs, privatization and wage-cuts continued. Shipyard workers, bank clerks, subway workers, autoworkers at Daewoo Motors, and hotel workers, particularly the courageous employees of the luxurious Lotte Hotel in Seoul, fought employers, government, and thousands of riot police. Many of these strikes involved workplace occupations and pitched battles with riot police. Then in 2004 came an inspiring campaign of organization and resistance by migrant workers in Korea. (In order not to get ahead of our story, I'll return to look more at those struggles in chapter 6.)

Mourning the loss of a dictator and with a wary eye on workers' resistance to the IMF in Korea, western elites were already having trouble sleeping. Then resistance exploded right in their faces – in the tear-gas filled streets of Seattle.

Seattle: "The spirit that makes revolution possible"

To make history – to change the actual course of world events – is intoxicating, inspiring and life-transforming. So it was for those in the streets of Seattle on Tuesday, November 30 and Wednesday, December 1, 1999. Capturing a crucial dimension of the experience, activist Vicki Larson reported, "The spirit that makes revolution possible was strong on the streets of Seattle."[13] Similarly affected by the moment, Luis Hernandez Navarro proclaimed, "The new century was born on November 30, 1999 with the revolt of the globalized in Seattle, Washington."[14]

Seattle transformed the political climate in the centers of capitalism. "The terms of the free trade debate have been forever changed," wrote a reporter for the *Seattle Times*. "No amount of tear gas or police harassment of demonstrators after the fact changed the bottom line. For one day a ragtag army of nonviolent global citizens spoke – and the world listened." Indeed they did. In workplaces and schools, in *barrios* and pubs, millions of conversations took place about what had transpired in the streets of Seattle. People with only a foggy notion of the World Trade Organization (WTO) understood the elementary fact that presidents, prime ministers and their entourages had been challenged and shut down by young people and their labour and community supporters.

In an important sense, the editors of *In These Times* were right when they opined that "the real story of Seattle was the youth."[15] Organized into small, democratic affinity groups coordinated through the Direct Action Network, thousands of activists chose to put their bodies in the way of the WTO delegates and their convention centre. They danced, sang, and chanted in the streets, locked themselves down and withstood tear gas, pepper spray, police truncheons, and over 500 arrests – all to make sure people throughout the world heard their message. And hear it they did.

In the pre-dawn hours of Tuesday, November 30, around two thousand direct action protesters hit the streets, staking out all the main intersections that approached the Convention Center where WTO delegates were due to converge. For the next five or six hours their numbers would steadily grow. At 10:00 a.m. the police launched their first major attack with tear gas and rubber bullets, followed by baton bashes to heads and bodies. Demonstrators had their eyes washed out, and their wounds bandaged, but they would not be moved. Four hours later, all the intersections had been held. "By darkness on Tuesday," recorded one observer, "the 2,000 or so street warriors had won the day."[16]

It was a tremendous victory. But it was also a tainted one – tainted by the knowledge that forty thousand labour demonstrators had been led away from the protest zone by their leaders – a tactic that would be repeated a year and a half later in Québec City. A few thousand union activists did break away to join the young activists in the streets, but a glorious opportunity to put up to fifty thousand people on the streets outside the convention centre was lost, as was the opportunity to build greater unity and solidarity between organized workers and a diverse group of environmentalists, students, anarchists and socialists committed to direct action against corporate rule.

Not everything about the labour mobilization was a lost cause, however. To begin with, getting more than forty thousand union activists out for the event was a major achievement. The union crowd was also highly diverse, with significant numbers of women and workers of colour. In addition, one labour leader's speech even went so far as to identify capitalism as the problem: "The system turns everything into a commodity, a rain forest in Brazil, a library in Philadelphia, a hospital in Alberta. We have to name that system: It is corporate capitalism," one union leader told the rally.

The labour rally also had an internationalist flavour, with guests and speakers from the Dominican Republic, Barbados, El Salvador, Brazil, Mexico, South Africa, India, Malaysia and China. That's not to say nationalist protectionism of the "save American jobs" variety was not in evidence. It was, as were some US flags. But, the atmosphere of the event was much more internationalist than any substantial US labour gathering in many years. Notwithstanding these achievements, the decision of labour leaders to divert their demonstration from the protest zone was a terrible betrayal of those resisting in the streets.

Still, more than one thousand activists took to the streets the next day, Wednesday, December 1. As chants of "Whose streets? Our streets!" and "This is what democracy looks like!" echoed throughout downtown Seattle, it was clear that police repression had failed to break the movement.

Meanwhile, WTO delegates from the poorer countries of the South, perhaps sensing that activists in the street would not be bullied, became more assertive, denouncing the backroom manipulations of the richest nations. In particular, these delegates attacked the process by which they were denied access to the "Green Room" meeting where the WTO Secretariat held informal discussion among the richest nations. As the protests in the streets became more defiant, so the attacks on lack of transparency and accountability inside the conference grew louder. With their public relations exercise blowing up in their faces, then-US president Bill Clinton and his advisers decided to cut their losses and send everyone home. As news leaked out that the WTO talks had been canceled, euphoric celebrations began in the streets.

Despite a barrage of media condemnation denouncing the protesters and associating them with "violence" – facilitated by repeated images of "the same broken window taken from various angles," as one newspaper columnist put it – a majority of Americans polled indicated that they sympathized with the rebels in Seattle.[17] The effect of young people, students, and workers taking the streets, as well as the headlines, away from the rich and powerful was electrifying. The demonstrators had succeeded in dramatically redefining the "free trade" debate by putting issues like the environment, jobs and social programs on the agenda. But they had done more than that. They had established – for every person angered by what corporate rule has done to health care, communities, schools, jobs, the environment, the plight of the poor and the homeless – that resistance is possible. And not just token resistance – but effective, coordinated resistance that can upset the plans of the world's rulers.

After Seattle, radical protest became a credible strategy even in the world's dominant nation. A whole new way of doing politics was now on the agenda. For, if one thing stood out about the victory of the Seattle resisters, it was that they achieved it through militant direct action. A perceptive commentator summed it up nicely right after the events:

> In the annals of popular protest in America, these have been shining hours, achieved entirely outside the conventional arena of orderly protest and white-paper activism and the timid bleats of the professional leadership of big labour and environmentalism. This truly was an insurgency from below ...[18]

And that is what unites the Seattle protesters, the Zapatistas, the French students and workers of December 1995, the Indonesian students who toppled Suharto and the South Korean workers waging mass strikes – they are all insurgents from below. More than anything else, this is the key to the new radical movements that have emerged since the Zapatistas rode out of the hills of Chiapas. A new movement based on insurgency from below is emerging, and with it a new model of radical democracy is taking root.

As the Zapatistas' Sub-Commandante Marcos put it in his March 11, 2001 speech in Mexico City:

> We are not those who, foolishly, hope that from above will come the justice that can only come from below, the freedom that can only be won with all, the democracy which is struggled for at all levels and all the time.

After September 11, 2001: Repression, War, Resistance

Exactly seven months after Marcos' speech, the dynamics of world politics shifted once more, this time to the benefit of ruling classes. The terror attacks on the World Trade Center and the Pentagon created a golden opportunity for global elites to squelch political dissent. After several years during which public opinion was moving into closer synch with global justice protesters, governments were able to use fear, lies and patriotism to create a "law and order" mentality that discredited protest movements and justified escalating levels of police repression. Unions and non-governmental organizations (NGOs) that had once been prepared to flirt with street protests, quickly abandoned youth activists. In North America and most of Europe, demonstrations grew smaller and state repression intensified. The global justice movement in the North went into marked decline.

But the post-9/11 neoliberal offensive, led by the government of George W. Bush in Washington, did not have everything its way. In fact, Bush's belligerent imperial agenda soon reignited opposition movements.

First, disgusted by the Bush administration's campaign of lies and deception about Iraq's alleged "weapons of mass destruction" and ostensible links to al-Qaeda, and horrified by the impending destruction of Iraq, millions of people rallied to worldwide protests. On February 15, 2003, in the build-up to war, between 15 and 30 million people took to the streets in 800 cities around the world. February 15 represents the largest day of anti-war protests in world history. Indeed, the demonstration of three million people in Rome is listed in the *Guinness Book of World Records* as the biggest anti-war rally ever. These events clearly indicated that lies and repression had not stifled the spirit of resistance and that millions of people remained determined in their opposition to the globalization of poverty and war.

The second great problem for global rulers has been the continuing havoc that the globalization wreaks on the lives of the world's poor. Unwilling to accept condemnation to lifetimes of hardship and suffering, millions of people have continued to fight back. And in Latin America, huge popular movements have periodically broken through the neoliberal agenda, toppling governments and rolling back privatization policies. In countries like Argentina, Venezuela and Bolivia, mass movements are rejecting neoliberal globalization and searching for alternatives to capitalism. During the World Social Forum of the Americas in Caracas in early 2006, which I was fortunate to attend, thousands of participants engaged in spirited discussions over the idea of "a socialism for the twenty-first century" that would provide an alternative to war and exploitation.

So, even if global justice movements have been damaged in much of the North, political and street level opposition to globalization, empire and war have continued to grow in much of the world. Sooner or later, these struggles may reignite protest movements in the North, as have struggles in countries like Cuba, Vietnam and South Africa in the past. The winds of change blowing from the South may yet sweep another storm of protest into the North.

From Bolivia to France: The Resistance That Will Not Die

The early months of 2006 saw two great victories for popular movements – proving decisively that global resistance, however shaken by repression, remains unbroken.

In January of the year, the battle of the people of Cochabamba to de-privatize their water supply won a crucial legal victory, when Bechtel Corporation dropped its suit before the World Bank. After a popular uprising in 2000 (which I discuss in chapter 6) had forced Bolivia's government to tear up a water privatization contract, Bechtel had sued, demanding $50 million in damages from the Bolivian people. But the workers, indigenous peoples and urban poor of Bolivia would not yield. Mass protests continued year after year, expanding their demands to include public ownership of natural gas. Then, on December 18, 2005, Evo Morales of the Movement Toward Socialism was elected president, becoming the first indigenous person elected as head of state anywhere in the Americas. Recognizing that the whole political climate in the country had shifted against multinational capital, Bechtel dropped its legal suit, an extraordinary action from a $17 billion company with close ties to the Bush administration in Washington.

None of this, including Morales' election, would have been possible without absolutely heroic levels of self-mobilization by the lower orders in Bolivia. Claudia Lopez, an organizer for the Cochabamba chapter of the Federation of Factory Workers of Bolivia, explains:

> ... the happiness that Bolivia is experiencing ... is nothing less than the result of a tense struggle of resistance first, followed by the offensive of that gigantic conglomeration of men and women, young and old,

21

who embodied the Water War of 2000. This process, begun in 2000 has put a human fence of struggle around the plunder of our common goods such as water, hydrocarbons, by expelling transnationals, rejecting the overwhelming advance of transnational capital, an d also rejecting the impositions of financial organizations such as the World Bank, the IMF and the WTO.

And here too, insurgency from below has been decisive:

We have shut out and defeated the claims to perpetual power of those interests throughout these heroic past six years by means of: road blockages, closing off the city, uprisings and insurrections and marches, land occupations, closing the valves of the gas pipelines, occupation of oil wells. It has been six years filled with struggles, bravery, and indignation turned into public protest.[19]

Three months after Bechtel dropped its case in the face of popular resistance, youth, students and workers scored a major victory against neoliberalism in France. For more than a decade, the French government's efforts to implement an aggressive globalization agenda encountered powerful opposition. Student protests and mass strikes defeated the Juppé plan in 1995, as we have seen. Nevertheless, despite widespread protest, in 2003 the French government managed to cut social entitlements by raising the retirement age and inflicting major cuts to health care. Then, in early 2006, it introduced a Youth Labour Contract scheme (known as CPE by its French initials) which gave employers the power to fire workers under 26 years of age without having to give cause.

Not surprisingly, students launched a series of protests, beginning with a day of action on February 7, which drew 400,000 into the streets. A month later, one million people filled the streets. A million and a half turned out on March 18. Then the numbers soared – as three million joined the demonstrations on March

22

28, while even more did so on April 4. Especially ominous for the government, hundreds of thousands of workers began taking strike action in concert with the protests.

But it wasn't only the size of the demonstrations that shook the government. It was also the militant forms of self-organization that did so. More than three-quarters of the 88 universities in France were shut down by student strikes. Many were occupied, as student assemblies of thousands deliberated over how to advance the struggle, and students organized "open university" programs on everything from globalization to sexual liberation and the conditions of women workers. In the middle of March, huge numbers of high school students joined the movement. Hundreds of schools were closed by student strikes, including half the high schools in Paris. Notable here were schools in communities with large concentrations of immigrants. The government had been rocked by powerful protests against racism and unemployment in November 2005. Once again, students from these communities took up the battle in March and April.

As in every genuine mass struggle, there was a great and exciting ferment of ideas and self-organization. At many universities and some high schools, student assemblies chose commissions to write leaflets, connect with trade unions, organize film showings and stage political debates. New structures of democratic discussion and action were created, among them a Student Coordination, to which students from every striking university elected delegates, and which met every weekend at a different school.

Then, at the end of March, workers began to move, joining the demonstrations and launching protest strikes. Vital links between students and workers were forged, the likes of which had not been seen for decades.

By early April, it was clear that the CPE would have to go. Opinion polls revealed that seventy per cent of the French people – and 80 per cent of the youth – opposed the plan. Opposition to globalization and neoliberalism had grown to such heights that the *Economist* magazine lamented at the end of March that only 36 per cent of the French people though the "free market" was the best conceivable economic system.

With workers on strike, universities and high schools occupied, and the streets overflowing with protesters, the French government gave way, withdrawing the CPE. Another crucial battle against globalization had been won.

Searching for a Political Model

Among the greatest strengths of the new movements is their reliance on the self-activity and self-mobilization of thousands upon thousands of participants. The emphases on direct action, on participatory democracy (often organized through mass assemblies), and on the festive and celebratory side of political protest distinguish this as a truly popular, not elitist, movement. And, as I will discuss in later chapters, this is especially true in some of the most oppressed regions of the world where daring and innovative politics – mass strikes and uprisings, land occupations and new popular organizations – are fostering opposition to globalizing capitalism. This is a movement, in other worlds, in which the oppressed of the South, as it is often described, are playing a leading role.

Moreover, as Naomi Klein has pointed out, one of the things that makes this movement a radical one is that, rather than just opposing an individual corporation or institution, it is developing a "systemic critique" – one that locates the problem in a whole system of social life.[20] It follows from such a critique that meaningful social change will require much more than changing governments or heads of state. For, if it is the system that is rotten, then only a sweeping transformation that uproots the very structures of oppression can offer hope of an entirely different form of life.

It is still early days in this struggle. As with all great social movements, activists are learning, debating and deepening their analysis as they fight to change the world. They are coming up against serious obstacles – betrayals by governments that campaign against neoliberalism then do its dirty work, massive police repression, and, particularly in the North, lack of solidarity from trade unions. And they are encountering major debates and questions they have yet to resolve. Can organized labour, or its rank-and-file members, become a genuine part of a radical movement to change society? Are there alternatives to organizing social and economic life through the market? Is the system we seek to uproot globalization, neo-liberalism, capitalism, or all of these? If we oppose capitalism, what sense do we make of those socialisms that have failed to advance human rights and participatory democracy? Where do racism and patriarchy fit into global capitalism? Is it possible to build a mass movement for global justice in the rich countries of the world?

In the chapters that follow, I hope to suggest some ways of thinking about these and other questions. While not for a moment pretending to have all the answers, I am convinced there are important resources from the history of anti-capitalist struggles that can aid us in tackling these problems. Any such effort must start, of course, with the beast we seek to vanquish. So, I propose to begin with that buzzword of our era, "globalization." If we can unpack what it's about, we will be better equipped to figure out what it will take to build another world.

Notes

1 "Mayhem in May," *The Economist*, April 28, 2001.
2 Jerry Useem, "There's Something Happening Here," *Fortune*, May 15, 2000.
3 CSIS, *Anti-Globalization – A Spreading Phenomenon*, August 22, 2000.
4 Brian D. Johnson, "Naomi and the Brand-New Left," *Maclean's*, March 12, 2001.
5 Of course, globalization did not begin with NAFTA. In using the term "globalization regime" I refer to a set of legally enforceable agreements designed to "lock in" the neoliberal policies associated with "globalization."
6 Much of the information in this paragraph is drawn from the excellent article by Richard Roman and Edur Velasco Arregui, "Worker Insurgency, Rural Revolt, and the Crisis of the Mexican Regime" in *Rising from the Ashes? Labor in the Age of "Global" Capitalism*, eds. Ellen Meiksins Wood, Peter Meiksins and Michael Yates (New York: Monthly Review Press, 1998).

7 The Zapatistas, *Zapatista Encuentro: Documents from the 1996 Encounter for Humanity and Against Neoliberalism* (New York: Seven Stories Press, 1998), pp. 11-13.

8 Erik Izraelwicz, "La premiere revolte contre la mondialisation," *Le Monde*, December 7, 1995.

9 My account of the student protests and the mass strikes is indebted particularly to two accounts: Raghu Krishnan, "December 1995: 'The First Revolt Against Globalization'," *Monthly Review*, v. 48 (December 1996), and Brett Cemer, "France: Students and Workers Fight Back," *New Socialist*, n. 1 (January-February 1996).

10 Krishnan, p. 6.

11 Bertrans Leclair, "Roger Callois, la greve et les totems," *Politis*, December 14, 1995.

12 Much of the analysis I offer here draws on my article "Globalization on Trial: Crisis and Class Struggle in East Asia," *Monthly Review*, v. 50, September 1998, reprinted in Rising from the Ashes?

13 Vicki Larson, "Notes from the Editors," *Monthly Review*, v. 51, n. 8 (January 2000), p. 64.

14 Luis Hernandez Navarro, "The Revolt of the Globalized" in *Globalize This! The Battle Against the World Trade Organization and Corporate Rule*, eds. Kevin Danaher and Roger Burbach (Monroe, Maine: Common Courage Press, 2000), p. 41.

15 Craig Araron, "The Kids are All Right," *In These Times*, January 10, 2000.

16 Jeffrey St. Clair, "Seattle Diary," *New Left Review* 238 (November/December 1999), p. 89.

17 For a good overview of the cynical mainstream media coverage see Seth Ackerman, "Prattle in Seattle: Media Coverage Misrepresented Protests" in *Globalize This!*, pp. 59-66. John Machlachlan Gray's observation on the repeated use of the image of one broken window can be found in his article "Will the real Tim Leslie please stand up?" *Globe and Mail*, July 4, 2001.

18 St. Clair, p. 96.

19 Claudia Lopez, "Cochabamba's Water War: The Start of Other Struggles," May 1, 2006, posted at www.upsidedownworld.org

20 Naomi Klein, *No Logo: Taking Aim at the Brand Bullies* (Toronto: Vintage Canada, 2000), p. 338.

GLOBALIZATION:
IT'S NOT ABOUT FREE TRADE

"These deals aren't about trade. They're about the right
of these guys to do business the way they want, wherever they want."

– Eugene Whelan, Canada's former Agriculture Minister

A favorite pastime of the globalizers has been to label their opponents "anti-trade." *US News and World* Report, for instance,
mocked the Seattle protesters with the headline "Hell No, We
Won't Trade." In the same vein, a *Washington Post* article began
with the sentence, "A guerrilla army of anti-trade activists took
control of downtown Seattle today." And a business writer for the
Globe and Mail ridiculed "anti-free trade" critics who drink coffee, or eat fresh vegetables in the winter, since without trade they
would not be able to enjoy these things in Canada.

Having seized on trade as the issue, pro-globalization types
often shift into near-hysterical overdrive. Suggesting that humanity has progressed by "trading" and "sharing" goods and knowledge, they claim their anti-trade opponents will destroy human
culture and civilization. WTO head Michael Moore, for instance,
pronounced that the Seattle demonstrators represented "an um-
brella for everything that is wrong with the twenty-first century."

Yet, the more intelligent of the globalizers must know that
these arguments are bogus. After all, global justice activists do
not oppose the exchange of goods and services around the world.
They do not object to goods crossing national borders. What they

27

criticize is the framework in which global production and trade takes place: the way it empowers a few and exploits so many.

As all but the most ignorant of neoliberal pundits surely know, corporate globalization and the economic agreements designed to entrench it have little to do with trade. To prove this point, let's look at some of the main myths globalization advocates have developed.

The Myth of Globalized World Trade

Among the main claims made by globalization advocates are that recent decades have seen an unprecedented rise in the significance of world trade, and that, as a result, we are moving toward a much more open world. Neither of these claims is supported by the evidence.

From its beginnings, in the sixteenth and seventeenth centuries, capitalism has sought to profit from the exploitation of the peoples and natural resources around the globe. Enormous world movements of cotton, sugar, tobacco – and, most unconscionable, of enslaved Africans – fueled the accumulation of capitalist wealth. The colonization of huge areas of the globe – Ireland, India, the aboriginal lands of North and South America, China, much of Africa – were all central aspects of capitalist development. In chapters 3, 4 and 5, I will look at the dimensions of all this. For the moment, I merely want to underline the fact that capitalism has always been global in orientation.

Over 150 years ago, Karl Marx highlighted this in his dissection of modern capitalism. Of the emerging capitalist class, or bourgeoisie, and its new economic system, he wrote:

> The discovery of America, the rounding of the Cape, opened up fresh ground for the rising bourgeoisie. The East Indian and Chinese markets, the colonization of America, trade with the colonies ... gave to commerce, to navigation, to industry, an impulse never before known ...

> The bourgeoisie has through its exploitation of the world market given a cosmopolitan character to production and consumption in every country... All old-established national industries have been destroyed or are daily being destroyed ... by industries that no longer work up indigenous raw material, but raw material drawn from the remotest zones; industries whose products are consumed, not only at home, but in every corner of the globe.

> The bourgeoisie ... compels all nations, on pain of extinction, to adopt the bourgeois mode of production; it compels them to adopt what it calls civilization into their midst, i.e. to become bourgeois themselves. In one word, it creates a world after its own image.[1]

These passages are even more pertinent today. And they ought to disabuse a fair-minded reader of the notion that the development of world markets and world trade are new phenomena. In fact, the evidence strongly suggests that, in terms of trade, the world capitalist economy nearly a century ago was probably more internationalized than the global economy today.[2]

Economists customarily gauge the degree to which economies are globalized by measuring their imports and exports – the volume of goods sold outside the country in which they are produced (which is known as merchandise trade) – as a proportion of all national production (normally measured as gross domestic product, or GDP). A largely self-sufficient economy receives few imports and sends out few exports and thus has a low ratio of merchandise trade to GDP. In an economy highly integrated into world markets, on the other hand, imports and exports will comprise a considerable proportion of overall GDP. And economies becoming more globalized – our central concern for the moment – will show a rising ratio of merchandise trade to GDP. With these considerations in mind, let's consult the following Table which looks at major countries at a 60-year interval, taking 1913, the year before the disruption of the First World War, as the starting point.

Table 2.1 – Ratio of merchandise trade (imports and exports) to GDP at current prices

	1913	1973
United Kingdom	44.7	9.3
France	35.4	29.0
Germany	35.1	35.2
United States	11.2	10.5
Japan	31.4	18.3
Netherlands	103.6	80.1

Source: A. Maddison, "Growth and Slowdown in Advanced Capitalist Economies." [3]

These data indicate that the world's major economies did not become more internationalized over the course of the six decades following the First World War. In fact, by this measure, all except Germany became less globalized during this period. It's true that after about 1950, following the dislocation of the Great Depression and the Second World War, world trade expanded as a share of global production. But, as the Table above shows, as late as 1973, most major economies were less internationalized than they had been 60 years earlier. Since 1973, there has been a partial trend toward increased reliance on world trade – but not for the economically developed nations. Instead, it is countries in East Asia and parts of Latin America that have become more integrated into global trading systems.

In fact, economist John Weeks has shown that during the key decades of "globalization" – the 1980s and 1990s – the high income countries of the world had lower export shares than their postwar trends would have suggested. In an important sense they became less globalized.[4] Throughout the 1990s, for instance, exports represented about 12 per cent of the GDP of the economies of the United States, Europe and Japan, not particularly high by historic standards. If anything, then, the trade of the richest countries has been less globalized in recent years, not more so.

Moreover, if we turn to the late nineteenth century as a point of comparison, we find a world in which people travelled without passports, and in which governments imposed no controls on currency movements. By historic standards, then, there is little basis for saying that world trade is more globalized today than in the past. Whatever is going on with the rush to strengthen the WTO or create a Free Trade Area of the Americas, it has little to do with the fact that we live in a more integrated world economy today.

Managed Trade and Protectionism: The Myth of Freer World Trade

Since it is untrue that the richest nations are more globalized today, it would be convenient for the globalizers if they could show that world trade had become "freer," subject to fewer restrictions. Unfortunately for them, the evidence does not support that claim either. If anything, trade today may be more restricted than it was twenty years ago.

It is true that there has been a decline in the most conventional of trade restrictions – tariffs, a sort of tax slapped on imports or exports when they cross borders. However, at the same time as tariffs are being reduced, quotas and other non-tariff barriers are rising. Between 1975 and 1992, for example, the share of imports into the US subject to such barriers rose from 8 to 18 per cent. In fact a wide range of trade restrictions, as well as special subsidies given by governments to exporters based in their territory, have been on the rise. As a result of a variety of non-tariff restrictions – quotas, production and export subsidies, international strategic alliances, local-content rules and import-limiting agreements – huge chunks of world trade today are managed. So widespread are such non-tariff barriers that one expert estimates only about 15 per cent of world trade is truly "free" in the classical sense. Perhaps most significant, the evidence suggest, as the authors of *Managing the World Economy* argue, that trade becomes more managed the more globalized firms become.[5]

31

This should come as little surprise, since close to half of all world trade consists of transfers of goods and services between divisions of multinational corporations, that is, between different units of the same firm.[6] These are anything but open market transactions. Instead, they are internal transfers of parts, components and services from one unit of a corporation to another unit based in a different country. Technically, this is "trade." But in fact, there is no ordinary open market sale going on at all; "prices" of these goods are doctored in ways that work best for the multinational corporation when it comes to evading taxes and manipulating financial statements. So when we hear about world trade, it's important to remind ourselves that about half of it consists of little more than goods and services circulating inside powerful global companies.

This half of world trade is also clearly managed, not "free," i.e. not the result of the undirected play of market forces. As for the remaining half, as we've seen, much of this is subjected to a whole slew of non-tariff restrictions. And then there is the outright protectionism in which nations, particularly the most powerful ones, regularly engage.

In fact, none of the world's nations are committed to free trade, if by that we mean the unrestricted flow of goods and services in open markets. "Free trade" is a slogan used to attack practices designed by competitor economies to protect their own interests. It is not a policy to which any of the dominant powers adhere, but a battering ram for conquering each other's markets. The dominant nations advance the idea of free trade for industries in which they have an advantage, and they try to evade it wherever they are at a disadvantage. As a result, "free trade" is a policy imposed on the weakest and evaded by the most powerful.

Rich nation programs designed to give preferred treatment to firms based in their own countries are nowhere more blatant than in agriculture. As I discuss below, the rich countries massively subsidize agricultural production. Beyond agriculture, they squabble about trade in everything from lumber to steel. In early

2006, for instance, the French government proudly defended its "economic patriotism" when it cobbled together a deal to block the sale of energy company, Gaz de France SA by an Italian power company. But such moves are by no means unique to France. All major national governments engage in economic nationalism, using financial maneuvers, legal action, political pressure and intimidation to promote banks and corporations based In their own countries. In fact, governments in Europe, North America and Japan systematically subsidize and protect their auto, aerospace and defence industries, among others.

In June 2001, for instance, the US government of George W. Bush launched a sweeping trade action to protect America's steel producers by curbing imports of cheaper steel and offering financial subsidies to US firms. Bush did so by utilizing a piece of US trade law known as section 201, which allows him to restrict imports, ban them entirely, or provide financial aid to American companies. Of course, America's biggest competitor, the European Union (EU), where eighteen steel companies affected by the US action are based, immediately responded with trade actions of its own. Rather than being exceptional, trade disputes like these are the norm, with one major power after another engaging in deception and hidden practices in order to support its own multinationals. Often, these conflicts involve charges by one nation that another is "dumping" exports into its market below cost in order to hurt local firms. "Anti-dumping" claims are then invoked in order to impose duties against foreign importers or to subsidize local companies. Most of these claims are pure and simple bully tactics, attempts to protect domestic firms from foreign competition. Even the World Bank concedes that anti-dumping cases are a "packaging of protectionism to make it look like something different."[7] And this way of evading "free trade" is on the rise. In 2000, for instance, the number of such cases brought before the WTO hit a record of 328, up from 232 cases a year earlier.[8]

But anti-dumping cases are far from the only form taken by such economic disputes. In June 2001, the WTO ruled in favour of a European Union (EU) complaint against multi-billion dollar tax breaks the US government provides to major exporters such as Microsoft and IBM. The EU charges that these tax breaks represent illegal subsidies of these US companies to the tune of $4 billion in recent years As one of a number of retaliatory moves, Bush responded In 2004 by grieving the very nature of the EU itself. [9]

One of the most interesting things about these disputes is that they do little to eliminate world trade barriers. In fact, those who lose cases before the WTO have the option of removing their restrictions on trade or accepting the imposition of contravening trade sanctions by the competing nation. Most offending countries have chosen the latter option. As a result, instead of reducing trade restrictions, WTO rulings have the effect of increasing them. In what must seem a gigantic paradox to those who believe the rhetoric of free trade, the WTO has created an environment in which, as one commentator notes, nations are "effectively raising barriers to trade in the name of freer trade."[10] In a world of gigantic capitalist monopolies, many of these trends can be expected to get worse, not better. After all, as Canada's federal competition watchdog put it recently, "The impact of cartels is much more severe in a globalized economy."[11]

The Globalizing Monopolies

While globalizers are famous for the hymn they sing to the virtues of open, liberalized, competitive market economies, the reality of the world economy they defend could scarcely be further from this image. Like free trade, the terms "openness" and "competition" are purely ideological constructions designed to conceal immense concentrations of power. The more globalized the world becomes, the more control of wealth and resources becomes concentrated in fewer and fewer hands. At the heart of the globalization agenda is the creation of corporate monopolies with global reach, enormous firms that are able to write the rules of economic life on the planet.[12] Consider the following:

- As of the year 2000, a tiny minority of the world's companies – 500 corporations – accounted for 70 per cent of world trade. That makes these corporations more powerful global economic actors than the vast majority of nation-states.
- According to a December 2000 report by the Institute of Policy Studies, fifty-one of the one hundred largest economies in the world are corporations, and only forty-nine nation-states.[13]
- In fact, many of these corporations have assets greater than the GDP of large nations. Judged in these terms, by late 1999 Microsoft was as big as Spain, General Electric the same size as Thailand, Wal-Mart as large as Argentina, Cisco Systems as big as Iran, Lucent Technologies the size of South Africa, and IBM equal to Colombia.[14]
- As of 1997, according to the United Nations Conference on Trade and Development, the world's one hundred largest non-financial corporations held assets of $1.8 trillion, employed six million people, and exported products worth $2.1 trillion.
- As a result of mergers (where companies combine) and acquisitions (where one company buys another), the big just keep getting bigger – and they're doing so at ever-faster rates. In 1980, for instance, the top twenty pharmaceutical drug companies held roughly five per cent of the world trade in prescription drugs. Twenty years later, they controlled well over 40 per cent.
- The agricultural chemicals industry offers an even more dramatic example. Twenty years ago, sixty-five companies were competing in this industry's world markets. Today nine of them account for 90 per cent of international sales of pesticides.[15]
- In 1983, Ben Bagdikian estimated, in his book *The Media Monopoly*, that fifty firms dominated the mass media. Seventeen years later, in the 2000 edition of the work, he put the number

at ten, among them Disney, Time Warner, General Electric, Viacom, and Sony.

It should be obvious that most medium-sized businesses, never mind small ones, have no chance of survival in competition with these global behemoths. We can see this clearly if we take two of the Latin American nations that have most religiously followed the globalization model. In Argentina over the course of the 1990s, 38,000 medium-sized enterprises went bankrupt or were effectively destroyed by crippling debt. In Mexico, meanwhile, fully 750,000 firms have in recent years joined an organization of bank-indebted companies.[16]

These effects are particularly dramatic in agriculture at the moment. As I document in more detail in the next chapter, western governments subsidize their agri-businesses to the tune of $360 billion per year while demanding that Third World nations open their markets. Having forced open agricultural markets in countries like India, the Philippines, and Mexico, western nations then dump farm products at subsidized prices that are impossible for Third World farmers to meet. (In the next chapter, I will explore the specific effects these practices have in impoverishing cotton growers, sugar producers and others in the Global South.) In this way, "free trade" policies are used by the West to manipulate agricultural prices and drive small farmers from their lands. So, while Third World farmers struggle to survive on less than $400 a year on average, every farmer in the US, Canada and Europe receives between $16,000 and $21,000 from their governments per year In order to undercut producers elsewhere – all In the name of "free" trade.[17] On one count after another, rather than markets becoming more competitive, they are continually becoming less so. Contrary to the neo-liberal myth of a free and open world market, therefore, we live in a world in which an ever-smaller number of multinational corporations dominate the global economy – and as a result of new trade rules their wealth and power is increasing at unprecedented speed.

Andrew Shapiro of the Harvard Law School's Center for Internet and Society twigged on to the sheer hypocrisy of the global monopolizers in an open email message to Bill Gates. Reflecting on the hype about the liberating effects of the so-called Internet revolution, Shapiro challenged Gates: "If the whole idea of this revolution is to empower people, Bill, why are you locking up the market and restricting choices?"[18]

The answer is that the Internet revolution is not about empowering people anymore than are globalization and "free trade." They are about helping the richest economic actors in the world to become richer and ever more powerful. As Canada's former Agriculture Minister, Eugene Whelan, put it, "These deals aren't about free trade. They're about the right of these guys to do business the way they want, wherever they want." And judged in those terms, they are a wonderful success.

Freeing Capital, Not Trade

If we want to actually understand the economic agreements that are proliferating, we need to look behind the obfuscating rhetoric of "free trade" to decipher what's going on behind the scenes. Once we do so, clues as to what is occurring are not hard to come by.

Consider, first, an article by former Canadian Prime Minister Brian Mulroney who presided over Canada's initial "free trade" agreement with the United States. Writing in a national newspaper on the eve of the April 2001 Summit of the Americas in Québec City, Mulroney rhymed off a series of ostensible benefits of the current NAFTA accord. At the end of his list he reminded his readers that NAFTA "establishes a regime to protect investors."[19] Next, take the aggressive push in the late 1990s to negotiate a comprehensive economic pact known as the Multilateral Agreement on Investment (MAI). While these negotiations collapsed in 1998, in large measure because of public opposition, it is worth contemplating what the world's richest nations hoped to achieve. Especially instructive for our purposes is that, rather than refer to trade, the very name of the failed agreement specifically mentions investment.

Reflecting on these clues, we could be forgiven for thinking that the major purpose of global economic agreements is not so much freeing trade as it is protecting the rights and privileges of international investors. Once we investigate the globalization agenda in these terms, a lot of things start to fall into place.

As an initial observation, we should note that what distinguishes the era of globalization since the mid-1970s is not the growth of world trade (which as we've seen is not much greater in relative terms than it was in 1913) but, rather, the explosion of foreign direct investment and, most crucially, the emergence of the multinational corporations that drive it. It is here that we find the unique features of the globalization era.

Prior to the 1950s, there were few corporations that actually invested directly outside their home country. Until then, most foreign investment took the form of various kinds of financial loans (often known as "portfolio investment"). Capitalists would put up large sums of money to be loaned to foreign governments, banks or investors (in return for tidy profits). But these loans were in "liquid" form – advances of sums of cash in return for paper assets (like stocks and bonds) which provide interest payments. These investments are considered liquid because they can almost always be turned back into cash (and withdrawn from the country in which they are held) quite quickly by selling the paper assets, like stocks or bonds, to another buyer. Thus, while foreign capitalists profited handsomely from the exploitation of labour and natural resources in the colonial world and elsewhere, rarely did they involve themselves in long-term fixed investments such as factories, mines, or communication systems. Such investments are considered fixed, rather than liquid, since they often can't be converted back into cash overnight (there's not always a buyer for a factory or a mine, after all, but there almost always is for a stock or a bond, especially if the seller is eager to sell and willing to lower the price).

After the Second World War, however, US-based firms saw tremendous opportunities for investing directly in foreign countries. With much of Europe just beginning to recover from the ruination of war – which had destroyed factories, roads, airports, and houses along with millions of people – American firms were eager to enter those markets. In many cases, investing directly in foreign countries by building factories and other business operations was highly attractive since, by so doing, US companies could position themselves near large markets (thus ensuring low transportation costs) and draw upon skilled labour supplies. In this way, American corporations hoped to capture markets from companies in war-torn Europe and elsewhere. Throughout the1950s and 1960s, this sort of expansion of US-based firms (largely into Europe and Canada) led to the rise of the modern multinational corporation.[20]

If anything has defined the era of globalization, it has been large-scale foreign direct investment (FDI) and the growth of the financial flows that accompany it. Not only is this a relatively new phenomenon, but FDI has also been growing much more rapidly than the world economy as a whole. Put simply, capitalists are now setting up shop in other parts of the globe at a faster rate than the international economy has been expanding. During the 1960s, for instance, FDI grew twice as fast as the output of goods and services, and during the 1980s it increased four times as fast. But the truly staggering acceleration comes in the 1990s. Across that decade, FDI soared by 314 per cent, utterly eclipsing the 65 per cent increase in world trade and the 40 per cent increase in world gross domestic product.

This is the context in which multinational corporations desperately wanted new rules governing world-wide investment. By 1998, total outward foreign direct investment hit a record level of $649 billion in a single year; the following year it jumped to $865 billion, pushing the world stock of FDI (the total value of direct investment in foreign nations) to US$5 trillion. According to experts at the United Nations, outward FDI hit US$1 trillion in 2000. Once we understand foreign direct investment by multinational corporations as driving the "globalization" process, then foreign trade rightly recedes into the background. Since the early 1980s, after all, global firms have done much more business through their foreign-based affiliates than by exporting goods from their home countries. In order to grab a share of foreign markets, in other words, they more typically set up shop there, rather than ship goods to the intended market. By 1998, in fact, the total sales of foreign-affiliates hit $11 trillion, massively eclipsing world exports which totaled $7 trillion. All of this, as the World Investment Report notes, makes "international production globally more important than trade in terms of delivering goods and services to foreign markets."[21]

If international production, not trade, is the key process driving globalization, the multinational corporation is its principal institution. Looking at the previous period of globalization (roughly 1880-1914) we discover that there were at most a few hundred multinational firms in 1914; today there are about 60,000. These firms account for virtually all FDI and, as we've seen, their internal cross-border transfers of goods and services comprise about half of all world trade. In fact, just the largest 100 of these corporations hold over 40 per cent of all foreign assets (In excess of $2 trillion), making some of the largest wealthier than sizable nations. With all this in mind, one of the most thorough analysts of globalization states that the multinational corporation today "is the single most important force creating global shifts in economic activity."[22]

Again, we need to remind ourselves about some of the misleading connotations of the term globalization. It is simply untrue, after all, that these firms are "trans-national" in character. While they do indeed conduct business in many regions of the globe, their head offices are based in specific countries and the bulk of profits flow there. In 2004, for instance, the *Financial* Times of

London published a comprehensive ranking of the world's 500 largest multinational firms. Of these, nearly half are based in the United States and about one quarter in Western Europe. In short, fully three-quarters emanate from the traditional centers of world capitalism. Another 18 per cent are based in Asia, notably Japan. If we narrow the list to the top 100 multinationals, we find that 75 are US-based, 20 are housed in Europe, while the remaining five are based In Japan.[23] In short, "multinational" firms are overwhelmingly based in the dominant capitalist nations, and they conduct the bulk of their business their, or in other "developed" countries.

Nonetheless, there have been significant trends toward investment by multinational corporations in *parts* of the so-called "developing world," particularly Asia. Between 1975 and 1985, for instance, the share of FDI going into Asia increased from 5.3 percent of the world total to 7.8 percent. But the really large flows of FDI into developing countries happened in the 1990s. In the space of two years, from 1991 to 1993, foreign direct investment into developing countries doubled. Still, this foreign investment remained concentrated in a handful of countries. In 1994, in fact, half of all FDI flows to developing countries were going to East Asia, particularly Indonesia, Korea, Malaysia, China, and Thailand. By the later 1990s, parts of Latin America, especially Mexico and Brazil and to a lesser extent Argentina, had also become major recipients of FDI. Indeed, 55 per cent of all FDI in the developing world went to only five countries in the late 1990s: China, Brazil, Mexico, Singapore and Indonesia. (It is worth mentioning too that a large part of this investment in developing countries has involved takeovers of domestic companies by multinational ones, not investment designed to create new facilities and means of production, a point to which I shall return.) Meanwhile, the world's forty-eight poorest nations attracted only 0.5 per cent of world-wide FDI.[24] Rather than actually going global, international investment is still overwhelmingly concentrated in the dominant nations and a handful of select countries in the developing world. This is one reason, among many, that capitalist globalization is increasing world inequalities, not reducing them, as I will discuss later in this chapter.

Once we recognize that economic globalization is about an explosion in foreign direct investment by multinational corporations, not about trade, we are in a position to make sense of the global corporate agenda. While economic pacts may not have much to do with freeing trade, they have everything to do with freeing capital – with creating new global rules that make foreign investment and takeovers easier, and which give powerful legal protections to foreign investors anywhere in the world. In fact, an extensive international study of more than one thousand changes made between 1991 and 1999 to laws on foreign investment revealed that 94 per cent of these changes increased the rights and freedoms of foreign capitalists.[25] The "free" movement of capital – anywhere, any time, according to rules of its own making – is the real secret of the globalization agenda.

Alongside this goes a liberalization of short-term capital flows – money that moves around buying stocks, currencies, government bonds, real estate, and various sorts of complex financial instruments, for a matter of hours or days before selling again. Such investment is purely *speculative* in nature, since it consists of short-term bets as to which way prices will move for things like oil or currencies, but it doesn't invest in the productive infrastructure of a country (like machines of factories). With huge sums now flowing through these short-term markets (currency markets alone see movements of about $1.9 trillion US every day, about thirty times more than the daily exchange of goods and services), the whole of the global economy has become much more volatile, as countries like Korea and Argentina have painfully learned. Yet the globalizers insist that, whatever the consequences for the people of a country, world financial markets must be perfectly free for world traders and speculators.

Expanding the Rights of Property, Not People

Government and business leaders love to proclaim that international economic agreements are about extending democracy. Yet, not one clause in any of these accords – from NAFTA to the WTO agreements – establishes a single addition to the civil or human rights of people. What they do accomplish, however, is an unprecedented extension of the legal rights and powers of corporations.

Perhaps the clearest example of this is Chapter 11 of NAFTA, which allows investors to sue governments if they believe their firms have suffered a loss because of a breach of free trade and investment rules. In the past, most legal systems have given governments – as theoretical custodians of the public interest – the right to override private interests if they could demonstrate a clear public interest in doing so. Protecting the environment from corporate polluters is an obvious example, as are laws prohibiting private firms from using child labour. For generations, the only agents to international treaties have been nation-states. But NAFTA's chapter 11 changes all of this. For the first time ever in international law, it bestows on corporations the right to directly enforce a treaty to which they are not parties. Furthermore, it does so while imposing absolutely no obligations on them, such as to be good corporate citizens or respect the environment. As a result, NAFTA reverses the relationship that is supposed to exist between governments and private bodies (albeit a relationship that has often only existed in theory) by subordinating governments to international investment rules that are designed to protect the property rights of huge private corporations. A number of NAFTA decisions indicate just how insidious this elevation of property rights over the rights of the public can be.

One of the most notorious examples is the complaint brought against the Mexican government by the US toxic waste processing company, Metalclad. In 1992, the company received permission from Mexico to build a plant that would handle 360,000 tons of hazardous waste every year at a landfill site in San Luis Potosi in central Mexico. Three years later, as the company's plant was being constructed, area residents began a protest campaign, arguing that the firm had no right to proceed without the approval of local governments. Responding to mass pressure, the state's governor blocked local approval. Metalclad then notified Mexico that it would file a Chapter 11 complaint and in 2000 a NAFTA tribunal ruled in favour of the company, ordering Mexico to pay $16.7 million in damages to the corporation.[26] Under NAFTA, in other words, the right of corporations to bring thousands of tons of hazardous waste into local communities overrides the rights of residents to protect their health.

And the Metalclad case is just the beginning. In recent years a Canadian company, Methanex, which makes a methanol-based gasoline additive called MTBE, has sued the state of California for trying to phase out use of the additive after gasoline containing MTBE was found to have contaminated the water supply in Santa Monica – compelling the state of California to shut down most of the area's municipal wells. Similarly, a Canadian mining firm, Glamis Corporation, launched a suit against the state of California, demanding the right to undertake open pit mining that would destroy watersheds on native lands. In the same vein, United Parcel Service, America's largest courier company, has filed a $200 million Chapter 11 suit against the Canadian government alleging that Canada Post's monopoly on ordinary mail constitutes an illegal subsidy of the post office's courier services. In the largest – and what will probably be the most controversial – case, Sun Belt Water Inc. of California is suing the Canadian government for $14 billion in damages after British Columbia banned bulk water exports in 1993. So intimidated have governments become that the mere threat of a Chapter 11 suit is often enough to force governments to back down, as Canada did by withdrawing a ban on hazardous PCB imports after S. D. Myers, a US waste disposal company, launched a NAFTA complaint action.

None of these decisions are made by elected or accountable officials, nor are their procedures or rulings made public. Instead, they happen in secret, outside the scrutiny, never mind the control, of citizens. We shouldn't be surprised, then, when the president of the US consumer watchdog group Public Citizen charges that NAFTA tribunals represent a kind of "secret government." As a *New York Times* correspondent explains:

> Their meetings are secret. Their members are generally unknown. The decisions they reach need not be fully disclosed. Yet the way a small group of international tribunals handles disputes between investors and foreign governments has led to national laws being revoked, justice systems questioned, and environmental regulations challenged. And it is all in the name of protecting the rights of foreign investors under the North American Free Trade Agreement.[27]

The key to free trade agreements is the package of new legal rights and protections they give to investors. At the end of a twenty-five year period in which foreign direct investment has grown massively, multinational capital now seeks a new legal regime where the rights of global property owners – international investors – take precedence over all others.

"An Eye to Property": Deciphering the WTO Agreements

Capitalism, as I argue in the next chapter, has always been about the rights of property over people. Agreements like NAFTA and the WTO represent concerted efforts to move toward a capitalist utopia where multinational behemoths can get their way, riding roughshod over the laws, practices and traditions of communities.

Nowadays, however, political and business leaders like to pretend that what they're up to has to do with much more uplifting things: democracy, global prosperity, human rights. These claims for democracy are, in historical terms, quite recent. Only in the twentieth century did most mainstream political parties and heads of state come to embrace "democracy." I look at some of these issues with respect to democracy and capitalism in detail in chapter 6. For the moment, however, I want to look at a time when they did not couch their views in democratic terms, as doing so can clarify many issues about the present. When capitalism was in its infancy, a startlingly candid debate occurred about the conflict between the rights of property and the rights of the people – a debate that sheds much light on what is transpiring today.

The year was 1647, the country England. A king had just been defeated by an army of ordinary working men – farmers, artisans, sailors and the unemployed – presided over by a group of wealthy landlords who mistrusted the king's respect for their property. Known as the New Model Army, these forces of the people had vanquished the royal army and captured the king. Now they confronted the task of deciding what sort of constitutional order should replace the monarchy. Worried that wealthy leaders might betray them by bringing in a less than democratic system, rank-and-file soldiers convened a council and invited the two most important army generals, Oliver Cromwell and Henry Ireton, to meet with them at a church in Putney. Ably assisted by a radical group known as the Levellers, the soldiers had drawn up a document called the Agreement of the People which proposed that all adult males should have the vote.[28] Fortunately for posterity, someone kept a record of these discussions (which historians have come to call the Putney Debates). As a result, we have written documents of one of the most extraordinary debates in political history.

What happened at Putney is extraordinary in part because poor men were challenging their wealthy superiors. But it is equally so because of the terms in which the debate was cast: as a clash between property and democracy.

Stating the case for the democrats, Colonel Rainborough of the people's army told the generals: "I think that the poorest he that is in England hath a life to live, as the greatest he; and therefore truly, sir, I think it's clear, that every man that is to live under a government ought first by his own consent to put himself under that government." For Rainborough and the Levellers, such consent could only be accomplished by voting.

Speaking for the wealthy landowners and merchants, General Ireton directly attacked Rainborough's argument. "No person hath a right to an interest or share in determining or choosing those that shall determine what laws we shall be ruled by here – no person hath a right to this, that hath not a permanent fixed interest in this kingdom." And only a small group has such a permanent fixed interest, he maintained: "the persons in whom all land lies, and those in corporations in whom all trading lies."

And why should the right to choose the government lie exclusively with men of vast property? Because, if you grant that we are all politically equal – and therefore all ought to have the right to vote – then why not hold that we all ought to be socially and economically equal too? If "one man hath an equal right with another to the choosing of him that shall govern him," said Ireton, "by the same right of nature he hath the same [equal] right in any goods he sees – meat, drink, clothes – to take and use them for his sustenance. He hath a freedom to the land, to the ground, to exercise it, till it." In short, argued Ireton, if we adopt the equal right to participate in government, we will soon have to accept equality across the board, and that will be the end of unequal ownership of property. The reason he could not accept democracy, he proclaimed, "is because I would have an eye for property."[29]

An eye to property: here is the key to so many debates that have swirled across the history of capitalism – no more so than today as opposition to globalization builds. The confrontations that are taking place in the mountains of Chiapas, the villages of India and China, the city squares of Argentina and Bolivia, the barrios of Venezuela all hearken back to the debate at the church in Putney more than 350 years ago: do rights belong to people as people, or merely to wealthy property-owners?

For the architects of NAFTA, the MAI or the WTO accords the answer is clear: they intend to create new rights for multinational capital that will not be available to ordinary citizens. More than that, they seek a negotiating process – at world economic meetings – that is not even accessible to citizens' groups. As one senior WTO official admitted to the *Financial Times*, "The WTO is the place where governments collude in private against their domestic pressure groups."[30] Among other things, that collusion has resulted in the further impoverishment of millions of people.

Globalizing Poverty and Inequality

When supporters of globalization are confronted with evidence of the alarming new powers being bestowed on multinational corporations, they usually shift the terms of discussion. Whatever the weaknesses of these accords, they intone, the one great thing about globalization is that it spreads prosperity around the globe. *New York Times* columnist, Thomas Friedman, has been one of the foremost promoters of this view. "The driving force behind globalization is free-market capitalism," he writes. "The more you let market forces rule and the more you open your economy to free trade and competition, the more efficient and flourishing your economy will be." Almost every aspect of this statement is wrong. As we have seen, globalization is not about "free markets" or "competition." And it certainly hasn't made economies "more efficient and flourishing," as I shall show in a moment. Yet, the facts of the matter have not stopped a crescendo of mainstream voices that echo Friedman's views. The *Globe and Mail*, the most influential paper in Canada, for instance, ran a seven-part series prior to the 2001 Summit of the Americas in Québec City which sang this chorus repeatedly. "Globalization," proclaimed the paper's editors, "is a powerful force for good, with the potential to lift millions out of poverty and make the world a safer, richer, better place." They returned to the theme the next day: "For the first time in history, the end of mass poverty is in clear sight. For the hundreds of millions who live in want, there is finally a way out. That way is globalization." In the spirit of flogging a dead horse in the hope that it will move, the editors took up their tune again five days later pronouncing, "globalization is a force for good, with the potential to lift millions out of poverty."[31]

Now, if this was true, if globalization for all its unhappy effects actually raised millions out of poverty and hunger, if it truly made the world a safer and better place, then many opponents would feel obliged to think twice. Curiously, however, the globalizers are notoriously short on hard facts. Neo-liberal free trade rhetoric and ideology seemed to be enough to persuade them of their cause. But for millions the world over, rhetoric won't feed the children, provide clean drinking water, or stem the tide of disease. And once we look at the actual facts of the matter in these and other areas, the globalizers' arguments look highly unpersuasive.

Globalization has produced lower rates of economic growth

To begin with, there is no serious evidence that the changes associated with globalization have done anything to raise the rates at which economics expand. Indeed, the evidence overwhelmingly shows exactly the opposite. While we should not make a fetish of growth, especially given the environmental consequences of capitalist-style industrial growth (a point to which I return), it nonetheless remains significant that *on their own terms*, the globalizers' arguments fail. As the Washington-based Center for Economic and Policy Research has shown, compared with the previous twenty years, the globalization period has been characterized by sub-standard rates of growth. Placing all the world's countries into five groups according to wealth, the Center uses International Monetary fund data to demonstrate that all groups of nations, even the richest, have experienced slower growth throughout the era of globalization (1980-2005). And reduced rates of economic growth are a major cause of slower rises in living standards. Indeed, in many parts of the world, the growth slowdown of the globalization era has been associated with catastrophic *declines* in standards of living. For regions like Latin America and Sub-Saharan Africa, the results have been devastating, as Table 2.2 illustrates.

Table 2.2 – Growth of Per Capita Income, 1960-80 and 1980-2000

	1960-80	1980-2000
Latin America	+73 percent	+7 percent
Africa	+34 percent	-23 percent

Source: Murray Dobbin, "Democracy and the Québec Summit," *Financial Post*, April 30, 2001.

The impact of globalization on economic growth in these two regions has, in short, been disastrous. While Latin America, which "has led the world in trade liberalization," as the United Nations puts it, has undergone a devastating collapse in economic growth rates, Africa has experienced nothing short of outright calamity, with per capita income plummeting by nearly one-quarter, and life expectancy dropping in many countries.

Using more recent data, the Center for Economic and Policy Research has shown the dramatic dimensions of the slowdown of economic growth in these two regions.[32] In Table 2.3, I use their data to compare average annual growth in these regions during the pre-globalization (1960-79) and globalization eras.

Table 2.3 – Average Annual Growth in Income per Person, 1960-79 and 1980-2005

	1960-79	1980-2005
Latin America	+ 4 per cent	+0.7 per cent
Sub-Saharan Africa	+1.8 per cent	-0.75 per cent

Source: Data derived from Center for Economic and Policy Research, *The Scorecard on Development* (Washington, 2005).

Not only has the globalization period been one of less robust improvements in living standards, as these figures show; it has also produced poorer rates of improvements for infant and child mortality in most nations of the world. In short, more infants and children are dying worldwide than would have been the case if pre-globalization era trends had continued. The same is true for adults. In all these regards, then, globalization signals a cruel deterioration in human welfare for most of the world's people, and particularly for the poorest inhabitants of the planet. Translating these trends into more tangible human terms, we learn the following:

- According to the 2004 *Human Development Report*, the people of 46 countries are poorer today than they were in 1990.
- As a result, the number of countries with per capita incomes of less than $900 per year (the United Nation's cutoff for the category of "least developed" countries) has doubled since 1971 – from 25 to 49.[33]
- One of the results has been a decline in life expectancy in eighteen countries – ten of them in Africa, and eight in Eastern Europe and the former Soviet Union.
- According to the 2005 *Human Development Report* published by the United Nations, more than one billion people in the

world live on less than $1 a day. Another 1.5 billion struggle to survive on one to two dollars daily. That's 40 per cent of humankind condemned to unrelenting poverty and hardship. In addition, a billion people on the planet lack access to safe water. In fact, according to the definition used by major international agencies, more than seventy-seven per cent of the world's people are poor.

- Related to all of the above, every year more than 10 million children die before their fifth birthday. Again according to the UN, "most of these deaths could be prevented by simple, low-cost interventions" like vaccines for measles, diphtheria and tetanus.[34]

Globalization has increased world inequalities

At the same time as globalization has been associated with more sluggish economic growth (or with outright contraction) it has also generated greater inequalities in the distribution of wealth – precisely the opposite of what the globalizers claim. Drawing on new studies done for the World Bank, Robert Wade of the London School of Economics has shown that under the globalization regime the rich have gotten richer, the poor poorer. Looking at the distribution of world income over a mere five years (1988-93), Wade concludes that "the share of world income going to the poorest 10% of the world's population fell by over a quarter, whereas the share of the richest 10% rose by 8%." His basic results have been confirmed by study after study. The United Nations reports, for instance, that of 73 countries for which data are available, 53 of these – containing over 80 per cent of the world's population – have experienced increases in inequality. While a few countries have experienced declining inequality, they account for a mere four per cent of the planet's population. For ninety-six per cent of humankind, therefore, there has been no improvement in social equality. In fact, for four-fifths of the world, things have gotten more unequal in recent decades. The preponderance of such evidence has forced even conservative mainstream commentators, at least the honest ones, to take notice. William Easterly of the World Bank, for instance, now describes the globalization era as "the lost decades" for developing countries. Another World Bank economist, Branko Milanovic, has gone further, producing a series of highly comprehensive studies which show that globalization has substantially increased inequalities between rich and poor.[35] In fact, as the chart below indicates, Milanovic's research shows that international inequality, i.e. the inequality between nations (measured according to what is known as the Gini coefficient), has risen by more than 20 per cent during the globalization era, after having been relatively stable over the previous thirty years (1950-80).[36] Moreover, global inequality shoots up most sharply during the 1990s, when neoliberal globalization most fully came into its own. Put simply, inequalities between rich and poor nations have sharply increased throughout the globalization period.

Chart 2.1 – International Inequality, 1950 – 98, measured by the Gini Coefficient

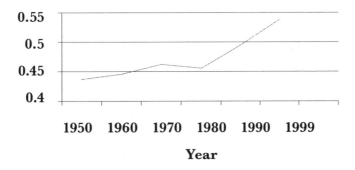

Year

Source: Branko Milanovic (2002) "The Two Faces of Globalization."

The human results of these trends are obscene:

- The richest two hundred people in the world more than doubled their net worth in the four years leading up to 1998 to more than $1 trillion.
- Merely three billionaires have assets greater than the combined gross national product of the world's "least developed" nations and their 600 million inhabitants.
- The world's 793 billionaires have a combined wealth greater than the gross domestic product of all but six countries in the world according to *Forbes* magazine's 2006 ranking of the world's super rich.
- The income gap between the one-fifth of the human population living in the richest countries and the fifth living in the poorest countries has gone from 30:1 in 1960, to 60:1 in 1990, and up again to 74:1 in 1997. Taking the richest ten per cent and the poorest ten percent of those on the globe as of 2005, we get an inequality ratio of 103:1.
- In the United States, the ratio of Chief Executive Officer (CEO) income to that of the average worker has risen from 35:1 in 1965, to 80:1 by 1980, and to an astonishing 450:1 today (2005).
- Microsoft CEO Bill Gates has more wealth than the bottom 45 of all American households. In fact, Gates is worth more than the combined Gross National Product of Central America – Guatemala, El Salvador, Cost Rica, Panama, Honduras, Nicaragua and Belize all combined. In fact, as of 1998, we could add Jamaica and Bolivia to this list and Gates would still come out on top.
- Executive pay at top US corporations rose 571 per cent from 1990 to 2000, at the same time as in the poorest countries one

billion adults are illiterate, 2.4 billion lack basic sanitation, and one billion have no access to safe water. [37]

As some of this data indicates, it's not just global inequalities between nations that have increased, so have inequalities within nations. Take the examples of the two most "globalized" economies in Latin America. In 1975, the income ratio of the richest 20 per cent of the population of Argentina compared to the poorest 20 percent was 8:1. As neoliberal reforms took hold, this ratio doubled by 1991; it then soared to 25:1 by 1997. In Brazil, meanwhile, the inequality ratio between these two groups has hit 44:1. [38] Put baldly, globalization has been nothing less than a mechanism for a massive transfer of wealth from poor to rich – in other words, exactly what is was designed to be.

World Trade has impoverished sub-Saharan Africa

While the globalizers love to claim that trade in world markets is the path to prosperity, they conveniently ignore the evidence from the world's most impoverished region, sub-Saharan Africa. After all, as Table 2.3 indicates, this region exports a much higher share of its output than does any other part of the world.

Table 2.4 – Share of GDP exported to foreign markets

OECD countries*	19%
Latin America	15%
Sub-Saharan Africa	29%

*The OECD (Organization for Economic Cooperation and Development) countries are the economically developed nations of North America, Western Europe and Japan.
Source: United Nations, *Human Development Report* 1999, pp. 2, 31.

Yet, contrary to the free trade mythology, high rates of exports have done nothing to help the people of the region. According to the World Bank, per capita incomes in sub-Saharan Africa fell by 25 per cent between 1987 and 2000. People on the African subcontinent have become even more impoverished, both absolutely and relatively, during the globalization period.. In 1950, Africans made on average 16 per cent of what people in the Global North earned. Yet, by 2001 their relative earnings had plummeted to less than seven per cent of average incomes in the North.[39] Not surprisingly, as we have previously noted, with falling incomes has come a decline in life expectancy throughout much of the region. In fact, four sub-Saharan African nations have seen staggering declines in life spans: a drop of 14 per cent in Botswana, 15 per cent in Uganda, and 17 per cent in both Zambia and Zimbabwe.[40] With world market prices for raw commodities from coffee to copper plummeting, these trends are likely to continue. Yet, desperately needing foreign currency to pay off debts to foreign banks and lenders such as the IMF, African nations have no choice but to continue mass production of those goods for which there is international demand, irrespective of the fact that their prices are collapsing. In fact, sub-Saharan Africa currently pays as much as $500 million *per day* in debt payments – an amount that completely eclipses any "aid" that comes from rich nations. The entire region is thus caught in a debt trap in which exports generate declining revenues that are sent to world banks and financial institutions instead of contributing to local investment, health care, or education. The results have been utterly – and tragically – predictable: with lower incomes, poorer diets and weakened immune systems have come cholera and tuberculosis epidemics, an HIV-AIDS pandemic, and the rising child mortality rates discussed above. Let us take just one example to put some flesh on these points. Since 1990, tuberculosis rates have tripled in 21 African countries. Every year, more than two million Africans are diagnosed with the disease and half a million die of it. In fact, most of the deaths of HIV-positive people in Africa are due to tuberculosis. Yet, a curative six month treatment costs a mere $15. Still they die, however, since global capitalism's imperative that

debts must be paid starves governments of desperately needed resources for health and education.[41] The idea that the rising tide of
world trade raises all boats is nothing less than an incredibly sick
joke where the peoples of most of Africa are concerned.

In fact, as we have seen, all the real evidence shows that
neoliberal policies are destroying lives across the continent. Let us
take just one recent case, the 2005 "famine" in Niger, the world's
second-poorest country, where hundreds of thousand died of
hunger. A British journalist recently described the reality of this
country's "free market famine":

> In Tahou market, there is no sign that hard times are
> at hand. Instead, there are piles of red onions, bun-
> dles of glistening spinach, and pumpkins sliced into
> orange shards. There are plastic bags of rice, pasta
> and manioc flour ...
>
> A few minutes drive from the market ... aid
> workers coax babies with spidery limbs to take sips of
> milk, or the smallest dabs of high-protein paste.
>
> Starving infants are wrapped in gold foil to
> keep them warm. There is the sound of children wail-
> ing, or coughing.
>
> ... This is the strange reality of Niger's hun-
> ger crisis. There is plenty of food, but children are
> starving because their parents cannot afford to buy
> it.
>
> The starvation in Niger is not the inevitable
> consequence of poverty or simply the fault of locusts
> or drought. It is also the result of a belief that the free
> market can solve the problems of one of the world's
> poorest countries.
>
> ... Prices have been rising because traders in
> the country have been exporting grain to wealthier
> neighbours ...
>
> The UN ... also declined to distribute free
> food. The reason given was that interfering with the

free market could disrupt Niger's development out of poverty.[42]

On the altar of free market dogma, in other words, the poor and the vulnerable have been sacrificed, permitted to starve in the midst of plenty. This, as we shall see in the next chapter, is anything but an aberration. Confronted with this sort of evidence, the globalizers tend to fall back on the claim that these nations just need to stick to the neoliberal road a bit longer, and sooner or later they'll see the payoff. Unimpressive as this argument is, let's examine it by looking at some of the developing nations that have most fully embraced the neoliberal model in recent years – South Korea, Argentina and Mexico. Then I will turn to the two latest cases embraced by the globalizers: China and India.

Global Integration and Economic Meltdowns: South Korea and Argentina

Developing on the basis of state-assisted industrialization from the mid-1950s, South Korea emerged in the 1970s as one of the world's most powerful "newly industrializing countries." By the 1980s, the country had become a significant force in global electronics, steel, automobile and shipbuilding industries.[43] At this point, the American government launched an offensive to force Korea to open its markets to foreign goods and investments. In 1983 US President Ronald Reagan visited Korea and issued ultimatums to that effect. Then the US government used its "Super 301" trade law – which authorizes Washington to retaliate against "unfair" traders – to break open the Korean economy. So effective was this offensive, all couched in neoliberal jargon, that Korean imports of US agricultural goods skyrocketed from $1.8 billion in 1985 to $5 billion by the end of 1991. In fact, Korea now consumes more American farm products than any other foreign nation.[44]

With Korea's markets pried open, international investors and speculators began pouring in, targeting other East Asian countries such as Thailand, Indonesia, Malaysia and the Philippines as well. Between 1990 and 1995, foreign capital flows into these five Asian countries nearly quintupled, soaring from $20 billion to $95 billion (US). But, as happens in all unregulated markets, the influx of speculative capital overshot all real opportunities for profits. As soon as that became clear, foreign capital started to flee the region. Economic troubles in Thailand then triggered an avalanche of fleeing capital. The inflow of foreign capital to the five countries did a dramatic U-turn, declining by $115 billion (resulting in a net outflow of $20 billion) in 1997, precipitating a catastrophic meltdown. In just a matter of a few weeks, a million people in Thailand and a staggering 22 million in Indonesia were rudely shoved below the poverty line.

Once the pride of the region, neoliberalized South Korea now found itself reeling from the effects of its open markets. At the peak of the crisis, 10,000 workers received layoff notices every day – a job loss rate of 300,000 per month.[45] Rather than see here a social and human tragedy, global capital – and the IMF, the US government and American-based corporations in particular – perceived an opportunity for pillage. As a condition for loans to nurse Korea through its crisis, they demanded new laws opening the country's banks and corporations to foreign ownership. With those changes in place, US businesses moved in for the kill, buying up twice as many Korean businesses in the first five months of 1998 as they had in any previous year – and at rock bottom prices as a result of the crisis. As a case in point, General Motors bought up the auto manufacturer, Daewoo Motors – a deal the American firm signed only after Daewoo agreed to lay off one-third of its 22,000 employees.[46] Similar transformations were forced upon Indonesia and Thailand, resulting in what some analysts believe is the largest transformation of domestic assets to foreign owners in half a century. Economic instability and insecurity, layoffs and falling living standards, and bank and industry takeovers by foreign capital: such are the rewards for following the neoliberal road.

But if any country has been perversely punished for accepting the globalization model, it is Argentina. Unlike Korea, which was beaten into submission, at the beginning of the 1990s, Argentina's rulers embraced neoliberalism with the fervour of a religious convert, chopping trade barriers and privatizing 400 public corporations. Having found the religion of the free market, Argentina's government became Washington's staunchest ally in Latin America. No other country in the region agreed to send troops to participate in America's 1991 war against Iraq; and only Argentina among Latin American states voted consistently with the US in international bodies. So enthused by its pro-US policies was the government that Argentina's foreign minister described his country's ties to the US as "carnal relations."[47]

On the economic front, the country pursued the whole gambit of neoliberal policies: privatization, opening of markets, vicious cuts to social spending. On top of that, the government agreed to dollarization – the policy of tying its currency (the peso) to the US dollar. As a result, every time the US dollar rose, so did Argentina's peso, even though this made its goods more expensive in world markets. As prices for its goods rose, Argentina's exports fell, and the country's trade deficit mounted. This compelled the government to turn to foreign borrowing to pay its way. With a cruel inevitability, the dollarization policy pushed by Washington, the IMF and the World Bank led to steadily mounting foreign debt, which hit $141 billion (US) in 2001.

While the country was sliding deeper into debt, the people were reeling from the effects of privatization, social service cuts, and mass layoffs. The *Wall Street Journal* estimates that during these years four million people fell below the poverty line, some ten per cent of the population.[48] At the peak of the crisis, 18 per cent of Argentines were officially unemployed, one of the highest rates of any industrial country in the world (and the real number was certainly much higher). And the IMF and World Bank managed to make a difficult situation desperately worse.

As the crisis worsened, a "Technical Memorandum of Understanding" was signed between the government and the IMF in September 2000 under which Argentina was required to make a $1.2 billion budget cut in 2001, at the very time it was obviously sinking into recession. In an astonishing section entitled "Improving the Conditions of the Poor," Argentina was directed to cut $40 per month from the salaries paid under the government's emergency employment program – thereby driving hundreds of thousands more into poverty.

With the economy in obvious collapse, and industrial production plummeting by 25 per cent, the World Bank president boasted that the country had slashed $3 billion in government spending and cut labour costs. Ignoring economic collapse, soaring poverty and mass layoffs, Bank President James Wolfensohn excitedly praised the country's new-found "labour market flexibility" (read lower wages).[49] Meanwhile, the official poverty rate soared to 44 per cent of the population, double its rate ten years earlier; at the peak of the crisis, more than half of all Argentines were impoverished.[50] As the downturn turned into an avalanche of poverty and despair, provoking riots that toppled successive governments, the Bank and the IMF refused to provide funds to address a debacle they had created. As in Korea, they did, however, encourage massive foreign takeover of the country's banks. For a decade of slavish devotion to American-style neoliberalism, the people of Argentina were rewarded with a financial collapse, bankrupt industries, soaring poverty and massive foreign debt. Neoliberalism had indeed produced what film maker Fernando E. Solanas called "social genocide" in his award-winning 2004 documentary on Argentina's collapse. These cases highlight one of the major consequences of the globalization model: full-fledged integration into global markets, alongside privatization and massive cuts to social spending make smaller economies incredibly vulnerable to financial and economic collapse – precisely the opposite of what globalization orthodoxy claims.

Fittingly, Argentina's economy began to recover only when its government openly rejected the policy prescriptions of the IMF.[51] But this move by government was merely a pale reflection of a popular radicalization throughout the country, and throughout much of Latin America, which has involved, as we shall see in Chapter 6, a growing revolt against neoliberal globalization.

NAFTA Devastates the Mexican People

If any nation should be a globalization success story, of course, it is Mexico. Closer than any other poor nation to the world's largest market, and the only developing country included in NAFTA, Mexico ought to be ideally located to reap the benefits of globalization. Moreover, unlike Sub-Saharan Africa, Mexico has received massive amounts of foreign direct investment in recent years. As I noted above, Mexico is one of the five largest recipients of foreign investment in the developing world. Indeed, the country's free-trade exporting zones, known as the *maquiladoras*, have seen new factories built at a staggering rate. By the end of 2000, there were 3,700 *maquiladora* factories employing 1.35 million people – an increase of a million jobs since 1987.[52] By globalization standards, then, Mexico is a boom town. Yet, for ordinary people, the results have been devastating. Since the implementation of NAFTA in 1994:

- The real minimum wage has fallen by 40 per cent;
- The gap between US and Mexican wages has grown by 30 per cent;[53]
- In the automotive industry – a major actor in the *maquiladora* zones – Mexican workers now earn one-twelfth of the wage of an American auto worker – down from one-third in 1980;
- Hundreds of thousands of people have left the land, as NAFTA-induced declining prices for rice, corn and coffee make it impossible for small farmers to make a living on their land.

- Thirty-six million people with jobs now live below the poverty line – 62 per cent of the working population;
- Since 1995, says the Organization for Economic Cooperation and Development, real wages in Mexico have declined by 10 per cent (probably a considerable underestimation) while workers' productivity has soared by 45 per cent.[54]

The last point is crucial. Soaring productivity and falling wages translate into massive profits. And that, as I've been emphasizing, is what NAFTA and similar agreements are all about. The very essence of the globalization agenda is a concerted campaign to raise the profits of multinational corporations by lowering wages, cutting taxes, loosening environmental regulations, and weakening labour rights. Not surprisingly, then, as one mainstream commentator notes, "Because of NAFTA's focus on cutting business costs, and because Mexico's workforce has grown so rapidly, Mexican workers have not benefited."[55]

What this comment leaves out is an essential aspect of the corporate bonanza in Mexico under NAFTA: police and military repression. After all, Mexican workers, peasants and indigenous peoples have fought back against the globalization agenda. But they have consistently been greeted with brutality by the state.

In the *maquiladoras*, attempts by workers to organize independent unions have been crushed repeatedly. In June 2000, for instance, police brandishing pistols and rifles attacked peaceful strikers at the US-owned Duro factory, beating workers and arresting their leaders. While an international campaign won the release of the strike leaders, the company fired more than one hundred of the strikers and the government refused to certify their union. Far from an isolated example, the use of police and thugs to injure, arrest, and intimidate workers in the *maquiladoras* is widespread. Moreover, belying all the pious claims about human improvement, in ten years not a single worker has been returned to her or his job, and not one independent union has been granted legal rights or a contract through NAFTA.[56]

And this, as the Zapatistas well know, gives us an important clue to one of the dirty secrets of the neoliberal agenda: that it rests on repression and violence. Indeed, without the use of police and troops, the globalization agenda could scarcely get off the ground. But before turning to this issue, let us first look at the cases of India and China.

India and China: Globalization Success Stories?

If a new mantra has been heard from the business press in recent years, it is that India and China prove the success of the globalization model. It is certainly true that each of these enormous nation-states, particularly China, has experienced growth rates higher than the norm. But before we pronounce these countries "success stories" for neoliberal globalization, we would be wise to look at the details – for it is there, as they say, that the devil lurks. Let's start with India.

Between 1980 and 2005, India's economy grew by about 3.8 per cent a year in per capita terms. And since 1990, the country's exports have grown by more than 10 per cent each year. But let's put this in perspective: as of 2005, India still accounted for just 0.7 per cent of world exports. In short, despite all the hype, it remains a very minor player in world markets.

Even if we grant, however, that India's growth is significant, the globalizers will have a hard time taking credit. After all, it was in 1991 that India's government undertook a rapid series of neoliberal reforms – privatization, reduction of trade barriers, greater opening to foreign investment, and so on. Yet, since that time, economic growth has not been as rapid as it was in the 1980s, prior to neoliberalization.

But it is when we turn to human welfare that the real picture comes into sharpest relief. For the growth of the export economy and the expansion of software engineering and call centers has done virtually nothing to improve employment and earnings. True, there is now a small middle class more capable of buying cell phones. But this has little to do with the lives of the vast majority. After all, fully 92 per cent of Indians who work do so in the "unorganized sector" – as street vendors, migrant labourers, farmers or truck drivers – where they lack job security, stable incomes or basic benefits. As the *Wall Street Journal* notes, across India "the poverty rate is more than 20 per cent and many people are chronically underemployed." In fact, in spite of the flurry of business articles on the topic, employment in "outsourced" industries, like customer service agencies and software engineering, amounts to a mere statistical blip: one quarter of one per cent of all jobs in India.[57]

And when we turn to rural India, where the vast majority live, the effects of the globalization era are especially disquieting. The effect of neoliberal reforms has been to open India to cheap (and heavily subsidized) agricultural imports from the Global North, while also pushing up costs for power and fertilizer, and making it more difficult for poor farmers to get credit in lean years. The result has been a crisis of falling incomes and soaring debt for millions of peasants. So desperate have farmers become that tens of thousands have committed suicide – up to 3000, for instance, in the state of Andhra Pradesh in a six year period. By and large, however, this story – of tens of thousands of suicides in response to neoliberal impoverishment – has failed to register in the mainstream press. One exception is a *New York Times* reporter who accurately observed, albeit with incredible understatement, that "the dead farmers are also the canaries in the mines for India's agricultural economy – indicators of dire straits."[58]

It comes as little surprise, then, to learn that the globalization era has seen no improvement in poverty in India. One in every 11 Indian children dies in the first five years of life. And malnutrition affects fully half the children in the country.[59] But try finding those stories in the world's business press.

Let us now turn to the case of China. Here, the record of economic growth is indeed exceptional, much more so than in India. Since 1980, for instance, China has tripled its weight in the world economy, now accounting for 14 per cent of world output, compared to five per cent twenty-five years ago. During that period, China's exports of manufactured goods rose 10 fold, generating worries in the United States and elsewhere about the emergence of a new economic powerhouse. Once again, however, growth figures taken on their own tend to obscure more troubling trends, especially with respect to poverty and social inequality.

In fact, as the World Bank has noted, in less than twenty years (from the early 1980s to 2000), inequality between rich and poor in China *doubled*. Incredibly, social inequality grew faster in China than in any other country in the world, making it one of the planet's more unequal societies and destroying whatever pretensions to "socialism" might still have existed.[60] As in India, poverty and hunger in the countryside have mounted precipitously. Even the World Trade Organization concedes that China's rural poor have suffered a "sharp six per cent drop" in living standards since China joined the WTO in 2001. For the poorest rural dwellers, the drop has been much more calamitous, with tens of millions falling into abject hunger and misery. Indeed, the World Bank estimates that over 200 million rural Chinese subsist on less than $1 a day, while other analysts believe the number is at least twice as high. According to one comprehensive report done in 2006, nearly 700 million people in China, or just under half the population, live on less than $2 a day – in short, they struggle to survive in conditions of "absolute poverty," to use the World Bank's expression.

At the same time, millions of urban dwellers – many of them recently displaced from the countryside – also struggle to survive. On top of this, some 36 million workers lost their jobs as a result of layoffs and plant closures by state-owned enterprises. Then, as millions flooded into the cities, struggles over urban space began. In Shanghai, for instance 1.5 million people were "relocated" between 1991 and 1997 in order to clear space for luxury apartments, skyscrapers and shopping malls. Amidst small pockets of extreme wealth, great concentrations of poverty have grown.

Some of the worst effects of poverty can be found in the health-care field. As China has climbed on the globalization bandwagon, medical care has been increasingly privatized. Today, fully 60 per cent of all healthcare spending in the country comes directly from people's pockets. Worse, more than three-quarters of those living in the countryside have no health insurance whatsoever; the same is true for nearly half of all urban dwellers. Studies suggest that at least half of these people cannot afford to seek medical attention when they are ill. Despite robust economic growth, like India, China's record on child mortality has worsened as its economy has increasingly adhered to the globalization model.[61]

Meanwhile, workers in the country's sweat shops generally work 60-70 hour weeks. Two-thirds have no medical insurance, and more than 90 per cent have no pensions. They also work in some of the world's most hazardous and unhealthy environments.[62]

What has happened in China in recent decades, therefore, is an accelerated process of *class differentiation*. Small numbers of Chinese have indeed become substantially wealthier – the country contributed eight new billionaires to the world list in 2006, for instance – while huge numbers have become poorer. As elsewhere in the world, neoliberal globalization has enriched a few while impoverishing the many. Hou Wenzhou, who heads a human rights organization called the Empowerment and Rights Institute, rightly observes that "Chinese society has evolved into something like Karl Marx's society, where some of the powerful and wealthy class are depriving the poor of the opportunity for justice or equality." And he further notes that this has led to intensified conflict between rich and poor.

The Chinese government acknowledges as much. Its own statistics show that the number of social protests, or "mass incidents," as it calls them, has soared from 8,700 in 1993 to 74,000 in 2004. Equally significant is the growth in the size of such protests. During the 1990s, typical "incidents" involved 10 or fewer protesters; by 2003, the average protest consisted of more than 50 people – and a growing number saw the mobilization of hundreds of thousands of participants. At the same time, the number of strikes and labour protests has also soared. Conflicts over seizures of land have become especially volatile. In 2004, for instance, up to 100,000 poor farmers fought thousands of police in a battle over the seizure of farmland to build a hydro plant. A particularly brutal struggle erupted in late 2005, when hundreds of villagers in the fishing town of Dongzhou confronted riot police bearing automatic rifles. At least 20 villagers appear to have been killed, and many more wounded, when police opened fire.[63] Here, Chinese authorities join hands with globalizers around the world for whom violence and repression are central instruments in the neoliberal arsenal.

Policing the City, Locking Up the Poor: State Violence and Neoliberalism

Given the way the globalizers spout off interminably about freedom, it is all the more important that we insist on this point. After all, the neoliberals are law and order fanatics. No voices are more vociferous than theirs when calls are heard to crack down on youth, create boot camps, clear parks of homeless people, lock up drug users, detain refugees, use the death penalty, criminalize political dissent, or justify torture and abuse of prisoners in America's "war on terror". Behind their fluffy rhetoric about free trade and free markets lurks a hostility toward freedom for ordinary people – and a love affair with police and prisons. Their heroes are not sweatshop workers standing up for their rights, indigenous peoples reclaiming their lands, or homeless people who resist a police beating. Such people give them nightmares. Instead, they adore jackbooting police with automatic weapons, and they rush to defend police who shoot unarmed protesters and beat the daylights out of youth of colour. Brutality, egregious violations of civil rights and freedoms, even murder are acceptable to them in the battle to utterly defend the "freedom" of propertied interests.

Anyone who has participated in global justice protests in cities like Seattle, Washington, Bangkok, Buenos Aires, Melbourne, Seoul, Prague, Québec City, or Genoa knows the truth of this. Under assault from riot cops bombarding them with tear gas, pepper spray, rubber bullets, water cannons and more, many sensed that it was only a matter of time before police murdered a protester at world trade meetings. That moment came on July 20, 2001 when twenty-three-year-old Carlo Giuliani was killed by police in Genoa, Italy. But, much as we need to remember Carlo and name his murderers, we must not treat his death as an isolated event. That would be an injustice to so many others killed in one country after another, from Vietnam to Colombia, to protect the property of the wealthy. I discuss many examples of this in the next two chapters. For the moment, however, I want to focus on the globalizers' infatuation with state repression.

Among the finest studies of the neoliberal cult of police and prisons is Christian Parenti's book, *Lockdown America*. Parenti documents how the current trend to paramilitary policing in the US began as a response to the social upheavals of the 1960s and early 1970s – the anti-Vietnam War movement, the Black Panthers, the early women's movement, militant workers' strikes, and so on. But it was during the Reagan-Bush-Clinton era that began in 1980 – the very time the globalization agenda emerged – that police and prisons became the preferred way of dealing with the inevitable fallout from massive cuts to social programs. As poverty and homelessness soared, billions were spent to contain "crime" by building prisons and giving police military weaponry.

Over the last twenty years, several key components of America's law-and-order crusade were carefully constructed: the creation of a public frenzy about drugs; social cleansing policies to get the poor off the streets in order to gentrify chunks of inner cities; a crackdown on immigrants and refugees, particularly on the Mexican border; and a racist law-and-order regime in the inner cities designed to intimidate those sections of the population who, with virtually nothing to lose, might be the most likely to rebel.

Not surprisingly, from New York to Cincinnati to Los Angeles, police violence – the shooting of a Black or Latino youth in particular – has often been the detonator for community uprisings.

There are several essential components to what is sometimes called "the prison-industrial complex."[64] First, a wave of US laws – with names like Violent Crime Control and Law Enforcement Act, 1994, or Anti-Terrorism and Effective Death Penalty Act, 1996 – gave police sweeping new powers (often in the name of the "war on drugs") and reduced the rights of the accused. Similar laws can be found in countries like Britain, Canada and Australia. Second, police have been increasingly militarized, receiving automatic weapons like M-16s, helicopters, grenade launchers, and armoured personnel carriers. Thirdly, America in the 1980s and '90s witnessed a massive wave of prison construction to the tune of $7 billion per year at its peak. The combined results of all this are shocking:

- Every week during the 1990s the prison population in the US grew by 1,000 bodies.
- In the year 2000, the number of people in American prisons and jails passed two million – up from 500,000 in 1980.[65]
- Two-thirds of the people imprisoned in the US are Black or Latino; the number of Black women in prison for drug offenses has soared.
- One in every three Black men in America is in prison or under some form of criminal surveillance (such as parole or probation).
- Of the 675 people sentenced to death in the US between 1995 and 2000, Blacks constituted fully half of that number and Latinos 20 per cent.[66]
- Of those in prison, only three in ten are there for alleged violent crime. The rest are there for drug offenses, property offenses (usually theft), or public disorder.[67]
- In 1998, 682 residents of the US per 100,000 people were in prison – eight times higher than the comparable figure for

France (where resistance to neoliberalism has been particularly strong).[68]

All of this has been happening at a time when crime rates are falling – although the public has been indoctrinated by media and government to believe otherwise.[69] In fact, what we have been witnessing is not an escalation of crime on the streets, but the systematic militarization of policing. As one commentator has noted, the new model for crime control "represents not the police but the military." As a result, crime is being "dealt with as if it were an insurgency."[70] And, as we have seen, the reason is not escalating crime. Instead, it is a key component of the neoliberal agenda: the enforcement of new regimes of discipline and social control on the working class and the poor. The poorest neighbourhoods and communities are treated as enemy territory that must be conquered and subdued, and the poor themselves as threats to law and order who must be intimidated and brutalized. Inevitably, then, while the impoverished – especially poor people of colour – are being effectively criminalized, those responsible for controlling and harassing them become more racist, brutal and bigoted. Consider just two recent US examples:

> *Washington* – An internal affairs probe uncovered more than one million racist, sexist and homophobic messages sent between officers through onboard laptop computers in police cars.[71]

> *Los Angeles* – A massive investigation of the Los Angeles Police Department uncovered shocking brutality, especially within the LAPD's Community Resources Against Street Hoodlums (CRASH) program. Evidence showed that LA police routinely took Black and Latino men to their headquarters where they would "tie their hands behind their backs and beat them bloody, break their limbs, choke them to the verge of unconsciousness or batter their heads into concrete walls." CRASH officers were awarded with plaques from their commanders every time they shot someone. As one reporter noted, "Routine activities

71

> included beating or coercing confessions out of sus-
> pects, intimidating witnesses into false testimony or
> silence, planting guns or drugs on people, shooting
> people without cause, tampering with death scenes
> and planting guns on people to justify improper shoot-
> ings, paying informants with drugs, lying in court and
> selling seized drugs."[72]

Lest anyone think cases like these are unique to the American criminal justice system, let us take a look at the case with which I am most familiar, policing in Canada. The following examples illustrate the trends.

Racist imprisonment of native peoples – In a scathing 1999 ruling, the Supreme Court of Canada blasted the use of incarceration as a weapon to dominate native people. The Court pointed out that a native male is twenty-five times more likely to be admitted to a provincial jail than a non-native, while a native woman is 131 time more likely to be behind bars than her non-native counter-part.[73]

Discrimination against Blacks in Ontario – The 432-page report of the Commission on Systemic Racism in the Ontario Criminal Justice System (1996) described the heightening trend to imprison black people as "shocking." The Commission judged that systemic discrimination toward blacks existed at every level of the criminal justice system in the province, particularly incarceration.[74]

Criminal, trigger-happy police in Toronto – As part of an investiga-tion into allegations of widespread police corruption in Toronto, a lawyer has alleged that the city's downtown drug officers are "members of a criminal organization, whose members habitually cheat, lie and steal." Another report showed recently that, when judged in terms of the city's murder rates, police in Toronto are much more likely to fire their guns than police in either Washing-ton or Los Angeles.[75]

Montreal cops return to work after conviction for killing cab driver – A twelve-person jury ruled that police killed taxi driver Richard Barnabé after assaulting him in detention in 1993. Barnabé suffered a fractured skull, broken nose and teeth, and such severe blows that one of his teeth was lodged in his throat. Despite the jury's verdict, a judge ruled that his killers could return to police duty.[76]

Refugees and immigrants have been especially mistreated by the repressive law and order agenda. Among the many sad ironies of globalization is that, while they argue for the free movement of capital, neoliberals overwhelmingly endorse clampdowns on the movement of people. And throughout the North, governments have moved to block, detain, imprison and deport more people crossing borders in search of a better life. Still, people desperately fleeing violence, civil war, repression and poverty continue to make their way to countries in the North. There they find themselves considered to be – and incarcerated. Let us look at just two of the more egregious examples: Britain and Australia.

The British government has been the most hardcore of European supporters of America's "war on terror," which I discuss in a later chapter. And this has involved a "national security" agenda that discriminates against people from the South. In fact, the British government has amended its Human Rights Act to make it easier to deport people without giving them adequate legal representation, and to return people to countries where they might face torture. Of course, governments across the whole of Europe, like their counterparts in Canada, the US and Australia, have been cracking down on the movement of poor people from the Global South (rich people, of course, typically have no problem crossing borders). More and more, refugees who arrive in the North find themselves thrown into huge prisons where they are denied access to lawyers and frequently subjected to racist and dehumanizing treatment. Britain's Yarl's Wood detention center, designed to hold 900 "asylum seekers," illustrates these trends. As religious leaders in Britain have testified, detainees at Yarl's Wood are often deprived of mattresses and covers and fed as if they were animals. Their religion and ethnicity is often mocked by guards. One such incident, in which guards prevented a woman named

Eunice Igbegwe from going to the prayer room, was one of the sparks for a riot in which parts of Yarl's Wood were burned down by irate detainees. As journalists covering the subsequent trial noted, almost everyone charged after the riot had been a victim of cruel and mean-spirited repression by immigration officials and the criminal justice system, and a number had atempted suicide in despair at their imprisonment.[77]

But few countries are more notorious for their brutal treatment of asylum seekers than Australia. That country has seen an upsurge of anti-immigrant bigotry in recent years. Perhaps no institution more symbolizes this bigotry than the Woomera detention camp, one of six such camps in the country, which has held as many as 1,500 refugees in intolerable conditions in the Australian outback. As one journalist describes it:

> The detention camp lies low on the desert, in rows of narrow barracks surrounded by three rows of fences topped by barbed wire, and razor wire lining the ground between. In summer, the temperature rises to well over 40 degrees.
>
> … Some of the detainees have climbed to the roofs of the barracks and jumped on the razor wire, lacerating their bodies in an attempt to escape.
>
> Hundreds have cut their arms with wires or hanged themselves.[78]

It is important to emphasize that these people are not accused of any act of violence. They have not robbed, assaulted or threatened anyone. In fact, about a third of them are children. Their "crime" is to have fled desperate conditions in search of a better life. Yet, the globalizers, who genuflect before "free trade," and an "open world", are only too happy to have these poor people from the South locked up, humiliated, criminalized, and deported back to frequently unsafe conditions. Somehow, they expect us to take seriously the claim that they stand for freedom and human well-being.

It's Not About Freedom Either

These examples could be multiplied many times over. Moreover, as I show in the next chapter, the picture is much worse when we consider the use of military forces, US-backed death squads, and paramilitaries to suppress dissent, crush indigenous peoples, smash unions, and protect the power of the rich in some of the world's poorest countries.

What all of this should make clear, however, is that just as globalization is not about trade, so it also has nothing to do with human freedom. Instead, it is about a regime of discipline and repression designed to more successfully control and exploit working class people. Like their predecessors more than 350 years ago, the globalizers have "an eye to property." That is what their trade deals are about. And it is why they meet at economic forums, why they invest in various parts of the world, and why they support the use of massive amounts of social wealth to police and lock up the poor.

Their order is a system of power, privilege, oppression and inequality. And they have backed it up with an infrastructure of police, courts, jails and prisons whose fundamental purpose is to intimidate and control the poor. Their order is a system of class domination, where police and prisons are instruments of class rule – of the organized power of the owning class.

About eighty years ago, the great American socialist Eugene Debs brilliantly captured how all this works. For leading mass strikes and carrying on radical agitation, Debs spent four years of his life behind bars. But prison did not stop his political work: as Prisoner No. 9653 he received nearly one million votes in 1920 as the Socialist candidate for the US presidency. In a book published after he died, Debs laid out his view on capitalism and prisons:

> Crime in all its varied forms and manifestations is of such a common nature under the capitalist system that capitalism and crime have become almost synonymous terms ...

The few who own and control the means of existence are literally the masters of mankind. The great mass of dispossessed people are their slaves...

To buttress and safeguard this exploiting system, private property of the capitalist has been made a fetish, a sacred thing, and thousands of laws have been enacted and more thousands supplemented by court decisions to punish so-called crimes against the holy institution of private property.

A vast majority of the crimes that are punished under the law and for which men are sent to prison, are committed directly or indirectly against property. Under the capitalist system there is far more concern about property and infinitely greater care in its conservation than in human life.[79]

As an example, Debs proceeded to describe situations where governments refuse to prosecute capitalists responsible for factory fires that kill workers. And this is no antiquated crime of the past. In the spring of 2001, fifty-two Bangladeshi women died in just this way in the country's thirtieth factory fire since 1995, a majority of which have taken human lives.[80] That so little has changed over seventy-five years when it comes to the priority of property over human life should tell us we are dealing not with accidental features of our society, but with deep-rooted social and economic structures and practices.

Debs clearly understood that it is these arrangements that are criminal – arrangements that protect the system by which the powerful grow rich through the exploitation of the majority: "Private appropriation of the earth's surface, the natural resources, and the means of life is nothing less than a crime against humanity."[81]

That criminal system has a name: capitalism.

Notes

1 Karl Marx and Frederick Engels, "Manifesto of the Communist Party" in Marx, *The Revolutions of 1848*, ed. David Fernbach (Harmondsworth: Penguin Books, 1973), pp. 68, 71.

2 Much of this evidence is nicely and convincingly summarized by Paul Hirst and Grahame Thompson, *Globalization in Question* (Cambridge, UK: Polity Press, 1996), pp. 26-31. An important contribution to this discussion is Robert Zevin, "Are World Financial Markets More Open? If So, Why and With What Effect?" in *Financial Openness and National Autonomy: Opportunities and Constraints*, eds. Tariq Banuri and Juliet B. Schor (Oxford: Clarendon Press, 1992), pp. 43-83.

3 Data derived from A. Maddison, "Growth and Slowdown in Advanced Capitalist Economies," *Journal of Economic Literature*, v. 25, n. 2, June 1987, pp. 649-98.

4 John Weeks, "Globalize, Globa-lize, Global Lies: Myths of the World Economy in the 1990s" in *Phases of Capitalist Development: Booms, Crises and Globalizations*, eds. Robert Albritton, Makoto Itoh, Richard Westra and Alan Zuege (New York: Palgrave, 2001), pp. 268-9

5 References for the claims in this paragraph are available in my article "Globalization, Trade Pacts and Migrant Workers: Rethinking the Politics of Working Class Resistance" in *Restructuring and Resistance: Canadian Public Policy in an Age of Global Capitalism*, eds. Mike Burke, Colin Mooers and John Shields (Halifax: Fernwood Publishing, 2000), p. 266.

6 The exact measurement of intra-firm trade, as it is called, is difficult. While Steven Shrybman puts it at 40 per cent of world trade in his book *WTO: A Citizen's Guide* (Toronto: Canadian Centre for Policy Alternatives/Lorimer, 2001), p. 3, Canada's former ambassador to the Organization for Economic Cooperation and Development, Kimon Valaskakis, estimates it at 60 per cent in his article "It's about world governance," *Globe and Mail*, April 19, 2001. The *Wall Street Journal* (July 5, 1991) claimed that more than half of all trade involving US companies consisted of intra-firm transfers. More recently, some American economists have put the figure at 42 per cent. See Timothy Appel, "Global firms give trade a new twist," *Wall Street Journal*, May 31, 2005. Taking all such estimations into account, it seems reasonable to suggest that close to half of all world trade falls into this category.

7 The World Bank as quoted by Alan Freeman, "Has the Empire Struck Back?" in *Phases of Capitalist Development*, p. 212.

8 Guy de Jonquiere, "EU leads surge in anti-dumping claims," *Financial Times*, April 17, 2000.

9 Adrian Croft "WTO rules against U.S.," *Globe and Mail*, July 24, 2001; Scott Miller, "U.S. files surprise complaint against EU," *Wall Street Journal*, September 22, 2004.

10 William Thorsell, "Energy, trade, crime and the Web," Globe and Mail, April 16, 2001.

11 Shawn McCarthy, "Global cartels a growing threat, watchdog says," *Globe and Mail,* July 9, 2001.

12 Some economists insist on the need to distinguish monopolies, single firms that control the whole market in a specific good, from oligopolies, enormous firms that share market control with a handful of others. For purposes of this discussion, I use the term monopolies in a looser sense to indicate giant firms that, with a handful of others, dominate markets.

13 Institute for Policy Studies, *Top 200: The Rise of Corporate Global Power* (Washington: IPS, 2000).

14 Gretchen Morgenson, "A Company Worth More than Spain?" *New York Times*, December 26, 1999.

15 Data on pharmaceutical and pesticides is drawn from Pat Roy Mooney, "The ETC Century: Erosion, Technological Transformation and Corporate Concentration in the 21st Century," *Development Dialogue*, 1999:1-2, p. 74.

16 James Petras and Henry Veltmeyer, *Globalization Unmasked: Imperialism in the 21st Century* (Halifax: Fernwood Publishing, 2001), pp. 84-5.

17 See Natividad Yabut-Bernardino, "An Impact Study of Agricultural Trade Liberalization in the Philippines" (Manila: International South Group Network, 2000), pp. 9-10, available at www.isgnweb.org; Michel Chossudovsky, *The Globalisation of Poverty: Impacts of IMF and World Bank Reforms* (London: Zed Press, 1998), p. 141; Walden Bello, *Dilemmas of Domination: The Unmaking of the American Empire* (New York: Metropolitan Books, 2005), p. 153.

18 As quoted by Naomi Klein, *No Logo: Taking Aim at the Brand Bullies* (Toronto: Vintage Canada, 2000), p. 164.

19 Brian Mulroney, "What's in free trade for Canada?" *Globe and Mail*, April 17, 2001.

20 Within the political economy literature there are differences between those who prefer the term "transnational corporation" and those who choose "multinational corporation" to describe firms with global operations. Both sides to this debate have scored some points. I have chosen to stick with the term multinational corporation, whatever its shortcomings, because I worry that "transnational corporation" suggests that these firms have direct operations in virtually all parts of the globe (when in fact they ignore most of the world) and that they have transcended links with specific nation-states, a highly misleading notion in my view. By and large, these companies are nationally based but operate in a number of strategically selected parts of the world economy (i.e., they are multi-national enterprises). For some useful evidence in this regard see Hirst and Thompson, *Globalization in Question*, and Paul N. Doremus, William W. Keller, Louis W. Pauly and

Simon Reich, *The Myth of the Global Corporation* (Princeton: Princeton University Press, 1998).

21 United Nations Conference on Trade and Development, *World Investment Report 1999* (New York and Geneva: United Nations, 1999), p. 14. Other data in this paragraph drawn from pages 9 and 12 of this report and updated on the basis of UN information presented by Peter Cook, "Who's winning the war over globalization?" *Globe and Mail*, October 9, 2000.

22 Peter Dicken, *Global Shift: The Internationalization of Economic Activity*, 2nd edn. (London: Paul Chapman Publishing, 1992), p. 47. Dicken prefers the term transnational corporation which, for reasons outlined in footnote 20 above, I choose not to use.

23 "Global 500: Special Report," *Financial Times*, May 27, 2004.

24 World Investment Report 1999, pp. 18-19, 11.

25 United Nations, *World Investment Report 2000* (New York and Geneva: United Nations, 2000).

26 A basic account of this case is provided by Anthony DePalma, "Nafta's Powerful Little Secret," *New York Times*, March 11, 2001.

27 DePalma, "Nafta's Powerful Little Secret."

28 Some radical groups known as True Levellers and Diggers also contemplated extending the vote to women. On the Levellers see H. N. Brailsford, *The Levellers and the English Revolution*, ed. Christopher Hill (Nottingham: Spokesman Books, 1976); G. E. Alymer, ed., *The Levellers in the English Revolution* (Ithaca: Cornell University Press, 1975); A. L. Morton, ed., *Freedom in Arms: A Selection of Leveller Writings* (New York: International Publishers, 1975).

29 A. S. P. Woodhouse, ed., *Puritanism and Liberty: Being the Army Debates (1647-49) from the Clarke Manuscripts*, 3rd edn. (London: J. M Dent and Sons, 1986), pp. 53,54, 58, 57.

30 As quoted by Barlow and Clarke, *Global Showdown*, p. 74.

31 Thomas Friedman, "Manifesto for a Fast World," New York Times Magazine, March 28, 1999; "The myths about globalization (1)," *Globe and Mail*, April 12, 2001; "The myths about globalization (2)," *Globe and Mail*, April 13, 2001; "The myths about globalization (7), *Globe and Mail*, April 19, 2001.

32 Mark Weisbrot, Dean Baker, Egor Kraev and Judy Chen, *The Scorecard on Globalization 1980-2000: Twenty Years of Diminished Progress* (Washington: Center for Economic and Policy Research), pp. 7-8, 16.

33 Richard Gwynn, "Global economy isn't global," *Toronto Star*, April 18, 2001; Constant Brand, "Poorest countries demand more help," *Globe and Mail*, May 15, 2001.

34 United Nations, *Human Development Report 2005*, pp. 24-25.

35 Robert Wade, "Global Inequality: Winners and Losers," *Economist*, April 28, 2001, p. 74; William Easterly, "The Lost Decades: Developing Countries' Stagnation in Spite of Policy Reform 1980-1998," World Bank, Febru-

ary 2001; Branko Milanovic, "The Two Faces of Globalization: Against Globalization as We Know It", World Bank Research Department, May 2002.

36 The Gini coefficient is expressed as a number between 0 and 1. A ranking of 0 means everyone has the same income, and a ranking of 1 means one person has all the income and everyone else has none. It is only one of a number of measures of inequality. Whatever its shortcomings, it does capture the basic trend towards an increase in inequality between nations. For more on its use in this regard see Branko Milanovic, *Worlds Apart: Measuring International and Global Inequality* (Princeton: Princeton University Press, 2005).

37 These data are drawn from *Human Development Report 1999*, p. 3 , *Human Development Report 2000*, pp. 30, 34, 82, and *Human Development Report 2005*, p. 38; Petras and Veltmeyer, p. 86.

39 World Bank, *World Development Report 2000/2001* (New York: Oxford University Press); Bob Sutcliffe, "World Inequality and Globalization," *Oxford Review of Economic Policy*, v. 20, n. 1 (2004), p. 23..

40 *Human Development Report 1999*, p. 130.

41 Karen Palmer, "TB in Africa a crisis, health experts warn," *Toronto Star*, August 27, 2005. See also Patrick Bond, *Against Global Apartheid: South Africa Meets the World Bank, the IMF, and International Finance,* updated edition (London: Zed Books, 2003), p. 26.

42 Jeevan Vasagar, "The hungry reality of free-market Niger," *Guardian*, August 2, 2005.

43 For a useful overview see Nigel Harris, *The End of the Third World* (Harmondsworth: Penguin Books, 1986), pp. 31-45.

44 Waldon Bello with Shea Cunningham and Bill Rau, *Dark Victory: The United States and Global Poverty*, 2nd edn. (London: Pluto Press, 1999), p. 77.

45 See David McNally, "Globalization on Trial: Crisis and Class Struggle in East Asia" in *Rising from the Ashes? Labor in the Age of "Global Capitalism,"* eds. Ellen Meiksins Wood, Peter Meiksins and Michael Yates (New York: Monthly Review Press, 1998), p. 142.

46 Sang-Hun Choe, "GM to acquire Daewoo," *Globe and Mail*, September 21, 2001. On the effects of the Asian crisis generally, see Walden Bello, *Deglobalization: Ideas for a New World Economy*, second edition (London: Zed Books, 2004), pp. 48-50; Peter Gowan, *Global Gamble: Washington's Faustian Bid for World Dominance* (Lodnon: Verso books, 1999), Ch. 6; and R. Wade and F. Veneroso, "The Asian Crisis: The High Debt Model versus the Wall-Street-Treasury-IMF Complex," *New Left Review* 228 (1998), pp. 3-23.

47 Larry Rohter, "Argentina And the U.S. Grow Apart Over a Crisis," New York Times, January 20, 2002.

48 Thomas Walkom, "Argentina a warning to Canada," *Toronto Star*, January 8, 2002.

49 See the excellent article by Greg Palast, "Argentina: World Bank President's Secret Plan for Bleeding Nation an Uncharming Mix of Self-Delusion and Cruelty," January 2002, at www.americas.org.

50 James Petras, "Road Warriors," February 2002, at www.americas.org.

51 Larry Rohter, "Economic Rally for Argentines Defies Forecasts," *New York Times*, December 26, 2004.

52 Data derived from John MacArthur, "The secret free trade agenda," *Globe and Mail*, April 12, 2001, and Linda Diebel, "Murder most foul," *Toronto Star*, May 23, 1999.

53 Alan Tonelson, "Bush's Latin American Trade Mirage," *Washington Post*, April 17, 2001.

54 The data in the last five points comes form the following sources: 1) Professor John Warnock, "Who Benefits from the Free Trade Agreements?" unpublished article Spring 2001. Warnock is the author of *The Other Mexico: The North American Triangle Completed* (Montreal: Black Rose Books, 1995; 2) Ginger Thomson, "Farms Unrest Roils Mexico, Challenging New Chief," *New York Times*, July 22, 2001. I suspect that the OECD estimation of a 10 per cent drop in real wages is too small since Tonelson, using US Department of Labor statistics, reports a 20 per cent drop in real wages in Mexico.

55 Tonelson.

56 Lynda Yantz, "Mr. Fox, does Mexican democracy include workers?" *Globe and Mail*, August 23, 2000; David Bacon, *The Children of NAFTA* (Berkeley: University of California Press, 2004).

57 Joanna Slater, "India: Job creation remains a weak spot," *Wall Street Journal*, April 5, 2004.

58 Amy Waldman, "Heavy Debt and Drought Drive India's Farmers to Desperation," *New York Times*, June 6, 2004.

59 *Human Development Report 2005*, p. 30.

60 World Bank, *China: Promoting Growth with Equity*, September 15, 2003, pp. 12-13.

61 *Human Development Report 2005*, pp. 63, 28.

62 International Confederation of Free Trade Unions, "Trade, Development and Employment in the People's Republic of China," April 2006.

63 Geoffrey York, "A burst of gunfire exploding in the darkness," *Globe and Mail*, December 17, 2005. On labour protests see Wong Kam Yan, "China's Worker Protests, *Against the Current*, March-April 2006, and Han Dongfang, "Chinese Labour Struggles," *New Left Review* 34, July-August 2005.

64 While there is something attractive about this term insofar as it underlines the centrality of incarceration to American capitalism today, it can mistakenly suggest that the military-industrial complex is now a thing of the past. For a thoughtful discussion of these issues see Parenti, *Lockdown America: Police and Prisons in an Age of Crisis* (New York: Verso Books, 1999), pp. 213-16.

65 Joseph T. Hallinan, *Going Up the River: Travels in a Prison Nation* (New York: Random House, 2001).

66 Associated Press, "Minorities overrepresented on death row," *Globe and Mail*, September 13, 2000.

67 Parenti, pp. 217, 239, 167.

68 John Ibbitson, "U.S. prison population numbers dropping," *Globe and Mail*, August 14, 2001. This article notes a small decline in the US prison population during the last six months of 2000. While it is too early to know if this represents a new trend, it is clear that some American states are now questioning the enormous sums they spend on imprisoning people.

69 Martin Woolacott, "The long army of the law," *Globe and Mail*, January 27, 1996; Timothy Appleby and John Saunders, "Growing fear of crime unfounded, data show," *Globe and Mail*, January 13, 1999. Timothy Appleby, "Murder rate at its lowest since 1967," *Globe and Mail*, October 19, 2000.

70 Woolacott, "The long army of the law."

71 William Walker, "Police-force racism shocks Washington," *Toronto Star*, April 18, 2001.

72 Doug Saunders, "How fierce war on L.A. gangs spawned police reign of terror," *Globe and Mail*, February 28, 2000.

73 Kirk Makin, "Top court appalled as natives fill Canada's jails," *Globe and Mail*, April 24, 1999.

74 Kirk Makin, "Black imprisonment trends 'shocking' says racism report," *Globe and Mail*, January 16, 1996.

75 Colin Freeze, "Mountie leads probe of city police," *Globe and Mail*, August 17, 2001; Nicole Nolan, "Metro cops more likely to shoot than LAPD," *Now*, July 11-17, 2001.

76 Ingrid Peritz, "Montréalers aghast at Barnabé ruling," *Globe and Mail*, March 9, 2000.

77 Jenny Matthews, "Some Kind of Asylum," *The Guardian Weekend*, September 6, 2003.

78 Campbell Clark, "Outback brutal for boat people," *Globe and Mail*, March 19, 2002.

79 Eugene Debs, *Eugene Debs Speaks* (New York: Pathfinder Press, 1970), pp. 305-6.

80 Barry Bearek, "Lives Held Cheap in Bangladesh Sweatshop," *New York Times*, April 15, 2001.

81 Debs, p. 305.

3. The Invisible Hand Is a Closed Fist: Inequality, Alienation, and the Capitalist Market Economy

"If you think the IMF is scary, wait until you hear about capitalism."

– Placard carried by an anti-IMF protester in Washington

Many in the anti-globalization movement, particularly in North America, have displayed a definite shyness about using the term "capitalism," though this has started to change, especially in Latin America. Perhaps fearing they will be seen as crazy radicals, or identified with the legacy of authoritarian Communist Party regimes, many global justice advocates in the North have tended to finger ideological beliefs such as "neo-liberalism" or "free-market economics" when assigning responsibility for the growing gaps between rich and poor, the destruction of the natural environment, and other ills of globalization.

Yet, this avoidance of the term "capitalism" comes with a cost: it encourages critics and activists to see the problem not as the system that organizes our lives, but merely as a set of policies pursued by those currently at the top. The effect is to de-radicalize the movement by proposing to change merely the ideology that drives government policy, not the system as a whole. Consistent with this, critics reluctant to name capitalism as the problem frequently confine their aims to building a citizen's lobby to revamp government policy within a capitalist framework.

Those who favour this approach typically call for replacing the free trade agenda with fair trade policies. This orientation, often associated with mainstream non-governmental organizations (NGOs) and social-democratic groups, holds out the hope that capitalism could be made to function fairly – without outrageous social inequalities, environmental degradation or growing disparities between nations. It maintains that there is nothing objectionable in principle about global trade agreements so long as they are fairly constructed.[1] Of course, there are limited circumstances in which producers and activists have been able to carve out fair trade practices through which Third World cultivators of goods like coffee and tea are guaranteed a basic subsistence price for commodities like coffee, sugar and cocoa regardless of fluctuations in world markets. While these practices are commendable, their results are often quite meager.[2] Furthermore, such practices can affect only a tiny proportion of all the commodities in the world. There is simply no way that these arrangements could be devised for trade in the likes of steel, oil, tool and dye machines, combine harvesters, automobiles and so on.

The idea that capitalism could be made to function according to fair trade was first advanced by Adam Smith (1713-1790), the celebrated founder of liberal economics. Contrary to liberal myth, Smith was not an apologist for capitalists.[3] He argued, in fact, that capitalists always seek "to deceive and oppress the public" by conspiring to inflate their prices and profits. As a result, Smith condemned "the mean rapacity, the monopolizing spirit of merchants and manufacturers," and urged that governments should always be on guard against their treachery.[4] Yet, these views did not make Smith a critic of capitalism *per se*. Instead, he maintained that a properly governed capitalist society could benefit the vast majority. So long as governments prevent monopolistic behaviour (such as cornering markets and rigging prices), said Smith, the "invisible hand" of the market will reward everyone.

In short, capitalists are the real threat to free trade. Protected from their deviousness, however, genuinely free trade, a market economy without monopolies or collusion by capitalists, could be made to function fairly.

Radical and socialist critics had little difficulty demonstrating the fundamental flaws in the analysis Smith developed in the *Wealth of Nations*. Even when capitalists don't collude and monopolize, the market system will systematically benefit them at the expense of the poor. This follows from the inherently unequal relations of exchange between large property owners and those who are propertyless. If the latter risk hunger and deprivation in the event that they cannot find a buyer for their labour, they are at a structural disadvantage. It is more than a little difficult to accept the fiction, familiar in mainstream economics texts, that we are all just buyers and sellers treated equally by the market; it is something of a stretch to believe that the invisible hand of the market is blind to the inequality of power between multinational capitalists and the world's poor. This is especially so when most of the poor are selling the only commodity they have to offer – their labour – and the global elite can find millions of these poor labourers in country after country. As we shall see, it is this structure of social inequality that makes labour markets systematically exploitative. This is why, for the world's poor, the invisible hand of the market feels a lot more like a closed fist.

By suggesting that meaningful rules and practices of fair trade can be constructed within capitalism, the fair trade theory fails to confront the systemic structures of inequality between capitalists and propertyless labourers that constitute the core of capitalism. Problems such as global poverty, sweatshops and lack of labour rights are treated as aberrations, susceptible to correction with a bit of fine-tuning, rather than as phenomena intrinsic to the system. Fortunately, growing numbers of global justice activists have become deeply skeptical about this approach. As Naomi Klein points out, activists increasingly recognize that "the conduct of the individual multinationals is simply a product of a broader global economic system."[5] And with increasing frequency, that system is being named. The *Economist* magazine, for instance, now speaks of global justice protests as "outbreaks of anti-capitalist sentiment."[6]

Yet, the word *sentiment* is significant here. The anti-capitalist feeling that frequently emerges is not the same thing as a full-fledged anti-capitalist *consciousness*. For that, we need a thoroughgoing critical analysis of capitalism.

Markets and Capitalism

It is a commonplace of liberal ideology that capitalist market economies are natural. Proponents of capitalism love to insist that humans have an instinct to trade, or what Adam Smith called "a natural propensity to truck, barter and exchange one thing for another." Since trade is said to be inscribed in our genes, it follows that capitalism accords with human nature. Every attempt to organize a human society on non-capitalist lines is by this logic doomed in advance to failure, and attempts to so reorder things can only be foolhardy, if not outrightly dangerous.

This argument is so widespread – trumpeted by the mass media, politicians, teachers and ostensible intellectuals – that it comes as a shock to realize that every bit of it is false. The liberal argument is nothing but a convenient fiction constructed on the most superficial and shoddy of theoretical arguments. There is simply no truth to the claim that most human economies have been organized on market principles. More than this, the liberal outlook completely confuses the exchange of goods with the regulation of economic life by market principles. Yet, the difference here is so fundamental that, once grasped, the whole liberal argument crumbles.

Examining a variety of human societies, the renowned economic anthropologist and historian Karl Polanyi observes that "never before our own time were markets more than accessories of economic life. As a rule, the economic system was absorbed in the social system … the self-regulating market was unknown."[7] Noting that throughout history market exchanges have usually been "accessories" to economic life, Polanyi distinguishes between markets and *market-regulation*. There Is no doubt that market exchanges have often played a role at the margins of economic life, but they have rarely been central to it. Non-market principles have generally predominated – which is what Polanyi intends with his claim that markets were generally "absorbed in the social system."

Polanyi demonstrates convincingly that most human societies have been organized according to two principles: *reciprocity* and *redistribution*. Reciprocity refers to the idea that every member of society has duties and obligations to all others. Coupled with this is the notion of redistribution, the principle that the community systematically transfers wealth to those who have less. Consequently, the idea that economic life should be organized to maximize individual accumulation had no place in these societies. Instead, the guiding principle was a collective one: ensuring the well-being of all the members of the community. In such societies, therefore, "the individual is not in danger of starving unless the community as a whole is in a like predicament."[8]

Consistent with this, as many anthropologists note, most human societies have accorded the greatest prestige not to individuals who accumulated immense private wealth, but to those who shared wealth most widely and generously. In fact, the only motive for accumulation recognized by most cultures is sharing. Summarizing the evidence from a range of societies and cultures, anthropologist Marshall Sahlins remarks: "The objective of gathering wealth, indeed, is often that of giving it away."[9]

In short, had they encountered them, most human cultures would have abhorred capitalist motives and values. The idea that individuals ought to hoard, exploit, cheat and deceive in order to amass private fortunes would have been considered bizarre, anti-social behaviour. Far from being eternal, market economics and the profit motive are recent developments, established only by forcibly extinguishing practices of reciprocity and redistribution. In Canada, for instance, governments outlawed the potlatch ceremonies in which native peoples would redistribute goods to those in need. Five years after first criminalizing the potlatch in 1884, the federal minister of Indian Affairs explained government policy in these terms: "The policy of destroying the tribal or communist system is assailed in every possible way and every effort made to implant a spirit of individual responsibility instead."[10] In other words, the spirit of individual self-seeking, acquisition and accumulation could only be promoted by destroying older communal and cooperative practices. Similar efforts to destroy indigenous communalism took place from the United States to Australia.

While it is important not to romanticize pre-capitalist societies, since they often had their own relations of inequality and domination, it is equally vital to recognize that the anthropological and historical records completely debunk claims for the naturalness of capitalism. It is only with capitalism that all goods and services become market commodities and, most significantly, that land and labour are commodified. Yet this – the systematic commodification of land and labour – is a phenomenon without historical precedent, one that requires destroying the fabric of all previous social life. While many societies accepted the buying and selling of some goods, most would have found repulsive the idea that the land or a person's labour could be bought and sold. Only thorough-going commodification of all aspects of life – most notably human labour – could produce a capitalist society in which literally everything has a price. How that immense revolution in human affairs came about is crucial to understanding the world in which we live today.

Creating a Market in Labour: Capitalism's First-War Against the Poor

The distinguishing feature of a capitalist society is the commodification of human labour – and it is this that differentiated early modern England from all other nations. England was not the first country to develop long-distance trade or to plunder other parts of the world; throughout the fifteenth, sixteenth and seventeenth centuries, countries like Portugal, Spain and Holland exceeded England in these regards. What set English society of the time apart from its European rivals, however, was that it alone established an extensive labour market, the key to capitalist development.

The very term *labour market* can be deceiving, however. There is a world of difference, after all, between a market in a particular good – such as grain, cars, or computers – and a market in labour. Only in the latter do we encounter the buying and selling of human powers and capacities. Labour markets, in other words, do not just trade a specific good but, rather, an essential part of the life-activity of human beings (which is sometimes described as human labour power). As Polanyi noted, one cannot buy and sell the commodity labour power "without affecting also the human individual who happens to be the bearer of this peculiar commodity."[11] On the labour market, every economic transaction touches directly on essential qualities of human life – material, social and moral. In exchange for wages, those who sell their labour power surrender to the capitalist ultimate control over the work to be done, its conditions, pace, and organization. Rather than treating our creative energies as a unique source of personal identity, "the owners of the conditions of production treat living labour-power as a thing."[12] The result is a profound personal alienation, a hollowing out of the meaning of life. This is why the poor, as we shall see, have historically resisted being driven into labour markets as their only means of survival.

Reflecting on this relationship, Karl Marx described work under capitalism as *alienated labour*: Relinquishing control over her labour, the worker suffers an estrangement from an essential part of her humanity.[13] As Marx put it in one succinct passage:

> But the exercise of labour power, labour, is the work-er's own life-activity, the manifestation of his own life. And this life-activity he sells to another person in order to secure the necessary means of subsistence. Thus, his life-activity is for him only a means to en-able him to exist. He works in order to live. He does not even reckon labour as part of his life, it is rather a sacrifice of his life. It is a commodity which he has made over to another.[14]

For the worker, in other words, work is a means to life, but not life itself. Real life begins after work, during "free time," i.e. time away from labour. The familiar expression, "Thank God It's Friday," is a depressing acknowledgment that work is, for the majority, oppressive, alienating, boring and dehumanizing. Of course, things look very different from the vantage point of the capitalist.

Since the worker alienates control of her labour to the em-ployer, the capitalist is in a position to exploit that labour – to force the labourer to perform an amount of work that exceeds the value of the wages paid. Indeed, this is the whole point of the transaction for the capitalist: to make a profit on the purchase of labour by getting workers to produce more value than what they are paid. And this difference between labour's output and the wages paid – called surplus value – is the secret to the massive inequalities of capitalism: enormous amounts of the wealth pro-duced by workers accumulate in the hands of the owning class.

But why should workers agree to this exchange? Why should they submit to exploitation? The simple fact is that across differ-ent societies people have always resisted this arrangement. Given virtually any other semi-viable option, people overwhelmingly prefer to cling to precarious conditions as farmers, fishers, hunters and the like rather than sell their human capacities to a buyer. It is only when there is literally no other way to survive – when, in short, all other economic options have been taken from them – that people reluctantly accept a life as wage-labourers.

In sixteenth- and seventeenth-century England, the creation of a class of wage labourers was accomplished by depriving millions of peasants of their land. Only when they were thoroughly dispossessed of both land held as personal possessions (often on some kind of lease basis) and of access to what were known as *common lands* did large numbers of the English poor turn to waged work and submit to the disciplines of the labour market.

In the feudal society that pre-existed capitalism, particularly in its earliest periods, villages consisted of land that belonged to the lord (most of which was worked by peasants in exchange for rent and services) and lands that belonged to the community as a whole, such as fields and forests, where all could graze animals, raise crops, hunt, fish and gather wood. Access to these lands was considered a common right, something everyone had simply as a result of membership in the village community.[15] These millions of acres of European common lands were indispensable to the very survival of the poor. Often having only a small plot for the personal use of their own families, they relied heavily on the game, fish, berries, wood, and grazing land (if they owned a cow, a pig, or a few sheep) that the common lands provided. In addition, much of Europe was organized in terms of open farming, where fields were not fenced in (or "enclosed"), and peasants had access to their own small plots or common fields by crossing land that was held by someone else.

As dramatic social and economic change swept the English countryside throughout the sixteenth and seventeenth centuries, the emerging class of capitalist landlords and rich farmers launched a battle to dispossess peasants of their lands. By driving up rents, disputing peasant ownership in the courts, and foreclosing on debts, English landlords forced hundreds of thousands of peasants to give up their lands. As rich farmers took over these plots, constructed large farms, and paid increased rents to land-lords, they also hired landless peasants as wage workers. Still, large numbers of dispossessed peasants resisted entering the labour market. Many erected small cottages on the common lands, hoping to survive there rather than sell their labour to an employer. As a result, the emerging capitalist class launched a war against the common lands, turning them wherever possible into their own private property.

A key part of the process was known as *enclosure* – literally the erection of fences and hedges to close off land that had previously been open to all – but pure and simple eviction also played a central role. It's not surprising to discover that most anti-enclosure riots consisted of peasants tearing down these fences. Yet, through extortion, intrigue, violence and manipulation, more and more English land was enclosed – perhaps 30 per cent of all the land in the country between 1600 and 1760. A social order in which common lands played a central role was systematically eroded by a regime of privatized ownership.

Once the rich and powerful had set in motion the destruction of the common land system (and the common rights that accompanied it), they sealed the process by turning to Parliament. There, in the midst of other rich landowners, they introduced private Enclosure Acts which enclosed the commons, gave legal title to it to rich landlords, and deprived the poor of vital sources of livelihood. Between 1760 and 1830, at least six million acres of common lands were enclosed by parliamentary decree.[16] These Acts often ignited a class war on the land as the rural poor fought desperately to preserve their livelihoods. But with the backing of Parliament, the courts, troops and superior weapons, the authorities crushed peasant resistance. The new capitalist order emerged, as Marx put it, "dripping from head to toe, from every pore, with blood and dirt."[17]

As is so often the case, the privatizers and enclosers tried to present their battle not as the greedy and violent property grab it was, but as a great moral crusade that would lift the poor out of poverty and idleness. Defending "the appropriation of the forests," one land surveyor claimed it "would be the means of producing a number of additional useful hands for agricultural employment, by gradually cutting up and annihilating the nest and conservatory of sloth, idleness and misery, which is uniformly to be witnessed in the vicinity of all commons, waste lands and forests."[18]

Yet, while presenting the greed of his class as an uplifting human service, the author of this tract also tipped his hand by acknowledging that the purpose was to produce "a number of additional useful hands for agricultural employment." The creation of a landless class of wage workers – people who had no means of survival other than the sale of their labour – was at the very heart of capitalist development since this working class, or proletariat, produces the surplus value (the excess of the value labour produces over the wages paid) that makes capitalist profit and accumulation possible. The following tables indicate the enormous scale on which such a class was created.

Table 3. 1 Number of Landless Peasants in England and Wales 1086-1640

Date	Population (millions)	Number of landless peasants
1086	1.1	66,000
1279	3.3	330,000
1381	2.1	42,000
1540-67	2.9	360,000
1600-10	3.7	1,312,500
1620-40	5.0	2,000,000

Source: Adapted from Table 1.1 in D. McNally, *Against the Market,* p. 9.

The hundred years from 1540 to 1640 saw an explosion in the number of peasants without land: from just over a third of a million to about two million; from about 10 per cent to 40 per cent of the population of England and Wales. In the course of a century, the conditions of life for millions of people had been dramatically and irreversibly transformed. No longer did they work land in village communities where their families had lived for countless generations; they were now uprooted members of the landless poor compelled to sell their labour on the market to rich buyers. As Table 3.2 shows, before the seventeenth century was out, a majority of peasants had become wage labourers.[19]

Table 3.2 Proportion of English Peasants Employed as Wage-Labourers, 1086-1688

Date	% of peasants employed as wage-labourers
1086	6
1279	10
1380	12
1540-59	11
1550-67	12
1600-10	35
1620-40	40
1688	56

Source: Richard Lachman, *From Manor to Market: Structural Change in England, 1530-1640*, p. 17

Of course, there was always an alternative to wage labour: begging. So, to close this option off, severely punitive Vagrancy Acts were passed to criminalize requests for alms by healthy individuals. In 1530, legislation decreed that sturdy vagabonds were to be whipped until blood streamed from their bodies, after which they could be imprisoned. A 1547 Act allowed a complainant to take as a slave anyone who refused work and to keep them in chains and whip them. According to a law of 1572, unlicensed beggars were to be brutally flogged and branded on the left ear.[20] The purpose of all these Acts was to drive people to labour for wages. Two centuries later, the battle continued: under the Vagrancy Act of 1744 magistrates were empowered to whip or imprison beggars, peddlers, gamblers, strolling actors, gypsies and "all those who refused to work for the usual and common wages."[21] Far from being natural, people had to be driven into wage labour. And, as today, those unable or unwilling to submit to labour market discipline were simply jailed; the numbers imprisoned and executed soared in the late-eighteenth century, the take-off period for the "industrial revolution" so crucial to capitalism.[22]

Capitalism emerged, then, through violent and bloody struggles against previous non-capitalist forms of life. Only by driving peasants off their land, enclosing the commons, tearing down the cottages of the poor, criminalizing "vagrancy," and erecting a new system of punishment was a capitalist labour market created. Rather than a natural form of social life that evolved spontaneously, "free market capitalism" was built by destroying previous social arrangements. Or, as Polanyi puts it with just a touch of irony, "*laissez faire* was planned."[23] And the same is true today. The neoliberal utopia of unrestrained capitalism is being created by a war against the poor and the commons. In fact, the "new enclosures" are a sign that the struggles that marked the birth of capitalism are still very much alive.

Globalization and Enclosure of the "Global Commons"

Just as the rise of capitalism saw widespread enclosure and privatization of community resources – the common lands in particular – so contemporary capitalism continues and intensifies these processes. While the capitalist economy has been around for a few hundred years, large parts of the natural, human and social environments have so far escaped being commodified – turned into privately owned commodities that can be bought and sold.

Throughout history, most societies have treated a wide range of essential goods and services as communal property, things that make up the common stock of the community. Oceans, lakes and rivers have usually been considered public goods, as have space and the atmosphere. A wide range of knowledge and human practices with respect to farming and seeds have similarly been treated as the traditional common "property" of various communities. Today, however, all these things are being privatized and commodified – from the genetic structures of the seeds farmers use, to the human genetic code. Items that have been part of the global commons – like water, plant seeds, rain forests, and the genetic make-up of life – are now bring privatized and marketed as commodities. In the same vein, social services such as education and health care, which have frequently been regulated as public goods accessible to all, are being rapidly commodified.

Common wealth is in the process of being transferred from the public domain to the private sector. Alongside the most iron-clad protection of the rights of private investors, globalization is extending commodification farther than most people ever imagined. Indeed, if we were to choose a shorthand definition of globalization, we could do much worse than selecting the term *global commodification*. Or, drawing on the original rise of capitalism, we could say that we are witnessing the "new enclosures."[24] The same drama that resulted in the birth of capitalism in Britain – massive property grabs, dispossession of the poor, and their displacement onto the labour market as propertyless workers – is being enacted in one part of the world after another.[25] And, once again, suffering is being inflicted on millions of lives.

Globalization, Agriculture, and the Struggle over Land

Few aspects of the globalization agenda are more cynical than WTO, IMF and World Bank approaches toward agriculture in the "developing world." These institutions have supported agricultural protectionism in the North while encouraging large-scale, export-oriented farming in the Third World. The results have been disastrous for self-sufficiency in food, and for the livelihoods of peasants and small farmers throughout the South.

The cynicism of the globalizers begins with the protection of western agriculture provided by ostensible "free trade" deals. As discussed in chapter 2, Europe, the United States and Canada massively subsidize their agricultural sectors to the tune of about $360 billion per year – subsidies that were effectively locked in to the WTO Agreement on Agriculture.[26] By financially under-writing huge numbers of farmers in Europe and North America, these subsidies generate a global glut of farm products that depress prices for agricultural goods. Third World producers are thus forced to compete on glutted markets against heavily subsidized commodities from the West, a competition they can never win.

Let me take just two examples: sugar and cotton. In the European Union, sugar producers are paid *four times* the world market price for the sugar they produce. Then the EU spends a billion dollars more in subsidizing exports of this sugar into world markets. Rather than "free," then, the market is rigged, with European producers receiving anything but the market price. But thanks to these subsidies, a huge glut of sugar drives world prices about one-third lower than they would otherwise be. And it is poor farmers in Mozambique, Brazil, Thailand and South Africa who lose out. The same thing takes place with the US cotton industry. There, the US Department of Agriculture provides nearly $5 billion in subsidies – more than all US aid to Sub-Saharan Africa – to America's 20,000 cotton farmers. As in the case of sugar, these cotton subsidies depress world prices and inflict untold hardship on poor farmers in African countries like Mali, Burkino Faso and Benin. Indeed, the drop in cotton prices due to US subsidies is believed responsible for a huge jump in poverty rates in Benin, from 37 to 59 per cent of the population, in 2001-2.[27] Behind the sickeningly hypocritical talk of free trade, millions endure poverty as a direct result of the protectionist practices of the world's strongest governments.

All of these dynamics are worsened when governments of poor indebted nations, desperate for foreign currency (without which these debts can't be paid), promote export-oriented farming. After all, production for local markets does not bring in foreign funds; only agricultural exports can do that. Yet, as one poor nation after another promotes exports, markets are flooded and prices plummet, often impoverishing Third World farmers. A vivid example of this trend can be observed in the world coffee market. Under pressure to finance its debts, Vietnam in particular has converted more and more land to coffee production and export, now eclipsing Colombia as the world's second-largest producer (after Brazil). Yet, the influx of massive new supplies onto the world market simply succeeded in driving prices down to a thirty-six-year low in mid-2001. Then, as bountiful rainfall in South America raised expectations of a record harvest, futures contracts for coffee (which track future prices) plummeted to record lows – as low as 42.5 cents per pound, compared to $3.05 a pound as recently as 1997. By 2002 in fact, coffee growers were taking in $8 billion less for their exports than they had only five years earlier.[28] All of this spells disaster for coffee producers and governments that depend on coffee revenues:

> In Nicaragua, coffee pickers with malnourished children beg for food at the roadside. In Peru, some families have abandoned their land, while others have switched to growing drug crops in search of cash, just as they have in Colombia. From Mexico to Brazil, tens of thousands of rural labourers have been laid off, swelling the peripheries of cities in a desperate search for work.[29]

Coffee is just the latest in a long line of agricultural commodities, from bananas to cocoa, that have followed this trend. As prices collapse and producers' earnings dive, poor farmers are driven into unsustainable debt. In such circumstances, they are often forced to sell their land, either to local rich farmers or to western agri-businesses. Just as their counterparts in Britain did a few hundred years ago, these landless peasants then move onto the labour market, swelling the ranks of the wage-earning poor. Land ownership becomes concentrated into fewer hands and capitalist employers find more poor people desperate for work at almost any wage. All these trends are encouraged by governments in the South because rich capitalist farmers export a larger share of what they produce (since poor farmers directly consume or barter much of their produce) and generate more foreign currency.

Taken together, western agricultural protection, Third World debt, glutted markets, falling agricultural prices, and policies promoting large-scale export-oriented farming converge to push millions of people off the land and into the labour market. Global and local capitalists thus find a growing pool of cheap labour available around the world. The proletarianization of ever-larger sections of the population is an inherent result of the struggle over the land.

Environmental Destruction in the Third World

Alongside the undermining of traditional agriculture and land use, globalization policies also inflict horrific damage on the natural environment. Desperate to raise cash crops in order to feed themselves and their families, Third World cultivators are under enormous pressure to adopt farming methods that undermine the soil, forest life and bio-diversity. The cumulative effects are mind-numbing.

A recent UN study warns that, given uncontrolled logging, it will take a miracle to save the world's remaining healthy forests. Loss of forests has a devastating effect on wildlife and biodiversity, as well as removing timberlands which capture rain water and prevent flooding. Despite the risks, half the forests in Asia are already threatened; rain forests in Brazil and Indonesia have been decimated; and Mexico has destroyed half its forests in a mere four decades. In fact, in just eight years (1993-2000), Mexico lost 2.78 million acres of land – a deforested area equivalent in size to the whole of Ireland.[30] Meanwhile, Brazil eliminates over 15,000 square kilometres of rainforest – an area nearly as large as Lake Ontario – every year. According to the 2004 meeting of the American Association for the Advancement of Science, the world's cropland has declined by 20 per cent per person over a single decade; altogether, an area of 300 million hectares, about 10 times the size of Britain, has been so severely degraded that it cannot produce food. Forest destruction combines with global warming – itself the result of greenhouse effects caused by industrial pollution – to pose a huge threat to world food production. As a result of climate change, the UN predicts that the world's poorest forty countries will lose roughly one-fifth of their capacity to grow food. By 2080, these countries will face shortages to the tune of sixty million tons of food, an astronomical figure for impoverished peoples.[31]

Rather than allow us to reverse these trends, contemporary globalization can only exacerbate them. The rush to produce exportable cash crops invariably inflicts further damage on the environment. To take just one example, in the early 1980s indebted nations were pushed to replace organic, shade-grown coffee with sun-tolerant varieties since the latter have high yields. Desperate for foreign currency in order to repay loans, countries like Brazil and Colombia did just that. While shade-grown coffees protect trees and preserve biodiversity, sun-tolerant varieties do not.[32] Consequently, deforestation has accelerated as growers abandon shade-grown coffee, thus worsening the environmental crisis – all at the urgings of the IMF and World Bank.

Similar trends are in play elsewhere. Haiti, for instance, has now lost 90 per cent of its forests, as 30 million trees are cut down each year by peasants desperate to make a living. And in the Congo, logging of rainforests destroys over 3,000 square miles of lush woods every year.

It is no accident that some of the worst environmental catastrophes are developing in the very Third World nations that have been coming under World Bank and IMF domination. Globalization has from the start had a neo-colonial character, with the Third World being seen as a ghetto of cheap labour and natural resources ripe for plundering, and as a place where the West can dump its garbage, industrial wastes and pollutants. In 1991, for instance, Lawrence Summers, then chief economist at the World Bank, distributed a memo in which he stated, "I think the economic logic behind dumping a load of toxic waste in the lowest wage country is impeccable."[33] So, while the biosphere is being destroyed, the damage gets unequally distributed – hitting the South and poor communities in the North especially hard.

For these reasons, there can be no environmental solutions without social solutions. Studying the legacies of imperialism and environmental destruction in Central America, Daniel Faber concludes, "like human poverty, the environmental crisis spreading through Central America stems from unequal distribution of land and natural resources." Environmental crisis and social inequality, he rightly concludes, "are two faces of a single process."[34]

Crisis on the Land: Agriculture and Rural Poverty in India

The interconnections of land distribution, environmental degradation and rural poverty are thrown into sharp relief in the case of India, one of the World Bank's agricultural "success stories." The so-called "Green Revolution" of the 1960s launched Indian agriculture down the road of large-scale, centralized, chemical-intensive farming. Because prices of pesticides and chemical fertilizers raised the costs of farming, many small peasants were unable to make ends meet. As a result, despite land reform programs in much of India that allowed more of the rural population to own land, peasants often found themselves burdened with heavy debts.[35] Consequently, even where land reform was genuinely pursued, it was often undermined by the promotion of large-scale commercial farming. One analyst claims that, whereas 18 per cent of India's peasants had no land prior to the Green Revolution, fully one-third became landless afterward.[36]

These trends were accelerated in 1991 when India's need for loans to refinance its foreign debt enabled the IMF to step in and impose its economic surgery (indeed, key policy documents of the Indian government were written directly by the IMF and World Bank for the country's Ministry of Finance). Invariably, these organizations promoted a heightened emphasis on export-oriented farming. Land that once produced food consumed by the local population was increasingly converted to cultivating cash crops for export:

> In Kerala, vast tracts of forests and paddy fields have been converted into rubber, coffee and coconut plantations. Every year about 25,000 hectares of good paddy land [for rice production] is diverted for non-paddy purposes. Such a structural transformation is not only peculiar to Kerala alone. It is happening in almost all parts of the country. Commercial crops are eating into the fertile land tracts meant for growing essential food grains ...[37]

As a consequence of the shift from subsistence to commercial farming, food supplies available for domestic consumption have contracted. Formerly self-sufficient Third World countries must increasingly import food, thereby giving European and North American agri-businesses the new markets they seek for their agricultural products. In such circumstances, the poor of the Third World, especially those driven off the land or struggling to hang on, find they cannot afford as much food as in the past – and this process triggers a rise in poverty and malnutrition. Calculated in terms of those whose diets are nutritionally deficient, the number of rural poor in India has gone up 10 per cent compared with the early 1970s.[38] One extensive study indicates that 47 per cent of Indian girls and boys, aged four and under, are malnourished, as are 48.5 per cent of adults.[39] These trends prevail even in parts of India that have enjoyed economic prosperity in recent years, such as the state of Haryana. As one analyst has shown, despite rising agricultural output and improving per capita income, the absolute number of people in poverty has risen throughout the 1990s. This can only mean that the benefits of economic growth are being shared more and more unequally – and that the gap between rich and poor is widening.[40] This is the context in which thousands of poor and despairing peasants have committed suicide, as we saw in the last chapter.

The globalizers' agenda has thus bred a reliance on export-oriented agriculture in an already-glutted world market, a dependence on food imports from the West, increasing social inequality and rising rural poverty and malnutrition. The overall pattern at work has rightly been described by one critic as "the economic re-colonisation of third world agriculture":

> The structural characteristics of the colonial syndrome in the agrarian sphere – the growth of exports and decline in the absorption of food staples by the poorer majority of local populations – is being replicated all over the developing world ...
>
> ... Rising export volumes are squeezed out at falling prices as more and more developing countries are required to follow the same policies and compete against each other to export similar products. What we are witnessing today is the economic re-colonisation of third world agriculture. . .[41]

A rise in the number of landless poor in the rural areas is a direct outcome of this agenda. And so is an increase in the number of members of rural households who, because their families cannot survive on the output of their own land, move into a variety of forms of labour for others. Women in particular have felt the brunt of this trend, particularly in the period of neoliberalism and structural adjustment that opened up in 1991.[42] As a consequence of the IMF-imposed structural adjustments of 1991, for instance,

India removed subsidies on chemical fertilizers, leading to a 40 per cent rise in their prices. As huge numbers of poor peasants saw their farms go under, or found they could no longer subsist without finding work for wages, they flooded onto labour markets, depressing wage levels much to the delight of capitalist farmers and foreign agri-businesses.[43]

Perhaps nothing has so dramatically contributed to the growth of landlessness as the obsession of the globalizers and successive Indian governments with constructing giant dams. These construction projects are attractive to many governments because they represent huge investments fueled by massive funds from the World Bank. On top of this, Indian governments claim that giant dams will divert water to dry areas and encourage agricultural development. On scientific grounds, this reasoning is dubious. Moreover, of the 4,000 large dams built in India, virtually none has ever lived up to its promises to deliver water to the masses. What giant dams have done, however, is provide water to huge plantations producing export crops, such as the sugar cane estates in drought-stricken Gujarat. What they also do with great effect is displace millions of people from their lands and livelihoods.

Since 1950, at least twenty-five million people in India have been displaced by large projects – and the actual number could be twice that high. In Bargi Nagar, for instance, a single dam submerged 162 villages and drove 114,000 people from the land on which they lived. Statistics indicate that of the millions displaced by these projects, at least half have been completely pauperized. Moreover, of those so displaced, 40 per cent are indigenous peoples – known as *adivasis* – although they represent only 8 per cent of India's total population. While those affected by giant dams have fought back with breath-taking courage and determination (as I discuss in chapter 6), they are up against the overwhelming forces of capitalist globalization. All too often, in the face of court orders, police and troops, they have been the losers.

Here again, we see a familiar story of enclosure and displacement being played out. Rising costs, falling prices, land grabs by capitalist farmers and western agri-businesses, and environmentally dangerous giant dam projects have all converged to accelerate the proletarianization of the rural poor and expand the labour pool available to global capital. As one elderly displaced farmer told a writer for *New Internationalist*: "From Khatedars [land-owners] we became day-labourers and paupers."[44] It is a refrain heard in one Third World country after another.

And the Beat Goes On: Proletarianizing Peasants and Indigenous Peoples

It would not be difficult to provide detailed examples of the same pattern in one country after another. A handful of examples, however, will illustrate just how far-reaching these trends are.

• **The Philippines** – As a result of WTO and IMF pressures to boost cash crops for export, the amount of land planted with corn declined by one million acres over a ten year period. Food production for domestic consumption has dropped drastically: between 1993 and 1998 alone, corn production fell by 20 per cent and rice output by 24 per cent.. The amount of land devoted to growing corn dropped by a massive 600,000 hectares between 1993 and 2000.[45] Meanwhile, output of export commodities such as coconut, cane sugar, bananas and pineapple has soared. At the same time, reliance on imports of food from the West has grown dramatically. During the first four years of WTO accords (1994-98), imports of corn jumped by 500 per cent. Rice imports now equal 40 per cent of domestic production; and imports of wheat (not a traditional part of the diet) total 30 per cent of domestic output of rice.[46] Here too we see the same processes of dispossession and proletarianization:

> To entice investments in export production, the government has provided foreign and local companies with concessions and licenses over land and coastal

105

resources in the public domain. As a result of such privatization of the commons, subsistence farmers and indigenous peoples living in upland areas are driven from their land to give way to large mining and timber plantation companies.[47]

- **Indonesia** – In a drive to clearcut huge sections of tropical rainforest and to provide extensive lands to mining companies, millions of people have been physically dislocated. Across the island of Kalimantan, 2.5 million indigenous peoples were displaced during the 1970s in order to facilitate logging and other commercial activities. On Java, the most populous island, another 3.6 million people were "resettled" to other islands. As deforestation proceeds at the pace of 1.3 million hectares per year, thousands upon thousands of people continue to be displaced.[48]

- **Colombia** – Under the guise of the war on drugs, military and paramilitary forces across Colombia routinely displace peasants, indigenous peoples and Afro-Colombian communities. Displacement is particularly severe in areas rich in oil, gas and other natural resources. According to one estimate made in 2002, on average 1,029 Colombians are driven off their lands *every day*.[49]

- **Mexico** – Well before NAFTA, farmers were shifting from production of foodstuffs such as corn or beans to raising animals for the more lucrative livestock industry which exports much of the meat it produces. NAFTA has accelerated the trends toward export-based farming and displacement of poor farmers. An analysis conducted by the Center for Economic Studies at the Colegio of Mexico indicates that 30 per cent of Mexico's small farmers will be driven off the land.[50] A recent article in the *New York Times* claims that "By the tens of thousands, peasants in Mexico are abandoning the small plots they considered their birthright." And, dissecting the causes, the author identifies NAFTA, plummeting prices and cuts to government support for agricultural producers.[51]

- **Papua New Guinea** – In outright capitulation to the IMF and the World Bank, the government of Papua New Guinea has embarked on a massive privatization campaign, including the demand that traditional landholders register their land claims. Since 90 per cent of all land is owned communally, the move to individual registration is a clear effort to introduce private land ownership and a commercial land market, both long desired by the World Bank and IMF. Student resistance to this program in June 2001 was greeted by brutal repression, with police killing at least three protesters.[52]

- **Honduras** – Seeing a great opportunity in Hurricane Mitch, which killed 5,000 people and displaced two million in 1998, the Honduran government repealed constitutional provisions that had prohibited the sale of indigenous lands and had blocked foreign ownership of lands within 25 miles of the coast. Reminiscent of English enclosures, private mansions in gated and guarded complexes have been built on lands belonging to the Garifunas, 150,000 descendants of African slaves who have lived on the Atlantic coast for over two hundred years. The Coordinated Black Organizations of Honduras and the Confederation of Autonomous Communities are now waging an historic battle to defend their commons.[53]

All of these processes are ways of carrying through the separation of producers from the land that is the key to capitalist development. Marx described this process of dispossessing peasants and creating a wage-labouring class as the original or primary accumulation of capital, a process that entails terrible episodes in which "great masses" of people "are suddenly and forcibly torn from their means of subsistence, and hurled onto the labour market as free, unprotected and rightless proletarians."[54]

The heart of this process is the commodification of human labour power. And what is called "globalization" centrally involves this process, be it in India, the Philippines, Mexico or any poor, indebted country. In fact, the acceleration of primitive ac-

107

cumulation is one of the most significant features of the neoliberal era. As Petras and Veltmeyer point out,

> ... the capitalist development process has separated large numbers of direct producers from their means of production, converting them into a proletariat and creating a labour force which at the global level was estimated to encompass 1.9 billion workers and employees in 1980, 2.3 billion in 1990 and close to three billion by 1995.

This represents a phenomenal growth in the size of the propertyless global working class in a remarkably short period of time. Globalization has meant dramatic dispossession and massive proletarianization of people – and the creation of a labour surplus for capitalists. As these people are forced off the land, they pour into cities, scrambling for the tiniest bit of substandard housing in the megaslums that now house the fastest growing section of humankind. And in these urban settings, close to half of this new proletariat is unemployed or under-employed "eking out a bare existence in the growing informal sector of the Third World's burgeoning urban centres or on the margins of the capitalist economy."[55] Globalization is thus also about global commodification of labour and globalization of poverty; it is about global proletarianization – the creation of a poor and dispossessed world working class for capital to exploit.

Enclosing Life Forms: "Charging a fee for what was once free"

Alongside the commodification of labour power, capitalism unleashes commodification throughout one sphere of human life after another. This logic of capitalism has been bluntly expressed by two mainstream economists who claim that "The history of economic progress consists of charging a fee for what was once free."[56] Of course, as Polanyi and others have shown, this claim is nonsense. But, if we substitute the phrase "the history of capitalist development," then the logic of the contemporary world system is grasped beautifully here. For under capitalism, one thing after another upon which human communities depend has been seized, privatized and commodified. In the era of global commodification, these processes are proceeding much the way they did during the epoch of colonial land-grabs, but today the new enclosures have extended into unprecedented areas.

Commodifying the human genome

Under the banner of "intellectual property rights," the WTO confers private patent rights on virtually any intellectual invention or discovery – even if this simply involves patenting something that people have known about and used for centuries (such as a plant form). Through its Trade Related Intellectual Property Rights (TRIPs) Agreement, the WTO establishes global patent rights whose violation can be punished by trade sanctions. Already, this is leading to major conflicts over medicines and medical treatments with respect to HIV-AIDS and other diseases.

These disputes originate in the fact that corporations can now "patent" specific human, animal and plant genes and claim intellectual property rights over them. As a result, anyone else dealing in any way with those genes – for research or treatment purposes, for instance – must pay the "owner" a royalty fee. Twenty percent of the human genome is now privately owned. A US-based biotech company owns the entire genome of the hepatitis C virus, while another firm owns the gene for diabetes. If you choose to do any research involving these genes, you must pay these firms for use of their "property." And the exercise of these property rights can have terrible effects on human well-being.

One particularly glaring example involves an American firm called Myriad Genetics. Having established patents on two genes that can indicate susceptibility for breast cancer, and on the process of comparing a woman's gene against the standard, the company has taken action against hospitals performing diagnostic testing involving these genes. Indeed, Myriad claims that it can block any woman from access to the contents of their own genes in this area, unless doctors treating them use the company's facilities. As a result, Canadian hospitals have been ordered to stop performing such tests (which cost about $1,300) and told they must pay for them to be conducted at a Myriad lab in Salt Lake City at a cost of $3,850. Unable to meet these costs, and frightened of having to pay Myriad large damages, cash-strapped hospitals in British Columbia have stopped the diagnostic test. That this could threaten the lives of thousands of women seems not to worry the corporation one bit: "We will protect our commercial rights," the Myriad president told a journalist.[57]

Firms with patents on human embryonic stem cells similarly threaten treatment of maladies such as diabetes and Parkinson's disease. With 45,000 biotech patents on file in the US (sixty of them to Myriad alone), the prospects are chilling. Says the director of genetic-testing at North York General Hospital in Toronto:

> There are hundreds of these patents coming. It's breast cancer today, prostate cancer and heart disease tomorrow. If they're all handled like this, it is the end of publicly funded health care.[58]

The battle over HIV-AIDS treatment in the Third World

One of the most contentious battles over intellectual property rights has to do with pharmaceutical drugs. WTO and other agreements have increased patent protection for drug manufacturers and waged war on cheaper generic drugs. Nowhere have the results been more devastating than in Africa, heart of the world's HIV/AIDS pandemic.

Of thirty-six million people around the world infected with HIV/AIDS as of the year 2000, twenty-five million of them live in sub-Saharan Africa. In South Africa, at least 16 percent of the adult population tests positive for HIV. For pharmaceutical companies, these people are a "growing market" for their high-profit commodities. In Kenya, for instance, the drug fluconazale, patented by Pfitzer and used in AIDS treatments, costs $18 per pill. On a typical regime of two per day for eight weeks, followed by one per day for life, a Kenyan would have to come up with $,1,080 for each of the first two months, then $540 a month for life – in a country where a police officer earns $43 per month.

Outraged by these impossible prices, the government of South Africa passed a Medicines Act in 1997, which allows for the use and import of affordable, generic drugs. In response, thirty-nine world-wide pharmaceutical firms launched a lawsuit defending their patent rights. Brazil and Thailand, facing major crises in treating HIV/AIDS, have enacted similar laws – all of them illegal under the WTO. In fact, in 2001 the United States won a WTO complaint against Brazil's violation of drug patents. The irony is that, by providing free anti-retroviral treatment to people, Brazil has had one of the most effective HIV/AIDS programs anywhere. In the case of Thailand, the government dropped plans to produce the anti-HIV drug ddI when it was threatened with trade sanctions. By policing its property rights in this way, the global pharmaceutical industry has enjoyed an explosion in sales from $22 billion in 1980 to more than $260 billion by the mid-1990s. A few of the global giants in the industry have filed thousands of patent applications

The battle over drug patents and the HIV/AIDS pandemic illustrates the contradiction at the heart of capitalism between private property rights and public needs and interests. While there are now noises about a "compromise" where AIDS/HIV drugs are concerned, the principle is clear: even when a life-threatening disease is at stake, the position of capitalist firms echoes the pledge of the president of Myriad that "we will protect our commercial rights."

Ownership of plant seeds and genes

Alongside monopolies in ownership of human genes, diagnostic testing and pharmaceuticals, other biotech firms have focused on plant life and seeds. As of the year 2000, patents had been granted or are pending on 500,000 genes and partial gene sequences in living organisms; and of these patents, fully three-quarters are owned by five life science corporations.[59] Many of these patent claims include plants and seeds that have been cultivated for centuries as gifts of nature, but over which nobody has claimed ownership. As of 2003, for example, about 7,000 patents had been issued based on indigenous knowledge in India, knowledge, which has long been the common property of society. The most notorious of the biotech firms in the agricultural sector, Monsanto, has filed a patent in eighty-one countries on soybeans containing certain genes or DNA segments from "wild" or "exotic" soybeans. The agreements that farmers must sign with Monsanto prohibit them from saving any seed for replanting, or supplying seed to another person. They must also agree to let Monsanto inspect their fields and to pay 120 times the technology fee plus legal fees if they are found guilty of violating the agreement. By February 1999, the biotech giant had brought 525 cases of legal action against farmers, and has added hundreds more since.

If any one development in this field perfectly captures the logic of capitalism in the biotech sector, it may be the development of terminator seeds, i.e. seeds genetically altered so that they do not reproduce. The world's farmers are being forced to buy these seeds year after year since nature's millennia-long gift to them has now been taken away. And, of course, as poor farmers struggle to meet costs, as they are forced to sell off their lands and enter labour markets, biotech firms will watch their profits and stock valuations soar.

Privatizing the world's water

Probably nothing will affect so many people in the coming years as the corporate rush to privatize water. According to the United Nations, more than one billion people lack clean drinking water at the moment. That number is expected to explode to 2.7 billion people, one third of humankind, within twenty-five years. In large cities in Asia, Africa and Latin America, fewer than half of all houses have running water. Salivating at the prospects of global water scarcity, multinational firms are moving to corner the market which is estimated at $1 trillion (US). And they have been aided by the World Bank which has financially supported at least 84 projects involving water privatization.

Privatization of water supplies has been rushing forward for some time already. In one part of India, for instance, Coca Cola has been granted a license for the contents of an entire water shed, making it illegal for people to use water in wells on their own lands.[60] And much more extensive developments are afoot. US President George W. Bush has pushed for bulk water exports from Canada to the American South. Should Canada be reluctant to comply, charges before the WTO are likely. Indeed, Sun Belt Water of California is already suing the government of British Columbia for refusing to let it export water in bulk. Moreover, William Cosgrove, a former vice-president of the WTO, has already promised that water will be "a major agenda item of future World Trade Organization talks."[61]

In this context, it's not surprising that Monsanto is also getting into the water business. A company document states that "since water is as central to food production as seed is, and without water life is not possible, [Monsanto] is now trying to establish its control over water." The company further indicates that it "has launched a new water business with India and Mexico, since both of these countries face water shortages."[62] And there we have it. Shortages drive up demand, prices, and profits. The fact that one or two billion people do not have ready access to clean water, without which "life is not possible," is not something to be bemoaned, but celebrated. Water-short countries like India and Mexico will be targeted for exploitation. Indeed, where water privatization has proceeded, costs have soared. While that is good for corporate profits, it has also provoked powerful resistance, since most people treat access to water as a right. This is deplored by the water industry. As a writer for Water Engineering and Management puts it, "water remains in many regions underpriced and oversubsidized."

In short, water is not yet fully commodified. But the WTO, IMF and World Bank, along with multinational capitalists, plan to change all that. In fact, at the WTO ministerial meeting in Doha, Qatar in November 2001, a clause was inserted into the final text that moves a considerable way toward privatizing the world's fresh water.[63] If the globalizers get their way, we will see terrible increases in disease and infant mortality throughout the poorest parts of the world. Fortunately, water has become a focal point for important resistance. Nowhere has this been more true than in Bolivia where, as I will discuss in chapter 6, an uprising of indigenous peoples and unions stopped privatization of the water supply in that country's second largest city. Undaunted thus far, the privatizers continue to enclose the world's water supplies. The consequences, should they succeed, will be enormous.

Commodifying the Psyche: Capitalism and Human Alienation

No concept is more central to Marx's critical analysis of capitalism than alienated labour. Marx condemns capitalism not simply because of the exploitation and inequality it breeds, but also because it impoverishes our inner lives and degrades relations among people. As the young Marx argued in 1844, conscious, creative activity that shapes the environment in which we live is central to what makes us human. But under capitalism, this essential life activity – social labour – is transformed into work done according to the dictates of capital. What is produced, how it is produced, according to what techniques and under what circumstances is determined by the logic of capitalist accumulation. Rather than an affirmation of our humanity, of our existence as creative beings making our lives together, labour under capitalism becomes drudgery, a detested, mind-numbing loss of life.

There are four essential aspects of alienated labour under capitalism. First the worker is alienated from the product of her labour, since this product goes into the hands of (or in the case of services is controlled by) the capitalist. Second, the worker is estranged from the process of production itself since this is controlled and determined by the employer, managers and supervisors. Third, the worker is alienated from her fellow-workers since, rather than cooperating in a shared and planned activity, she is divided from and pitted against other workers. And, finally, workers are estranged from their human capacity for creative self-development as members of a cooperative community.[64]

An essential feature of alienated labour is the reduction of work to a set of repeatable physical motions, in which different workers specialize, and whose speed is relentlessly increased. The use of "scientific management" to break every work process down into its component parts, each subjected to the stopwatch, is known as *Taylorism*, after the American Frederick Winslow Taylor. While Taylorism was initially used in assembly line systems of manufacture, it now dominates most sectors of the capitalist economy. Let me offer two examples. The first comes from *A Guide to Office Clerical Time Standards*, a manual used by the likes of General Electric and Stanford University. Almost every imaginable office activity is subjected to time standards (based on fractions of a minute). Opening and closing drawers, stapling, typing (per character and per inch), opening envelopes are all time calibrated. Getting up from a chair should take 0.33 minutes, while swiveling a chair in order to perform another task should take 0.009 minutes.[65]

My second example comes from Wendy's burger chain, part of the ever-expanding global fast food industry. According to the

Wall Street Journal, time is of the essence, nowhere more so than in the growing drive-through part of the industry. Every six seconds shaved off time serving each customer at the drive through translates into a one per cent increase in sales. So, grillers keep 25 burger patties on the grill and place one in a bun within five seconds of receiving an order, "Once the meat hits the bun, the griller hands off to the sandwich makers, who have no more than seven seconds to complete each customized option."[66]

An essential aspect of globalization has been a massive speedup of work processes, a drive to make production "lean," to use the jargon — that is, to get more and more work out of fewer and fewer workers.[67] The results, as more and more commentators acknowledge, include physically exhausted workers who struggle with ever higher levels of work-related stress.

As a result of all these aspects of alienation, the very fabric of human life becomes degraded. A single, alienated goal – the acquisition of money in exchange for estranged labour – becomes the central feature of our lives. Everything becomes concentrated on this debased and debasing goal. Sacrificing our human potential in exchange for money warps and deforms all parts of our lives. Instead of a rich social life characterized by creative work, play and recreation, artistic expression, intellectual stimulation, love, solidarity and cooperation, our lives are impoverished. The rich diversity of human possibilities is mindlessly reduced to one narrow, alienated goal: accumulating private wealth. Owning things replaces all the other forms in which we can enjoy and experience life. In Marx's words:

> Private property has made us so stupid and one-sided that an object is only ours when we have it, when it exists for us as capital or when we directly possess, eat, drink, wear, inhabit it, etc....all the physical and intellectual senses have been replaced by the simple estrangement of all these senses – the sense of having.

Inherent in this multi-faceted process of estrangement is that we are pressed to think of ourselves as commodities. "Selling yourself" becomes an art in this society. And more and more people are taking it literally. In the United States, for instance, growing numbers of people are agreeing, for a price, to have company logos tattooed to their heads. "Human billboards," they are called – and they sport logos of Toyota, among other companies.[68] And if our bodies are to be overtly commodified, then why not other essential features of our identities? In 2002, for instance, four Canadians whose last names are Dunlop agreed, for about $6,000 each, to change their last names to Dunlop-Tire in order to advertise Goodyear Corporations main brand of tires.[69]

So, while estranged labour is at the root of human degradation under capitalism, multiple forms of alienation pervade all aspects of life: our identities; our connections with nature; our sense of our bodies and our sexualities; our emotional well-being; relations between genders, between young and old, between peoples from different parts of the world. All these spheres of life become yet more areas in which we are estranged from others and from ourselves.

Then, in a vicious circle of alienation, capitalism promises us fulfillment, sense of purpose and belonging through commodities, the very markers of our alienation. Having robbed our lives of meaning, capitalism pretends to sell it back to us in the form of things. Mere means of life – cars, clothes, jewelry, and so on – are offered up as life's ends. The result is "an inverted world" in which things are substituted for human relations.[70] In fact, in a virtual parody of Marx's theory, a whole philosophy of contemporary marketing uses a model in which a consumer brand such as Nike, Pepsi or Ford is meant to represent an actual human relationship.[71] Rather than overcome alienation, these relationships with brands only deepen it. The more we pursue the things on offer from capitalism, the more estranged we become from the human qualities we most deeply seek – cooperation, sense of purpose, belonging, solidarity, creativity.

While Marx's analysis offers us the richest account of the deep roots of human alienation in capitalist society, many studies have confirmed much of what he has to say. A number of social scientists have been struck, for instance, by the fact that rising incomes in the dominant countries does not translate into higher levels of human happiness. Indeed, one analyst of this phenomenon chose to call his book *The Joyless Economy*. The author of this study noted that most people associate happiness with pleasures such as satisfying work, friendship, intellectual stimulation and so on – in other words, with non-commercial "goods."[72] A later study confirmed the same findings: "if the things that contribute most to well being are unrelated to money, we cannot buy them," its author wrote; "this is the principal cause of money's curious failure to produce happiness."[73] Rather than creating a high level of human fulfillment and happiness, capitalist wealth merely perpetuates the emptiness and loss of meaning built into the system of alienated labour and capitalist property. It comes as no surprise to learn, then, that a very large proportion of Americans who seek psychotherapy complain of forms of "psychic deadness" such as chronic boredom, purposelessness, meaninglessness, and alienation from themselves and others.[74]

Capitalism, Alienation and Destruction of the Natural Environment

An inherent part of capitalist alienation is that humans become estranged from their own bodies and their natural environment. After all, since it involves people sacrificing their physical, emotional and intellectual capacities in exchange for wages, capitalism encourages us to think of everything around us as commodifiable, as mere things that can be sold for money. The more alienated we are, the more we can treat our world and ourselves as detached, lifeless things with a commercial potential. Moreover, if we sell our bodies (even on a temporary basis), why not sell nature? As Marx wrote, "Nature is man's inorganic body ... and he must maintain a continuing dialogue with it if he is not to die."[75] Having been conditioned to sell our bodies and our human capacities, it is just a short step to doing the same with our inorganic bodies. The alienating outlook that permeates commodified social life conditions us to perceive the natural environment as a collection of resources ripe for commercial exploitation.

But there is more than merely an attitude at stake here. For capitalism is based upon laws of motion – social rules of behaviour, or imperatives – that require capitalists to minimize costs, exploit labour and degrade the environment. Because it is a system of competitive accumulation each capitalist must try to find a way of lowering costs, cornering the market and boosting profits. Those capitalists who can't keep up lose market share and risk going under. If they are to survive this competitive struggle, it is imperative that capitalists discover every possible means of reducing their costs and producing goods more cheaply. This means regularly introducing new technologies that speed up the labour process, and cutting costs anywhere and everywhere. In a parody on capitalism, Marx wrote that its commandment is: "Accumulate, accumulate! That is Moses and the prophets!"[76]

The cost-minimizing and profit-maximizing imperative of capitalism means that wind- and water-power, land, air, fossil deposits, rivers and lakes, trees, and minerals are treated as gifts of nature to be handled as ruthlessly as human labour. Consequently, industrial systems of high-speed production are created to exploit these elements of nature and then pump industrial waste-products back into them. Capitalists reject the idea that the social costs of degrading the environment should be imposed on them (since this would lower profits), so society as a whole suffers the consequences. Air and water systems are incessantly polluted, forests are leveled, fish and mineral stocks are exhausted to the point where the life-supporting capacities of the biosphere are imperiled.

A recent study determined, for instance, that when all social costs are tallied – including the costs of treating miners who contract black-lung disease – wind power is much cheaper than coal power. But, because both individuals and the wider society pick up the tab for healthcare, coal is still a cheaper energy source for private companies to market, as they need only absorb the private costs their business incurs, not the social costs they create, such as sick people. The irrational logic of capitalism – that private interests can benefit while the public loses – is here thrown into sharp relief. As one environmentalist puts it:

> From the point of view of society as a whole, sure, wind's a lot cheaper. But the utility [company] doesn't care about society as a whole. It only cares about its own profits and it's willing to sacrifice public health to increase its profits.[77]

The world environmental crisis is a result of that logic writ large. The pell-mell pursuit of private profit degrades everything in its path. And the scale of the ecological damage that has been inflicted as a result is difficult to contemplate. One environmentalist offers a chilling description:

> Everywhere on our planet, the picture is the same. Forests are being cut down, wetlands drained, coral reefs grubbed up, agricultural lands eroded, salinized, desertified, or simply paved over. Pollution is now generalized – our groundwater, streams, rivers, estuaries, seas and oceans, the air we breathe, the food we eat are all affected. Just about every living creature on earth now contains in its body traces of agricultural and industrial chemicals – many of which are known carcinogens or mutagens.[78]

In fact, one recent study calculates that in the course of 12 months humans now use up natural resources that the environment requires 15 months to replenish. Put differently, in 1961 humans used 70 per cent of the planet's annual biological productivity every year. By 2002 we were using 125 percent of that productivity. Simple arithmetic says this is not sustainable. So, fish stocks disappear, animal and plant species die out, Arctic ice melts (more than a million square kilometres between 1978 and 2000) the seas and coral reefs degrade, and life on the planet becomes less and less sustainable.[79]

At the same time, it is important to emphasize, as Dennis Soron does, that it is the behaviour of capitalist industry, not individual consumers, which is at the heart of the problem. Commercial agriculture and industry, for instance, account for 92 per cent of the world's water use, and the production of capital goods for industries is responsible for about 78 per cent of all energy use and 88 per cent of all toxic releases in the US.[80] The pell-mell industrialization of whole new regions of the globe, like huge parts of China, only worsens these problems. China is now the second largest consumer of oil among the countries of the world. Of the planet's 30 most polluted cities, 20 are to be found in China. Not surprisingly, given these figures, roughly 400,000 people are dying prematurely every year in that country due to air pollution.[81]

Rather than reversing these trends, rather than helping to save the planet and the species that inhabit it, the WTO and similar agreements have ominous implications in all these areas, since they make it illegal for governments to discriminate in favour of environmentally friendly products production processes. One trade ruling has decreed that nations cannot favour lumber from a selective cut of a managed second-growth forest over lumber from the clear-cutting of old growth forest. In another infamous ruling, the WTO (and its predecessor body, the General Agreement on Tariffs and Trade) declared it illegal for the US to restrict the import of tuna caught with nets that also trap and kill dolphins. The fact that laws protecting dolphins or old growth forests may be rational, humane, intelligent or far-sighted is irrelevant to bodies like the WTO. By deviating from the religion of "free trade" – which acknowledges only narrow economic efficiency, not social rationality – any trade policy based on societal or environmental goals is by definition "restrictive" and must be removed. Environmental protection is not to be an exception to the cult of the market, any more than is poverty or inequality. Not surprisingly, not a single environmental measure challenged before NAFTA, GATT or the WTO has survived; when the crunch comes, the environment is systematically subordinated to

121

the principles of the capitalist market.[82] That these principles are destroying the ecosystems that sustain life illustrates the irrational logic of capitalism.

The Irrational Logic of Capitalism

"Irrational logic" may seem self-contradictory, but it is an appropriate description. There is a logic to capitalism, by which I mean that the system operates according to a set of regular and predictable rules. Yet these lead to results that are destructive of the interests and well-being of humankind. In short, the rules of behaviour in capitalist society systematically produce irrational consequences.

To say that capitalism has a logic is to claim, in other words, that all of the trends I've been describing – from the privatization of the global commons to the destruction of the biosphere – exhibit a systemic pattern. Critics who fail to understand this simply cannot get to the roots of the problems they identify. As a result, while numerous commentators have discussed many of the phenomena I've described above, their criticism is often cast in exclusively moral terms. Of course, moral outrage is necessary and laudable. But a purely moral response ignores the fact that capitalism requires its dominant participants to behave in an exploitative and destructive fashion. No amount of moral lecturing or enlightenment will change the behaviour of capitalists as a group, since only by doing what they do will they survive as capitalists. If they do not exploit the poor, grab land and resources, commodify the globe, and act in environmentally destructive ways, they will not persevere in the war of economic competition. The imperatives of cost-minimization and profit maximization compel capitalists to do these things. If a given company stops doing them, it will simply be replaced by others who will do so. For this reason, in addition to condemning the behaviour of the world's dominant groups, we need to develop a critical understanding of the *laws of motion* of capitalism that dictate this behaviour. Once we do that, we can grasp the societal logic that links together such disparate phenomena as impoverishment of the poor, privatization of life forms, and destruction of the natural environment.

I describe capitalism as a contradictory system since what is apparently rational at the level of the individual unit (in this case the corporation) is demonstrably irrational for human society as a whole. Ruthless, competitive, cost-cutting behaviour is generally the only way for the owners and managers of a capitalist enterprise to keep their business afloat. But, as general principles of action, adhered to by millions of actors, capitalist economic "rationality" will ultimately destroy the foundations of human life. Because it is based upon estranged, atomized, disconnected competitors, capitalism cannot produce a genuine social rationality; there is an inherent gap between what seems rational for a part of the system and what is in fact rational for society as a whole.

At the root of the social irrationality of capitalism is the unique structure of alienated relations that define the system. As we have seen, capitalism could not exist without separating producers from means of production (particularly the land). Once alienated in this way, direct producers lose control over their work, the products of their labour, and their social inter-connections as workers and as human beings. Connected with this structure of alienation is a system of class antagonisms. On the one side, capitalists strive to intensify their control over workers and the labour they perform in order to exploit them to the maximum degree possible – and thus turn a profit sufficient to stay alive in the world of capitalist competition. Workers, on the other side, struggle to reassert some control over their working lives, to reclaim some dignity at work, and to limit their exploitation. The result is the class struggle between labour and capital that I discuss in chapter 6. For the moment, however, we need to concentrate on a crucial point: alienated social relations produce a social system that is out of control, one that is prone to self-destructive crises. And when these occur, it is the poor and working people of the planet who pay the highest price.

Economic Crisis and Social Irrationality

One need only think of the horrific economic crisis of the Great Depression of the 1930s, out of which grew fascism and a world war, to realize that economic crises are among the most devastating manifestations of the irrational logic of capitalism. As our analysis implies, crises of this sort are not historical accidents. They are inevitable outcomes of a system that compels capitalists to do everything possible to increase the productivity of their enterprises. In order to keep pace with the competition, capitalists must introduce new technologies such as computers and fiber optics, that speed up the pace of work and lower the costs of their products.[83] But with every capitalist purchasing new machines and equipment, and building the most modern plants they can, several things happen. First, they take on huge new costs, often financed by borrowing from the banks. Second, they develop massive new capacities for producing everything from cars to computer chips – capacities that often greatly exceed any reasonable expectation of market demand. This results in what Marx described as a crisis of *over-accumulation*, in which capitalists have accumulated more facilities and means of production than they can possibly use profitably. Faced with massive overcapacity (and the attendant costs) and inadequate sales and profits, some capitalists begin to teeter on the verge of bankruptcy, or collapse. The entry of whole new players, like China, into a vast array of global industries has exacerbated these trends. In fact, China itself is experiencing massive over-accumulation in 11 of its largest industries.

In the world automobile industry today, for instance, firms have the capacity to produce seven to eight million cars more each year than the existing demand requires. That's the equivalent of a world excess of about eighty state-of-the-art car factories. Not surprisingly, when the global economic slowdown hit in early 2001, auto firms begin to lay off workers, close factories and cut costs dramatically: Ford announced layoffs of 5,000 workers in North America, while General Motor's European company Opel gave pink slips to similar numbers. But even bigger shockwaves hit four years later, when GM alone announced plans to close 10 factories and lay off 30,000 workers. Ford followed with its own announcement of massive closures and job cuts. Before the shake-out in the auto industry is over, dozens of factories will close and tens of thousands of jobs will disappear.[84]

Similar trends have hit the telecommunications sector where one company after another has been melting down. In an analysis that confirms Marx's basic theory of capitalist over-accumulation, a *Wall Street Journal* article on the telecom crisis reported, "Oceans of cheap capital and competitive one-upmanship drove telecommunications and Internet service providers to build far more capacity than realistic forecasts of demand could justify. Now, many of those companies are bankrupt, or close to it."[85] So over-built is the world's telecommunications infrastructure that, by one estimate, more than 95 per cent of fiber optics capacity is unused.

Capitalism has a two-part solution to a crisis of over-accumulation and declining profits. First, a recession or depression is required to bankrupt a number of firms, reduce capacity, and enable the survivors to produce profitably once again. With some firms knocked out of business, the survivors can increase their market share, while mass layoffs and mounting unemployment drive down wages and, as a consequence, reduce the costs of doing business. Recessions, depressions, layoffs and unemployment are thus the inherent mechanism the capitalist market uses to "adjust" to a crisis situation. As one North American economist recently put it, "It's better to let the free market work and let there be a bloodbath and get rid of some excess capacity."[86] That the cost of such a blood-letting is usually millions of jobs lost, the impoverishment of millions of people, and the crushing of lives and hopes seems never to worry pro-business commentators. The second aspect of the capitalist response to crisis is to take advantage of the fear and insecurity caused by layoffs and unemployment to launch an all-out offensive against workers' wages and benefits, and the unions that are meant to protect them.

The deepest and most lasting crisis of the twentieth century was the Great Depression of the 1930s, a depression that ended only with the carnage and destruction of a world war. But in the early 1970s, another global economic downturn emerged. From the mid-1970s to the early 1980s, world capitalism stumbled from one crisis to another: recession (1974-75), outbreaks of double-digit inflation, further recession (1980-82), and debt crises in countries such as Mexico, Poland and Brazil. By the early 1980s, capitalists had launched a coordinated counter-offensive under the banners of neoliberalism and globalization. Led by the likes of British Prime Minister Margaret Thatcher and US President Ronald Reagan, western governments slashed social programs, smashed unions, launched a "trade offensive" against countries in the Third World to force them into the neoliberal model, and started locking the world economy into the globalization mold through mechanisms like the WTO.

Increasing Social Inequality: Globalization and the Closed Fist of the Market

Everything we have learned about capitalism should lead us to expect that the neoliberal globalizers would be intent on two things: driving more people into the ranks of the proletariat (in order to expand the pool of cheap labour) and launching a battle to drive down workers' wages (in order to boost profits). And, predictably, both of these processes have been central to the globalization agenda of the past twenty years or more.

As we've seen above, the number of propertyless labourers (proletarians) around the world increased from 1.9 billion in 1980 to nearly 3 billion by 1995. This massive growth — caused particularly by driving Third World peasants off the land — swelled the ranks of the poor, casual, and unorganized working class, thus offering global capital a terrific opportunity for heightened exploitation of labour. Alongside these developments went the neoliberal offensive against the wages, job security, and union rights of workers around the world.

Reagan's destruction of the US air traffic controllers' union at the beginning of the 1980s, and Thatcher's war in the middle of that decade against the British miners' union were just two of the most celebrated cases of a global offensive against the working class. In the US, the proportion of workers in unions fell from 25 per cent in 1980 to barely more than half that level by the mid-1990s. In France, the decline in "union density," as it's often described, was equally dramatic, plunging from 21 to 10 per cent. Workers in Spain experienced a staggering drop, from about 50 per cent to 10 per cent of all workers protected by unions.[87]

But nowhere was the war against workers more brutal and devastating than in parts of Latin America. The combination of military dictatorships, state repression, and IMF-directed structural adjustment has had devastating results. The weakening of labour laws has meant that more and more people work without contracts or with contracts that lack earlier protections. By 1996, for instance, the proportion of workers without contracts, or with weakened contracts, had jumped to 30 per cent in Chile, 36 percent in Argentina, 39 per cent in Colombia, and 41 per cent in Peru.[88] The consequences for workers' earnings have been devastating. In most western nations today, workers' wages make up about 40 per cent of the national income. In 1970 this was largely true of Latin America as well. But, as Table 3.3 indicates, the neoliberal era has witnessed a staggering reversal.

Table 3.3 – Wages as a percentage of national income

	1970	1980	1985	1989	1992
Argentina	40.9	31.5	31.9	24.9	n.a.*
Chile	47.7	43.4	37.8	19	n.a*
Ecuador	34.4	34.8	23.6	16.0	15.8
Mexico	37.5	39.0	31.6	28.4	27.3
Peru	40.0	32.8	30.5	25.5	16.8

* n.a. = not available
Source: James Petras and Henry Veltmeyer, Globalization Unmasked, pp. 85-6.

A contraction in working class earnings of this magnitude – a reduction by half of their share in national income on average – cannot take place without calamitous effects. These have been brutally evident in the form of soaring levels of homelessness, poverty and malnutrition. Inevitably, the poorest wage-earners suffer the worst effects. Take minimum wage levels, for instance: by 1994 they had lost between 62 and 86 per cent of their 1985 values in Peru and Mexico.[89] In this context, the number of people living in poverty increased by 50 million in the 1980s alone. Not surprisingly, throughout this period we have witnessed large-scale growth in the shanty towns on the outskirts of a large number of Latin American cities.

Alongside this growth of poverty, an unconscionable improvement in the fortunes of the rich has taken place. In Argentina, for instance, the earnings ratio between the top 20 per cent and the bottom fifth of income earners tripled in just over twenty years: from 8:1 in 1975 to 25:1 in 1997. In Brazil, the top 10 per cent now takes in forty-four times what the bottom 10 per cent earn. The discrepancies are so palpable that one finds "different worlds" inside the same nation:

> Today, 15-20 per cent of Latin Americans share a
> "First World" lifestyle: they send their kids to private

schools; belong to private country clubs ...; get face-lifts at private clinics; travel in luxury cars on private toll roads; and communicate via computer, fax, and private courier service. They live in gated communities protected by private police. They frequently vacation and shop in New York, Miami, London and Paris... They form part of the international circuit of the new imperial system.

The rest of the population lives in a totally different world. Cuts in social spending and the elimination of basic food subsidies have pushed peasants towards malnutrition and hunger. Large-scale redundancy of factory workers and their entry into the "informal sector" means a subsistence existence ... Cuts in funds for maintenance of water, sewage and other public services have resulted in a resurgence of infectious diseases. Declining living standards ... is the reality for two-thirds or more of the population.[90]

When examined on a global scale, the inequalities involved are so obscene that words seem inadequate to describe them. While more than a billion people do not have access to clean water or adequate food and shelter, there are now 793 billionaires in the world whose combined wealth, according to *Forbes* magazine, is an almost incomprehensible $2.6 trillion – more than the gross domestic product of all but six countries in the world.[91] In fact, the assets of the world's 200 richest people are greater than the combined income of 41 per cent of humankind.[92]

What globalization has done, therefore, is accelerate the increasing social inequality that is at the heart of capitalism. In the United States, for example, the top one percent of households owned 57.5 per cent of all corporate wealth in 2003 – up from 38.7 percent a mere twelve years earlier.[93] Because it continually transfers massive amounts of wealth (surplus value) from labouring people to the owning/employing class, capitalism produces inequalities that escalate without end. Those who are poor get locked into a poverty trap from which they cannot escape, while the wealthy continue to accumulate at their expense.[94] In Marx's words, "accumulation of wealth at one pole is, therefore, at the same time, accumulation of misery, the torment of labour, slavery ... at the opposite pole."[95]

Even the World Trade Organization admits as much. In its 1999 study, Trade, Income Disparity and Poverty, the WTO points out that in 1985 the average American earned "5,500% more than the average Ethiopian." It continues: "These gaps defy the imagination ... and will double in a century and a half at the current trend."[96] Worse, these statistics apply merely to the average American income compared to that of an Ethiopian. Yet, inequality inside the US has been escalating too throughout the globalization era. As *Business Week* reports, the compensation packages of Chief Executive Officers (CEOs) of American-based corporations went from 85 times the earnings of their average blue collar employee in 1990 to 475 times what a blue collar workers makes by 1999.[97] Were we then to compare the earnings of an American CEO to those of an average Ethiopian, we would be looking incomes nearly two and a half million per cent greater! What the globalization era represents, then, is an acceleration of the persistent increases in inequalities within and between nations that are endemic to capitalism. As Table 3.4 illustrates, the whole history of capitalism has been characterized by a continuous multiplication in the ratio of inequality between the richest and poorest countries.

Table 3.4 – Share of world income received by the richest 20 per cent of the world's countries relative to the share received by the poorest 20 per cent

1820 – 3:1	1960 – 30:1
1870 – 7:1	1990 – 60:1
1913 – 11:1	1997 – 74:1

Source: United Nations Development Program, *Human Development Report* 1999, p. 38.

This table demonstrates conclusively that the history of capitalism is one of increasing inequalities – which is exactly what our analysis would predict. And, as the huge jumps between 1960 and 1997 indicate, the globalization era is distinguished by an acceleration of this trend. Rather than lifting "countless millions out of poverty" and making "the world a safer, richer, better place," as its defenders claim, globalization has done precisely the opposite.[98] The world today suffers under the greatest global inequalities it has ever known – and the neoliberal agenda will only continue to exacerbate them. In doing so, globalization intensifies the historical legacy of colonialism, racism and imperialism that has marked capitalism since its birth. The next two chapters examine this legacy. Then we will shift gears and investigate the growing global revolt against all these forms of oppression.

Notes

1 For some representative samples of the fair trade perspective see "Fair Trade – Not Free Trade," Spring 2001 Newsletter of Canada's federal New Democratic Party; Deborah James, "Fair Trade, Not Free Trade" in *Globalize This!*, eds. Kevin Danaher and Roger Burbach (Monroe, Maine: Common Courage Press, 2000), pp.188-94; Maude Barlow and Tony Clarke, *Global Showdown. How the New Activists are Fighting Global Corporate Rule* (Toronto: Stoddart, 2001), p. 28. I should point out that a number of fair trade projects – such as those for coffee growers – are quite laudable initiatives. What I am questioning is a political perspective that couches its opposition to globalization in terms of fair trade.

2 Jennifer Alsever, "Fair Prices for Farmers: Simple Idea, Complex Reality," *New York Times*, March 19, 2006.

3 For recent mainstream explorations of Smith's legacy see Paul Mattick, "Who Is the Real Adam Smith," *New York Times Book Review*, July 8, 2001, and Jeet Heer, "Adam's Smith's Identity Crisis," *National Post* (Toronto), December 3, 2001.

4 Adam Smith, *The Wealth of Nations*, 2 vols., eds. R. H. Campbell and A. S. Skinner (Oxford: Oxford University Press, 1976), v. 1, pp. 267, 144. For a detailed discussion of Smith in these regards see David McNally, *Political Economy and the Rise of Capitalism* (Berkeley: University of California Press, 1988), Chs. 4 and 5, and McNally, *Against the Market: Political Economy, Market Socialism and the Marxist Critique* (London: Verso Books, 1993), Ch. 2.

5 Naomi Klein, *No Logo: Taking Aim at the Brand Bullies* (Toronto: Vintage Canada, 2000), p. 421.

6 "The case for globalisation," *The Economist*, September 23, 2000.

7 Karl Polanyi, *The Great Transformation: The Political and Economic Origins of Our Times* (Boston: Beacon Press, 1957), p. 68. Despite some quite valuable insights, Polanyi mistakenly attributes the emergence of capitalism to technological change, rather than class conflicts. On this point see Ellen Meiksins Wood, *The Origin of Capitalism* (New York: Monthly Review Press, 1999), pp. 103-4.

8 Karl Polanyi, *Primitive, Archaic and Modern Economies* (Boston: Beacon Press, 1968), p. 66.

9 Marshall Sahlins, *Stone Age Economics* (Chicago: Aldine Publishing, 1972), p. 213.

10 As quoted by Donald Purich, *Our Land: Native Rights in Canada* (Toronto: Lorimer, 1986), p. 127.

11 Polanyi, *Great Transformation*, p. 73.

12 Karl Marx, "Results of the Immediate Process of Production" in Marx, *Capital*, v. 1, trans. Ben Fowkes (Harmondsworth: Penguin Books, 1976), p. 989.

13 See Karl Marx, "Estranged Labour" in Marx, *Early Writings* (Harmondsworth: Penguin Books, 1975), pp. 322-34

14 Karl Marx, *Wage-Labour and Capital* (Moscow: Progress Publishers, 1952), p. 20.

15 For a wonderful description of the English commons see Jeanette M. Neeson, *Commoners: Common Right, Enclosure and Social Change in England, 1700-1820* (Cambridge: Cambridge University Press, 1993). A detailed account of these lands is provided by A. W. B. Simpson, *A History of the Land Law*, 2nd edn. (Oxford: Oxford University Press, 1986). For the meaning of common rights see E. P. Thompson, *Customs in Common* (New York: The New Press, 1991).

16 This discussion draws upon my earlier account in *Against the Market*, pp. 7-14.

17 Karl Marx, *Capital*, v. 1, p. 926. For discussions of resistance to enclosure see Roger B. Manning, *Village Revolts: Social Protest and Popular Disturbances in England, 1509-1640* (Oxford: Clarendon Press, 1988; Andrew Charlesworth, An Atlas of Rural Protest In Britain 1548-1900 (Philadelphia: University of Pennsylvania Press, 1983); Buchanan Sharp, *In Contempt of All Authority: Rural Artisans and Riot in the West of England, 1580-1660* (Berkeley: University of California Press 1980);

18 *General View of the Agriculture of Hampshire*, as cited by Thompson, p. 163.

19 Many of these peasants might have taken wage labour only on a part time or seasonal basis, but slowly but surely they were being proletarianized, i.e. rendered dependent on the labour market.

20 Marx, *Capital*, v. 1, pp. 896-7.

21 As quoted by McNally, *Against the Market*, p. 39.

22 See the data in Ibid., p. 40.

23 Polanyi, *Great Transformation*, p. 141.

24 The term "new enclosures" has been used by Pat Roy Mooney, "The ETC Century: Erosion, Technological Transformation and Corporate Concentration in the 21st Century," *Development Dialogue 1999*, n. 1-2, p. 83.

25 This is not to say that capitalism is just arriving in these countries, but that it is being intensified in the most dramatic of fashions.

26 See Natividad Yabut-Bernardino, *An Impact Study of Agricultural Trade Liberalization in the Philippines* (Manila, 2001) available at www.isgnweb.org.

27 *Human Development Report 2005*, p. 131.

28 Flavia Krause-Jackson, "Price of coffee futures plunges to 36-year low," *Toronto Star*, August 4, 2001; Anthony DePalma, "For Coffee Traders, Disaster Comes in Pairs," *New York Times*, October 28, 2001; Kim Bendheim, "Global Issues Flow into America's Coffee," *New York Times*, November 3, 2002.

29 "Drowning in cheap coffee," *The Economist*, September 29, 2001.

30 Alanna Mitchell, "Forests face global extinction, study says," *Globe and Mail*, August 21, 2001; Sam Dillon, "Mexican villagers rise to fight illegal loggers devastating forests," *New York Times*, April 30, 1999; "Mexican deforestation," *Globe and Mail*, December 12, 2001.

31 Alanna Mitchell, "Hungriest may turn to Canada, UN warns," *Globe and Mail*, July 11, 2001.

32 Julian Haber, "The real price of coffee," *Globe and Mail*, August 2, 2001.

33 Lawrence Summers, Memo, December 12, 1991, available at www.whirledbank.org/ourwords/summers.html.

34 Daniel Faber, *Environment Under Fire: Imperialism and Ecological Crisis in Central America* (New York: Monthly Review Press, 1993).

35 On the problem of debt for the rural poor see the following articles in *Journal of Peasant Studies* (Special Issue on Rural Labour Relations in India), v. 26, n. 2/3, January/April 1999: Lucia Da Corta and Davuluri Venkateshwarlu, "Unfree Relations and the Feminisation of Agricultural Relations in Andhra Pradesh, 1970-95," pp. 71-139; Jens Lerche, "Politics of the Poor: Agricultural Labourers and Political Transformations in Uttar Pradesh," pp. 182-241; J. Mohan Rao, "Agrarian Power and Unfree Labour," PP. 242-261.

36 Vandana Shiva, "The Green Revolution and After" in *The Great Grain Drain* (Bangalore: Books for Change, 1998), p. 17.

37 Devinder Sharma, "The Future Shock" in *The Great Grain Drain*, p. 83.

38 R. Nagaraj, "Indian Economy since 1980: Virtuous Growth or Polarisation?" *Economic and Political Weekly*, August 5, 2000, p. 283-288.

39 Madhura Swaminathan, "A further attack on the PDS," *Frontline*, February 2, 2001, p. 30.

40 Sheila Bhalla, "Liberalisation, Rural Labour Markets and the mobilisation of Farm Workers: The Haryana Story in an All-India Context," *Journal of Peasant Studies*, v. 26, n. 2/3 (January/April 1999), pp. 30-33.

41 Utsa Patnaik, "Export-Oriented Agriculture and Food Security" in *The Great Grain Drain*, p. 53.

42 See Da Corta and Venkateshwarlu.

43 Michel Chossudovsky, *The Globalisation of Poverty: Impacts of IMF and World Bank Reforms* (London: Zed Press, 1998), p. 128.

44 This quote and much of the data on giant dams in India is derived from a series of illuminating articles on Narmada dams by Maggie Black in *New Internationalist* 336, July 2001.

45 Yabut-Bernardino, p. 16; Walden Bello, *Dilemmas of Domination: The Unmaking of the American Empire* (New York: Metropolitan Books, 2005), p. 152.

46 Yabut-Bernardino, p. 17.

47 Yabut-Bernardino, p. 21.

48 Curtis Runyan, "Indonesia'a Discontent," *World Watch*, May/June 1998.

49 S. H. Larsen, "Uribe's Dictatorial Rule Suits Oil Companies," Znet Colombia, October 21, 2002.

50 Richard J. Barnet and John Cavanagh, *Global Dreams: Imperial Corporations and the New World Order* (New York: Touchstone, 1995), p. 254.

51 Ginger Thompson, "Farm Unrest Roils Mexico, Challenging New Chief," *New York Times*, July 22, 2001.

52 Sean Healy, "Papua New Guinea: People rebel against World Bank," *Green Left Weekly*, July 2001.

53 Kari Lyderson, "Land Sharks: The Honduran government is selling off indigenous lands," *In These Times*, January 10, 2000.

54 Marx, *Capital*, v. 1, p. 876.

55 James Petras and Henry Veltmeyer, *Globalization Unmasked: Imperialism in the 21st Century* (Halifax: Fernwood Publishing, 2001), p. 24. See also, Mike Davis's marvelous book, *Planet of Slums* (London: Verso Books, 2006).

56 B. Joseph Pine II and James H. Gilmore, *The Experience Economy* (Cambridge, Mass.: Harvard University Press, 1999), as cited by Harvey Schachter, "Have you been experienced?" *Globe and Mail*, May 5, 1999.

57 Lynda Hurst, "U.S. firm calls halt to cancer test in Canada," *Toronto Star*, August 11, 2001.

58 As quoted by Hurst. See also, Richard Gold, "My body, your patient," *Globe and Mail*, October 29, 2001. On ownership of embryonic stem cells see Andrew Pollack, "The Promise in Selling Stem Cells," *New York Times*, August 26, 2001.

59 James Meek, "The race to buy life," *The Guardian*, November 15, 2000. See also Birgit Muller, "On the Ownership of Nature" in *Not for Sale: Decommodifying Public Life*, eds. Gordon Laxer and Dennis Soron (Peterborough: Broadview-Garamond, 2006).

60 Robert Mata, "Coalition wants to make water the issue for antiglobalization forces," *Globe and Mail*, July 7, 2001.

61 Alanna Mitchell, "Canadian water on tap for future trade talks," *Globe and Mail*, August 13, 2001.

62 As quoted by Nate Dogg, "Oh Canada!," *Clamor* April/May 2001, p. 38.

63 Maude Barlow, "Don't swallow their water grab," *Globe and Mail*, November 30, 2001.

64 All these points are made by Marx in the manuscript on "Estranged Labour" in Marx, *Early Writings*, especially pp. 327-31. It is important to remember that workers resist these processes; nevertheless, they fundamentally define work in a capitalist society.

65 James W. Rinehart, *The Tyranny of Work: Alienation and the Labour Process*, 3rd. edn. (Toronto: Harcourt Brace, 1996), p. 85.

66 J. Ordonez, "An efficiency drive: fast food lanes are getting even faster," *Wall Street Journal*, May 18, 2000.

67 See Kim Moody, *Workers in a Lean World* (London: Verso Books, 1997).

68 Lisa Sanders, "Selling Scions with Forehead Ads: Human Billboards Prowl Times Square for Toyota," *Advertising Age*, April 7, 2004.

69 John Heinzl, "Four renamed Dunlops now big wheels," *Globe and Mail*, March 12, 2002.

70 Marx often uses this term to describe capitalism. See, for example, *Early Writings*, p. 379.

71 See Naomi Klein, *No Logo*, p. 176.

72 Tibor Scitovsky, *The Joyless Economy: An Inquiry into Human Satisfaction and Consumer Dissatisfaction* (London: Oxford University Press, 1976). While there are some serious theoretical shortcomings to this work, it serves an important purpose in highlighting these forms of human dissatisfaction in "advanced" capitalism.

73 Robert E. Lane, "Does money buy happiness?" *The Public Interest*, n. 113 (Fall 1993), p. 58. I have corrected the misspelling of "principal" in the passage cited.

74 John F. Schumaker, "Dead Zone," *New Internationalist* 336 (July 2001), p. 35.

75 Marx, *Early Writings*, p. 328.

76 Marx, *Capital*, v. 1, p. 742.

77 Jack Gibbons of the Ontario Clean Air Alliance, as quoted by Dawn Walton, "Wind power cheaper than coal, study says," *Globe and Mail*, August 24, 2001.

78 Edward Goldsmith, *The Way* (London: Rider, 1992), p. xi. Unfortunately, like many environmentalists, Goldsmith does not analyze the ways in which these trends are specifically embedded in the laws of motion of capitalism.

79 See the following articles by Alanna Mitchell: "Earth faces supply crisis, study finds," *Globe and Mail*, June 25, 2002; "Arctic ice melting much faster than thought," *Globe and Mail*, November 28, 2002; "Few of the world's

large fish remain, study says," *Globe and Mail*, May 15, 2003. For an excellent theoretical treatment of these issues see Joel Kovel, *The Enemy of Nature: The End of Capitalism or the End of the World?* (Halifax: Fernwood Publishing, 2002).

80 Dennis Soron, "Decommodifying Daily Life: The Politics of Overconsumption" in Laxer and Soron, pp. 219-37.

81 Geoffrey York, "Chinese subsidize nascent gridlock on the road to environmental ruin," *Globe and Mail*, March 31, 2006.

82 See Shrybman, p. 20, who also provides a good account of the tuna-dolphins case, pp. 20-22.

83 The lowering of costs refers to real costs. In an inflationary environment, nominal costs might go up while real prices fall.

84 Scott Miller, "Opel slashes capacity," *Wall Street Journal*, August 16, 2001; "Ford to slash up to 5,000 jobs," *Globe and Mail*, August 18, 2001; Gordon Pitts, "GM economic aftershocks," *Globe and Mail*, November 22, 2005.

85 Rebecca Blumenstein, Scott Thurm and Greg Ip, "Telecom sector's collapse disrupts entire food chain," *Wall Street Journal*, July 25, 2001.

86 Financial analyst John Tumazos as quoted by Greg Keenan, "Steel markers melt down over more than imports," *Globe and Mail*, May 2001.

87 Kim Moody, *Workers in a Lean World* (London: Verso Books, 1997), p. 183.

88 United Nations Development Program, *Human Development Report 1999* (New York: Oxford University Press, 1999), p. 37.

89 Henry Veltmeyer, "The World Economy and Labour," *Canadian Journal of Development Studies* 20 (1999), p. 693.

90 Petras and Veltmeyer, *Globalization Unmasked*, p. 88.

91 "The World's Richest People," *Forbes*, March 27, 2006.

92 United Nations Development Program, *Human Development Report 1999*, p. 38.

93 David Cay Johnston, "Corporate Wealth Share Rises for Top-Income Americans," *New York Times*, January 29, 2006.

94 Of course, there are the exceptional cases in which a poor person becomes rich, or a rich person loses a fortune. But as social scientists have shown repeatedly, these cases are so rare as to be statistically without significance.

95 Marx, *Capital*, v. 1, p. 799.

96 WTO, *Trade, Income Disparity and Poverty* (1999), available at www.wto.org.

97 See the report on executive compensation in *Business Week*, April 17, 2000.

98 These are the editorial claims of the *Globe and Mail*, April 12, 2001.

4. THE COLOUR OF MONEY: RACE, GENDER, AND THE MANY OPPRESSIONS OF GLOBAL CAPITAL

You can't have capitalism without racism.

– Malcolm X

"I would annex the planets if I could," remarked Cecil Rhodes, who conquered much of southern Africa in the name of the British empire more than a century ago. Rhodes' statement encapsulates a crucial feature of capitalism – its limitless drive to appropriate land and to turn more and more people into propertyless labourers. Already, corporations are exploring ownership of parts of outer space. Yet, there is nothing qualitatively new about this; from the start capitalism had a globalizing impetus, systematically bringing more and more of the world into its orbit. Rather than the tranquil process of liberal myth, the internationalization of capitalism has been accomplished by means of invasion, conquest, war and plunder. The violence inflicted on the English peasantry during the birth of capitalism would soon pale by comparison with what was done to non-European peoples. With the British leading the way, European capitalism invaded Ireland, the Americas, Asia and Africa, exhibiting a barbarity and cruelty that is almost incomprehensible. The rivers of blood that capitalism dug grew ever wider and deeper, defying all but the most murderous imaginations. In the process, a colonial system and an ideology of modern racism were constructed – abominations that continue to haunt the world in which we live.

It is the job of the pundits of the dominant class to deny this history, to weave a narrative about the advance of capitalism as the march of human freedom. But there have been, and continue to be, too many mass murders, too many acts of genocide, for the voices of the victims to be forever silenced.

Gold, Silver, Slavery and Murder: The Legacy of Columbus

In the fall of 2001, a great brouhaha was raised in the media about a handbook produced by the student union at Concordia University in Montreal. A number of organizations came together in a press conference to denounce the publication, while incensed right-wing editorialists denounced the student union as, among other things, "anti-globalization zealots" guilty of "sullying the university's name."[1] Among the features of the handbook singled out for condemnation at a press conference was its entry for October 8, 2001 which reads "Thanksgiving – Colonialist Holiday."

But what is it to which the right-wingers object? After all, native peoples certainly didn't initiate Thanksgiving Day, nor do they celebrate it. As Ward Churchill of the American Indian Movement has asked about the annual celebrations on this day:

> Should we be thankful for the scalp bounties paid by every English colony – as well as every US state and territory in the lower 48 – for proof of the deaths of individual Indians, including women and children? How might we best show our appreciation of the order issued by Lord Jeffrey Amherst in 1763, requiring smallpox-infested items be given as gifts to the Ottawas so that 'we might extirpate this execrable race?'... It's no mystery why Indians don't observe Thanksgiving Day. The real question is why do you feast rather than fast on what should be a national day of mourning and atonement.[2]

138

Given that it is not a day of mourning and atonement, what is the holiday if not a celebration of European colonization of North America? Here the outraged conservatives turn evasive. And for good reason. For the legacy of European colonization of the Americas, beginning with the "voyages" of Christopher Columbus, is not quite the uplifting affair they choose to celebrate.

As a number of commentators have pointed out, Columbus was less interested in discovery and adventure than he was in gold. In fact, his preoccupation with the metal could be described as obsessive. One expert points out that the word gold appears in his diary 140 times on his first trip to the Americas: "It was the one constant of his Journal, the one recurring goal, and on some days he seemed hardly able to get it out of his mind."[3] Alas, the great discoverer came up empty on his first two trips to the "New World" (1492 and 1493). Five years later, however, his luck turned: gold was discovered in the new colony of Espanola (what is today Haiti and the Dominican Republic). As extensive mining began, the colony turned out from one to three tons of the yellow metal every year between 1504 and 1519. "Gold is most precious," exuded Columbus. "Gold is treasure, and with it, whoever has it may do what he wants in the world, and may succeed in taking souls to Paradise."[4]

Paradise is not what would be visited upon the area's indigenous peoples, however. On his first and second voyages, despairing of finding gold, Columbus had hit upon another commodity that he could use to satisfy the king and queen of Spain, who had financed his journeys: slaves. Worried by his failure to locate gold, he sent several dozen natives back during his first voyage. Then, during the second trip, he captured 1,600 Tainos from the interior of Espanola and proposed to the Spanish royals that these men, women and children could be traded for cattle and supplies. With the discovery of gold on his third voyage came the decision that would shape all the early chapters of colonial history in the Americas: the great "discoverer" decreed that indigenous people would be enslaved and forced to mine gold.[5] In time, slavery would become the preferred labour system for every major commodity in the "New World": gold, silver, sugar, tobacco.

Of course, the indigenous peoples were unlikely to submit readily to this new arrangement. In order to conquer their resistance, terror was pursued as a routine part of colonial policy. Gallows were erected in every Spanish town, 340 of them in the valley of the Vega Real alone.[6] And these gallows were used with bloody results. Bartolomé de Las Casas, who came to the Americas as a Catholic missionary, chronicled the savagery of the Spanish. One historian summarizes parts of his findings:

> De las Casas reports how they made low, wide gallows on which they strung up the Arawaks, their feet almost touching the ground. Then they put burning green wood at their feet. These executions took place in lots of thirteen. Thirteen Arawaks were hanged each time. Why? This was "in memory of Our Redeemer and His twelve Apostles."

> De las Casas continues to say that chiefs and nobles were usually not hanged like that, but burned to death on grids of rods. Once, he writes, a captain complained that he couldn't sleep because of the cries and he ordered the victims strangled. But the constable … instead put sticks over their tongues so that they could not make a sound, and "roasted them slowly, as he liked." Men, women, and children on Columbus' Hispaniola were hacked to pieces, and those pieces were sold from stalls to the Spaniards for feeding their dogs.[7]

Murder, death by overwork, and disease ravaged the indigenous peoples. The scale of the human destruction is staggering. Scholarly research now suggests that there were about eight million Tainos when Columbus first arrived in 1492. Four years later, only three million remained. By the time Columbus left his duties as governor of the colony in 1500, a mere 100,000 of these indigenous peoples had survived. By 1542, perhaps 200 were alive. In short, within 50 years of European conquest, more than 99.9 per cent of the Tainos population had perished.[8] An apocalypse had occurred, bringing in its wake a wave of human annihilation that would reverberate throughout the Americas.

"They crave gold like hungry swine"

Columbus retired from colonial ventures in 1504. But his withdrawal did nothing to stem the tide of colonizing destruction. The lure of precious metals drew the Spanish, then the Portuguese, into one part of the Caribbean and South America after another. "They lifted up gold as if they were monkeys," said the Nahuatl, "with expressions of joy, as if it put new life into them … Their bodies fatten on it and they hunger violently for it. They crave gold like hungry swine."[9]

Then came the discovery of silver, and the earth was gorged to bring this sparkling metal to Spanish shores. Between 1503 and 1660, 185,000 kilograms of gold were shipped to Spain. But this pales by comparison with the 16 million kilograms of silver that arrived.[10] Alongside the mountains of silver, grew the piles of human corpses.

The devastation of the native peoples of Potosi – once a thriving economic and cultural hub, now an impoverished part of Bolivia – is just one graphic illustration of the ruinous "silver cycle." After tons of silver were dug from the ground, eight million Indians had perished, and the region was left impoverished.[11] Yet, as if it were a contest to exceed previous massacres, each mass slaughter merely paved the way for the next. Few are as tragic and stomach-turning as the destruction of the Aztec people of Mexico by the Spanish conquistador Cortés. Having captured the Mexican Aztec capital of Tenochtitlan in 1519, Cortés launched a first attack, followed by a pause to let a smallpox epidemic run its course, after which the conquistador launched another merciless assault. Twelve thousand people were slaughtered in one afternoon; the following day the death toll soared to 40,000. Ravaged by disease and overwhelmed by the death all around them, the people of the city were incapable of meaningful resistance. Still, Cortés attacked again and again until roughly two-thirds of Tenochtitlan's population of 350,000 lay dead.[12]

Having completed the conquest of the Mexicas by 1525, the conquistadors set their sights on the Mayans and other indigenous peoples to the south. Led by Pedro de Alvarado, a lieutenant of Cortés, Spanish troops advanced, according to Las Casas, "killing, ravaging, burning, robbing and destroying all the country." Referring to the "massacres and murders" committed, Las Casas wrote of Alvarado that "He and his brothers, together with others, have killed more than four or five million people in fifteen or sixteen years, from the year 1525 until 1540, and they continue to kill and destroy those who are still left."[13]

Massacres in order to control land and resources were compounded by mass death as a result of enslavement and overwork – all in imitation of the pattern first established by Columbus. Having founded the colony of "New Spain" in central Mexico, for instance, Cortés built an economy based on terror and slavery. Chained together at the neck, Indians were marched to the mines. Decapitation was routine punishment for stumbling or falling; children who walked too slowly were stabbed to death. So severe was the labour, and so weakened the slaves, that Spanish officials estimated between one-third and one-half of workers on the cocoa plantations died as a result of their five months of forced labour.[14] The mountains of corpses kept rising. Within the area of the former Mexican kingdom, a population of 25 million in 1519 was reduced to 1.3 million by 1595. In the Andes, out of a population of 14 million prior to the colonial invasion, barely a million indigenous peoples remained by the end of the of the sixteenth century.[15]

Meanwhile, refusing to be left out of the action, Portuguese colonialism had moved into the act in the area of Brazil, enslaving 300,000 Indians in the quest for "white gold" (sugar) and the yellow metal itself. By the time the sixteenth century was over, the native population had been reduced by 90 per cent. Desperate for slave labour, the Portuguese turned next to the trade in enslaved Africans – importing up to 10 million black slaves referred to as "coins of the Indies."[16] And the Portuguese found a seller who appeared to possess an infinite supply of enslaved Africans: Britain, which had entered the African slave trade in 1672 with the creation of the Royal African Company. Within forty years they would be the principal suppliers of African bond-labour to the Western Hemisphere. At the peak of the trade, shipments of gold to pay for slaves were arriving in London to the tune of 50,000 English pounds per week. But the British were not simply sellers of enslaved Africans; British colonies in the "New World" would soon be the world's largest buyers of slaves as well.

Capitalism and Slavery: The Legacy of British Colonialism

The role of Britain in colonial slavery is especially significant since it was the leading capitalist power of the age. In fact, a case can be made that many, perhaps all, of the other colonial powers of the period – particularly Spain and Portugal – were still essentially feudal societies, albeit of an aberrant sort. As a result of a European-wide crisis in the fourteenth-century, feudal ruling classes had turned to war, foreign trade and the looting of colonized lands as ways to preserve their powers. By the sixteenth century, a number of European monarchies were sponsoring overseas exploration (such as Columbus's voyages) in order to find the booty to fund military campaigns. In this respect, European colonialism grew out of feudalism. But Britain's colonial project differed in important ways from that of Spain or other European powers. In fact, the British empire of this period represents the purest form of capitalist colonialism. This becomes clear when we examine some of its key differences from the colonial system of its rivals.

Historian Sidney Mintz observes that while the Spanish "concentrated their colonizing efforts in the New World on the extraction of precious metals," Britain focused on "the production of marketable commodities" such as cotton, indigo, coffee, sugar and tobacco.[17] This distinction is more significant than might appear at first glance. Spanish colonialism was based overwhelmingly on tearing precious metals from the ground and shipping them home to finance wars; when the supply of silver or gold was exhausted, the land was abandoned. Spanish colonialism thus left defunct mines and dead labourers in its wake. British colonialism, however, was largely premised on developing means of production – land that was cleared, improved and cultivated; storehouses, mills, curing houses and distilleries that were used to process or "manufacture" raw commodities; and the infrastructure of roads and trading houses necessary to producing commodities (largely with slave labour) and shipping them to world markets. Consequently, Britain's colonial system favoured patterns of capital investment and production of commodities that were, as Mintz further notes, essentially "industrial" in form. While agricultural operations such as planting, sowing and harvesting were at the heart of Britain's colonial plantation economy, these were performed by hundreds of bond-labourers working on large estates according to exacting standards of production and labour discipline.[18] Britain thus pioneered, from the middle of the seventeenth century, what has rightly been described as "systemic slavery, linked to plantations and commodity production" – something radically different from the Spanish and Portuguese search for precious metals.[19]

Once we understand these uniquely capitalist features of the British colonial system, we can make sense of the claims by contemporaries that Britain's slave system was more oppressive than those elsewhere in the "New World." The less harsh treatment of slaves in the Spanish colonies had precious little to do with culture or religion, and everything to do with systems of exploitation. For one of the areas in which capitalism completely surpasses feudalism is with respect to the efficiency of exploitation. Unlike capitalism, feudal society does not subject the producers – usually peasants – to systematic supervision, control and regulation of their work process. Instead, peasants work largely by themselves on their plots and pay rents and taxes later. But capitalism increases the "efficiencies" of exploitation by seizing control of the work process itself and systematically subjecting wage labourers to the most intricate and invasive systems of supervision, direction and management. In so doing, it exploits labour more intensively than has any other social system.

These tendencies can be seen at work in the systemic slavery of the Anglo-American plantation economies. As David Brion Davis, who questions the greater humanity of the Spanish, observes: "There is little doubt that slavery in Latin America, compared with that in North America, was less subject to the pressures of competitive capitalism."[20] Anglo-American slavery, in short, was what Marx described as capitalist slavery, a system based on the use of slave labour to produce commodities for world markets. As a result, it exhibited unique forms of control and discipline of enslaved labour that struck observers as especially harsh.

Having established the model of a commodity-producing plantation economy based on systemic slavery, Britain proceeded to conquer the most territory and import the most slaves, quickly emerging as the dominant colonial power in the world. Only France had the military reach and economic resources to try its hand at the same game, but it was never able to seriously challenge Britain's hegemony. By 1770 the British-style plantation system in the colonial world involved "nearly two and a half million slaves toiling in the fields, mills, mines, workshops and households of the New World colonies," producing commodities, such as sugar and tobacco, equal in value to one-third of all European commerce.[21] By this point in time, enslaved Africans performed the overwhelming bulk of all plantation labour. The plantation economy was now constituted on the basis of racial oppression. But the racial oppression of Africans in the Americas emerged out of a complex system of bond-labour that had originally included other groups. Particularly significant in this regard were the Irish and the indigenous peoples of the Americas.

Irish, Indians and Origins of Racial Oppression

In September of 1880, a writer in the Times of London commented on English depictions of the Irish. The largest English newspapers, he wrote, "allow no occasion to escape them of treating the Irish as an inferior race – as a kind of white negroes."[22] This observation is doubly significant – first, for what it tells us about the racial oppression of the Irish and, second, for the light it sheds on the social construction of race and racism.

That the Irish were racially caricatured should come as no surprise since, as the adage has it, Ireland was Britain's oldest colony. Yet, over several centuries, English domination was never fully secured. It was only with the emergence of agrarian capitalism in the sixteenth and seventeenth centuries that England established a new regime of colonial domination that secured its control, a regime that was to become the model for its ventures in America. This new system of control emerged tentatively in the sixteenth century when four wars were fought and a number of colonizing initiatives launched. The turning point came in 1649-52, when an army under Oliver Cromwell routed Irish resistance. The key to the Cromwellian conquest involved more than superior military power, however. For the first time, Irish landholders, rich and poor alike, were evicted from their lands and a new capitalist landowning class, of English and Scottish descent, was settled in their place. By 1665, Irish Catholics, who had held two-thirds of the land in 1641, now clung to merely one-fifth.

The British ruling class applied in Ireland the methods of eviction it had pioneered against the English peasantry. Huge expanses of land changed hands, creating a new landed ruling class – known to historians as the Protestant Ascendancy – which, unlike absentee owners, could directly oppress and control the Irish peasantry. Firmly ensconced, this ruling group moved to consolidate its hold. A series of anti-Catholic statutes were passed, known as the Penal Laws, that forbade Irish Catholics from sitting in parliament, voting in parliamentary elections, possessing arms, operating a school, attending university, or practicing law. Under these laws, Catholics lost yet more land until they owned a mere one-sixteenth of the country. A virtual system of apartheid was created. But, while religion was the badge that differentiated exploiter from exploited, as one Anglo-Irish historian pointed out, "The penal code as it was actually carried out was inspired much less by fanaticism than by rapacity, and was directed less against the Catholic religion than against the property and industry of its professors."[23] It was, in short, a massive property grab orchestrated under religious guise.

This marriage of plunder with ethno-racial discrimination established the basic structures of racial oppression as it would come to be practiced in America. Violence and terror, systematic discrimination and enslavement were all employed. During the anti-Irish wars of conquest, the heads of those killed during the day would be publicly displayed.[24] Moreover, at the end of the 1650s, up to 40,000 Irish men were sold by British adventurers to foreign armies for use as soldiers, a practice that would be repeated throughout the century. Young Irishmen were also kidnapped by English adventurers and sold as indentured servants to plantation owners in Virginia and elsewhere.[25] Even much of the legal framework of racial domination that would be applied to African-Americans had its Irish parallels. As Theodore Allen points out:

> If a law enacted in Virginia in 1723 provided that "manslaughter of a slave is not punishable," so under Anglo-Norman law it sufficed for acquittal to show that the victim in a killing was Irish. Anglo-Norman priests granted absolution on the grounds that it was "no more a sin to kill an Irishman than a dog or any other brute."[26]

Of course, a regime of oppression and discrimination of this sort requires some sort of ideological justification. English colonizers were initially troubled in this regard for two reasons. First, English law dating back to 1366 granted Irishmen the same legal status as English subjects. Secondly, it had long been considered sinful for Christians to persecute or enslave other Christians. In working their way around these problems, the English ruling class laid crucial building blocks for racism as a belief system.

A key ideological move was to claim that, because they were not civilized, the Irish were not in fact Christians. Since the dominant world-view held that "savages" could not be Christians, apologists for the conquest of Ireland set about to prove Irish barbarity. To that end, a whole series of racist stereotypes were constructed depicting the Irish as licentious, incestuous, pagan and uncivilized. Enslavement of Muslims, pagans and Africans throughout parts of medieval Europe had been justified on just this basis.[27] Now, the same rationale was being used to justify colonial domination – including terror and slavery – as the basis for civilizing a "savage" people in Ireland. In developing this argument, English writers drew freely on Spanish justifications for murder and pillage against native peoples in the Americas.[28] At the very origins of the European colonial era, then, the Irish joined American Indians as an "uncivilized" group against whom almost any and all forms of violence and oppression were justified.

Race, Class and Unfree Labour in the Rise of Capitalism

The Irish experience provides an important confirmation of the pioneering argument made by the Trinidadian historian Eric Williams in his landmark book, *Capitalism and Slavery* (1944). Arguing that slavery must be understood principally as an economic institution out of which racism grows, Williams wrote that

> Slavery in the Caribbean has been too narrowly identified with the Negro. A racial twist has thereby been given to what is basically an economic phenomenon. Slavery was not born of racism; racism was born of slavery. Unfree labor in the New World was brown, white, black and yellow; Catholic, Protestant and pagan.[29]

Williams' argument, while one-sided in some respects, contains a profound truth: that unfree labour in the Americas was not initially based upon race. Only through a long period of trial and error did plantation capitalists settle on a strategy of racial oppression of enslaved Africans. At its beginnings, bonded labour in the Americas was, as Williams says, "brown, white, black and yellow." In fact, as it became clear that indigenous peoples would not be a sufficient foundation for New World labour – either because of their ability to resist or because of their catastrophic disappearance due to disease and murder – the planters turned largely to Europe for bonded or indentured labourers. These bonded labourers were obliged to work for a master for a defined period of time, often for five to seven years. Typically, their legal status did not differ considerably from that of black slaves: they could not marry without permission and they could be sold, put up as stakes in bets, inherited or used to pay debts.[30] Considered property in law, indentured servants lacked the rights due to legal subjects; they could be "beaten, maimed and even killed with impunity."[31]

In the decades prior to large-scale importation of enslaved Africans, white indentured servants formed a class of unfree labour which, far from being of marginal importance, was absolutely central to many of the early plantation economies. Indeed, for more than 150 years, over half the white emigrants to North America came as indentured servants – large numbers of them transported convicts, kidnapped Irishmen, or poor English youth conned into thinking that a better life awaited them. Between 1607 and 1783, more than 350,000 "white" bond-labourers arrived in the British colonies, at least 250,000 of them landing in British North America.[32]

Considered in light of this history, Williams' claim that "White servitude was the historic base upon which Negro slavery was constructed" looks entirely convincing, as does his claim that the origin of black slavery "had to do not with the color of the laborer, but the cheapness of the labor." The planter class, he wrote, "would have gone to the moon, if necessary, for labor. Africa was nearer than the moon, nearer too than the more populous countries of India and China. But their turn was to come."[33]

We should not be surprised to discover, then, that racial categories were quite unstable at this point in the history of colonial capitalism. Indeed, the modern discourse of race had not yet developed, at least in part because differences in skin colour did not yet map onto the distinction between the free and the unfree. After all, the Americas knew both unfree whites and free blacks. The latter group, while a definite minority, exercised basic rights in law (until the period of systematic racialization arrived); they could buy, sell and own land and slaves, and they could purchase European-American bond-labourers.[34] At the same time, the racial identity of the poor Irish in Britain and its colonies remained unclear. In 1690, for instance, the Barbados Colony Council requested that the colonial government provide "white servants;" yet, they proceeded to exclude "Irish rebels," explaining that they did not want "labourers of that Colour to work for us."[35] This remarkable passage underlines just how much race is a social construction. Here we have the Irish, who would eventually attain "whiteness" in America, designated as of a "Colour" different from "white servants." So long as labourers from the British isles were being kidnapped, indentured and sold, the line between the free and the unfree was not clearly racialized. Consequently, everyday language in Anglo-America used the term "servant" to indicate a wide variety of whites as well as blacks, adding "adjectives like perpetual and negro" to identify slaves.[36] Attempting in 1770 to define what it meant to be a slave, Benjamin Franklin did not use any racial criteria at all; in fact, he argued that there were thousands of "slaves" in Britain, by which he clearly meant bonded labourers.[37]

In principle, emerging capitalism in the New World could have functioned quite happily with a variety of ethno-racial groups forming a stock of unfree labour. And, for a considerable period of time, the planters tried to organize colonial societies on just this basis. But a key problem – control of the labouring class – eventually forced them to choose a strategy of racial domination. The result would be new forms of oppression whose wretched effects continue to shape the world in which we live.

How to Tame a "Giddy Multitude": The Dilemma of Colonial Capitalism

Too often, the development of racial slavery and doctrines of white supremacy are simply attributed to the available supply of unfree labour. The African slave trade, it is suggested, was the only reliable source for the large numbers of bonded labourers required by the New World colonies. Yet, as Theodore W. Allen shows in his major study, *The Invention of the White Race*, these supply-side explanations are highly deficient. Ignoring the evidence that the planter class was quite happy to exploit a "mixed" population of unfree labourers, they neglect this ruling elite's problems in trying to discipline rebellious groups of white servants, Indians and black slaves that populated the Anglo-American colonies.

The difficulty of relying largely on enslaved natives was two-fold. First, on continental land masses, such as Brazil and North America, indigenous peoples, if they survived disease, had significant capacity for resistance or flight to "unsettled" territories. Small island colonies might function effectively with enslaved Indians, but this strategy was deficient where land masses were much larger. Secondly, native societies were not sufficiently stratified for a privileged layer of indigenous peoples to be "bought off" and integrated into the structure of domination. In most of Ireland outside of Ulster, by contrast, the English eventually hit on the solution of co-opting the Catholic bourgeoisie into a neo-colonial arrangement. This social stratum then served as a "buffer group" – a sort of junior partner in the colonial relationship – which administered systems of social control no longer seen as originating outside Irish society .[38] But native societies were simply not unequal enough to facilitate such a strategy. Resistance to enslavement thus tended to provoke uprisings of whole peoples.

While tens of thousands of native peoples were enslaved in British North America by the early 1700s, the costs of extensive enslavement – in terms of Indian wars that imposed great damage on the fledgling colonial societies – tended to be prohibitive.[39]

These social and economic costs first became clear to the planters of Virginia on March 22, 1622 when the Indians of the Powhatan Confederacy launched a war to halt Anglo-American expansion onto Indian lands. In the aftermath of the devastation caused by that battle, the planters backed off enslavement of natives and set out instead to impose bondage on all Anglo-American labour.[40] The same dilemma reared its head in southeast Anglo-America during the so-called Yamassee War (1715-17), a rebellion of Indian nations that came close to toppling the colony of South Carolina. After this native uprising, the use of Indian slaves quickly disappeared.[41] The social costs of trying to discipline unfree native labour had proved too high. Natives would eventually be genocidally eliminated, once population settlement and military power made victory more or less certain; for the time being, however, different sources of bond labour had to be found.

Throughout most of the seventeenth century, indentured labourers from the British isles were imported in ever-larger numbers for this purpose. More than 90,000 European immigrants, three-quarters of them chattel bond-labourers, were brought to Virginia and Maryland between 1607 and 1682.[42] Then, as a result of the establishment of the Royal African Company in 1672, a steady supply of African slaves was secured. Yet, while the supply of labour was now guaranteed, its control was not. As new problems of social unrest erupted, the plantation bourgeoisie moved in fits and starts toward a strategy of strict racial oppression.

The essential problem for the planters had to do with the rebellious culture of the lower classes. Especially worrying was the way this popular culture crossed ethno-racial lines. In the Virginia of the 1660s, for instance, the ruling class bemoaned the character of the "giddy multitude" which consisted, as one historian puts it, of "an amalgam of indentured servants and slaves, of poor whites and blacks, of landless freemen and debtors."[43] This mixed "rabble" of the lower classes regularly resisted the violence and oppression of unfree labour. On occasion, this resistance could pass over into insurrection as it did in 1676.

Bacon's Rebellion of 1676 was the largest popular upheaval in the history of colonial America. The crisis started as a quarrel within the colonial elite over enforcement of anti-Indian policies, but, as so often happens in popular rebellions, division and conflict at the top of society created the opening for the lower orders to mobilize on their own behalf. Of 15,000 participants in the tumultuous events, a majority were bond-labourers – 2,000 African-Americans and 6,000 European-Americans. These well-armed rebels plundered property and set the capital ablaze, in the process sending the royal governor and his entourage into hiding.[44] Perhaps most significant, they demanded freedom from chattel servitude. The ruling class now confronted a rebel army composed of "freemen, searvants, and slaves."[45] That such a diverse group of labourers could resort to common insurrectionary action was especially disconcerting. Sent to intervene at one point in the conflict, English naval captain Thomas Grantham described being met by "about foure hundred English and Negroes in Armes."[46] Such images of a joint uprising of black and white, slave and bondsman, proved traumatic. In the face of a united rebellion of the lower orders, the planter bourgeoisie understood that their entire system of colonial exploitation and privilege was at risk.

Social Control in the "New World": The Emergence of White Supremacy

Determined to eliminate the threat of revolution from below, the planters devised a new system of social control. As the English bourgeoisie had done in Ireland, they sought to create a buffer group that could reinforce the established order. To this end, they relaxed the servitude of white labourers, intensified the bonds of black slavery, and introduced a new regime of racial oppression. In so doing, they effectively created the white race – and with it white supremacy.

Again, it is important to insist that the problem of social control drove this strategy. The fundamental issue was not colour prejudice, although this certainly existed, but the establishment of stable structures of oppression that would be secure against rebellion. In the British West Indies, for instance, the promotion of a "colored" middle class was used to develop a buffer group as a counterweight to lower-class revolt.[47] "Rebellion, or the threat of it," wrote Orlando Patterson, "was an almost permanent feature of Jamaican slave society." In addition to wars with Maroons (escaped slaves who established colonies of free blacks in the hills and mountains), large slave revolts, or intended uprisings, occurred in 1760, 1776, 1784, 1823, 1824 and 1831. The last of these uprisings involved about twenty thousand rebellious slaves.[48] Because of "white" emigration to British North America, the European population of the West Indies was not sufficiently large to serve as an effective disciplinary force. The development of a substantial group of "free blacks and coloureds" emerged as the default strategy. By the early 1830s, this group owned nearly one-quarter of the bond-labourers in Jamaica.

In British North America, however, Europeans were generally a majority of the colonial population. To establish a stable regime of social control, the planter bourgeoisie eased white servitude and debased the status of African-Americans. Most historians agree that the conditions of white and black servants began to diverge considerably after 1660. Prior to then, many black servants appear not to have been indentured for life. From about 1660, however, a steady stream of legislation sought to separate black and white servants and to prevent "mixed" marriages and the procreation of "mixed-race" children (a crime known as "miscegenation").[49] Yet, law is one thing, practice another. And the evidence suggests that the behavioural changes – exemplified particularly in the decline of united rebellions by white and black servants – date in the case of Virginia from about 1680.[50]

Increasingly, colonial law imposed lifetime bondage for black servants – and, especially significant, the curse of lifetime servitude for their offspring. These became the defining features of slavery in America.[51] Legal decisions in Virginia in the 1660s reflect this trend, as does a law enacted in Maryland in 1664. Another Virginia law of 1691 curbed racial intermarriage; it would be duplicated by North Carolina in 1715. Meanwhile, South Carolina moved in 1712 to classify all blacks, Indians, or mixed-race peoples as slaves unless they could prove otherwise. Twelve years later, that colony also deprived men of those groups of the right to vote even if they were legally free and owned property. In fact, a Virginia act of 1723 denied African-Americans the right to hold any public office, to be witnesses against whites in a court of law, to raise their hand against any European-American (a crime whose punishment was thirty lashes at the public whipping post), or to bear any kind of arms. As Governor William Gooch explained, the Virginia Assembly had decided "to fix a perpetual Brand upon Free Negroes and Mulattos."[52] Across the board, laws were being redesigned in ways that drew sharper lines between the rights and conditions of European- and African-Americans. Central to this process was political disenfranchisement: the denial of the right to vote. Interestingly, most Anglo-American colonies had previously granted the vote to free blacks. But now this too was rescinded: in Virginia in 1723, in Georgia in 1761, in Louisiana in 1812 and so on.[53] Looking back on these developments, we can observe the ruling class of colonial America "in the act of inventing race."[54] A system of white supremacy and black inferiority was being constructed – one that crossed class lines and incorporated poor Europeans into white privilege. The planters had "consolidated their class position by asserting white racial unity."[55] Freedom was increasingly identified with race, not class. And a new mental universe – the ideology of modern racism – was constructed as an inherent part of this process.

155

Colonial Capitalism and the Invention of Race

Racial oppression emerged in Anglo-America as a strategy for capitalist control of the labouring class. The claim that modern racism developed as part of this process is often met with disbelief, however. One reason for this is that various forms of prejudice toward outsiders and foreigners have existed throughout different human societies across many historical periods. Yet, it is important to distinguish hostility toward those who are different – which is sometimes referred to as *heterophobia* – from modern racism, even where these hostilities involve colour prejudice. What is unique to the world of modern capitalism is the idea that there are physically distinct races of humans with radically different characteristics and attributes.

If we look at the ancient societies of Greece and Rome, for instance, bondage was not associated with skin colour or physical appearance. The same is true of Islam when it began expanding beyond Arabia in the seventh century: while there were black slaves in Egypt, skin colour was not used as a means of legitimating bondage. Similarly, Caucasians and other light-skinned peoples were enslaved at various times in European history. While both Islamic and Christian societies condoned slavery, it was seen as an exceptional condition and seems never to have been justified on the basis of colour.[56] What one historian has written of the ancient Mediterranean world appears also to have been true of most societies: they "developed no theories of white superiority."[57]

For a millennium, the Mediterranean world was torn between two hostile civilizations, Islam and Christendom. But this conflict was constructed in religious terms, not racial ones. Moreover, religion was seen as a set of beliefs and practices, not an inherent trait. By changing those beliefs and practices – through religious conversion – persecuted individuals could lose their oppressed status. Throughout this entire epoch, then, "religion was a matter of faith, not race."[58] Only in the era of modern capitalism did persecution get accounted for in terms of inherent and unchangeable features (the "race") of a specific group. For instance, Jews were persecuted for centuries in parts of the Christian and Islamic worlds because of their religion, but only in the last hundred years or so do we see claims that Jews are inherently, biologically different. Contrasting modern anti-Semitism with its earlier (religious) forms, Hannah Arendt notes that previously "Jews had been able to escape from Judaism into conversion; from Jewishness there was no escape."[59]

In fact, the same thing applied to European attitudes toward Africans and native peoples in the early stages of colonization. To be sure, these groups were considered "savage," "barbarian," and inferior to Europeans. And, because they were deemed to be "uncivilized," it was said to be acceptable to enslave and terrorize them – so long as this was done in order to "civilize" them. But violence, prejudice and bigotry were not justified by depicting these groups as separate races which were less than fully human. As one theorist of racism observes, "prior to the late eighteenth century, it was rarely claimed that the African was less than human." Christian doctrine held that, while Africans and Indians were "heathens," they could ultimately be raised to the level of European-Christian civilization. Only in the eighteenth-century was this view largely dropped in favour of the doctrine of racial inferiority.[60] What was it, then, about the development of capitalism that gave rise to modern racial ideology?

The key issue here has to do with the contradiction generated by capitalist claims for "freedom." Since its inception, capitalism in many societies has mobilized large groups of people in order to break down pre-capitalist forms of power and privilege – and thereby to elevate the principles of capitalist property and power. In early modern England, for instance, capitalism could only consolidate itself through the revolutions of the seventeenth century which sought to crush the right of the monarchy to tax wealth or interfere with property without the consent of property owners. Capitalist property was to be "freed" from the depredations of the throne – and this meant claiming the ground of "liberty" in a war on tyranny. Similarly, the French Revolution 150 years later mobilized the poor against the monarchy in the name of "liberty, equality and brotherhood."

Capitalism can successfully employ this rhetoric of freedom and equality because it eliminates "extra-economic" bases of social domination. In pre-capitalist societies, the power to demand wealth or labour services from others derived from the different political status of each group. Feudal lords, for instance, hold noble titles granted by the monarchy. These political titles or offices came with specific perks such as the right to demand land rents from peasants, to run local courts and so on. Similarly, being an exploited peasant (or serf) had to do with the status of the group into which one was born. One's economic position was not determined by purely economic factors; instead, it was set in advance by "extra-economic" factors such as whether one was born into a noble or peasant household.

For two key reasons, capitalism is hostile to these earlier structures of domination. First, the system of political titles and offices often kept capitalists – who had amassed fortunes through farming, trade or industry – from having a decisive influence on governments. If they weren't part of the aristocracy, capitalists tended to be excluded from the circles of political power. Secondly, certain hereditary rights – particularly access to common lands – gave poor peasants an alternative to full participation in the market economy. Seeking to commodify everything, capital is hostile to these customary limits to buying and selling.

As a result, bourgeois ideologists claim that capitalism is based on freedom and equality. Drawing up a theory of market liberty, they assert that every individual has an equal right to buy and sell goods on the market; no law shall be allowed to deprive anyone of this right. For the majority, of course, this means the "freedom" to sell their labour to a capitalist – or risk hunger and poverty should they fail to find a buyer. Thus, this freedom is often a form of deprivation. As the radical leader Jacques Roux put it in 1793 at the height of the French Revolution: "Liberty is no more than an empty shell when one class of men is allowed to condemn another to starvation without any measures being taken against them."[61] Still, this "empty shell" is often identified with freedom since the market exchange between capitalists and workers involves, in the words of Ellen Meiksins Wood, a "contractual relation between formally free and equal individuals." For this reason, emerging capitalism "carried with it an ideology of formal equality and freedom."[62]

But if everyone is free and equal, how then to justify chattel slavery? How is it possible that some people should be deprived of freedom and equality in a society that claims these ideals? In pre-capitalist societies, this was not a problem. Slavery was just one of a number of relations of inequality. And these unequal relations were justified according to ideologies that decreed that the divine power had created certain hierarchies – between gods and humans, kings and subjects, men and women, lords and peasants, masters and slaves – because this is the way human society was naturally meant to be. But these justifications can't work in a society that claims to be based on liberty and equality. As a result, Wood explains, "in capitalism, the criterion for excommunication seems to be excommunication from the main body of the human race."[63] If certain people are denied freedom and equality, this is because they aren't really human, because they are barbaric creatures, members of inferior races.

And so, as bondage became associated with Africans in eighteenth-century America, the concept of race was created. Even to describe themselves as white was an innovation for European-Americans. As a rule, they referred to themselves in terms of nationality (as Englishmen or Spaniards, for example) or, with reference to religion (as Christians). The appellation white was still quite rare. Yet, by the early eighteenth century, that term was occurring with some frequency.[64]

In the forefront of this development were members and associates of the planter class. As Peter Fryer explains in his marvelous study, *Staying Power: The History of Black People in Britain*, early claims by planters that Africans were not part of the same human race as Europeans were treated as religious heresy at odds with scripture. Because colonialism was justified as a Christian mission, it was held that Africans should be baptized and converted. Increasingly, however, the planters refused these policies. Fearing that baptism and Christian education would lead their slaves to rebel in the name of equal rights, they argued these practices were as absurd as baptizing horses. At first their arguments offended the dominant thinking. When the English naval surgeon John Atkins insisted in 1734 that "White and Black must have descended of different Protoplasts [i.e., human lines]," for instance, he acknowledged that this line of argument was out of step with religious orthodoxy. Forty years later, however, when Edward Long's *History of Jamaica* stated baldly that "the White and the Negroe are two distinct species," the author was by no means out of step with the views of the dominant class.[65] In the period between 1734 and 1774, modern racism had emerged.

The historical reasons for this transition are multiple. In the first instance, it had to do with the planters' anxieties about rebellions of African-American slaves. As William Knox, who had been a government official in Georgia and Florida, wrote in 1768, if slaves were taught to read, there would be "a general insurrection of the Negroes and the massacre of their owners."[66] Secondly, it owed something to the establishment in 1773 of British government control over Bengal, a development that raised questions about the basis on which Britain would rule a society of "natives." Thirdly, it had much to do with the doctrines of freedom and liberty associated with the agitation leading up to the American Revolution for independence from Britain in 1776.

This last factor is especially important because so much of the discourse of the struggle for American independence was organized in terms of the opposition between freedom and slavery. Britain was said to be intent on ruling Americans as if they were slaves; but freedom, claimed advocates of independence, was the natural right of humankind. This powerful rhetoric had a profound resonance among lower-class whites, many of whom were trying to escape servile status and claim rights as free men. Yet, the rhetoric of liberty, independence and natural rights had a radical logic to it which, at least implicitly, challenged the whole moral and political basis of any and all forms of slavery. This was especially clear to Thomas Paine, author of the best-selling work *Common Sense* (1776), which spelled out the case for American independence. On the same basis as he opposed British colonial rule over America, Paine denounced the enslavement of African-Americans. "We have enslaved multitudes, and shed much innocent blood," Paine wrote, "and now are threatened with the same."[67] In short, having practiced slavery, Americans were now confronted with enslavement themselves; the only decent response would be to renounce the entire "wicked and inhuman" institution. But that, of course, the slave-holders were not prepared to do. And so, the ideology of racism – of inherent difference and inequality among races – was systematically created in order to provide "the means of explaining slavery to people whose terrain was a republic founded on radical doctrines of liberty and natural rights."[68]

In fact, as colonial law subjugated African-Americans to a regime of discrimination and oppression, and as concepts of liberty and freedom became widespread among European-Americans, a pseudo-scientific racism emerged, by which I mean the effort to use methods associated with the natural sciences to "prove" the inherent differences among various "races" of humans. Again, we see this development taking place in the middle of the eighteenth century.

In the first edition of his *General System of Nature* (1735), the great naturalist Charles Linnaeus had made no attempt to classify humans. But this would soon change as the literature of racism – travelogues, histories and the like – grew in influence. Five years later, Linnaeus' second edition offered a four-part classification of human types. In his tenth edition of 1758, he expanded this to six groups. More significantly, with that edition Linnaeus moved beyond physical description to ascribe distinct character traits to each group. Anatomical differences were now linked to fundamental differences in moral character.[69] Soon, other natural scientists began challenging the dominant Christian view, known as monogenism, which held that all humans derived from a single source (Adam and Eve). "Scientific" racism now took up the cause of polygenism, the very doctrine the planters were promoting, according to which different human "races" were in fact separate biological creations.[70] It followed that the rights appropriate to humans need not apply to these "sub-human" species.

The construction of modern racism also identified races according to distinct colours. Whereas, prior to the eighteenth-century, American Indians generally had been considered whites at a lower stage of social evolution, they were now increasingly characterized as "redskins."[71] Having a different colour became the identifier for belonging to a separate race/species, and thus being subject to unequal treatment. In its crudest terms, racism blatantly justified violence and oppression. In 1764, for instance, Benjamin Franklin reported that "The Spirit of killing all Indians, Friends and Foes, [has] spread amazingly thro the whole country."[72] It would seem to be no accident that the escalation of anti-native violence coincided with the period in which the ideology of modern racism was being consolidated.

After the American Revolution, the pseudo-scientific discourse of race became the official position in American intellectual life, actively promoted by the likes of naturalist Louis Agassiz, professor at Harvard University and founder and director of the Museum of Comparative Zoology.[73] When the influential *United States Magazine and Democratic Review* asserted in 1850 that "the dark races are utterly incapable of attaining to that intellectual superiority which marks the white race," it did not say anything that would have surprised its (white) readers.[74] And the British ruling class, deeply entwined with colonialism and plantation slavery, rallied to the cause, as did colonial powers elsewhere. Deeply rooted relations of racial oppression were now integral to Anglo

American capitalism – and with it, as we shall see, the whole of international capitalism.

Race and Empire

Throughout the nineteenth and twentieth centuries, racism became a centerpiece of the new age of empire. While the scramble for control of the Americas had dominated colonial conflicts among the European powers in the early going, the rest of the world would not long be spared. Parts of coastal Africa had been ravaged for hundreds of years by the European trade in slaves, and the Dutch had developed extensive colonial projects in India and Indonesia, as these countries are now known. Building upon the record of the East India Company, British capitalism seized Bengal in the middle of the eighteenth century, bleeding the riches of the land, inducing famine and devastating the system of agricultural production. But it was in the final quarter of the nineteenth-century that the age of empire really took hold and, with it, a mad scramble for colonial territories among a half dozen of the world's major capitalist powers. Huge chunks of the planet and tens of millions of peoples who lived there were drawn into the orbit of European domination. The age of classic imperialism had begun. As historian Eric Hobsbawm explains,

> Between 1880 and 1914 ... most of the world outside Europe and the Americas was formally partitioned into territories under the formal rule or informal domination of one or a handful of states: mainly Great Britain, France, Germany, Italy, the Netherlands, Belgium, the USA and Japan ...
>
> Two major regions of the world were, for practical purposes, entirely divided up: Africa and the Pacific ...
>
> ... Between 1876 and 1915 about one-quarter of the globe's land surface was distributed or redistributed as colonies among a half dozen states. Britain increased its territories by some 4 million square miles, France

by some 3.5 millions, Germany acquired more than
1 million, Belgium and Italy just under 1 million
each.[75]

The imperialist powers of the age had an ideology ready-
made for the justification of colonial conquest and plunder: racism. If it was the conquest of India (Bengal) that needed legiti-
mation, then a new race, "the Hindoos," could be created and
a whole series of retrograde characteristics attributed to them.
George Coombe, claiming he could discover racial characteristics
by studying heads, declared that "The Hindoo brain indicates a
manifest deficiency in Combativeness and Destructiveness" and
that people of this race "are remarkable for a want of character."[76]
With these pseudo-scientific stereotypes in hand, imperial powers
proceeded to execrable acts of violence and plunder.

Reading the accounts from India or parts of Africa makes
depressingly familiar reading. Huge amounts of land are seized;
mining and agricultural production are developed, often using
bonded labour; the local population is impoverished and driven
into labour for the colonizers; a system of bloody terror is introduced. As the British established their East African Protectorate,
local tribes were ground under the wheel of imperial "progress."
Writing to the Foreign Office in London in 1904, for example, Sir
Charles Elliot, Commissioner for the Protectorate, informed his
superiors: "There can be no doubt that the Masai and many other
tribes must go under. It is a prospect I view with equanimity and
a clear conscience."[77] And it was racism that cleansed such consciences. As 40 million black Africans were brought under British
domination, Cecil Rhodes could console himself that "the British
were the best race to rule the world."[78] In the same spirit, the
British people were called upon to celebrate the royal coronation
in 1902 by recognizing the crown "as a symbol of the world-wide
dominion of their race."[79]

But, while the British were the most accomplished practitio-
ners of colonial violence, they were far from alone. King Leopold
of Belgium, for instance, harboured an obsession with develop-

ing colonial holdings. To this end, he studied the history of the conquistadors in America and visited the British possessions in Ceylon, India and Burma. Then, in the 1880s, he used a combination of deception and bribery to procure an enormous African colony that would be known as the Congo. Having studiously absorbed the legacy of Columbus, Leopold used enslavement and forced labour to produce enormous quantities of ivory, then rubber. As world demand for rubber soared – for use in producing tires, hoses, wiring and tubing – Leopold made astronomical profits. Maintaining a disciplined labour supply was a problem, however, since rubber workers must disperse widely throughout rain forests. But Leopold had learned his lessons well. He devised a scheme by which his troops would invade a village, kidnap the women, and hold them until the men produced a certain quota of rubber. Then, after the quota was delivered, the women would be returned to the men of the village – for a price. In order to create the appropriate climate of terror, Leopold's soldiers massacred tribal peoples and left severed heads and decaying bodies for all to see. "My goal is ultimately humanitarian," declared one of his officers. "I killed a hundred people ... but that allowed five hundred others to live."[80] By these methods, in combination with starvation, disease and over-work, ten million people were killed in Belgian-controlled Africa between 1880 and 1920.[81]

There was nothing terribly unique about the human destruction carried out by Leopold in the Congo. In the rubber-rich forest areas of France's colonies in equatorial Africa, the population decline was of the same order: 50 per cent. Around the same time, US troops in the Philippines massacred anti-colonial rebels, burned villages and tortured prisoners in a crusade that saw 200,000 Filipinos perish.[82]

Just like Sir Charles Elliot, the leaders of Belgium, America, France and Britain had clear consciences. Imbued with the doctrine of white supremacy, they were not troubled that the creation of their empires entailed rivers of blood. So ingrained was racism in their worldview that the rule of the "white races" seemed a law of nature. While racism was no longer tied to slavery, it had become the ideology of imperialist conquest and racial discrimination against the most oppressed sections of the world's population. Notions of white supremacy also served to create powerful differences and divisions within working classes, thereby weakening their resistance to capital. This is not to suggest that racism was only a strategy of manipulation, however; the European and North American ruling classes have utterly absorbed its prejudices and assumptions, thus enabling them to justify the most shocking acts of barbarity against peoples of colour.

After the First World War, for instance, when world leaders were debating a Covenant for the League of Nations, Japan's proposal that it include the principle of racial equality was strenuously opposed by US president Woodrow Wilson. Wilson's objections were supported by British Foreign Secretary Arthur Balfour who explained that the principle that "all men are created equal" meant that people *within* any given nation were equal, "not that a man in Central Africa was created equal to a European."[83] Slavery may have been abolished, but the slaveowners' eighteenth-century claim that there were different "races" with distinctive characteristics and unique rights lived on, legitimating the inequalities and oppressions of the age of imperialism.

The same is true of those nation-states created under the guise of European colonialism, particularly the "white settler states" such as Australia and Canada. In 1901, for instance, a "White Australia" policy was established which built upon "Coloured Races Restriction and Regulation" bills developed by several British colonies. Australia's racist policies on immigration and settlement were supported by the Colonial Office in London which expressed its sympathy with the desire to avoid "the permanent presence of a considerable element of an inferior race."[84]

Canada too, notwithstanding its current rhetoric of multiculturalism, was constructed along the lines of white domination.[85] The racial segregation and oppression of native peoples, institutionalized under the Indian Act (1876), the development of a pass system for Indians on reserves – which was studied and copied by the racist apartheid government in South Africa – and the horrific policy of residential schools which tore native children from their parents, are all part of a legacy of official racism that continues to scar Canadian society.[86] And, like Australia, a "White Canada" policy governed immigration and settlement. Chinese labourers in particular felt its effects.

While thousands of young Chinese men were brought in to build the transcontinental railroad in the 1880s, the Canadian government soon moved to prevent further Chinese immigration. A $50 head tax, an enormous amount of money for the time, was imposed in 1885 in the hope that it would be prohibitive. The head tax was raised twice more, hitting $500 by 1903. Finally, the government moved to an outright ban with the Chinese Exclusion Act of 1923; and those Chinese who had settled in the country were denied the right to vote until after the Second World War. Moreover, during that war, Canada refused entry to ships carrying Jews fleeing Nazi-occupied Europe. As far as Jews were concerned, in the words of the country's prime minister, "none is too many."[87]

This racist legacy was openly articulated by a series of the country's political leaders. In 1885 Sir John A. Macdonald, Canada's first prime minister, proclaimed, with respect to people from Africa and Asia, "It is not desired that they should come; that we should have a mongrel race; that the Aryan future of British America should be destroyed by a cross or crosses of that kind."[88] More than sixty years later, Prime Minister Mackenzie King (of "none is too many" fame) declared, "There will, I am sure, be general agreement with the view that the people of Canada do not wish, as a result of mass immigration, to make a fundamental alteration in the character of our population. Large-scale immigration from the Orient would change the fundamental composition of the Canadian population."[89] In somewhat more subtle guise, a racially biased policy continues to govern immigration into Canada.[90]

The Wages of Whiteness

One shortcoming in the account I have offered until now is that it might lead us to see racism as entirely something imposed from above, as merely a conspiracy of the powerful. It is true that modern racism was devised as a means of disciplining a labour force. Initially, it was used to control bonded labour in the colonial plantation system. Subsequently, it became the ideology of classical imperialism, legitimating violence and plunder on an extraordinary scale. Moreover, it became a powerful weapon for dividing working classes in the imperial countries and getting large numbers to identify with the racial and national traditions of "their" nation-states.

But to accomplish the latter, to mobilize the identifications of many workers, racism must have become more than a tool of the elites; it must have become integral to the outlook of large numbers of working class peoples in Europe and North America who have often been only too happy to see themselves as "white." In important respects, in other words, significant numbers of "white workers" must have made racism central to their own self-understanding.

This dimension of racism, its power of attraction for "white workers," was brilliantly analyzed by the historian W. E. B. Dubois in a famous passage in his book, *Black Reconstruction in America*. Explaining the widespread racism of poor whites in the US South, Dubois wrote:

> It must be remembered that the white group of laborers, while they received a low wage, were compensated in part by a sort of public and psychological wage. They were given public deference and courtesy because they were white. They were admitted freely with all classes of white people to public functions, public parks, and the best schools. The police were drawn from their ranks ...[91]

Dubois' notion of a public and psychological wage has informed some major discussions of the "wages of whiteness," the idea that white supremacy affords exploited white workers a sort of psychological compensation, based upon public recognition, for their inferior economic status.[92] Smarting from their treatment as dispensable wage-labourers, white workers are allowed to bask in the significantly better treatment they receive in public places, before the police and the courts, in schools and job interviews, and as members of the dominant cultural group.

Some within the ruling class have long recognized the advantages of conferring such a psychological wage on white workers. An eighteenth-century Virginia planter, for instance, observed that poor whites did not reap significant economic gains from white supremacy. They have "little but their complexion to console them for being born into a higher caste," he noted.[93] Yet, this little matter of complexion, the public recognition that comes with membership in the "superior race," could become all the more precious precisely because poor white workers had so little else. In fact, study after study has shown that white workers in the US South, where racial segregation was most marked, lived much more poorly than their white counterparts elsewhere. Not surprisingly, the attractions of whiteness have been especially powerful for those oppressed groups whose racial status in America and Europe was markedly insecure. This has been the case more for the Irish in America than perhaps any other group.

The utterly downtrodden status of Irish immigrants to America in the seventeenth, eighteenth and nineteenth centuries often comes as something of a shock to students of history today. Given Ireland's history as a British colony, it should not be surprising. Huge numbers of the millions who left Ireland – as indentured servants or "economic refugees" – were not only poor, they were also members of a despised and ostracized group. Once in America, they often found themselves with no option but to take the worst and toughest jobs. Indeed, it was not uncommon to hire the Irish to do jobs that were considered too dangerous for black slaves, since the slave owner had made a long-term investment in purchasing a slave. An Alabama shipping company that hired the Irish explained, for instance, that blacks "are worth too much to be risked here; if the Paddies are knocked overboard, or get their backs broke, nobody loses anything."[94] So poor were the Irish, so ghettoized into the most dangerous jobs, that on average they lived six years after their arrival in America.[95]

Furthermore, the Irish had closer personal relations with African-Americans than did any other group at the time. Blacks and Irish often lived together in squalid apartments, and in cities like New York and Boston, the majority of "mixed" couples involved Irish women and black men. Into at least the 1830s, Irish and African-Americans lived and socialized together in many American cities, creating a vibrant popular culture. Black celebrations, such as Negro Election Day, where slaves came to town and, together with whites, elected black "governors" were hugely popular with the Irish in particular, part of a carnivalesque popular culture whose festivities would go on for days.[96] It was in the context of these close interconnections that the Irish were often referred to as "smoked Irish," "white negroes," or "niggers turned inside out." Indeed, some commentators argued that the Irish were part of a "dark" race, one that had probably originated in Africa.[97] To racists, then, it made perfect sense when both blacks and Irish were targeted by rioting whites in Boston in 1829.[98]

As racism was reorganized in the middle of the nineteenth century – a result of the intensification of industrial capitalism in the US North and the demise of slavery in the South after the Civil War – the Irish found that social advancement might be possible if they could stake a claim to whiteness and respectability. This was no easy matter. Irish Catholics in particular found the transition to the disciplinary regimes of industrial capitalism particularly wrenching. In contrast to many other "white" immigrant groups, the Irish Catholics had not had generations of cultural adjustment to the "Protestant work ethic" – the exacting disciplines of industrial labour, and the repression of sexuality, recreation and festivity that accompany them.[99] Like others who came from societies that retained elements of non-capitalist cultural life, Irish Catholics were considered unruly, dirty, lazy, rebellious and lascivious. With the deepening of industrial capitalism in the northern states, however, they were subjected to a social and cultural onslaught, ridiculed and humbled as inept and not truly American: "Young Irish indentures, apprentices and child laborers in mills often suffered a psychological battering from Protestant employers bent on reforming the children, sometimes in front of their parents."[100]

As the Irish in nineteenth-century America sought a place for themselves, then, they were driven to intensify the internal psychic repression that is part of industrial capitalism – the subordination of desires for recreation, drink, festivity, sex, and social celebration to employers' demands for a sober, industrious and disciplined workforce. Yet, as invariably happens, severe internal repression involves projection. Seeking whiteness and respectability, the Irish projected onto blacks the very characteristics they strove to repress in themselves. The more they undertook to discipline themselves, the more they came to hate African-Americans as fantastic repositories of the very desires and behaviours they hoped to control in themselves. In particular, they soon entered into the racist construction of blacks as having an unbridled and insatiable "primitive" sexuality.[101] As Frantz Fanon noted about this phobia: "The civilized white man retains an irrational longing for unusual eras of sexual license ... Projecting his own desires onto the Negro, the white man behaves 'as if' the Negro really had them."[102]

Racist psychology thus nurtures powerful desires to reclaim the very things – eros, joy, festivity – that capitalism and imperialism deny. Yet, because they are repressed, these desires reappear (in racist projections) as larger than life, as monstrously destructive. The more powerful these desires, the greater is the anxiety that giving in to them will invite public scorn, humiliation and loss of status. Whiteness comes, therefore, at a great psychological cost, which in part explains its pathological and violent dimensions. In many respects, the primitive racist mentality is at war with a repressed identification with the forbidden Other, with the non-white who represents fantasies of gargantuan bodily prowess and appetites. As David Roediger points out with respect to the incredible popularity of "black face" minstrel shows in nineteenth-century America, in painting themselves black and behaving with the license and lack of inhibition they projected onto African-Americans – or in applauding entertainers who did this – white crowds both entered into their longing for "blackness" and took their distance from it. They were allowed a ritual participation in "blackness" precisely because they simultaneously scorned and ridiculed it.[103]

At the heart of racism is a profound anxiety (often related to sexuality), a fear among whites that, were their secret desires known, they might be identified as outsiders to civilization – as black. Bourgeois culture, particularly during the age of classical imperialism, when one non-white people after another was being conquered, thus enacted bizarre rituals designed to cleanse itself of the dirt and stench of real human bodies. Attitudes toward dirt became profoundly phobic: soap and other cleansers were constantly promoted, while maids and servants were required to engage in obsessive cleaning of door handles, doors, windows and so on.[104] The more imperialism conquered, the more did fear of powerful (sexualized) non-white peoples mount. Often the working classes of the dominant nations, along with other oppressed groups, were more or less thrown into the mix and inferiorized as degenerate and uncivilized. The idea that white women secretly longed for black men was a staple of the imperialist mentality, for instance. Racist crowds were especially horrified by rumours of sexual relations between white women and black men. And in the US states and the British colonies, new laws against miscegenation, sexual relations between the races, were regularly enacted.

Of course, these sexual anxieties also merged with fears of insurrection. Throughout the colonial world, for instance, "the term 'Black Peril' referred to sexual threats, but it also connoted the fear of insurgence."[105] Moreover, trepidation about sexual relations among blacks and lower class whites spoke powerfully to ruling class fears that, should these two "peoples of the body" make common cause, revolution would be inevitable.[106] As Victor Kiernan puts it, for the ruling class "discontented native in the colonies, labour agitator in the mills, were the same serpent in alternate disguises."[107]

To a culture that publicly abhorred the body (while secretly fantasizing about it), sweat, dirt and all "body-peoples" were dangerous. For this reason, there was a phobic campaign to "feminize" women, those ultimate people of the body, by inserting them into a cult of domesticity. Indeed, one of the most remarkable campaigns in mid-nineteenth-century Britain involved a concerted effort to stop women from working in the mines. Anne McClintock demonstrates that this had little to do with concerns for their safety and much to do with anxieties created by women covered in dirt and sweat, wielding shovels and – perhaps the greatest of the expressed horrors – wearing trousers.[108] Working class, slave and colonized women represented the deepest anxieties of the imperial ruling classes – fears of being surrounded by hordes of immensely powerful, sexually insatiable savages who could tear them apart with their bare hands or devour them with their sex organs.[109] All these non-bourgeois others – Africans, Irish, Orientals, women, homosexuals, prostitutes, and the labouring poor of Europe – were animalized, feminized and racialized, constructed as members of dangerous races/classes who posed a threat to the totality of bourgeois civilization.[110] A perceived breakdown in gender relations symbolized fears for the disintegration of the order of life that the ruling class claimed as natural: one in which the bourgeois western male dominated the world. Preservation of gender order thus became a centerpiece of capitalist rule – and nowhere has this been more true that in the colonized and imperialized parts of the world system.

Capitalism, Patriarchy and Colonial Rule

The subordination of women did not emerge with capitalism, of course; it appears to have arisen thousands of years ago in many parts of the world, alongside the emergence of structures of social and class inequality. Truly egalitarian societies have functioned without gender oppression.[111] And a variety of societies have known divisions of labour between the sexes that did not generate systematic female subordination. But wherever systems of class differentiation developed, male-dominated kinship networks became the form in which private property was accumulated and transmitted across generations.[112] Certainly, there is no record of a class-divided society which is not also male-dominated.

To say this is not to reduce the order of gender to the structure of class. Instead, it is to insist on their interconnection and interaction, to claim that they are dialectically interrelated, not ordered on the basis of simple cause-and-effect. Moreover, to say this is also to draw attention to their historicity, to the way in which class and gender relations change as part of overall patterns of social transformation. So, while we can trace a continuity of female subordination across all class-divided societies, we can also map crucial shifts and discontinuities in the way this domination is organized, shifts that are related to changes in forms of social production and family life. The concept of *patriarchy* – which typically refers to the systematic subordination of women and children to husbands and fathers – is a crucial case in point. For, if it is to be a truly powerful explanatory concept, it must help us make sense of the way in which women in most peasant economies have been dominated by their fathers and husbands while, in capitalist society, women's oppression assumes forms far beyond the reach of fathers and husbands, such as gendered wage- and employment-relations at work and subordination to sexist laws and state regulations.

Initially, as the rise of capitalism generated economic activities outside the (patriarchal) household, considerable numbers of women managed to establish greater independence. With market relationships becoming more central to life in villages, towns and cities, spaces opened up in which single and married women could take goods to market, buy, sell, enter into contracts and run business operations. While they often did this as wives of small farmers, women also entered the market economy as widows, daughters, or single women who had left the countryside and now lived as peddlers, craftswomen, or small traders. So long as petty capitalist operations were predominant in many parts of England, particularly during the fifteenth, sixteenth and seventeenth centuries, considerable numbers of women seem to have enjoyed increased mobility and independence.[113] Then, as capitalism consolidated itself – and petty capitalists were increasingly ground under in the face of the greater productivity of the factory system – women were inserted into much more restrictive social relations. With factory production displacing work done in households, women and children were shunted out of a whole range of economic activities. As a broad generalization needing many qualifications, men increasingly went to work for wages while women performed household work.[114] Well into the eighteenth century, for instance, women in England had been apprenticed as goldsmiths, stonemasons, engravers, weavers, doctors and dentists. Yet most of these doors closed in the nineteenth-century as a stricter division of labour and sharper demarcation between household (private) and economic (public) spheres set in.[115]

As white workers did with racism, male workers often became complicit in the new gendered division of labour. Early working class organizations were typically masculinist in character, stressing the virtues of labour, skill and brotherhood as male virtues from which women ought to be excluded. The exclusions created by capital were claimed as markers of male identity which craft unions in particular often sought to defend.[116]

Henceforth, the position of the vast majority of women – women outside the privileged classes – would be defined by a central contradiction. On the one hand, capital would use women as a source of cheap labour in textile mills, sweatshops and the homes of the rich. On the other hand, because it also needs a steady supply of new labourers, capitalism reinforced the special role of women as breeders and nurturers, as members of the sex which births and raises the next generation. This reproductive role is powerfully emphasized by the dominant ideology since capital benefits substantially from having healthy educated workers available whose upbringing it does not pay for. Despite many variations, capitalism has always tended to assign women unique responsibility for the social-biological reproduction of the future working class.[117] The tension between women's productive and reproductive roles manifests itself as the famous "double burden" – the expectation that women should be both wage-earners and keepers of the household. More than this, women are subjected to an oppressive ideological and cultural barrage which, as part of maintaining their primary responsibility for domestic life, depicts them simultaneously as objects of male sexual gratification and as loving, nurturing caregivers who raise children. Women who try to break out of these roles by living independently or challenging bourgeois sex roles have often been subjected to the most vicious forms of oppression, among them rape and sexual violence.

We see all of these dimensions of women's oppression played out with horrifying severity in the slave-economies of colonial America. So long as the supply of enslaved Africans was ample and the cost relatively low, slave women were prevented from bonding with African-American men in order to prevent them from becoming pregnant (being raped by their masters was a different matter, however). Seeking the best return on their investment, planters wanted female slaves constantly at work in the fields, rather than taking time out to birth and nurture newborns. Under these conditions, "breeding" was discouraged and relationships among male and female slaves prohibited. In addition, determined not to see more black children enslaved, many slave women deliberately aborted or allowed their newborns to die.[118] But, when the supply of slaves slowed down – as a result of pressure applied by the anti-slavery movement and by the great slave rebellions, particularly those in Haiti – many African-American women were turned into breeders.[119] They were then subjected to laws designating their children the property of the slave-master – just like the offspring of pigs and horses.[120] Enslaved African-American women experienced the most extreme form of the contradiction between the capitalist functions of women as labourers and breeders. As slave-labour, they were driven into the fields and whipped when their productivity sagged; as breeders, they were forced to procreate, only to have their children stolen from them, sometimes to be sold, always to be enslaved. The practices of oppression inflicted on slave women formed a pattern that would be replicated across the colonial world.

It is crucial to underline that women's oppression in most parts of the world does not derive primarily from the patriarchal bent of traditional cultures. Time and time again, western capitalism pretends that it seeks the liberation of women but is constrained by the weight of traditional society. Most recently, western governments have tried to perpetuate this fraud in their barbaric war against Afghanistan; having funded and supported the Taliban movement, imperialism suddenly discovers oppressed women when it needs a justification for war. Yet, while traditional societies clearly were male-dominated, western capitalism both preserved structures of female oppression and compounded them with new forms of suffering and hardship.

In many pre-colonial African societies, for instance, women had active roles as cultivators – sometimes working alongside men, other times on their own – and they could barter or sell their surplus products. Indeed, in southwestern Nigeria, women ran courts that set prices and resolved disputes.[121] In Sri Lanka, social relations among both Tamil and Sinhalese populations accorded women meaningful economic power and some real freedom in choice of sexual partners. These possibilities derived in large part from practices of communal land ownership; in the absence of private ownership, women had some genuine economic alternatives.[122] The impact of colonialism was to systematically degrade the status of women. As private property and western legal systems were introduced, women generally lost access to land (since only men were recognized by the colonizers as its private owners). When western capital removed men from the villages to work in mines or on plantations, women were left on their own to raise children and eke out a living.[123] The impact of colonialism thus tended to reduce women's economic independence, heighten their responsibility for child-rearing, and subject them to sexual violence from the colonizers who regularly used rape as a weapon to intimidate whole populations and to break the resistance of the men.[124] Colonialism had the effect of depriving women of traditional rights and supports while constructing new relations of capitalist patriarchy which intensified previous systems of male domination. Allying itself with the patriarchal features of pre-colonial societies, colonialist capitalism exacerbated them in several ways: through new property relations which adversely affected women; through systems of labour control which often heightened female responsibility for children; and through racialized forms of sexual violence and control (rape and prostitution). All of these aspects of gender and racial domination are key features of the age of capitalist globalization.

Gender, Race and Globalization

The dispossession of Third World peoples from the land has been particularly devastating for women. The suffering that comes with rural displacement and urban poverty has had a catastrophic impact on female life spans in many countries in tropical Africa and South Asia. In addition, the infant mortality rate has risen markedly for girls, who are often underfed relative to boys (whose employment and income prospects are better). These higher mortality rates for women and female children cannot simply be accounted for by traditional biases since these rates have been increasing in the course of capitalist "development."[125]

Alongside rising mortality rates, we also see a frightening escalation in violence against women. In India, for instance, a number of studies indicate a significant increase in wife-battering and the killing of young brides who fail to bring an acceptable dowry (cash or goods given to the groom's family at marriage and other occasions).[126] While this sort of violence clearly has roots in certain traditional practices, its dramatic increase has to be put in the context of rural displacement and the drive toward capitalist agriculture. As Maria Mies notes, "the most brutal forms of violence and of sexist terror are to be found in areas where agriculture has been rapidly 'developed' in recent years."[127] In one area, women are now beaten up for the long-standing practice of cutting grass on the edge of landlords' fields since grass cuttings have now become a commodity sold to dairy farms. When there are major disputes over land ownership, rural wages and the like, in addition to burning down the huts and beating men from the labouring classes, landlords and police regularly rape poor women as a way of breaking the resistance of peasants and rural labourers. As violence against women becomes a central feature of the class struggle in the countryside, the inextricable connections between sexual and economic violence are thrown into sharp relief.[128]

Another trend that can be observed, particularly in India, is for women to become a specially oppressed sub-proletariat in the countryside. In the Indian state of Andhra Pradesh, for instance, as commercialization, falling prices for agricultural goods and rising costs for fertilizers have made it impossible for small farming families to survive on their land alone, women have been driven into some of the most oppressive and demeaning forms of agricultural labour. Under "tied labour" arrangements, women are required to work for landowners at sub-standard rates of pay in return for loans necessary to keep the family farm afloat. Because these demeaning "tied labour" set-ups are reminiscent of bonded labour, men often refuse to accept them, sending wives and daughters while they and their sons work the family plot.[129]

Rather than fostering "development," then, in much of the world the age of globalization brings decreasing life expectancy, rising mortality rates for female children, escalating violence against women and highly oppressive work arrangements. Related to these trends are four others that are especially discernible: ghettoization in the informal economy; the rise of a sex trade catering to western clients; the emergence of global sweatshops exploiting the labour of young women; and the exodus of Third World women to serve as domestic labourers in the imperialist countries.

Ghettoization and the informal sector

No matter how desperately they seek it, millions of women throughout the world cannot find waged work. Operating outside of regular waged employment – whether it's producing or selling flowers in Colombia, peddling fruits and candies as street vendors in Mexico, or crocheting lace in India – these women participate in the so-called informal economy. This term indicates the absence of standard jobs with regular hours and wages (the form of employment that is measured and taxed by the state); instead, informal employment takes place on the streets or in the home, with virtually no official records. Yet, what is often ignored is that women in the informal economy are, in the words of one analyst, "disguised industrial proletarians." Rather than independent vendors, most are working in the employ of a capitalist stratum of thugs and sweatshop employers.[130]

Despite their non-standard forms of work, these female labourers make an essential contribution to the economic reproduction of family members, be they husbands, parents or children, some of whom are wage workers in the formal economy. In fact, one of the things enabling capitalists in the Third World to keep wages so low is precisely the supplements to household income provided by the earnings of women in the informal sector. In many cases, it is middle-aged and elderly women who do this work because they are seen as lacking the physical attributes for prostitution, waitressing, or domestic service.[131] Moreover, being "informal" does not mean being part-time. Huge numbers of women in this sector work from dawn to dusk to make a pittance. And sometimes, this employment is highly routinized according to exacting standards of production. In the crochet lace industry which is widespread in Indian villages around Naraspur, West Godavari district, Andrha Pradesh, as many as 150,000 women work in the home, subjected to strict terms and rules of production.[132] So, while these women are not engaged in standard waged employment, they are essential parts of proletarian households whose labour ensures the material and social reproduction of those working directly for capital in the formal economy.

Work in the informal economy is not regulated by any of the legal rules which govern things like hours of work, minimum wages, health and safety regulations in the formal economy. Lacking rudimentary protections, women in the informal ghettoes often make the most trivial amounts for their labour. They are also subject to harassment by police, particularly in places like Mexico City, since their blatant poverty is considered bad for business and tourism.

There are, of course, men working in the informal sector as well, as well as millions of children. Nevertheless, it remains a heavily gendered sector of the world economy, an economic ghetto inhabited primarily by women. And sexist ideology plays a central role in this, pivoting as it does on the idea that women's real role is not to be primary (waged) providers but, rather, to look after husbands and children first and supplement the family income where possible.

Women in the Global Sex Trade

Nowhere, perhaps, do relations of racial and gender oppression converge so clearly as in the global sex trade. After all, this industry operates primarily to provide the bodies of young women of colour to a wealthy male clientele of tourists and business travelers largely from the West.

While prostitution emerged in the earliest days of colonization, in many regions it developed as an actual industry with the rise of multinational corporations after World War Two.[133] But it is in the era of globalization that the sex trade has really taken off. Alongside the growth of a world-traveling international business class have arisen networks of luxury hotels, nightclubs and sex shops in many parts of the Third World. Indeed, those areas of the "developing world" that have been most fully incorporated into the circuits of global capital, such as East Asia, have also experienced the most explosive growth in the buying and selling of sex. In Thailand, for instance, there are probably one million women between the ages of fifteen and thirty-four selling sex in nightclubs and massage parlours.[134] The Philippines too has a huge sex industry: as long ago as 1979 that country's Ministry of Labour and Employment had issued 100,000 licenses and health certificates for "hospitality girls," a number that has certainly been surpassed since then and that would dramatically increase were unlicensed sex trade workers included in the figures.[135]

For the western male traveler, a place like Thailand is just another colonial garden of exotic delights, a place outside the West (but clearly subordinated to it) where the bourgeois male can indulge "naughty pleasures" with a few dollars thrown the way of poor women, the majority of them teenagers who have only recently left the village for a city like Bangkok. These countries are considered "virgin territory" whose natural resources, labour and young female bodies can be exploited without guilt. It is no small irony that the Thai sex trade has its roots in the demand generated by US soldiers on leaves from active duty during the Vietnam War, just as the industry in the Philippines derives from the long-time presence of US military bases there.[136] But the male tourist and business traveler has no trouble walking in the footprints left by US soldiers. Whether it's making war or business deals, the colonial world operates both as a site of systematic plunder and a fantasy space for the satisfaction of forbidden de-sires. "Sun, sex and sand as goals of travel correspond to those of colonial travelers," write two perceptive commentators, once again marking countries like Thailand as "pleasure spots on the world map of desire."[137]

The nightmarish underside of the western bourgeois male fantasy is, of course, exploitation and suffering. Many of the young women selling sex in Third World cities are the offspring of poor peasant families whose fathers have sold them to brothel owners in the cities. The precious dollars they earn are often sent back to the village to keep the peasant household afloat. The link between peasant indebtedness and dispossession brought about by western agribusiness and agricultural protectionism, on the one hand, and the growing numbers of sex trade workers in Third World cities, on the other, is a blatantly direct one. To make a bad situation worse, the western male's lack of regard for these women (and the peoples of which they are a part) has spawned an HIV/AIDS pandemic. According to some estimates, perhaps half the child prostitutes in Thailand are HIV positive. The num-bers appear to be similar in Brazil, another hot spot of Third World development favoured by western capital.[138] Once again, as western capitalism enriches itself at the expense of the non-white world, women pay a special price, one that often spells premature death. It is perhaps only the most perverse irony among many that western multinationals refuse to allow these countries to produce or import cheap, generic AIDS-fighting drugs. Having helped to create an appalling health crisis, western capital sees nothing but a growing market for pharmaceutical drugs.

Women in the Global Sweatshop

While the informal economy and the sex trade have been the lot of huge numbers of women, global capital has also sought out poorly paid women's labour for exploitation in manufactur-ing industries. Particularly in the maquiladora zones of Mexico and in Asian countries like Malaysia, Korea, Indonesia, the Philippines and Bangladesh, a new female proletariat has emerged, concentrated in sweatshop production. In most of these countries, young women, usually unmarried, are sought out for employment by such footwear and apparel companies as Nike, Reebok, Esprit, Ralph Lauren and the Gap, electronics firms supplying parts to Sony, JVC and others, and auto parts firms working on contract for the likes of Ford and GM.

Sweatshops such as these have proliferated in Export Processing Zones (EPZs) in one "developing" country after another as duty-free and tax-free havens where western multinationals (or their sub-contractors) can establish virtually any hours, conditions of work and wage structure they choose. So popular with governments in the South is the EPZ strategy for attracting foreign investment, and so enticing to global capital the prospects for exploiting the labour of young women of colour, that there are now about 1000 EPZs in at least seventy countries, employing as many as twenty-seven million workers.[139]

The exploitation of young female labour in EPZs is the dirty secret of so many of the development "miracles" in East Asia and elsewhere. The scale on which global capital has incorporated women into production is truly staggering. Between 1956 and 1986, for instance, the proportion of women in the working class in Taiwan jumped from 20 to 45 per cent. Similar trends can be observed in countries like Mexico, Egypt, Hong Kong, Korea, Malaysia, Philippines and Singapore.[140] In Mexico, more than 2,000 maquiladora plants have opened, employing more than half a million workers, at least 70 per cent of whom are women.[141] And in some cases, such as Bangladesh, where the economy turns on an export-oriented garment industry, women are so preponderant that "industrial production has been visibly feminised." About 1.5 million garment workers toil in more than 3,000 factories in Bangladesh – between 80 to 90 per cent of whom are women, the vast majority between the ages of 14 and 25.[142] Of course, the growth of the Bangladeshi garment industry has done nothing to change the fact that the country is one of the poorest in the world. Women garment workers in that country take home about $35 (US) per month, a bit less than male workers who earn about $40, according to the Bangladesh Institute for Development Studies.

So low are the wages paid to this new sweatshop proletariat that many commentators use the language of slavery to describe the conditions. One human rights group discovered thirty-three Bangladesh workers in a Honduran EPZ sewing shirts for eighty hours per week at a pay rate of 20 cents an hour. Astonishingly, that rate is higher than what their counterparts make in parts of China where some earn as little as 13 cents per hour working for Wal-Mart, Ralph Lauren, Adidas, Nike and others.[143]

Unquestionably, women's labour has been central to the globalization of manufacturing industries over the past twenty to twenty-five years. Recognizing that they have a great thing happening, employers go to extraordinary lengths to avoid extra costs. Young women in "free trade" zones are often subjected to draconian levels of surveillance, including having to turn in bloody tampons every month to prove that they are not pregnant (and therefore won't qualify for maternity benefits).These women are clearly wanted for productive, not reproductive purposes. Indeed, in many maquiladora plants it is common for supervisors to distribute birth control pills.[144] Of course, one way global capital can get around the problem of young women getting pregnant is to get them while they're children; in India and Pakistan, for instance, at least a million and a half children are at work stitching and sewing products for sale in the US.[145] As if these sorts of practices are not enough, many EPZ firms in Thailand and Central America fire workers at the end of the year, only to hire them a few weeks later, a piece of subterfuge designed to insure they don't achieve "permanent" status and the legal rights that is supposed to confer. Alongside these practices, in Mexico, Indonesia, Guatemala and many other places, police and troops regularly crush union organizing drives and break strikes.[146] One perceptive commentator offers a general summary of the conditions of these workers:

> Regardless of where the EPZs are concentrated, the workers' stories have a certain mesmerizing sameness: the workday is long – fourteen hours in Sri Lanka, twelve hours in Indonesia, sixteen in southern China, twelve in the Philippines. The vast majority of the workers are women, always young . . The management is military-style, the supervisors often abusive, the wages below subsistence and the work low-skill and tedious.[147]

The dangers of working in these sweatshops are also extreme, as the most devastating industrial fires in the history of capitalism have taken place in such plants. The worst of these burned down the Kader toy factory on the outskirts of Bangkok, Thailand on May 10, 1993. The official death toll was 188, but it was undoubtedly higher, as many incinerated bodies were never identified. All but fourteen of those who died were women, some of them as young as thirteen years of age. As in so many cases, the main doors to the factory were locked and many windows barred (ostensibly to prevent employee theft), and highly flammable materials like stuffing and fabrics were piled everywhere. When the flames were finally doused, the bodies of nearly two hundred people, mainly young women, were found scorched lying next to dolls of Disney and Sesame Street characters. Not only was this was the third or fourth fire that had broken out at this plant, but there were no fire alarms or sprinkler systems. Two months later a fire at a Bangkok shirt factory killed ten women. Four months after that, eighty-four women perished in a fire at another toy factory in Shenzhen, China. These fires have become sickeningly predictable. And there has been no decline in their frequency. Between 1995 and 2000, thirty fires occurred in Bangladeshi garment factories, seventeen of them involving loss of human life; one, in November 2000, killed at least fifty-two workers.[148] In every case, the circumstances are chillingly similar: locked doors, barred windows, absence of fire alarms and sprinkler systems, flammable materials sitting next to electrical equipment. One analyst of the Kader fire writes that it "was ordained and organized by the free market itself."[149] The same could be said of all the others.

It would be a mistake to imagine, however, that sweatshops like these are solely a Third World affair. Many Americans were horrified to discover in August, 1995 that seventy-two Thai women had been held in bondage in a California apartment complex for up to seven years, sewing clothes for top US manufacturers and retailers. In fact, millions of immigrants toil in homes and sweatshops across the United States in wretched conditions; hundreds of thousands more pick lettuce, strawberries and the like as migrant farm labourers, constituting a Third World proletariat In the North.

In Los Angeles, more than 120,000 workers, three-quarters of them immigrants from Mexico, many of them undocumented, produce garments in over 5,000 factories. Thousands more, including many children, do industrial work in homes. In the San Francisco-Oakland area, it is Chinese immigrants who do much of this sweatshop labour.[150] Ten, twelve, even fourteen hour days are common; wages and working conditions are obscene. In the case of the seventy-two Thai women, the circumstances in which they lived and worked approximated slavery: they would sweat through eighteen hour shifts in a barbed wire-enclosed compound surrounded by armed guards. All food and toiletries were purchased from their captors at massively inflated prices. Communication with the outside world was closely monitored. Then, when the situation was exposed, the immigrant women were arrested and imprisoned by the Immigration and Naturalization Service (INS).[151]

A concerted campaign by immigrant rights groups, unions and human rights organizations did make some important gains for these workers. And this is the danger that globalizing capitalism confronts. While it has created an enormous pool of cheap female labour which it exploits brazenly − indeed pundits like

Harvard professor Jeffrey Sachs have proclaimed that there are too few sweatshops in the world[152] – world capitalism has also conjured up a potentially powerful opponent: a female sweatshop proletariat. In the face of draconian repression, as I show in chapter 6, this new working class has fought and won some impressive battles. Should it be able to organize itself effectively, we will see momentous struggles that could transform global workers' movements.

Migrant Female Labour: The Case of Disposable Domestics

As should now be clear, sweatshop workers are often global migrants. Every year, in fact, millions of Asian women emigrate – from the very countries that are alleged to be the success stories of globalization – in order to work as sex workers, domestics, service workers and nurses in the West. In some countries, women workers have become the favoured national export. In the Philippines, for instance, about 700,000 people emigrate in search of work every year, roughly 70 per cent of them to work as domestic servants in Europe and North America. Altogether, more than 4 per cent of the country's total population consists of overseas contract workers.[153] Large numbers also migrate out of Mexico and Central America. While emigration in search of work is often presented as a choice, it is clearly driven by economic necessity. Statistics show, for instance, that between 30 and 50 per cent of the people of the Philippines are dependent upon the financial remittances that migrant workers send back home.[154]

No one should delude themselves that these people are picking up and leaving because of the wonderful life awaiting them in the West. One study of Chinese, Filipina and Latina women working predominantly as house cleaners and domestics in the San Francisco/Bay area found that nearly 60 per cent were making between $250 and $500 per month, many of them supporting between one and six people on these wages – and all the while

sending money back home too.[155] These workers leave largely because of the limited (and deteriorating) opportunities available to
them in their countries of origin. In most cases, it is the combination of neoliberalism, western protectionism and IMF/World
Bank structural adjustment programs that drives them out.

The Dominican Republic is an interesting case in point. US
protection of its own sugar industry to the tune of $3 billion annu-
ally has decimated sugar production in the Caribbean. In less than
a decade, sugar exports from the Dominican Republic to the US
collapsed to one-quarter of their previous level; in the Caribbean
Basin as a whole, 400,000 jobs were lost between 1982 and 1988.
During this period, there was a marked increase in out-migration
from the region to the US.[156] We observe the same pattern in large
parts of Asia, particularly the Philippines, which has been almost
continuously subjected to IMF/World Bank structural adjustment
programs since 1980. As lands that traditionally produced foods
like rice and corn for local consumption have been converted to
producing pineapples, or exotic flowers for export, and as small
farms have collapsed in the face of rising costs and falling prices
for farm products, women in particular have left the land – and
the country. Structural adjustment programs (SAPs) have a particularly devastating impact on poor women. Pushed off the land,
they often move into poorly-paid seasonal work in the fields or
into local sweatshops. When SAP conditions for loans to Third
World nations require governments to eliminate food subsidies
that have kept down prices for bread or rice, it is women who often
cut their consumption in order to feed their children. As healthcare budgets are cut, girls are often pulled out of school to care
for ill family members. When none of this is enough to keep the
family from drowning in poverty and debt, young women move
to the sweatshops or the sex trade in large cities, or emigrate in
search of work abroad.[157]

In the case of Asian and Latino domestics, it is clear that
race plays a major role in organizing the flow of female migrant
labour to countries like Canada, the United States and Australia

(where 93 per cent of all emigrants from the Philippines go, for instance). Patterns of gender, racial and class subordination all intersect in the massive phenomenon of poor immigrant women of colour serving well-off white families. Indeed, capitalist globalization simply reworks an old pattern: "The immigrant woman serving the white middle-class professional women has replaced the traditional image of the black female servant serving the white master."[158] The female domestic lives the contradiction between capitalism's dual demands on women: her productive labour is prized as a means of providing for the bio-social reproduction of the children of middle- and upper-class white women. At the same time, a whole battery of laws have been erected to make it difficult for her to settle in countries like Canada and the US, bring over family members, or raise children of her own. In short, "while immigrant women's labor is desired, their reproduction – whether biological or social – is not."[159]

It is clear then that globalizing capitalism is a system of gendered and racialized class inequalities. Within the world working class, a sub-category of migrant labourers are policed, documented, harassed and subjected to galling forms of inequality. These global migrants constitute what has rightly been described as "the new untouchables."[160]

The New Untouchables: Migrant Labour in the Age of Globalization

The plight of migrant workers from the Third World exposes a dirty secret about capitalist globalization: while constraints on the movement of capital are being eased, restrictions on the movement of labour are being systematically tightened. It's not that global business does not want immigrant labour to the West. It simply wants this labour on its own terms: frightened, oppressed, vulnerable. To that end, migrant workers are subjected to an apartheid system which denies them fundamental rights – to change jobs, move, receive social services, vote, join unions – available to most other inhabitants of the countries in which they work. The fundamental truth about globalization – that it represents freedom for capital and unfreedom for labour – is especially clear where global migrants are concerned.

Again, there is nothing new about labourers being moved around the world in the interests of capital. As we have seen, between ten and twenty million Africans were stolen from their homes in West Africa to serve as plantation slaves. Perhaps fifty million Indian and Chinese labourers were recruited by the colonial powers (and their junior partners, like Canada) to work in North America, Southeast Asia, the Caribbean and Africa. Then, during the long wave of western economic expansion after the Second World War, a variety of "guest worker" programs were created. Germany and France each imported about two and a half million immigrant workers between 1955 and 1973, drawing in labourers from Greece, Morocco, Italy, Turkey and other nations.[161] In the United States, hundreds of thousands of Mexican men were brought in every year from 1942 to 1964 under the Bracero program, which became the model for "guest workers" programs today.[162]

As rising living standards and the availability of contraception have produced falling birth rates in the North, the demand for foreign labour has risen steadily. While immigrant workers represent only 7 per cent of the US workforce, they are responsible for fully 22 per cent of its growth since 1970.[163] Western capital desperately needs immigrant labour. The United Nations Population Fund forecasts that, without immigration, by 2050 the population of Europe's thirty-one countries will drop to 603 million from its current level of 726 million; Germany alone will see its population decline from 82 million to 60 million over the same period unless it opens up immigration.[164] Similar concerns have led a former Canadian government economist to call for a doubling of the number of new immigrants Canada receives to 500,000 per year.[165] And, as more and more commentators in the US are acknowledging, it is only because of an inflow of up to 500,000 "illegal" immigrants each year that whole sectors of the economy can function. One *New York Times* writer noted recently: "Immigrants are increasingly coveted by corporate America: were the nation's six million illegal immigrants expelled tomorrow, thousands of hotels, restaurants, meat-packing plants, landscaping companies and garment factories would likely close."[166]

Yet, this profound need for immigrant labour does not go hand-in-hand with a welcoming approach – anything but. "Illegal" immigrants may be absolutely necessary to the economy, but they are also subject to systematic legal persecution. The US spends $2 billion per year to build walls and post armed patrols along its border with Mexico in order to terrify the very migrant labourers it seeks. By 2006, the US Border Patrol had three times as many agents as it did in the early 1990s. None of this has slowed the movement of people desperate for jobs and income, nor has it stopped businesses eager to employ them. But border patrols and high tech surveillance have made crossing the Mexico-US border increasingly hazardous: in just three years from 1993 to 1996 nearly 1,200 people are believed to have died trying to cross that border.[167] Those workers who do survive the journey live as undocumented labourers in fear of the Immigration and Naturalization Service (INS), which regularly raids workplaces in response to phone tips from employers trying to stamp out union drives or demands for unpaid back wages.[168] Moreover, recent Immigration Acts in the US have effectively blocked immigrants from accessing welfare, Medicaid and other social services for a period of five years. California's Proposition 187 bars undocumented immigrants from sending their children to public schools or from having them immunized.[169]

The US is not alone in this sort of crackdown on immigrants. The British government passed two immigration bills in recent years that restrict immigrants from Central Europe and limit the social services available to refugee applicants. In Canada, new immigration legislation enacted in 2001, which has been widely denounced by lawyers and human rights organizations, removes basic civil and legal rights from refugees and permanent residents, allowing for their deportation without appeal. Meanwhile, Canada relies increasingly on migrant labour programs that drastically curtail the rights and freedoms of workers from the Third World.[170] Not to be outdone, Germany has passed laws allowing for the deportation of immigrants on suspicion of a criminal offense. And in a remarkable piece of bigotry and cultural chauvinism, a recent policy paper in that country asserts that all foreigners must adhere to "the values of our Christian culture." Meanwhile, the government of the Netherlands passed a law that allows it to expel 26,000 refugee claimants.[171]

In all these senses, migrant workers are the new untouchables, a stratum of despised and persecuted poor workers. Undertaking costly, often dangerous journeys in search of work in a foreign country, they are treated like criminals, trapped into job ghettoes where they work exorbitant hours at pitiful wages, deprived of basic human and civil rights. So, while capital roams the world with ever fewer restrictions, migrant labour finds itself increasingly constrained, regulated and restricted. And global capital profits handsomely from the low wages and political and economic insecurity that plagues these workers. We encounter here one of the fundamental truths about globalization: that capital's freedom is built on the *unfreedom* of millions of the world's poor.

In fact, the unfreedom of migrant labour intersects with broader trends in the neoliberal era toward the curtailment of human freedom. The Anti-Slavery Society estimates there are 200 million people worldwide who might be described as "slaves" – people performing bonded labour to pay off a variety of debts. In India, more than 100,000 boys aged six to 14 are sold as carpet makers in the Varanasi area each year. Some experts contend that there may be as many as eight million bonded labourers in Latin America, more in sub-Saharan Africa, perhaps five million in India.[172] And, as we have seen, increasing numbers are being shipped to sweatshops in other parts of the world or sold into global prostitution rings. The growth of child labour is an integral part of these processes. And there is something eerily familiar about it all:

> Where once peasants labored from dawn to dusk cutting sugar cane that enriched local oligarchs and built the Fifth Avenue mansions and Manhattan skyscrapers of the American sugar barons, now the children and grandchildren of these peasants sit at sewing machines from dawn to dusk, and sometimes well into the night, making bras and jeans and blouses that through the magic of the market are transmitted into multimillion dollar CEO compensation packages and handsome profits for the privileged few.[173]

This is the reality of what globalization promises hundreds of millions of people on the planet. For a long time, this structure of global inequality had a more pointed name: imperialism. It is time we revived this term as part of the contemporary debate about the world in which we live today.

Notes

1 Jonathon Kay, "Concordia disgraced by its student union," *National Post*, September 28, 2001. The CSU Agenda is entitled Uprising 2001-2002.

2 Ward Churchill, "A Day to Give Thanks," November 15, 2000 (circulated on the world wide web).

3 Kirkpatrick Sale, *The Conquest of Paradise: Christopher Columbus and the Columbian Legacy* (New York: Plume/Penguin Books, 1991), p. 106.

4 As quoted by Sale, p. 181.

5 Initially, Columbus tried a forced tribute system, but before the 1490s were out he had settled upon outright enslavement.

6 Sale, p. 154.

7 Hans Koning, *Columbus: His Enterprise* (New York: Monthly Review Press, 1991), p. 117. Note that "Hispaniola" is the same colony as Espanola.

8 Ward Churchill, *A Little Matter of Genocide: Holocaust and Denial in the Americas 1492 to the Present* (Winnipeg: Arbeiter Ring Publishing, 1998), pp. 85-87; Sale, pp. 160-61.

9 Cited by Eduardo Galeano, *Open Veins of Latin America: Five Centuries of the Pillage of a Continent*, trans. Cedric Belfrage (New York: Monthly Review Press, 1973), p. 29.

10 Galeano, 33.

11 Galeano, 42-43.

12 Churchill, *A Little Matter*, p. 98.

13 As quoted by Churchill, *A Little Matter*, p. 99.

14 For the sheer scale of colonialist barbarism see William L. Sherman, *Native Forced Labor in Sixteenth Century Central America* (Lincoln: University of Nebraska Press, 1979); David E. Stannard, *American Holocaust: Columbus and the Conquest of the New World* (New York: Oxford University Press, 1992); and John Hemming, *The Conquest of the Incas* (New York: Harcourt Brace, 1970).

15 Churchill, *A Little Matter*, pp. 101-103.

16 Galeano, pp. 64-68.

17 Sidney W. Mintz, *Sweetness and Power: The Place of Sugar in Modern History* (New York: Penguin Books, 1986), pp. 35-36. Mintz wants to include France with Britain in this regard, but the situation seems to me to be slightly more complicated at this time.

18 Mintz, pp. 48-52.

19 Robin Blackburn, *The Overthrow of Colonial Slavery 1776-1848* (London: Verso Books, 1988), p. 9.

20 David Brion Davis, "Patterns of Slavery in the Americas" in *American Negro Slavery*, eds. Allen Weinstein and Frank Otto Gatell (New York: Oxford University Press, 1968), p. 203. For an interesting comparison of slave systems in Spanish- and Anglo-America see Herbert S. Klein, *Slavery in the Americas: A Comparative Study of Cuba and Virginia* (Chicago: University of Chicago Press, 1967).

21 Blackburn, p. 3.

22 As quoted by L. Perry Curtis, *Apes and Angels: The Irishman in Victorian Caricature* (Newton Abbot: David and Charles, 1971), p. 1.

23 W. E. H. Lecky, *History of Ireland in the Eighteenth Century*, 2nd edn., 3 vols. (London, 1881). My account in the previous paragraphs relies on Liam de Paor, *Divided Ulster*, 2nd edn. (Harmondsworth: Penguin Books, 1971), pp. 5-12; and Maire O'Brien and Conor Cruise O'Brien, *A Concise History of Ireland*, 2nd edn. (London: Thames and Hudson, 1973), pp. 56-78.

24 See Nicholas P. Canny, "The Ideology of English Colonization: From Ireland to America," *William and Mary Quarterly*, 3rd series, v. 30 (1973), p. 582.

25 On the impressment of Irish men into foreign armies see William Petty, "The Political Anatomy of Ireland" [1672] in *The Economic Writings of Sir William Petty*, ed. Charles Henry Hull, 2 vols. (New York: Augustus M. Kelley, 1963), p. 150. On the sale of Irishmen for bonded labour in America see

John W. Blake, "Transportation from Ireland to America, 1653-60," *Irish Historical Studies*, v. 3 (1942-43), pp. 267-81.

26 Theodore W. Allen, *The Invention of the White Race, Volume One: Racial Oppression and Social Control* (New York: Verso Books, 1994), pp. 46-47.

27 Charles Verlinden, *The Beginning of Modern Colonization*, trans. Yvonne Feccero (Ithaca: Cornell University Press, 1970), Ch. 2.

28 See Canny, pp. 584-95 for an insightful discussion of these issues.

29 Eric Williams, *Capitalism and Slavery* (London: Andre Deutsh, 1964), p.7.

30 David Brion Davis, "The Evolution of Slavery in British America and Latin America" in *American Negro Slavery*, p. 27. See also Williams, p. 16. For an overview, see Abbot E. Smith, *Colonists in Bondage: White Servitude and Convict Labor in America, 1607-1776* (Gloucester, Mass: P. Smith, 1965). It is important to note that, unlike the African slaves who would begin arriving in considerable numbers after 1680, European labourers could not be bonded for life; this often amounted to little, however, since huge numbers died before their periods of indenture expired.

31 Barbara Jeanne Fields, "Slavery, Race and Ideology in the United States of America," *New Left Review* 181 (1990), p. 102.

32 My figures here are derived from Blackburn, p. 11 and Theodore W. Allen, *The Invention of the White Race, Volume 2: The Origins of Racial Oppression in Anglo-America* (London: Verso Books, 1997), p. 314n10.

33 Williams, pp. 19, 20.

34 Allen, v. 2, pp. 181-9; and Kenneth Wiggins Porter, "Negroes on the Southern Frontier, 1670-1763," *Journal of Negro History* 33 (1948), pp. 74-75; Fields, p. 104.

35 As quoted by Allen, v. 2, p. 353n57.

36 David Roediger, *The Wages of Whiteness: Race and the Making of the American Working Class* (London: Verso Books 1991), p. 25.

37 Benjamin Franklin, "Conversation on Slavery," *Public Advertiser,* January 30, 1770, as cited by Roediger, p. 29.

38 Allen, v. 1, pp. 99-112.

39 The estimate that some tens of thousands of native peoples were enslaved by the early eighteenth-century in Anglo-America comes from Gary B. Nash, *Red, White and Black: The Peoples of Early America* (Englewood Cliffs, N. J.: Prentice-Hall, 1974), p. 152.

40 Allen, v. 2, pp. 84, 101-2.

41 William S. Willis, "Divide and Rule: Red, White and Black in the Southeast," *Journal of Negro History* 68, 3 (1963), p. 158; Allen, v. 2, p. 44.

42 Allen, v. 2, pp. 119, 314n4.

43 T. H. Breen, "A Changing Labor Force and Race Relations in Virginia," *Journal of Social History* (Fall 1973) p. 3.

44 Allen, v. 2, p. 211; Fields, p. 105.

45 Both quotes from Breen, p. 10. See also Peter Linebaugh and Marcus Rediker, *The Many-Headed Hydra: Sailors, Slaves, Commoners, and the hidden history of the Revolutionary Atlantic* (Boston: Beacon Press, 2000), pp. 136-39.

46 As quoted by Allen, v. 2, p. 214.

47 Again, I want to record my debt to Theodore Allen's important two-volume study. Much of the rest of this paragraph draws on Allen, v. 2, pp. 224-38.

48 Orlando Patterson, *The Sociology of Slavery: An Analysis of the Origins, Development and Structure of Negro Slave Society in Jamaica* (Rutherford, N.J.: Fairleigh-Dickinson University Press, 1969), pp. 266, 271-3.

49 The early historiography is reviewed by Winthrop Jordan, "Modern Tensions and the Origins of American Slavery," *Journal of Southern History* 38 (February 1962), pp. 18-30. Jordan identifies 1660 as a clear turning-point. As Barbara Fields points out, this is roughly the date at which legislation markedly shifts; social practices appear not to have changed significantly until about 1680.

50 Breen, p. 7.

51 Jordan, p. 19.

52 Vaughan, 934-5; Allen, v. 2, p. 250; Gooch quoted by Allen, v. 2, p. 242.

53 W. E. B. Dubois, *Black Reconstruction in America 1860-1880* (New York: Touchstone Books, 1992), pp. 6-7.

54 Fields, p. 107.

55 Ira Berlin, "Time, Space, and the Evolution of Afro-American Society on British Mainland North America," *American Historical Review* 85 (1980), p. 72.

56 David Brion Davis, *Slavery and Human Progress*, pp. 33, 37, 38. See also William McKee Evans, "From the Land of Canaan to the Land of Guinea: The Strange Odyssey of the 'Sons of Ham,'" *American Historical Review* 85 (1980), pp. 15-43.

57 Frank M. Snowden Jnr., *Blacks in Antiquity* (Cambridge, Mass.: Harvard University Press, 1970), p. 183.

58 Erna Paris, *The End of Days: A Story of Tolerance, Tyranny and the Expulsion of the Jews from Spain* (Toronto: Lester Publishing, 1995), p. 33.

59 Hannah Arendt, *The Origins of Totalitarianism* (New York: Harcourt-Brace, 1951), p. 87.

60 Robert Miles, *Racism* (London: Routledge, 1989), pp. 28, 29-30.

61 As quoted by Albert Soboul, *The French Revolution 1781-1799*, trans Alan Forrest (London: New Left Books, 1974), v. 1, pp. 255-6.

62 Ellen Meiksins Wood, *Democracy Against Capitalism* (Cambridge, U. K.: Cambridge University Press, 1995), p. 269.

63 Meiksins Wood, p. 269.

64 Vaughan, p. 931.

65 Peter Fryer, *Staying Power: The history of Black people in Britain* (London: Pluto Press, 1984), pp. 146, 144, 158.

66 As quoted by Fryer, p. 154.

67 Thomas Paine, "African Slavery in America" in *The Thomas Paine Reader*, ed. Isaac Kramnick (Harmondsworth: Penguin Book, 1987), pp. 55, 53.

68 Fields, p. 114.

69 See Vaughan, p. 944, and Stephen Jay Gould, *The Mismeasure of Man* (New York: W. W. Norton, 1981), p. 35.

70 On this doctrine see Gould, pp. 39-72.

71 See Vaughan for an interesting treatment of this transformation.

72 As quoted by Vaughan, p. 937.

73 Gould, pp. 42-50.

74 *United States Magazine and Democratic Review*, new series, v. 27, n. 145 (July 1850), p. 48.

75 Eric Hobsbawm, *The Age of Empire 1875-1914* (London: Sphere Books, 1981), pp. 57-59.

76 As quoted by Miles, p. 35.

77 As quoted by G. Bennett, "Settlers and Politics in Kenya" in *History of East Africa, v. 2*, eds. V. Harlow and E. M. Chivier (Oxford: Clarendon Press, 1965), p. 271.

78 As quoted by Fryer, p. 183. See also Victor G. Kiernan, *The Lords of Human kind: European Attitudes to the Outside World in the Imperial Age* (Harmondsworth: penguin Books, 1972).

79 As quoted by Hobsbawm, p. 70.

80 As quoted by Adam Hochschild, *King Leopold's Ghost: A Story of Greed, Terror and Heroism in Colonial Africa* (New York: Houghton Miflin, 1999), p. 166.

81 Hochschild, p. 233.

82 Hochschild, pp. 280, 282.

83 As quoted by Paul G. Lauren, *Power and Prejudice – The Politics and Diplomacy of Racial Discrimination* (Boulder: Westview Press, 1988), p. 84.

84 As quoted by A. T. Yarwood, "The 'White Australia' Policy: A Reinterpretation of its Development in the Late Colonial Period," *Historical Studies* 10 (1962), p. 263.

85 For a marvelously perceptive critique of multicultural policy in Canada see Himani Bannerji, *The Dark Side of the Nation: Essays on Multiculturalism, Nationalism and Gender* (Toronto: Canadian Scholars Press, 2000).

86 See Donald Purich, *Our Land: Native Rights in Canada* (Toronto: Lorimer, 1986); Howard Adams, *Prison of Grass: Canada from a Native Point of View*, rev. edn. (Saskatoon: Fifth House, 1989); and Howard Adams, *A Tortured People: The Politics of Colonization*, rev. edn. (Penticton, B. C.: Theytus Books, 1999).

87 See Irving Abella and Howard Troper, *None is Too Many: Canada and the Jews of Europe*, 3rd edn (Toronto: Lester Publishing, 1991).

88 Canada, House of Commons, *Debates* (May 4, 1885), p.1,588.

89 Canada, House of Commons, *Debates* (May 1, 1947), p. 2,645.

90 See Lisa Marie Jakubowski, *Immigration and the Legalization of Racism* (Halifax: Fernwood Publishing, 1997).

91 Dubois, p. 700.

92 Roediger offers the most sophisticated treatment of this concept.

93 As quoted by Allen, v. 1, p. 154.

94 As quoted by Noel Ignatieff, *How the Irish Became White* (New York: Routledge, 1995), p. 109.

95 As quoted by Ignatieff, p. 109.

96 Joseph P. Reidy, "Negro Election Day and Black Community Life in New England, 1750-1860," *Marxist Perspectives* 1 (Fall 1978), pp. 102-17.

97 See Carl Wittke, *The Irish in America* (New York: Russell and Russell, 1970), p. 34; Jonathon A. Gluckstein, *Concepts of Free Labor in Antebellum America* (New Haven: Yale University Press, 1991), p. 340; Ignatieff, p. 41; Roediger, p. 133.

98 Roediger, p. 134.

99 The classic statement of the Protestant work ethic thesis is Max Weber, *The Protestant Ethic and the Spirit of Capitalism*, trans. Talcott Parsons (New York: Charles Scribner's Sons, 1958). For a particularly insightful analysis of the rise of capitalist work discipline see E. P. Thompson, "Time, Work-Discipline and Industrial Capitalism" in Thompson, *Customs in Common: Studies in Traditional and Popular Culture* (New York: The New Press, 1991), pp. 352-403.

100 Roediger, p. 152.

101 This argument builds upon the powerful insights of Joel Kovel, *White Racism: A Psychohistory* (New York: Columbia University Press, 1984), especially pp. xlv, 186-9, 193-5. Roediger nicely incorporates this sort of analysis into his account of the wages of whiteness.

102 Frantz Fanon, *Black Skin, White Masks* (New York: Grove Press, 1967), p. 165.

103 Roediger, Chs. 6-7.

104 See the wonderful study by Anne McClintock, *Imperial Leather: Race, Gender and Sexuality in the Colonial Contest* (New York: Routledge, 1995).

105 Ann Laura Stoler, "Carnal Knowledge and Imperial Power: Gender, Race and Morality in Colonial Asia" in *Gender at the Crossroads: Feminist Anthropology in the Postmodern Era*, ed. Micaela di Leonardo (Berkeley: University of California Press, 1991), p. 68.

106 I take the wonderful expression "people of the body" from Himani Bannerji, "Gender, Race, Class and Socialism: An Interview," *New Socialist* 3, 1 (February-March 1998).

107 Kiernan, p. 316.

108 McClintock, pp. 114-17.

109 On the physical strength of female slaves in America, and one traveler's perception of it, see Angela Davis, ˆ (New York: Vintage Books, 1983), p. 11.

110 See David McNally, *Bodies of Meaning: Studies on Language, Labor and Liberation* (Albany: State University of New York Press, 2001), pp. 4-5.

111 See for example Maria Lepowsky, *Fruit of the Motherland: Gender in an Egalitarian Society* (New York: Columbia University Press, 1993).

112 For one account see Evelyn Reed, *Woman's Evolution: From Matriarchal Clan to Patriarchal Family* (New York: Pathfinder Press, 1975). Many subsequent commentators have preferred to describe earlier human societies as "matrilineal" or "matrifocal" rather than matriarchal; nevertheless much of Reed's argument has garnered support. Reed builds upon, but radically revises, some of the claims made by Frederick Engels, *The Origin of the Family, Private Property and the State* (Moscow: Progress Publishers, 1972). For further considerations on Engels' theses see Janet Sayers, Mary Evans and Nanneke Redclift, *Engels Revisited: New Feminist Essays* (London: Tavistock Publication, 1987). See also Evelyn Reed, *Sexism and Science* (New York: Pathfinder Press, 1978).

113 Rodney Hilton, "Women in the Village" in Hilton, *The English Peasantry in the Later Middle Ages* (Oxford: Clarendon Press, 1975), pp. 106-10; Maria Mies, *Patriarchy and Accumulation on a World Scale: Women in the International Division of Labour* (London: Zed Books, 1986), pp. 78-81.

114 This process took place quite unevenly, however, and there were certain industries where women's labour remained central.

115 See Ivy Pinchbeck, *Women and the Industrial Revolution 1750-1850* (London: Virago Books, 1981); Mary Lynn McDougall, "Working Class Women During the Industrial Revolution" and Theresa M. McBride, "The Long Road Home: Women's Work and Industrialization" both in *Becoming Visible: Women in European History*, eds. Renate Bridenthal and Claudia Koontz (Boston: Houghton Mifflin, 1977).

116 See, for instance, Anna Clark, *The Struggle for the Breeches: Gender and the Making of the British Working Class* (Berkeley: University of California Press, 1995).

117 For an illuminating treatment of capitalism and the specific role of women in the social-biological reproduction of the working class see Lise Vogel, *Capitalism and the Oppression of Women: Toward a Unitary Theory* (London: Pluto Press, 1983).

118 Rhoda Reddock, *Women, Labour and Struggle in 20th Century Trinidad and Tobago 1898-1960* (The Hague: Institute for Social Studies, 1984), pp. 16-18. The theme of infanticide as a form of resistance to enslavement is at the centre of Toni Morrison's novel, *Beloved*.

119 On the slave rebellions see especially Blackburn and C.L.R. James, *The Black Jacobins: Toussaint L'Ouverture and the San Domingo Revolution*, 2nd edn. (New York: Vintage Books, 1963).

120 A. Davis, p. 7.

121 Margaret Snyder and Mary Tadesse, "The African Context: Women in the Political Economy" in *The Women, Gender and Development Reader*, eds. Nalini Visvanthan, Lynn Duggan, Laurie Nisonoff and Nan Wiegersma (London: Zed Books, 1997), pp. 75-76.

122 Jean Grossholtz, *Forging Capitalist Patriarchy: The Economic and Social Transformation of Feudal Sri Lanka and its Impact on Women* (Durham, N. C.: Duke University Press, 1984), pp. 109-10.

123 Snyder and Tadesse, pp. 76-77.

124 Amina Mama, "Sheroes and Villains: Conceptualizing Colonial and Contemporary Violence Against Women in Africa" in *Feminist Genealogies, Colonial Legacies, Democratic Futures*, eds. M. Jacqui Alexander and Chandra Talpade Mohanty (New York: Routledge, 1997), pp. 51-53.

125 Janet Henshall Momsen, *Women and Development in the Third World* (London: Routledge, 1991), pp. 9-17; Maria Mies, "Capitalist Development and Subsistence Production: Rural Women in India" in Maria Mies, Veronika Bennholdt-Thoomsen and Claudia von Werlhof, *Women: The Last Colony* (London: Zed Books, 1988), pp. 30-31.

126 See Uma Shankar Jha and Premlata Pujari, *Indian Women Today: Tradition, Modernity and Challenge, Volume 2: Women in the Flames* (New Delhi: Kanishka Publishers, 1996); and Truti Shah and Bina Srinivasan, "The Effect of Capitalist Development on Gender Violence: Dowry and Female Feticide" in *Women's Lives in the Global Economy*, eds. Penny Duggan and Heather Dashner, Notebooks for Study and Research, n. 22 (Amsterdam: IIRF/IIRE, 1994).

127 Mies, "Class Struggles and Women's Struggle in Rural India" in *Women: The Last Colony*, p. 137. See also *Human Development Report 2005* for data on the declining health and education prospects for girls and young women.

128 Mies, "Class Struggle," pp. 135-38.

129 See Lucia Da Corta and Davuluri Venkateshwarlu, "Unfree Relations and the Feminisation of Agricutltural Labour in Andhra Pradesh, 1970-95," *Journal of Peasant Studies* 26, 2/3 (January-March 1999), pp. 71-139.

130 Cythia Truelove, "Disguised Industrial Proletarians in Latin America: Women's Informal Sector Factory Work and the Social Reproduction of Coffee Farm Labor in Columbia" in *Women Workers and Global Restructuring*, ed. Kathryn War (Cornell: ILR Press, 1990). See also Davis, *Planet of Slums*, pp. 176-85.

131 Lourdes Arzipe, "Women in the Informal Labour Sector: The Case of Mexico City" in *The Women, Gender and Development Reader*, p. 235. See also Julia Cleves Mosse, *Half the World, Half a Chance: An Introduction to Gender and Development* (Oxford: Oxfam, 1993), pp. 70-76.

132 Mies, "Capitalist Development and Subsistence Production," pp. 39-40.

133 See for instance the data in Maria Rosa Cutrufelli, *Women of Africa: Roots of Oppression*, trans. Nicolas Romano (London: Zed Press, 1983), pp. 30-36.

134 Ryan Bishop and Lillian S. Robinson, *Night Market: Sexual Cultures and the Thai Economic Miracle* (New York: Routledge, 1998), p. 8.

135 The 1979 number comes from Lourdes Beneria, "Gender and the Global Economy" in *Instability and Change in the World Economy*, eds. Arthur MacE-

201

wan and William K. Tabb (New York: Monthly Review Press, 1989), p.251.

136 Mies, *Patriarchy*, p. 138 and Bishop and Robinson, pp. 98-99.

137 Bishop and Robinson, p. 4.

138 Bishop and Robinson, p. 4; and Mosse, pp. 75-76.

139 Data from the International Labour Organization cited by Naomi Klein, *No Logo: Taking Aim at the Brand Bullies* (Toronto: Vintage Canada, 2000), p. 205.

140 Rita S. Gallin, "Women and the Export Industry of Taiwan: The Muting of Class Consciousness" and Susan Tiano, "Maquiladora Women: A New Category of Worker?" both in *Women Workers and Global Restructuring*, p. 179; Beneria, p. 244.

141 Carmen Valadez Prez, "NAFTA versus Human Rights" in *Women's Lives in the Global Economy*, p. 51.

142 Dina M. Siddiqi, "Miracle Worker of Womanmachine? Tracking (Trans)national Realities in Bangladeshi Factories," *Economic and Political Weekly*, May 27, 2000. I have increased the number of garment workers in Bangladesh in line with the figures provided by Barry Bearak, "Lives Held Cheap in Bangladesh Sweatshop," *New York Times*, April 15, 2001.

143 Alan Howard, "Labor, History and Sweatshops in the New Global Economy" in *No Sweat: Fashion, Free Trade and the Rights of Garment Workers*, ed. Andrew Ross (New York: Verso, 1997), p. 156; Klein, p. 212.

144 June Nash, "Cultural Parameters of Racism and Sexism in the International Division of Labor" in *Racism, Sexism and the World System*, eds. Joan Smith et. al. (New York: Greenwood Press, 1988), p. 27.

145 Howard, p. 158.

146 International Confederation of Free Trade Unions, *Behind the Wire: Anti-Union Repression in the Export Processing Zones* (Brussels: ICFTU, 1996).

147 Klein, p. 205.

148 Bearak, p. 1.

149 William Greider, *One World Ready or Not: The Manic Logic of Global Capitalism* (New York: Simon and Schuster, 1997), p. 344. My discussion of the Kader fire relies on Greider, pp. 337-40.

150 Steve Nutter, "The Structure and Growth of the Los Angeles Garment Industry" in *No Sweat*, pp. 199, 207.

151 Julie Su, "El Monte Thai Garment Workers: Slave Sweatshops" in *No Sweat*, p. 143-44.

152 As quoted by Klein, p. 228.

153 Grace Chang, *Disposable Domestics: Immigrant Women Workers in the Global Economy* (Cambridge, MA: South End Press, 2000), p. 129.

154 Chang, p. 130.

155 Chang, pp. 56-57.

156 Saskia Sassen, *Globalization and its Discontents* (New York: The New Press, 1998), p. 13.

157 See Natividad Yabut-Bernardino, *An Impact Study of Agricultural Trade Liberalization in the Philippines* (Manila: International South Group Network, 2000), available at www.isgnweb.org; and Chang, p. 124.

158 Sassen, pp. 90-91. See also Evelyn Nakano Glenn, "From Servitude to Service Work: Historical Continuities in the Racial Division of Paid Reproductive Labor," *Signs* 18, 1 (1992), pp. 1-43.

159 Chang, p. 10.

160 Nigel Harris, *The New Untouchables: Immigration and the New World Worker* (Harmondsworth: Penguin Books, 1995).

161 Harris, pp. 3, 9.

162 See Linda Jacobs Altman, *Migrant Farm Workers: The Temporary People* (New York: Franklin Watts, 1994), pp. 43-47, 50-53.

163 Sassen, p. 33.

164 John Shaw, "Australia Wants More People, but Without More Immigration," *New York Times*, November 25, 2001; Roger Cohen, "How Open to Immigrants Should Germany Be? An Uneasy Country's Debate Deepens," *New York Times*, May 13, 2001.

165 Shawn McCarthy, "Doubling of Immigrants urged," *Globe and Mail*, March 3, 2001.

166 Eric Schmitt, "Americans (a) Love (b) Hate Immigrants," *New York Times*, May 27, 2001. See also Eduardo Porter, "The Search for Illegal immigrants Stops at the Workplace," *New York Times*, March 5, 2006.

167 Robert Biel, *The New Imperialism* (London: Zed Books, 200), p. 260.

168 Chang, pp. 67, 110-11, 179.

169 Chang, pp. 61, 1.

170 Campbell Clark, "New immigration law called Draconian," *Globe and Mail*, March 16, 2001; John Herron, "Immigration bill seriously flawed," *Toronto Star*, May 1, 2001; Sandro Contenta, "Anti-Immigrant fever runs high," *Toronto Star*, February 29, 2004; Alan Freeman, "Dutch join Europe's anti-refugee tide," *Globe and Mail*, February 18, 2004.

171 Hannah Behrend, "Germany's War Againt Aliens," *New Politics* 7, 1 (Summer 1998), pp. 25-32; Cohen; Nandita Sharma, *Home Economics: Nationalism and the Making of 'Migrant Workers' in Canada* (Toronto: University of Toronto Press, 2006).

172 Harris, pp. 81-83.

173 Howard, p. 159.

5. THE MARINES HAVE LANDED: WAR AND IMPERIALISM IN THE AGE OF GLOBALIZATION

> Because we are the biggest beneficiaries of globalization we are unwittingly putting enormous pressure on the rest of the world ... producing a powerful backlash from all those brutalized or left behind... The hidden hand of the market will never work without a hidden fist – McDonald's cannot flourish without McDonnell Douglas, the builder of the F-15. And the hidden fist that keeps the world safe for Silicon Valley's technologies is called the United States Army, Air Force and Marine Corps.
>
> – Thomas Friedman, New York Times correspondent[1]

"The marines have landed and we now own a piece of Afghanistan," exclaimed US General James Mattis on November 26, 2001. The general's declaration managed in a single sentence to encapsulate the very spirit of imperialism: the idea that the world's dominant economic and military powers can claim ownership and control of a part of the world by virtue of military force. The Greek philosopher Plato may have rejected the idea that "might makes right" some 2,500 years ago, but America and its allies today make it the cornerstone of foreign policy.[2] In fact, so thoroughgoing is their embrace of this doctrine that US President George W. Bush claims the right to declare who shall live and who shall die. "The Bush administration today gave the nations of the world a choice," declared the *New York Times* on September 14, 2001, "Stand with us against terrorism … or face the certain prospect of death."

This doctrine – the right of the mighty to decide who shall live and who shall die – has been a cornerstone of imperialism throughout its history. Of course, those who exercise the power of life and death claim to do so for an exalted purpose: the defense of "civilization." Thus, Bush can declare that "civilization itself, the civilization we share, is threatened" and that the bombs he drops on Iraq or Afghanistan are in the service of "a war to save civilization."[3] It helps that the people who will be bombed in the name of civilization are brown-skinned adherents of Islam. After all, fear of Muslims has been central to the Euro-American identity since the Middle Ages. As one scholar notes, for centuries the Islamic prophet Muhammad was seen in Europe as "an Antichrist in alliance with the Devil."[4] So, when Bush invokes the defense of civilization while the bombs fall on the people of Baghdad, or on poor farmers and city-dwellers in Afghanistan, he taps into powerful racist associations of Muslims with evil. "We will rid the world of the evil-doers," he told an audience five days after the destruction of the World Trade Center. Indeed, he even employed the word "crusade" in one of his early speeches, until warned off by handlers nervous about offending US allies in Islamic countries.[5]

To invoke the defense of civilization is simultaneously to paint the enemy as uncivilized, savage, barbaric – all the standard motifs of racism. Having so dehumanized one's opponents, they can then be dismissed as beasts with which neither discussion nor negotiation is possible. "There's no need to negotiate. There's no discussions," Bush intoned shortly after September 11, 2001. In this spirit, when Pakistan's two Islamic parties negotiated a deal in late September and early October 2001 under which Osama bin Laden would be extradited to Pakistan to face an international tribunal, the US blew off the proposal.[6] America's version of justice, and it alone, would prevail – "no discussions." And what

better instruments of American "justice" than the B-52 bombers of Vietnam infamy, the state of the art F-15s and the widely
condemned cluster bombs? That these weapons would take the
lives of thousands of innocent Afghan and Iraqi citizens is of little
consequence. "I want justice," a bloodthirsty Bush proclaimed.
"There's an old poster out west, as I recall, that said, Wanted:
Dead or Alive."[7] Thousands of dead Afghans later, over 100,000
dead Iraqis later, America continues to inflict its "justice." And
there is no end in sight: US officials insist they will continue to
invade countries and launch missiles for years to come. Some
American policy makers openly describe the current conflict as
a permanent war, one "without constraint of either time or geog-
raphy."[8] So much for the claims that "globalization is a powerful
force for good" that will "make the world a safer, richer, better
place."[9] Welcome to the new world of globalization: war without
end.

From Classic Imperialism to US Dominance

Of course, anyone familiar with the history of capitalism
should not be surprised by any of this. After all, only in the era of
capitalism have we had world wars. No other form of human society has managed to globalize military conflict in this way. And
the internationalization of military conflict – which accompanies
the rise of the modern world economy – has involved its growing technological sophistication. As a result, we live in a world
that has raised the art of destruction to new levels of complexity;
humans can now be killed on a massive scale by means of com-
puter-guided missiles and weapons involving the use of advanced
chemistry, biology or atomic science.

Not only can humans be so killed, they have been with brutal
regularity. Perhaps the ugliest thing about it all is that these periodic acts of mass murder have been entirely predictable. In fact,
the bloodiest wars in human history – the world wars of 1914-19
and 1939-45 whose combined death toll is in the range of sixty-

five million – were virtually inevitable outcomes of the age of classic imperialism. Beginning about 1875, as we saw in the previous chapter, there commenced a massive scramble to conquer most of the globe in the name of the dominant capitalist powers. Over the next forty years, "Britain increased its territories by about 4 million miles, France by some 3.5 millions, Germany acquired more than 1 million, Belgium and Italy just under 1 million each."[10] By the time these four decades of imperial expansion had drawn to a close, war was inevitable. Capitalist competition had provoked a struggle to control huge chunks of the globe. This was especially so for Germany which, having made an enormous leap forward as an industrial power, found itself constrained by the vast colonial empires of its main rivals, France and Britain. As a result of their territorial holdings, the latter were able to frustrate Germany's drive for world markets and sources of raw materials. Something would have to give: either Germany would have to seize territories from its rivals, or it would have to be defeated in the war for markets and colonies.

Serious historians have never supported the claim that the First World War had no underlying cause, nor did intelligent political analysts at the time. When war broke out in 1914, they had been expecting it for some time. The Russian Marxist Nikolai Bukharin, writing at the outset of the conflict, argued that the roots of the war were to be found in the contradiction between the expanding forces of economic production of the major powers, on the one hand, and their efforts to use tariffs to restrict access to their own domestic and colonial markets on the other. Given the enormous scale of monopoly firms, all the dominant powers desperately needed foreign markets; economic rivalries thus intensified, forewarning the resort to arms. "Tariff wars, however, are only partial sorties," Bukharin wrote. "In the long run the conflict is solved by the interrelation of 'real forces,' i.e. by the force of arms ... the last word belongs to military technique."[11] It was not the approach of war that surprised commentators at the time, but its unprecedented barbarity. Grenades, flame throw-ers and poison gas turned Europe into a continental landscape of corpses. By early 1917, Russia alone had seen nearly six million of its soldiers die. The death toll for other combatants was similarly massive and shocking: 2.6 million for France, one million for Britain, nearly 900,000 for Italy.[12] Before the war was out, millions more would perish.

The root cause of the war was the conflict between the early imperialist colonizers and the "late-comer" industrial powers who lacked colonial empires on the scale of their rivals: "the older, colonizing states such as Britain and France still held the lion's share, and German capitalists envied the older established imperial powers ... Britain possessed a vast colonial empire, while Germany had captured a relatively minute share; nevertheless, Germany recently had achieved superior industrial strength."[13] Intensifying pressure to re-divide the globe between these contending powers made war virtually inevitable. Understanding these root causes, the radical left declared it an imperialist war.[14]

Yet, this barbaric war – "the war to end all wars" – did not settle matters in the least. Once defeated, Germany was severely punished, forced to pay war reparations to those who had humbled it. The economic weight of these reparations was debilitating. When a world economic slump hit in 1929, the German economy began a catastrophic meltdown, with unemployment doubling to more than six million. Within three years, Hitler's Nazi movement would goose-step to power, smashing militant trade unions and leftist parties, stirring up hatred of foreign powers and demonizing Jews and Roma people ("Gypsies"). A mere twenty years after the previous war had ended, its horrifying sequel broke out and perhaps fifty-four million more were slaughtered in the struggle for control over the world's markets and territories.[15] In many respects, the Second World War was a continuation of the First, a conflict triggered by the mismatch between industrial power and imperial reach. To be sure, Hitler was the aggressor. But for the victorious Allies, it was certainly not a war against fascism. Much of the western ruling class – from Canada's Prime Minister

William Lyon Mackenzie King to Henry Ford, a leading spokesman for American capitalism – initially welcomed Hitler and the services he might perform in crushing the German working class movement. In 1937, for instance, the US State Department argued that fascism "must succeed or the masses ... will again turn to the left."[16] If Hitler was the weapon with which to stop such a turn to the left, he would encounter no foreign interference. The sight of Communists, Jews and trade unionists being rounded up certainly did not cost US, Canadian or British elites a wink of sleep. Indeed, US investment poured into Germany after Hitler's seizure of power. When they went to war, it was not fascism the Allies set out to defeat, but German expansionism. Moreover, the victorious Allies conspired in the atrocity of the US use of atomic bombs against the people of Hiroshima and Nagasaki in 1945, when Japan's defeat was already inevitable.

Thirty years of war, between 1914 and 1945, finally broke the old structure of imperialism. But it did so in a way that few had anticipated, as the center of gravity of world capitalism shifted from Europe to America. What triggered this shift was the devastation wreaked by war in Europe and Japan – the latter had lost one-quarter of its factory buildings and one third of its industrial plant and equipment, while Germany lost more than 17 per cent of its capital stock.[17] But underlying the shift was a long-term process of US economic growth that dated back to the end of America's Civil War, and which rested on a continual process of territorial expansion. Capitalist America had become immensely more powerful than any other nation-state, and its population and resource base eclipsed all its rivals. Sooner or later, it would have emerged as the dominant power. What thirty years of war in Europe did was to seal the process in dramatic style. Table 5.1 gives an indication of the decline of Britain and rise of the US that had been at work since 1880.

Table 5. 1 –Shares of World Manufacturing Output, 1880-1938 (per cent)

	1880	1900	1913	1928	1938
Britain	22.9	18.5	13.6	9.9	10.7
United States	14.7	23.6	32.0	39.3	31.4
Germany	8.5	13.2	14.8	11.6	12.7
France	7.8	6.8	6.1	6.0	4.4

Source: Paul Kennedy, *The Rise and Fall of the Great Powers*, p. 259.

At the end of World War II, this reality was codified and America became the recognized leader of the world system. Urgently needing American funds in order to rebuild, Europe was cajoled into accepting US leadership exercised through a new set of international economic and political institutions. And American capitalism saw a clear interest in "helping" Europe recover. US big business was deeply troubled by the credibility the parties of the left – Communists and Socialists – in Italy, France and Greece, derived from their resistance to fascism and Nazi occupation. An aide to the US State Department expressed the anxieties of American capital in early 1947, musing that "if every other nation were to go Socialist, it would be extremely difficult, if not impossible, to preserve real private enterprise in the United States."[18] To that end, US dollars were used to buy influence, rebuild discredited conservative and liberal parties, and subvert the left.

But even with such high political stakes, US capital could not resist pushing its short-term business interests at the same time. In a series of bilateral treaties that provided American funds to war-torn Europe the US insisted on clauses giving American citizens the same treatment as nationals when it came to accessing the raw materials of the receiving nation. In fact, even during the war, America's loans to its allies were made contingent on the recipients eliminating "all forms of discriminatory treatment in international commerce" – i.e., on opening markets to US goods and investment.[19] In a pattern that has become familiar in the age of globalization, "aid" was offered in exchange for the right of US corporations to buy up world resources.

The United States was now in a position to pioneer a new form of imperialism, organized through multinational corporations and, as we shall see, overwhelming military power. The old style imperialism, based upon control of colonial territories, was coming under powerful attack at the same time as the successes of popular anti-fascist movements had given a boost to anti-colonial movements, the largest of which won independence for India, China and Indonesia in 1949. Pressure for de-colonization swept large parts of Asia and Africa. As the old empires increasingly gave way – save the Portuguese whose control over colonies in Africa would be overthrown only in the 1970s – the United States made little effort to return to direct political control. Instead, it constructed a new form of empire which, with some important shifts, continues to define the world in which we live.

American Imperialism: From Indian Wars to Subordinating the Third World

Many discussions of American imperialism lose sight of its roots in territorial expansion driven by genocidal wars against native peoples on the continent. It is impossible to fully understand the development of American capitalism, however, outside a brutal *internal colonialism* through which land and resources were violently expropriated from aboriginal peoples. From the start, in fact, colonies like Virginia legalized the enslavement of American Indians. And from the early seventeenth century, numerous armed conflicts broke out between white settlers and indigenous peoples. In 1637, for instance, colonists surrounded a community of Pequod in Connecticut, setting fire to the area. Four hundred people were burned alive, or killed while trying to escape the inferno. Following the American Revolution, George Washington ordered "destruction and devastation" of the Iroquois. In the early nineteenth century, "Indian wars" swept the US South, notably against the Seminoles of Florida who had provided safe harbour for runaway Black slaves. Then in 1830 President Jackson pushed through a Bill permitting transportation of Indians beyond the Mississippi River. Of the many appalling acts of cruelty that followed, the deportation of the Cherokee Nation to Oklahoma was particularly heart-wrenching. But it was in the second half of the nineteenth century that American colonialism surpassed its own bloody record as it pushed into the West, crushing Indigenous societies in California, New Mexico, Oregon, Oklahoma and the plains with dizzying violence. The Navajos, the Sioux, the Cheyennes and Comanches fought bravely against superior forces. On those occasions where they could amass sufficient numbers, native peoples mobilized courage, daring and intelligence to defeat US forces, most memorably when the Sioux, the Cheyennes and others routed General Custer at Little Big Horn in 1876. But those heroic occasions were too few. American capitalism had great material resources with which to crush, humiliate and inferiorize indigenous peoples, and white racism gave it the cruelty of character to commit shameful genocidal crimes.[20]

The seizing of Indian lands went hand in hand with other strategies of territorial expansion. By negotiation, purchase, annexation and war, the US state grabbed one part of the continent after another: Florida in 1819, Missouri a year later, Texas in 1845, northern California and New Mexico a few years later. Indeed, the mid-1840s were a time of outrightly expansionist wars against Mexico. In the end, as Texas, New Mexico and parts of California were seized, total US land mass jumped from 1.8 million square miles in 1844 to 3.0 million four years later. Further expansion was to follow.

Alaska, purchased from Russia, was gobbled up in 1867, while Hawaii was simply annexed thirty years later. Then came war with Spain and the occupation of the Philippines, America's most sustained experiment in colonial occupation. Yet, the Philippines exercise, alongside others such as an occupation of Cuba from 1906-9, soured America's rulers on direct colonial control. Instead, they found their approach in Central America and the Caribbean to be much more profitable. Combining economic domination with periodic military invasions, they were able to make the region a goldmine for US capital.

As American businesses poured investments into Central America and the Caribbean, so they regularly poured in troops. In 1912, Cuba was re-occupied. Over the next four years, Nicaragua, Guatemala, the Dominican Republic, Mexico and Haiti would be reacquainted with soldiers wearing the stars and stripes. Yet, in none of these cases did American governments seek permanent occupations. Instead, they installed ruthless generals and dictators, aided by US money and troops, to police their nations in the interests of wealthy elites and US banks and corporations. And it was this strategy – economic domination backed up by troops and marines – that America's rulers cultivated after the Second World War.

There were several key components to American policy after 1945. Foremost was "free trade" imperialism, the insistence that other nations open their markets to US goods and investment by American-based multinationals. The US Assistant Secretary of State put it bluntly a year after the war's end: "We need markets – big markets – around the world in which to buy and sell. We ask no special privileges in any of those markets."[21] Of course, special privileges were beside the point. The American economy was immensely more powerful than any other; were markets to be opened to it, it would inevitably ride roughshod over the competition. And, for the next twenty years or so, that's more or less exactly what happened. Foreign trade and foreign investment – organized through multinational corporations – became central to the workings of the US economy. In fact, during the heyday of American capitalism in the 1950s and 1960s, foreign investment by US-based firms rose much more quickly than did their investments at home. Between 1960 and 1965, American firms nearly tripled their spending on factories and equipment outside the US – a rate of increase six times faster than the growth of their domestic investments. Throughout the better part of the 1960s, foreign sales by US firms grew more than twice as fast as sales at home. And rates of profit on foreign investment were higher than on domestic operations too.[22]

Supporting the American multinational corporation and its invasion of world markets was an institutional architecture for the world economy that made the US dollar the international reserve currency – that is, the currency all countries agreed to accept as payment between nations. This system, in which the dollar was "as good as gold," officially established US hegemony over the global economy. Inevitably, the headquarters of the newly created International Monetary Fund and World Bank were located in the United States, a symbolic expression of the post-war hierarchy of world capitalism.

The dominant power in the world system ultimately rules by virtue of its military might. Given its wealth and population base, the US was clearly the only western nation capable in the post-1945 period of acting as a global cop. Consequently, international relations in the post-war period largely conformed to the foreign policy interests of the United States (although they were constrained to a degree by the former Soviet Union).

At the outset, American capital's biggest worries were about the future of Western Europe. Because the Russians had played such a decisive role in smashing the German war machine – single-handedly destroying forty-five German divisions – eastern Europe would be theirs, so long as they reined in Communist parties in Greece and elsewhere. This was the agreement that American President Franklin D. Roosevelt, British Prime Minister Winston Churchill and Russian leader Josef Stalin came to at Yalta in February, 1945. The atmosphere at the dinner meeting where the three leaders finalized the division between the Russian and American spheres of influence "was as that of a family," Roosevelt intoned.[23] Still, while Churchill and Roosevelt were prepared to hand chunks of eastern Europe to Stalin, they deeply feared the resurgence of Communist and Socialist parties in their own sphere. Washington was intent on stabilizing capitalism in Western Europe by subverting the region's leftist parties. But, as a result of social upheaval in Korea that began in 1945 and the revolution in China four years later, Asia soon became Washington's central preoccupation. Henceforth, the Cold War would be less about direct confrontations between East and West, than about Washington and its allies organizing to crush insurgence in the South. The rhetoric of anti-communism directed at Moscow was primarily meant for radical movements in the Third World. This became especially clear as conflict unfolded in Korea.

Like China, Korea had been occupied by Japan. As Japanese surrender became inevitable in 1945, resistance forces were emboldened and a new independence struggle, led by the left, broke out. By the end of August 1945, Peoples' Committees had been established in 145 cities and towns throughout the country and began to operate as organs of self-government. One week later, a Korean People's Republic was proclaimed. However, the American military, which was moving into Korea as Japan prepared its surrender, had no tolerance for a popular movement undertaking redistribution of land to poor peasants. Initially, the US declared its support for the hated Japanese military government in Korea. Then, when the American army of occupation had accumulated sufficient forces to form its own government, it retained Japanese personnel and engaged in looting, quickly alienating the local population.

The Americans were well aware of the popularity of the parties and movements of the left. A January 1946 report in the *Christian Science Monitor* observed, for instance, that "the so-called People's Republic, composed of Socialist and Communist elements, enjoys far more popular support than any other single political grouping."[24] Yet, in a pattern that stretches across the history of US foreign policy, Washington was not going to let democratic concerns obstruct its aims. Instead, while Korean living standards plummeted, Washington began a massive troop buildup and cracked down on dissent. Then, in an effort to avoid looking like an occupation government, as the hated Japanese had been, the Americans appointed an advisory council led by the corrupt politician, Syngman Rhee.

In response, a powerful movement of resistance erupted. In September 1946 the railworkers in Pusan launched a protest strike which soon escalated into a general strike of 300,000 workers. Police attacks on picket lines resulted in forty-one deaths. In early October, when the American Military Government (AMG) declared martial law, more than 100,000 students walked out of classes to express their solidarity with the strikers. Soon the revolt spread to the countryside. It would be contained only through mass repression – and Rhee was the man for the job. By October 1948 he had "closed all opposition newspapers, jailed editors, and put even his right-wing critics under more intense surveillance … By September, according to official data, there were 36,000 political prisoners in South Korea" (which had recently been divided between Russia and America at the thirty-eighth parallel).[25]

The US government and its army of occupation, led by General Douglas MacArthur, did not blink in the face of these ugly realities. In a blunt declaration of American policy, MacArthur proclaimed, "We must help anyone who will fight communism. I would help the devil, if he would come to this earth and offer to help fight the Communists."[26] As civil war raged, the pact with the devil soon involved war with Russia and China on Korean soil. The "Cold War" had suddenly turned very hot.

The Korean War resulted in tens of thousands of deaths and left a country forcibly divided. It also provided the pretext for a massive escalation in military spending. The world now found itself embroiled in a manic arms race that involved $120 billion in spending on weapons every year by 1962 (prior to the increases that accompanied war in Vietnam) – an amount equal to nearly 9 per cent of all the goods produced on the planet at the time, or the equivalent of half of all global spending on economic infrastructure, like factories and equipment, that can produce goods to satisfy human needs.[27] The United States and the Soviet Union became military superpowers, possessed of vast stocks of nuclear weapons, each policing parts of the globe. America remained the considerably more powerful of the two, however, and as the Cold War between the two camps escalated, a permanent war economy developed as an integral component of American imperialism. The war machine it generated was now increasingly aimed at the South.

Imprisoning the South: Guatemala, Cuba, Indonesia, Vietnam

In a candid statement, the historian of the US Central Intelligence Agency (CIA), Gerald Haines, wrote that "out of self-interest," the US took "responsibility for the welfare of the world capitalist system."[28] In the most basic terms, this entailed protecting American business anywhere and everywhere – and with a ruthlessness only the CIA might appreciate. Indeed, the millions of people who perished in the face of US aggression might be forgiven for thinking they were indeed victims of pacts with the devil. While a full documentation of the use of force by the US to defend its business interests would require several books, for our purposes, four particular episodes are especially worthy of attention.

1954: Mass Murder in Guatemala

In the waning years of WW II, Jorge Ubico's brutal dictatorship in Guatemala was overturned by a revolt of the liberal middle class. The new government reformed the education system and introduced a labour code that allowed trade unions to develop. Its successor, formed in 1951, initiated a land reform program that distributed unused lands to peasants, while landowners were compensated for their loss. Within three years, over 100,000 families had received new land.

But while peasants were improving their lot in life, an immensely powerful and wealthy US corporation was doing a not-very-slow burn. The United Fruit Company owned huge estates stretching from ocean to ocean, along with the railway and the port (while paying almost no taxes on bananas and other fruits it exported). Because it used only 8 per cent of the land it owned, the company was threatened with large chunks of its lands being distributed to peasants. Outraged by this attack on property, US media soon entered a frenzy of denunciation. A Guatemalan colonel trained in the US and backed by American-piloted F-47 bombers attacked the country in a fury of vengeance for which officials in Washington proudly claimed responsibility. In a fitting bit of irony, it turned out that the director of the CIA at the time, Allen Dulles, had been on the United Fruit board of directors, a tradition that was continued by other CIA and American government officials.[29]

Rather than an aberration, the overthrow of the reformist government of Guatemala was just part of a long line of US military interventions throughout the early twentieth century, including coups, occupations or mass murders in Haiti, Nicaragua, Cuba, Mexico and El Salvador. In a particularly candid reminiscence, US General Smedley D. Butler recalled in 1935:

> I spent thirty-three years and four months in active service as a member of our country's most agile military force – the Marine Corps... And during that period I spent most of my time being a high-class muscle man for Big Business, for Wall Street, and for the bankers. In short, I was a racketeer for capitalism... Thus I helped make Mexico and especially Tampico safe for American oil interests in 1914. I helped make Haiti and Cuba a decent place for the National City Bank to collect revenues in ... I helped purify Nicaragua for the international banking house of Brown Brothers in 1909-1912. I brought light to the Dominican Republic for American sugar interests in 1916. I helped make

Honduras "right" for American fruit companies in 1903.[30]

What was done to Guatemala in 1954 may have been easily recognizable as just another act of US imperialism, but few could have predicted the longevity of the violence. To this day, the country continues to live in the shadow of the slaughter that stopped land reform and crushed opposition to American big business. The execution of trade unionists, dissident intellectuals, peasants and indigenous peoples is unceasing. Whenever popular opposition resurfaces, the brutality escalates: between 1974 and 1978, for instance, troops and death squads assassinated 124 union leaders.[31] But the worst year may have been 1967 when, according to a Catholic priest from the US, right-wing terrorists killed 2,800 peasants, students, intellectuals and union activists.[32] In a campaign uncompromisingly backed and funded by the US, the military went on a killing spree reminiscent of the conquistadors:

> All the men of the village of Cajon del Rio were exterminated; those of Tituque had their intestines gouged out with knives; in Peidra Parada they were flayed alive; in Agua Blanca de Ipala they were burned alive after being shot in the legs. A rebellious peasant's head was stuck on a pole in the center of San Jorge's plaza. In Cerro Gordo the eyes of Jaime Velazquez were filled with pins... In San Lucas Sacatepéquez, the wells yielded corpses instead of water. On the Miraflores plantation the men greeted the dawn without hands or feet.[33]

This US-backed terror regime – whose murder toll has now hit 200,000, the majority indigenous people – remains in place to this day.[34] And the consequences are utterly predictable: 76 per cent of rural Guatemalans live in poverty (defined as less than $2 per day); 39 per cent live in extreme poverty (less than $1 a day); fewer than 3 per cent of workers are unionized.[35] But business is good, particularly for the heirs of United Fruit, the banana and coffee barons.

1961: On the Verge of Nuclear War over Cuba

Not far from Guatemala sits the island nation of Cuba, invaded by the United States in 1898 and run for sixty years on behalf of a small clique of American drug lords, sugar barons and organized criminals who turned the city of Havana into a private fiefdom for gambling and prostitution. In order to keep up appearances, this bunch installed a helpful dictator named Fulgencio Batista as head of state in 1952. At the time, thirteen US companies owned half of all the land devoted to sugar production, pocketing about $180 million every year in sugar profits. By 1958, a year before Batista's dictatorship was overthrown, Cuba had more registered prostitutes than mine workers, half of its children did not go to school and a million and a half Cubans were wholly or partially unemployed.[36]

In the face of a small but well-organized rebellion, the corrupt pro-American dictatorship collapsed like a house of cards in July 1959. Yet, while the new government headed by Fidel Castro declared no socialist or communist aims, the mere fact that it would defy America and reclaim some of its lands whipped the US ruling class into a frenzy of denunciation. First, the Eisenhower administration committed itself to reconquering Cuba and began air attacks. Then, upon taking office in 1960, newly elected US President John F. Kennedy exhibited an extraordinary obsession with bringing Castro to his knees – well before the Cuban leader decided to forge an alliance with the Soviet Union. One particular study of Kennedy's policies toward Cuba is especially instructive, as it was written by someone who spent five years as the principal United Nations correspondent for the US propaganda system, Voice of America.[37] After studying the historical record, Richard J. Walton concluded that:

- the Kennedy administration was the systematic aggressor "undertaking a military, political and economic offensive against a Cuba that had pitifully few weapons with which to respond" (p. 41);

- Kennedy sent 1,400 right-wing Cuban exiles into a ludicrously unsuccessful attempt to invade Cuba at the Bay of Pigs in April 1961 (pp. 44-47);
- Kennedy and his advisors regularly discussed plans to assassinate Castro – in complete violation of international law (p. 48);
- "the Bay of Pigs invasion was the major cause of the Cuban missile crisis" in which, threatening the Soviet Union for having sent Cuba missiles for defense against aggression, Kennedy brought the world perilously close to nuclear war (p. 104);
- when Cuba and the Soviet Union proposed a withdrawal of missiles in exchange for a US pledge not to launch further invasions, "the United States flatly refused to talk" (p. 116);
- when the US threatened to intercept Russian ships – again in violation of international law – it was the Soviet leader Nikita Khruschev who made a reasonable proposal "to avoid nuclear war and it was Kennedy who was pushing the world to the brink of nuclear catastrophe" (p. 134).

Walton's book is especially significant precisely because he worked for the American government and believed its version of events – that is, until he took the opportunity to investigate. What he does not account for, however, is the obsession of Kennedy and all successive US governments with crushing Cuba. To this day, as Noam Chomsky points out, "The US sanctions against Cuba are the harshest in the world, much harsher than the sanctions against Iraq" during the last years of Saddam Hussein's regime.[38] There is not another country in the world that supports the US in this regard (even Israel, which does so on paper, breaks the sanctions in practice). In fact, the United Nations, the European Union, the Inter-American Juridical Community and others have repeatedly condemned the US sanctions. None of these bodies buys the claim that the sanctions are necessary to defend the United States or to oppose violations of civil rights in Cuba.[39] The idiosyncratic American campaign against Cuba rests on a simple maxim of imperial policy: let a rebel get away with defiance and the disease will spread.

As Chomsky indicates, US motives become clear on reading the report written at the time by one of Kennedy's advisers, Arthur Schlesinger. The problem in Cuba, Schlesinger explained, is "the spread of the Castro idea of taking matters into one's own hands." Unfortunately, he continued, this idea is vastly popular throughout Latin America, where "the poor and underprivileged, stimulated by the example of the Cuban revolution, are now demanding opportunities for a decent living."[40] Taking matters into one's own hands and aspiring to a decent living – the principles of self-determination and material well being – are the subversive ideas that the United States is determined to quash. And so, more than forty years after winning its independence, Cuba remains besieged and bullied by the most powerful nation on the planet.

1965: Slaughter in Indonesia

While Indonesia had long been a Dutch colony, it was occupied by Japanese forces during the Second World War. As the war wound down and Japan prepared its surrender, a struggle erupted for Indonesian independence from all colonial powers. In the face of a joint British-Australian invasion to support the Dutch, a four-year revolutionary war developed, in the course of which the people of Indonesia adopted a new constitution, created new state institutions and ended the colonial system of forced labour. After independence in 1949, the dominant political figure was Sukarno (who, like most Indonesians, went by just one name), whose movement combined nationalism with authoritarian tendencies. In 1958, Sukarno created a political system called Guided Democracy according to which all social classes were to unite in a common national project under his leadership. At the same time, he made vaguely socialist noises and was prepared to cooperate with the sizable Indonesian Communist Party (PKI). As mass movements, often associated with the PKI, began to organize demonstrations and strikes calling for the seizure of Dutch factories, Sukarno moved to nationalize these industries without offering financial compensation to the previous owners.[41]

From the start, Washington was deeply distressed by Indonesian developments. However, in part because of its growing military involvement in Vietnam, the US decided to assist anti-Sukarno forces rather than intervene directly by opening up a second military front in Southeast Asia. Central to its strategy were efforts to influence the country's army. With the PKI continuing to grow in strength – its peasant organization embraced nine million members by the early 1960s –Indonesian military officials grew increasingly hostile toward Sukarno. In September 1965, a clash between sections of the PKI and the army created the opening for which military officers had been waiting. Led by General Suharto, the army crushed trade union and communist organizations. In a murderous frenzy, about 500,000 people were killed while hundreds of thousands more were imprisoned.

Indonesia's slaughter of 1965 remains one of the most barbaric events anywhere since the Second World War. True to form, Washington welcomed the mass murderers to power, the country's American ambassador proclaiming that his "Embassy and the USG [US Government] are generally sympathetic with and admiring of what [the] army is doing."[42] In the same spirit, *Time* magazine informed its readers that the destruction of Indonesia's Communist Party was "the West's best news for years in Asia."[43] For more than thirty years, a dictatorship headed by General Suharto basked in the sun of US approval, keeping Indonesia safe for foreign investors and mercilessly crushing all dissent. After a catastrophic financial crisis and student-led uprisings toppled Suharto in 1997, a *New York Times* correspondent deigned to tell his readers that the Suhartos had been "the most corrupt, venal, greedy, ruling family in the world."[44] But for the thirty-two years he kept Indonesia safe for business, Suharto was a valued friend and ally, "our kind of guy," as the Clinton administration described him, aided and armed by the US, and feted and pampered by Canada's prime minister at the Asia Pacific Economic Community summit in Vancouver in 1995.

1959-75: War in Vietnam and the Destruction of Indochina

But when it comes to human crimes, nothing in the post-World War II era can compare with what the United States did in Vietnam. It was, quite simply, mass murder carried out behind a veil of lies.

After an historic struggle against French colonialism, the Vietnamese people reached a peace settlement with France in 1954. Yet, the United States had no intention of honouring the peace agreement. Within a few days of the signing of the Geneva accords between France and Vietnam, the National Security Council in Washington proclaimed its right to use military force in the event of "local Communist subversion or rebellion not constituting armed attack."[45] In yet another violation of the UN Charter, any kind of radical rebellion – protest strikes, land reform, mass demonstrations – could be used to justify American military intervention. Consistent with this policy, Washington imposed a client government in South Vietnam (the country having been temporarily divided until an election scheduled for 1956 could create a unified government). The US puppet-leader proceeded to block the elections and launch a terror campaign that killed about 155,000 people between 1957 and 1965. Meanwhile, under the presidency of John F. Kennedy and that of his successor, Lyndon Johnson, the US directed bombing raids and engineered a massive troop buildup which saw half a million American troops prosecute a barbarous war.[46]

Recognizing that the people hated its military presence and the corrupt puppet government in the South, the US army simply decided to wage war against the whole Vietnamese people. Ordinary peasants became the enemy as the world's most powerful state used chemical weapons to destroy crops and poison people and water supplies, while dropping more bombs than had been used in all previous wars in history. When the forces of Vietnam's National Liberation Front (NLF) employed lightning strikes to capture large parts of the South in early 1968 – even briefly seizing the US embassy in Saigon – American troops and their South Vietnamese client army (ARVN) openly slaughtered civilians. As one journalist in the region reported:

> The U.S. and the ARVN forces responded to the attack with the fury of a blinded giant. Forced to fight in the cities, they bombed, shelled and strafed the most populous districts as if they saw no distinction between them and the jungle. . .
>
> Surveying the corpses and shattered buildings of Ben Tre, one America officer told an AP reporter, "We had to destroy it in order to save it." ... By the end of three weeks the Allied command estimated the toll of civilian dead at around 165,000, and the number of new refugees at two million.[47]

Destroy it they did – along with large chunks of Laos and Cambodia, invaded at the direction of US President Richard Nixon in his 1970 extension of the conflict throughout Indochina. By then, the official numbers for Vietnamese killed exceeded 1.4 million. Before the conflict was over, at least two million would perish, alongside another 600,000 in Cambodia.[48] Even these figures are almost certainly underestimates, as the devastation carried out by the US war machine led to epidemics of hunger and disease. One reporter noted at the time: "In the refugee camps and isolated villages, people die of malnutrition and the children are deformed. In the cities where there is no sanitation and rarely any running water, the adults die of cholera, typhoid, tuberculosis, leprosy, bubonic plague, and their children die of common diseases of dirt, such as scabies and sores."[49] We now know that Nixon also discussed using nuclear weapons against the Vietnamese people.[50]

Equally perverse, hundreds of thousands continue to perish long after the last US troops vacated Saigon. As recently as 1997, the *Wall Street Journal* reported an epidemic of dioxin-related deformities that had affected as many as half a million newborns – a result of the millions of tons of chemicals Washington dumped on South Vietnam.[51]

Despite the American savagery, the NLF and its supporters would not break. As protest movements erupted in the streets of America, the heroic resistance of the people of Vietnam, supported by a powerful global anti-war movement, inflicted a humiliating defeat on American imperialism. In 1975, the last US military advisers scrambled onto helicopters fleeing Saigon. Although eight million American troops had been dispatched to Southeast Asia and $141 billion spent on the war, the US government had failed to crush the Vietnamese people. America now found itself suffering from what came to be known as "Vietnam syndrome," hesitant to commit massive ground troops to fight guerrilla armies in the Third World. In the meantime, however, it had discovered a new weapon with which to discipline the South: debt.

Debt Crisis, Neoliberalism and "Market Colonialism"

The revelation that debt could be a weapon with which to systematically discipline the Third World came to the US ruling class in the early 1980s. With a world awash in American dollars – as a result of US government deficits to finance the Vietnam War and mounting US trade deficits with the rest of the world (which were covered by printing dollars) – global financial institutions in the 1970s were sitting on huge stockpiles of dollars and eager to find borrowers. As lending opportunities in the North dried up, they turned to the South where they found governments and firms eager for investment funds. In the span of a decade, from 1971 to 1980, Third World external debt grew eight-fold – from $70 billion to $560 billion.[52] Then, in 1979, the US and British governments decided to drive up interest rates in order to induce a recession, break labour militancy, and tame inflation. For Third World borrowers, the results were catastrophic: while export markets contracted (as a result of the recession), debt payments tripled due to massively higher interest rates.[53] In the midst of the world recession of 1980-82, both Mexico and Poland effectively declared bankruptcy, informing lenders that they could not make payments on their debts.

Western banks and governments now confronted a risk and an opportunity. The risk was that a debt default by a country like Mexico could send shock waves through the international financial system. But western leaders also perceived that desperate circumstances might represent an opportunity to force debtor countries to agree to almost any terms in order to get new loans. Always adept at smelling blood, the government of Ronald Reagan (1980-88) pushed the World Bank to shift from traditional lending to Structural Adjustment Loans (SALs). If the right conditions were imposed, SALs could compel Third World government to adopt pro-western economic and social policies. One US Treasury official explained, "Only countries that commit to market-oriented economic reform will get the help."[54] Since the early 1980s, World Bank and IMF loans have increasingly required that recipient countries agree to Letters of Intent committing themselves to a Structural Adjustment Program (SAP) which typically has the following features:

- massive cuts to government spending, particularly in areas such as health and education;
- mass layoffs of public employees;
- liberalization of trade and removal of restrictions on foreign investment;
- withdrawal of subsidies on basic goods consumed by the poor such as bread, rice and oil;
- cuts to wages of all public employees;
- devaluation of the local currency – which cheapens exports, but makes imported goods on which the population depends more expensive (and thus represents a further cut in living standards);

- privatization of state-owned companies such as oil and gas companies and public telephone, railway and hydroelectricity systems.

As one African political economist argues, SALs effectively constitute a process of "recolonisation."[55] They utterly subordinate the Third World debtor nation to the dictates of global capital, irrespective of the protests of the local population, which are often massive. Indeed, SALs represent a blatant denial of the sovereignty of the people of the debtor nation. Policies on public spending, health, education, the environment, foreign ownership and more are all dictated by the IMF and World Bank, the "new masters" of the Third World as they've been described.[56] In 1987, the Managing Director of the IMF triumphantly proclaimed, "Adjustment is now universal."[57] Since then, dozens more countries have been "structurally adjusted"; in fact, more than 100 of the 190 countries in the world have now been subjected to SAPs.[58]

Some commentators have assumed that these loan programs are designed to reduce Third World debt. Nothing could be further from the truth. As Table 5.2 illustrates, throughout the whole SAL era, the indebtedness of the South has soared.

Table 5.2 – External Debt of Third World Countries

Year	Total external debt (in $US billions)
1980	586.7
1990	1,459.9
2000	2,527.5

Source: World Bank, *Global Development Finance 2001*, p. 246.

Rather than alleviating debt, twenty years of structural adjustment has exacerbated it: the nations of the South are now 4.5 times more indebted than they were in 1980. What structural adjustment has succeeded at, however, is remaking the Third World along neoliberal lines while transferring huge amounts of wealth from the South to the North. Every year, between $160 and $200 billion flows out of the South as debt repayment, the bulk of it in the form of interest payments. From 1980 to 1992, Third World countries paid $1.7 trillion on their debt – only to end up owing massively more than they had owed before coughing up such a tremendous sum in debt repayment.[59] Global debt and IMF/World Bank programs have thus been enormous imperial hoses, siphoning wealth from the poorest nations to the richest. As a former director of the World Bank declared, "Not since the conquistadors plundered Latin America has the world experienced a flow in the direction we see today."[60]

The IMF/World Bank offensive has remade the South according to the whims of western capital, impoverishing it in the process. In the four years immediately following Mexico's debt crisis of 1982, for instance, average incomes dropped in twenty of twenty-five Latin American countries and in most of sub-Saharan Africa.[61] As we have seen, the globalization program also intensifies inequalities inside debtor nations. When a new debt crisis in the early 1990s brought a fresh round of SALs, the resulting liberalization of finance and privatization of state enterprises shifted huge fortunes into the pockets of the rich. Twenty-four Mexican families, for instance, had joined the list of the world's richest families by 1996 – at the same time as thirty-five million Mexicans were living on less than $1 per day.[62]

In some cases, the effects of SALs have been nothing short of catastrophic. The "Fujishock" – named after President Alberto Fujimori – imposed on Peru in August, 1990 destroyed life for millions. The price of bread increased over 1,000 per cent and the price of fuel by nearly 3,000 per cent in a single day. By the middle of 1991, real earnings had fallen by 85 per cent from their 1974 level, more than 83 per cent of the population was not meeting the minimum requirements for calories and protein, and 38.5 per cent of all children were malnourished.[63]

Meanwhile, halfway across the world, World Bank and IMF intervention in Rwanda helped prepare the ground for genocide against a million people of Tutsi descent. With the country's foreign debt multiplying twenty times between 1976 and 1994 to more than $1 billion, the Rwandan regime reached an SAP agreement with the IMF and World Bank (who hold three-quarters of its debt). Fuel prices rose by 79 per cent while the price that coffee farmers could charge was frozen. As hundreds of thousands of coffee farmers were ruined and 80 per cent of public employees slipped below the poverty line, massive social tension built up. Desperately clinging to power, a European-trained political elite deliberately fomented ethnic hostilities as a way of deflecting anger. As the 900-page report, *Leave None to Tell the Story*, demonstrates, the three-month long slaughter that ensued was anything but spontaneous; it was instead systematically orchestrated by a corrupt ruling group.[64] There is nothing more offensive, however, than the role the IMF and World Bank played in providing the funds for massive arms purchases which facilitated the genocide. While demanding "adjustments" that destroyed the livelihoods of millions of people, these global lenders handed out money to a regime that tripled military spending between 1990 and 1992 and committed massacres that were widely condemned by human rights organizations. In the ultimate irony – a fitting testimony to the age of globalization – those who survived are now expected to pay back the loans used for the arms with which the crimes were committed.[65]

It should come as no surprise by now that the most devastating effects of the debt offensive have occurred in Africa. By 1990, the UN Development Program reported that in the world's thirty-seven poorest countries, most of them in Africa, health spending had plummeted by 50 per cent since 1975. As a consequence, one million Africans die of malaria every year, 70 per cent of them children under five years old. More than half of the African population lives in poverty.[66] The human effects of structural adjustment are shockingly evident: rising malnutrition, especially among children; rising infant mortality rates in several countries; huge increases in deaths due to preventable diseases; and escalating debt burdens that will be borne by future generations. Perhaps most telling, sub-Saharan Africa is the only region of the world where food production per capita has fallen in recent decades.[67]

Western capitalism has undoubtedly found in structural adjustment a powerful weapon with which to discipline the South. While it may not be so blatant as slavery or the use of colonial armies, it is a weapon that takes human lives on a frightening scale. In the future, writes one expert, "the painful consequences of the exercise of that power by the lending countries and their international agencies, the IMF and the World Bank, will be interpreted by Historians in the same terms used to describe the evils of slavery in Africa."[68] Let us hope so.

The WTO Offensive and "Violent Peace" in the South

In the post-Vietnam period, American policy shifted away from land wars in the Third World. While military campaigns would still be waged, the imperial focus shifted to global economic policy more than ever before. The rebuilding of America's world dominance in the past twenty years relied in the first instance on economic restructuring: first at home, with the war against unions and social service spending and, secondly, with the "free trade" offensive against the South.

While America's global economic offensive began in earnest during the Reagan era (1980-88) and continued under the first George Bush (1988-92), it was codified and given the name *geoeconomics* in the Clinton era. In the words of Clinton's US Trade Representative, Mickey Kantor, military security and economic power are two sides of the same coin: "National security and our national economic security cannot be separated."[69] In this spirit, Clinton set up a National Economic Council alongside the National Security Council in order to coordinate economic and military policy.

If a moment were to be selected as the beginning of the new economic offensive against the South, it might well be Ronald

Reagan's visit to Korea in 1983 when the US president demanded that Korea open its markets and improve protection for property rights. Reagan's visit was followed by a campaign to break open Korea's markets through aggressive use of anti-dumping suits and the US Congress's "Super 301" trade law that empowers Washington to retaliate against "unfair" traders. In the name of free trade, these powerful new weapons of economic protectionism were launched against the South. As the US invasion escalated, Korean imports of American agricultural goods soared from $1.8 billion in 1985 to $5 billion by the end of 1991; Korea now consumes more US farm products per capita than any other foreign nation.[70] Soon, Indonesia, Thailand, Brazil and India found themselves on the US hit list. One of the crowning moments of the globalization offensive came with India's 1991 capitulation to the IMF and the World Bank which, as part of a structural adjustment process, proceeded to colonize the country's finance ministry. As we saw in chapter 2, new weapons were added to the arsenal when intellectual property rights (TRIPs) and services (GATS) were incorporated into the WTO onslaught.

The economic offensive coincided with two historic events that gave the United States unparalleled dominance in the world system: the disintegration of the Soviet Union and its sphere of influence beginning in 1989; and the crash of the Tokyo stock exchange in the early 1990s, the start of a decade-long crisis that is not yet over. In the span of a few years, America's most dynamic economic competitor (Japan) and its major military rival (the Soviet Union) were in severe disarray. At the same time, the debt offensive was paying big dividends in the South as structural adjustment opened markets to western goods and investment. The stage was set for a free trade offensive which included the incorporation of Mexico into NAFTA (1994); the attempt to implement a Multilateral Agreement on Investment (1994-98); the launching of the Millennium Round of the WTO (1999); and the convening of a Summit of the Americas to launch a Free Trade Area of the Americas (2001). All of these were integral parts of a design for redrawing the world economy in the image of the United States and its closest allies by locking the South into the "free trade" mold.

The United States had now consolidated a formidable economic, political and military hegemony reinforced by neoliberal fundamentalism. Yet, as a number of commentators observed, this also made the US decidedly unpopular – particularly in those parts of the world that were being hammered by the globalization juggernaut. *New York Times* correspondent and globalization booster Thomas Friedman put it bluntly, albeit with ludicrous imagery, in his infamous 1999 manifesto:

> To the rest of the world, American Gothic is actually two 20-something software engineers who come into your country ... kick down your front door, overturn everything in the house, stick a Big Mac in your mouth, fill your kids with ideas you never had or can't understand, slam a cable box onto your television set, lock in the channel to MTV, plug an Internet connection into your computer and tell you, "Download or die."
>
> We Americans are the apostles of the Fast World, the prophets of the free market and the high priests of high tech. We want enlargement of both our values and our Pizza Huts...
>
> No wonder, therefore, that resentment of America is on the rise globally.[71]

Friedman has a solution to that resentment, however, and to the "powerful backlash from those brutalized or left behind" that it provokes. It's a deadly serious one:

> The hidden hand of the market will never work without a hidden fist – McDonald's cannot flourish without McDonnell Douglas, the builder of the F-15. And the hidden fist that keeps the world safe for Silicon Valley's technologies is called the United States Army, Air Force, Navy and Marine Corps.

I say Friedman's imagery is ludicrous because a majority of people on the planet have never made a phone call, never mind seen MTV or logged onto the Internet. Nevertheless, he does manage to capture something of the manic logic of global capital, its relentless drive to colonize new markets, to kick in doors and turn cultures upside down in the name of McDonald's and Pizza Hut. Equally important, he acknowledges the centrality of military force to globalization. Lurking behind the US banker and industrialist or the IMF official is a fleet of F-15s, B-52s and naval destroyers, along with stockpiles of cruise missiles and cluster bombs. Those "brutalized or left behind" shall be dealt with.

Still, so damaging is the brutalization that, in defiance of all odds, people do fight back. This is the threat that haunts Jacques Attali in his book, *Millennium: Winners and Losers in the Coming World Order.* The former chairperson of the European Bank for Reconstruction and Development has no qualms about dismissing billions of people in the South as "millennial losers." Latin America is sinking into "terminal poverty," he intones, and Africa is nothing more than a "lost continent." The problem, however, is that rather than slink away to die while the rich get richer, these ingrates can be expected to make trouble. Washed aside by the tide of history, they are likely to strike back with a "war unlike any other seen in modern times," a conflict resembling "the barbarian raids of the seventh and eighth centuries."[72]

Interestingly, similar scenarios preoccupy US defense strategists. In a 1988 report, for instance, Washington's Commission on Integrated Long-Term Strategy made comparable arguments in a more dispassionate jargon. "Nearly all the armed conflicts of the past forty years have occurred in what is vaguely referred to as the Third World: the diverse countries of Asia, the Middle East, Africa, Latin America and the Eastern Caribbean," the authors wrote. "In the same period, all the wars in which the United States was involved – either directly with its combat forces or indirectly with military assistance – occurred in the Third World."[73] The report goes on to claim that the main problem confronting the US

is "low intensity conflict," which it defines as "insurgencies, organized terrorism, paramilitary crime, sabotage, and other forms of
violence." Then comes a particularly stunning assertion in light of
the recent rhetoric of the Bush administration about permanent
war:

> To defend its interests properly in the Third World,
> the United States will have to take low intensity con-
> flict much more seriously. It is a form of warfare in
> which "the enemy" is more or less omnipresent and
> unlikely ever to surrender. In the past we have some-
> times seen these attacks as a succession of transient
> and isolated crises. We now have to think of them as a
> permanent addition to the menu of defense planning
> problems.[74]

Let's take a moment to unpack this remarkable passage. First,
Washington acknowledges that it can now increasingly expect to
do battle not with well-equipped, modern armies, but with insurgents, guerrilla groups and "terrorists" in the South. Secondly, it
expects that its enemies will be anywhere and everywhere ("omnipresent") and that they will never surrender. As a result, thirdly,
these conflicts ought to be seen as a "permanent" feature of the
age of American-led globalization.

This particular document cannot be dismissed as an aberration. A study undertaken for the US Strategic Air Command two
years later (1990) also focused on threats from the South, arguing for a Nuclear Expeditionary Force "primarily for use against
China or Third World targets," as well as earth-penetrating war-
heads to destroy bunkers too well protected to be eliminated by
conventional bombs.[75] Another two years on and a Navy/Marine
Corps White Paper of September 1992 affirmed, "Our strategy
has shifted from a focus on a global threat to a focus on regional
challenges and opportunities." As if to underline the point, the
Marine Corps conducted planning and training exercises in
which Cuba, Libya, North Korea and Iraq were imagined targets.[76] The Bottom-Up Review (BUR) carried out by Clinton's

Defense Secretary in 1993 struck a similar tone. Rather than focus on confronting a single enemy (such as Russia during the Cold War era), the BUR argued for preparing to deal with two simultaneous "major regional conflicts" – Iraq and North Korea being given as examples of potential regional enemies. To cap off this survey of American military strategizing, let's consider the Quadrennial Defense Review undertaken by the US Defense Secretary in 1997. That document too talks of "the continuing need to maintain overseas presence to shape the international environment and to be better able to respond to a variety of smaller-scale contingencies and asymmetric threats."[77]

There can be little doubt that Washington has been planning at the highest levels for a "permanent" war against the South, one based on containing the endless conflict and violence globalization produces. The US ruling class intends to police the globe, to crush desperate acts by "those brutalized or left behind." And since these folks do not have modern armies or equipment, and because they literally can be found in a hundred or more countries, it now expects military engagements to be more fluid, shifting from one country and region to another, pitting the US against "asymmetric threats," i.e. small fighting forces lacking air forces, air defense or modern weapons systems. US military policy now entails intervening anywhere such low intensity opposition flares up – proponents of the new "war on terrorism" talk of military interventions in up to sixty countries – in a never-ending campaign whose front shifts constantly. The US goal is not to stop war, but to keep it localized in the Third World.

This entails what US military strategists call "keeping the violent peace."[78] Behind this oxymoron is the notion that America can live in "peace" – that is, security for its investments and its institutions – if it can keep the violence where it "belongs." War is not objectionable if dark-skinned people die in some part of the world that most Americans could not find on a globe. Indeed, George W. Bush's Defense Secretary, Donald Rumsfeld, made a remarkably revealing statement in this regard in the early stages of the war against Afghanistan. In a Pentagon briefing he told reporters, "We can no longer count on wars being waged safely, in their regions of origin."[79] In short, wars are safe when they take place in poor countries, where they belong; they become unsafe when Americans might be hurt.

Of course, planning for permanent war in the South does not mean a retreat from nuclear weapons. The US military consistently refuses to rule out a resort to nukes. And this is meant as both a real threat and a deterrent. A 1995 Pentagon document, for instance, argues that America should never appear too cool or rational: "That the U.S. may become irrational and vindictive if its vital interests are attacked should be part of the national persona we project."[80] The twenty million people in the South who have died in wars since 1945 are testimony to American success in this regard.

Imperialism and "War Without Boundaries"

The age of globalization has ushered in a new era of imperialism. The United States continues to exercise imperial power, but it does so in a more globalized way than ever before. No longer is imperialism simply about policing an identifiable territory or region; now it entails securing the entirety of the world market. In Friedman's words, "we are in a new international system ... called globalization... The driving idea behind globalization is free-market capitalism ... Sustaining globalization is our overarching national interest ..." The problem is that, rather than having an "immediately visible threat" (such as the former Soviet Union), the US is confronted "with many little threats and an abstract globalization system to maintain." Consequently, if it is to preserve that "abstract globalization system," the American empire needs a military strategy focussed not on specific territories, but on the globe as a whole.[81] And this gives a new dimension to imperialism today.

One radical theorist who has grasped the geometry of the new imperialism with exceptional insight is Ellen Meiksins Wood. Writing about the North Atlantic Treaty Organization (NATO) war in Kosovo in 1999, Wood argued as follows:

> Imperialism is taking place today in the context of what can be called the "universalization" of capitalism. It is not now primarily a matter of territorial conquest or direct military or colonial control ... Now it is more a matter of ensuring that the forces of the capitalist market prevail in every corner of the globe ... It is not just a matter of controlling particular territories. It is a matter of controlling a whole world economy and global markets, everywhere and all the time.[82]

Commenting on Bush's new war on terrorism, Wood notes that we now have "war without boundaries ... military action with no clearly attainable objective, identifiable enemy, geographic target, or endgame."[83] In many respects, "terrorism" is the ideal enemy in the age of globalization: a protean entity, it is constantly changing form and identity – yesterday, Serbia's Slobodan Milosevic or Iraq's Saddam Hussein, today Osama bin Laden and tomorrow whoever the US selects as "the new Hitler" – and can be found virtually wherever it chooses. An ostensible war on terrorism provides the cover for the "permanent" military conflict against an "omnipresent" enemy that US planners have been discussing since at least 1988. Rather than an innovation adopted by Washington as a result of the horrific attacks of September 11, 2001, the doctrine of permanent war – "a task that never ends," to quote Bush – has been gestating for a considerable period. September 11 simply gave US policy makers carte blanche to unveil it in a quick series of legislative and military moves. As Aijaz Ahmad explains:

> Taking advantage of the anger and human anguish arising from the tragedy, and exploiting the fear and frustration arising from the prospect of massive economic recession, the U.S. administration moved

quickly to a new, globalized, permanent war; to ex-
pound what amounts to a new doctrine of America's
right to use its might as it pleases; to expand the war-
making powers of the presidency; to put in place a
new regime of infinite surveillance; and to demolish
whatever restraints had been introduced after the
Vietnam War on America's right to undertake assassinations and covert actions across the globe ...

The U.S. Congress swiftly passed a resolution authorizing Bush to use wide powers in pursuit of this
war on terrorism, asserting that "all necessary and
appropriate force" could be used against nations, organizations and individuals. No nations were named,
nor were any organizations, let alone individuals; the
president could determine which was to be attacked
as he went along. Nor was there a time limit ...[84]

Permanent global war is the inevitable expression of the logic
of capitalist globalization. Just as the IMF, World Bank and WTO
represent the imposition of a universal regime of capitalist property rights (appropriately weighted in the interests of the North),
so the new imperialism represents a doctrine and a practice of
universal war. In order to police and control "those brutalized
and left behind," the globalization of poverty is coordinated with
the globalization of war.

Imperial Hypocrisy

As we have seen, the rulers of the US, Britain, Canada and
other western powers regularly invoke the defense of "civilization"
as the basis for military action. Former US president Bill Clinton
tended to excel at making such pronouncements, but few surpass
British Prime Minister Tony Blair when it comes to combining
imperial warmongering with moral bombast. Defending NATO's
bombing campaign in Yugoslavia, for instance, Blair asserted that
the debacle was "a just war, based not on any territorial ambitions
but on values."[85] Fortunately, his friend Clinton gave away the
ruse. In a speech delivered the day before the bombing began,

Clinton proclaimed that a strong US relationship with Europe "is what this Kosovo thing is all about." He elaborated: "If we're going to have a strong economic relationship that includes our ability to sell around the world, Europe has got to be a key."[86] In short, the US will go to war for market access. True, this explanation does not betray any territorial ambitions, but this is what we should expect in the age of "imperialism without frontiers." The point is to keep the world safe and open for business and investment.

Generally speaking, world leaders prefer loftier sounding phrases. War to defend market access sounds just a bit too crass, even imperialistic. Consequently, heads of state have taken to invoking human rights, freedom and defense of civilization as the touchstones of military policy. These uplifting phrases have been buttressed by the claim that the latest military intervention has the support of "the international community" – which usually means that various nations have been bullied or bought off (Pakistan's support for the war in Afghanistan came at the cost of $1 billion in aid from the Bush government).[87] What they will never admit is that their actions are driven by a fundamentalism – in this case, neoliberal market fundamentalism – every bit as dogmatic and cruel as those they claim to oppose.

Consider the interesting statement by a professor of Islamic Studies reported by a major Canadian newspaper shortly after September 11, 2001. Asked to explain the mentality of those who carried out the terror attacks in New York and Washington, he explained: "They believed this is the fight of good and evil, of the forces of darkness and the forces of light ... The only way you can justify such a horrendous act is by convincing yourself you're making the right interpretation of a particular message ... Everything else becomes irrelevant. You can ignore your victims."[88] Without a doubt, the professor captures something of the fanaticism that fuels things like suicide attacks. But there are two features of the explanation that are particularly intriguing: first, the idea that the fanatic sees these conflicts as a "fight of good and evil" and, secondly, the notion that, once you have such a mindset, "you can ignore your victims." Both of these observations beautifully describe the conduct of the United States government and its allies. Let us take two examples to illustrate this point: the US wars in Colombia and Afghanistan. Then I will turn to the nauseating story of the ongoing war in Iraq.

Colombia: Blood, Land and Power

In 1999, Colombia became the world's biggest recipient of US military and police aid, with the exception of Israel and Egypt which are in a category of their own. What had the government of Colombia done to earn this distinction? Consider the following:

- Over 4,000 political murders occur every year in Colombia. Nearly 300 massacres of civilians, overwhelmingly carried out by paramilitaries linked to the Colombian army, happen each year.
- In the ten year period beginning in 1986, 45,000 people died — 36,000 of them civilians — as a result of the country's civil war.
- Over 3,000 Colombian trade unionists have been assassinated since 1990 (more than half the total of trade unionists killed around the world).
- According to both Human Rights Watch and the United Nations, the bulk of these murders are carried out by right-wing paramilitaries closely connected to the Colombian armed forces.[89]
- In addition, a 1999 US Defense Department report concluded that "government forces continued to commit numerous, serious abuses, including extrajudicial killings."[90]
- Eighty percent of the country's indigenous people live in conditions of extreme poverty, as does 40 per cent of the population as a whole.

Colombia's story is a heartbreaking one. A country of immense natural wealth, it has been dominated by a corrupt oligarchy and bourgeoisie closely allied to the United States. Its ruling class often resorts to violence to settle its own internal disputes; it invariably does so to suppress dissent by the poor. In the Thousand Day War at the turn of the century (1899-1902), when landless peasants, indigenous peoples and the urban poor formed guerrilla groups to fight for a viable future, at least 100,000 were killed. The middle of the century then saw the barbaric episode known as *La Violencia* (1948-65) when, following the assassination of a liberal-populist president who had pledged to roll back the power of the oligarchy, a popular uprising was again met by mass murder. Fourteen thousand people were killed in 1947, more than 43,000 the following year. By 1953, 200,000 people had died.

In a pattern that has become drearily familiar, each wave of violence drove hundreds of thousands of poor peasants off their lands. Over the course of *La Violencia*, about one million people were forced from their lands by right-wing gunmen, enabling the rich to accumulate ever larger estates.[91] Today, Colombia has more displaced people – around 2.75 million – than any country except Sudan and Angola. And the number keeps growing with every new incursion by the paramilitaries, one of whose main purposes is to "serve as a means to violently expropriate land from indigenous people, peasants and settlers."[92] For one hundred years and more, primitive accumulation of capital in Colombia – the dispossession of the peasantry – has been written, as Marx described it, "in letters of blood and fire."[93]

All of this has made the country especially attractive to the United States. The World Bank established a close working relationship with the Colombian government in the early stages of *La Violencia* (1949) and the country emerged as one of the Bank's top borrowers. Three years later, a Mutual Defense Agreement was signed with the US and Colombia became the site of Washington's first counter-insurgency training school in Latin America.[94]

While the structure of violence allowed a corrupt ruling class to accumulate immense wealth through the development of coffee, coal and oil, the mass of the people shared little in the riches. By the mid-1980s, more than half the urban population worked in the informal sector – collecting rubbish for resale, shining shoes, selling flowers and newspapers, or working as prostitutes and thieves. Four and a half million children under fourteen are hungry – fully half the country's youngsters. In the countryside, the growing of coca is frequently the only way for peasant families to make ends meet.

So obscene are the socio-economic inequalities and so murderous the elite that resistance has never disappeared. Courageous movements of women, trade unionists, Afro-Colombians, peasants and indigenous peoples persistently brave violence and oppression in order to mobilize the exploited and excluded. And leftist guerrilla groups – particularly the Revolutionary Armed Forces of Colombia (FARC) and the National Liberation Army (ELN) – continue to control significant parts of the country and, despite authoritarian tendencies of their own, often provide peasants with protection from right-wing paramilitaries.

But Washington will not tolerate the sight of well-organized guerrilla movements developing a power base. The US government now envisions the northern region of South America – Colombia, eastern Ecuador and Venezuela – as an arena of anti-imperialist resistance that must be conquered. Its growing obsession with the region rests on two overriding preoccupations: first, the desire to control an area rich in oil, a major strategic resource; and, secondly, fears about the effects that a "radicalized and well-organized opposition to U.S. hemispheric hegemony" might have throughout the continent.[95] To this end, the Clinton administration designed a $1.6 billion "emergency aid" package for Colombia for 2001-2. Known as Plan Colombia, the package provides massive military assistance to an army directly involved in terror and murder. It also pledged "assistance" for thousands upon thousands of rural poor who will be displaced by the preposterous "war on drugs" – the smoke-screen for a war on the guerrillas and the peasantry. Many progressive activists in Colombia believe the subtext of Plan Colombia is the dispossession of indigenous peoples and Afro-Colombians from lands Washington and the Colombian elite would like to "develop." In the resource-rich and strategically located Pacific Coast in particular, where Afro-Colombians have legal recognition of "untransferable and inalienable" lands, the ruling class hopes to use war as a means to displace people and expropriate land.[96] Promises of assistance for the displaced are designed as a self-fulfilling prophecy: force peoples from their lands, seize them for "development," and then offer them token compensation.

Since September 11, 2001, the Colombian government and the US military have exploited the "war on terrorism" to advance their agenda of crushing the leftist guerrillas, decapitating popular resistance movements, displacing peasant, indigenous and Afro-Caribbean peoples and moving toward World Bank-style development programs. October 2001 saw nearly 200 civilians killed by paramilitaries, two congressmen kidnapped, and a trade union leader kidnapped and executed.[97] By late November 2001, a total of 121 trade unionists had been assassinated and sixty-seven had disappeared. In early November, police killed a medical student involved in an anti-war protest at Colombia National University. A few days later, paramilitaries destroyed the house of the Popular Women's Organization in Barrancabermeja which operated such dangerous services as a communal kitchen, psychological counseling and technical training classes. Kidnappings and massacres of peasants continue unabated.[98]

Once again, there can be no confusion about the US government's knowledge of such state-sponsored atrocities; its own documents discuss them in detail. Indeed, Bush pressured Colombia to pass legislation granting immunity from prosecution to any US official in that country. But, then, US governments have ideals they hold infinitely higher than peace and human rights. They have "an eye to property." And in its name, all resistance will be broken. As one commentator notes,

> Plan Colombia is about maintaining the mystique of the invincibility of empire and the irreversibility of neo-liberal policies ... Once U.S. dominance is tested and successfully resisted by popular struggle in one region, the mystique is eroded ... Plan Colombia is about preventing Colombia from becoming an example that demonstrates that alternatives are possible and that Washington is vincible.[99]

And so, the people of Colombia too shall be sacrificed – all in order to defend "civilization."

"Collateral Damage" in Afghanistan

There is a simple truth about the US led war against Afghanistan that cannot be repeated too often: without US weapons and funds, there would be no well-armed Islamist groups in Central Asia and the Middle East. For a decade, the US (and its allies in Saudia Arabia) poured billions into arming Islamic fundamentalist forces – known as the *Mujaheddin* – in order to defeat a left-liberal reform government in Afghanistan that leaned toward Moscow.

The successive governments of Noor Mohammed Taraki and Babrak Karmal (1978-1992) established a minimum wage, introduced equal rights for women, legalized unions, encouraged girls to attend school and mused about a land reform program.[100] The US was not going to stand for any of this. By 1979, as former US National Security adviser Zbigniew Brzezinski boasts, America's Central Intelligence Agency (CIA) had begun funding counter-revolutionary forces, well before any Russian troops entered Afghanistan.[101] Then, in 1986, CIA director William Casey won high-level backing for building up the Mujaheddin. As one highly knowledgeable analyst reports, Casey

persuaded the US Congress to provide the Mujaheddin with American-made Stinger anti-aircraft missiles to shoot down Soviet planes and provide US
advisers to train the guerrillas ... Casey committed
CIA support to a long standing ISI [Pakistani intelligence service] initiative to recruit radical Muslims
from around the world to come to Pakistan and fight
with the Mujaheddin ...

Between 1982 and 1992 some 35,000 Muslim radicals
from 43 Islamic countries in the Middle East, North
and East Africa, Central Asia and the Far East would
pass their baptism under fire with the Afghan Mujaheddin ...

Among these thousands of foreign recruits was a
young Saudi student, Osama bin Laden.[102]

So taken was the US government with Islamic militants like
bin Laden that then-president Ronald Reagan called them heroes, "the moral equivalents of the Founding Fathers." As Eduardo Galeano wryly observes, Hollywood agreed, making Afghan
Muslims the heroes of Rambo 3.[103] When the Soviet Union was
forced to withdraw in 1989 and the left-leaning government was
defeated three years later, Reagan's successors began to play foot-
sies with the Taliban. To be sure, oil was a central concern here,
as the Caspian region, which borders on Afghanistan, is home
to some of the largest unexplored and untapped reserves in the
world. In fact, Washington worked throughout the 1990s to give
US companies control of that oil and to influence how it would
be piped out of the region. In all of its calculations, Afghanistan
figured centrally.[104] But beyond oil, the US had long been com-
fortable with authoritarian Islamic regions (as in Saudi Arabia)
and looked forward to doing business with the Taliban.

From 1994 to 1997, the US edged close to the Taliban as the
group's forces captured major Afghan cities. After the movement
seized Kabul in 1996, US Assistant Secretary of State for South
Asia Robin Raphael, claimed it was not in US interests "that the
Taliban be isolated," while State Department spokesman Glyn

Davies announced that the US found "nothing objectionable" in the Taliban's imposition of Islamic law.[105] In late 1997, a Taliban delegation led by the "one-eyed Mullah Mohammed Ghaus," was wooed in Houston by US oil executives with close ties to the Bush family, enjoying the luxury of a five-star hotel at corporate expense.[106] So protective of the Taliban was George W. Bush, according to former FBI agent John O'Neill, that the US State Department blocked attempts to prove bin Laden's involvement in 1993, 1996 and 1998 bombings of US targets. O'Neill, who resigned from the FBI in frustration and died in the attacks on the World Trade Center, claimed that US oil corporations close to Bush were hostile to anything that might offend the Taliban.[107]

Then came the horrific events of September 11, 2001. Bush now made it his mission to punish bin Laden and the Taliban, conveniently ignoring the fact that he and his predecessors had built them up in the first place. Rather than accept responsibility for having created the very forces that had just taken the lives of almost 3,000 American civilians, Bush simply declared former hero bin Laden "the evil one," and the war was on. With only rare honourable exceptions, the western media, long ago having surrendered critical intelligence and moral purpose, dutifully fell into line.[108]

And so, B-52s, F-15s, cruise missiles, two-ton cluster bombs and more were unleashed on one of the poorest peoples on the earth, a people suffering from twenty years of war, drought and a famine that threatens up to seven million of them with starvation. By completely disrupting humanitarian relief, US bombing insured that many of these people would perish. Meanwhile, the US slaughter of Afghan innocents commenced. Within eight weeks of bombings, the US war machine probably killed more civilians than perished in America on September 11. A few examples give a small sense of what transpired:

- In late October, 2001, US warplanes bombed the village of Chowkar-Karez, killing as many as thirty-five civilians according to Human Rights Watch. Asked to explain the situation, a Pentagon spokesman replied, "The people there are dead because we wanted them dead."[109]

- In mid-November, US bombings around Kunduz killed around 150 civilians, according to refugees fleeing the area. "We dug a mass grave and put in all the bodies," reported one twenty-year-old. "My neighbour died, I have relatives who died. I saw twenty dead children."[110]
- Two weeks later, seventy-year-old Haji Mohammed fled Kandahar along with thousands of others, telling reporters that more than two hundred civilians had died in the bombing raids and up to a quarter of the city's population had fled for their lives. "People know they are going to die," he said. "What can they do?"[111]
- On December 1, American bombers hit three villages near Tora Bora, killing at least seventy people according to witnesses. "The village is no more," sobbed one survivor about the place he had lived. "All my family, twelve people, were killed. I am the only one left in this family. I have lost my children, my wife. They are no more."[112]

Reports on the numbers of civilians killed by US action vary, but even the *New York Times* concedes that "perhaps thousands of innocent Afghans have lost their lives during American attacks."[113] On the basis of an extensive survey, Professor Marc Herold of the University of New Hampshire estimates that more than 3,000 documented civilian deaths had occurred by March 2002.[114] Alongside these deaths are the massacres carried out by the Northern Alliance and the US military, most notably, that of four hundred bound prisoners at Mazar-I-Sharif in late November 2001 in complete violation of the Geneva conventions.[115] Of course, America's new-found allies in the Northern Alliance had butchered an estimated 50,000 people between 1992 and 1996, so its leaders, like their US advisers, were old hands at mass killing.[116] Moreover, up to six million people fled their homes as a result of the massive US bombardment of Afghanistan, untold thousands of them, largely children, perishing as a result of hunger and disease.

Meanwhile, in detention centres across Afghanistan, American guards have specialized in the sort of torture tactics that became infamous at Abu Ghraib prison in Iraq. In one case reported by the *New York Times*, a 22 year-old Afghan taxi driver known as Dilawar was beaten repeatedly and humiliated by guards: "At the interrogators' behest, a guard tried to force the young man to his knees. But his legs, which had been pummeled by guards for several days, could no longer bend. An interrogator told Mr. Dilawar that he could see a doctor after they finished with him. When he was finally sent back to his cell, though, the guards were instructed only to chain the prisoner back to the ceiling." Several hours later he was declared dead – one of many victims whose deaths US officials went to great pains to cover up.[117]

In the face of torture, displacement and the killing of innocent civilians, the Afghan people could be excused for asking how to tell terrorist from anti-terrorist. As Eduardo Galeano eloquently put it,

> There is a lot of similarity between homemade terrorism and high-tech terrorism, that of religious fundamentalists and that of fundamentalist believers in the market, that of the desperate and that of the powerful, that of the crazies on the loose and that of the military in uniform. They all share the same disdain for human life ... In the name of Good against Evil, in the name of the Only Truth, all of them resolve everything by killing first and asking questions later.[118]

*****

Slaughter of the Innocents: From "Western Infanticide" to Illegal War in Iraq

The story of how the United States put Saddam Hussein's Baath Party in power and provided his government with massive amounts of military assistance has been well documented elsewhere. Saddam was one of the many devils aided in the fight against communism. As the *National Catholic Register* reported in 1999, "throughout the 1970s and 1980s, the government of Iraq ... led by Saddam Hussein, was an ally of the United States. Iraq was a recipient of massive amounts of weapons of mass destruction, most notably biological weapons stocks."[119] In fact, when reports first surfaced of Saddam's use of chemical weapons against the Kurds in northern Iraq in 1988, Washington vigorously denied it (only to revive the story two years later when it declared the Iraqi leader it had protected to be the "new Hitler"). Washington's pre-1990 denials persisted even after an investigative team appointed by the US Senate's Foreign Relations Committee claimed "overwhelming evidence" of Iraqi use of chemical weapons against civilians.[120] Of course, Saddam was a key ally at that point, having waged a US-sponsored war against Iran in 1987-88. Indeed, so close was the US friendship with the Iraqi dictator that when Saddam informed the US ambassador to Iraq about his dispute with Kuwait in late July 1990, she told him, "We have no opinion on the Arab-Arab conflicts, like your border disagreements with Kuwait."[121] Believing he'd been given a green light, the Iraqi leader launched his invasion, only to discover that, having built him up, Washington now wanted to teach him a lesson – a lesson for which the Iraqi people continue to pay with their lives.

So determined to inflict a beating on Saddam was the US government that it repeatedly refused to discuss Iraqi offers to negotiate a withdrawal from Kuwait. As the *New York Times* reported, Washington dismissed these offers for fear they might "defuse the crisis."[122] After all, without a crisis, the case for war would have looked specious. Determined to make Saddam pay for acting without proper authorization, the US unleashed its war machine against Baghdad. After up to 150,000 Iraqi military personnel had perished, Saddam sued for peace. But peace is not what he — or, more importantly, his people — got. Britain and the US continued to bomb the country on almost a daily basis, without any authorization by the United Nations. Alongside bombing went the military and economic sanctions imposed in August 1990, which functioned as a weapon of mass destruction against the Iraqi people — all before the recent war and occupation.

Under the sanctions, the UN blocked half of the medicines and equipment requested by the Iraqi Health Ministry. Items prohibited from entering the country included "spare parts for kidney-transplantation equipment, refrigerators, numerous medicines, artificial limbs and spare parts for x-ray equipment."[123] With the health care system decaying and clean water effectively disappearing, death rates soared, particularly for children. The United Nations Children's Fund (Unicef) reported that, after the imposition of sanctions, the child mortality rate increased two and a half times: from 50 to 125 deaths per thousand live births. This amounted to an extra 500,000 dead children between 1991 and 1998.[124] At the same time, leukemia and other cancer rates skyrocketed in the aftermath of the first Gulf War, particularly in southern Iraq where US warplanes dropped bombs tipped with depleted uranium. The area is now soaked with about 800 tons of depleted uranium, with a half-life of 4.5 billion years. Perhaps another half million people have died as a consequence. All told about 1.5 million perished due to the sanctions.[125]

There is, of course, a question of foreknowledge: did Washington know that sanctions would have these effects? Westerners, after all, were particularly horrified — and rightly so — by the release of a video tape showing Osama bin Laden claiming to have calculated the number of casualties in advance of the attacks on the World Trade Center. Yet, there can be no doubt that Washington similarly knew mass suffering and death would be imposed on the people of Iraq as a result of the sanctions. They calculated these as a cost they could live with. Consider the following statements from US government agencies, all of which brazenly enumerate the suffering and deaths due to sanctions:[126]

- Failure by Iraq to procure specialized equipment and certain heavy chemicals could "lead to increased incidences, if not epidemics of disease" (US Department of Defense, "Iraq's Water Treatment Vulnerabilities," January 22, 1991);
- "Increased incidence of diseases will be attributable to degradation of normal preventive medicine, waste disposal, water purification/distribution, electricity, and decreased ability to control disease outbreaks" (US Department of Defense, "Subject: Effects of Bombing on Disease Occurrence in Baghdad," January 1991);
- Diseases are now more common as a result of "poor sanitary conditions (contaminated water supplied and improper sewage disposal) resulting from the war," notes one report. Observing that diarrhea and respiratory infections are rising, it adds, "children particularly have been affected by these diseases" (US Department of Defense, "Medical Problems in Iraq," March 1991);
- Asked on the CBS television program 60 Minutes if sanctions that have killed "more children than died in Hiroshima" are "worth it," Clinton's Defense Secretary, Madeleine Albright, replied: "we think the price is worth it."[127]

The appalling, murderous cruelty of the sanctions against Iraq produced serious disaffection within the UN itself. Denis Halliday, former UN Humanitarian Coordinator for Iraq, resigned in protest in September 1998 after thirty-four years with the agency. Similarly, Scott Ritter, a UN weapons inspector in Iraq from 1991 to 1998, also left in order to expose the atrocities. In a 1990 interview, Ritter said of Saddam Hussein, "He is a brutal dictator. He may torture to death 1,800 people a year. That's terrible and unacceptable. But we kill 6,000 a month. Let's put that on a scale."[128] In the run-up to the recent Invasion of Iraq,

Ritter spoke out against US attempts to justify a new war against Iraq on the grounds that it has weapons of mass destruction. Writing in Britain's largest newspaper, Ritter explained:

> Under the most stringent on-site inspection regime in the history of arms control, Iraq's biological weapons programmes were dismantled, destroyed or rendered harmless during the course of hundreds of no-notice inspections. The major biological weapons facility – al Hakum, which was responsible for producing Iraq's anthrax – was blown up by high explosive charges and all its equipment destroyed. Other biological facilities met the same fate if it was found that they had, at any time, been used for research and development of biological weapons.[129]

None of this made one bit of difference in Washington. Nor did it matter that even US officials conceded that "few targets" remained in Iraq after almost daily bombing for more than a decade. "We're down to the last outhouse," admitted one government official.[130] Washington was determined to concoct evidence, no matter how preposterous, to justify an invasion – for a time it tried to blame Saddam for the spate of anthrax attacks in the US until even domestic experts acknowledged this was not possible. As if the one and a half million who have died as a result of the sanctions was not enough, they were soon to be joined by at least 100,000 more. But then, as the experts have told us, when you are a fanatic, "you can ignore your victims."

Still, the scale of US government deceit was shocking. It started within hours of the September 11, 2001 attacks. According to CBS news, five hours after American Airlines Flight 77 hit the Pentagon, US Defense Secretary Donald Rumsfeld instructed his aides to manufacture a link between Saddam Hussein and the attacks inside the US. Notes taken by his aides quote the defense secretary as saying he wanted "info fast. Judge whether good enough to hit S. H.," in reference to Saddam. "Go massive," Rumsfeld ordered. "Sweep it all up. Things related and not."[131]

The last statement is the real give away: in instructing his staff to connect "things related and not" to 9/11, Rumsfeld cynically exploited fear and anger over American deaths to launch an illegal war. And, as all thinking people now know – and ought to have known at the time – the Iraqi regime of Saddam Hussein had no connection at all to the 9/11 attacks. Yet, so effective was the US government's campaign of lies and deception that today a huge chunk of American still believe Saddam was "involved' in 9/11.

Next came the lies about Saddam possessing weapons of mass destruction (WMD). While even the US government knew it couldn't get away with the claim that Iraq possessed nuclear weapons, it declared that the Iraqi leader possessed stockpiles of chemical and biological weapons. This was in defiance of its own best available intelligence – including that given to the CIA by a brother in law of Saddam who had defected to the US – which indicated that the Iraqi leader had ordered the destruction of such weapons after the 1991 Gulf War. Comprehensive and intrusive UN weapons inspections overwhelmingly confirmed those reports. No matter. American president George W. Bush and his circle wanted war. Armed with phony evidence, they failed to convince most governments of the world. But the US Congress and American mass media were another matter.[132] Each quickly jumped on the bandwagon – and the Iraqi people once again paid the price.

And some price it has been. At least 100,000 Iraqis have paid with their lives for the US invasion of 2003 and the continuing military occupation. As a result of direct military conflict alone, between 35,000 and 39,000 Iraqis had been killed by the spring of 2006.[133] Among those killed are civilians who almost certainly were massacred by US forces. In 2006, for instance, word broke about two separate civilian massacres in which US troops were alleged to have engaged. The first, which took place in November 2005 in the town of Haditha, involved house to house execution of 24 civilians when US Marines sought revenge for an explosion. The second incident, based on reports from the British Broadcasting Corporation, claims that US soldiers rounded up and killed 11 people, five of them children, in a house in Ishaqi. American reporters also allege that US military brass tried to cover up these murders.

On top of the 100,000 or more who have died as a direct result of action by military forces, twice as many civilians have died from diseases caused by destruction of water and sanitation systems and damage to medical and hospital infrastructure and the like. According to a wide-ranging survey of mortality rates conducted by the Center for International Emergency and Refugee Studies at the Johns Hopkins Bloomberg School of Public Health in Baltimore, at least 100,000 Iraqis had perished by mid 2004 as a result of the consequences of US war.[134] Moreover, the rate of death and injury due to conflict has been *rising* over time, entirely counter to US government claims that Iraq is making "progress" toward peace and stability.[135] Small wonder that it has become common for Iraqis to refer bitterly to "the so-called 'liberation'" of their country.

Masters of Torture

Perhaps nothing so exposed the actual nature of the US occupation as the shocking photos from Abu Ghraib prison in Baghdad. The International Committee of the Red Cross reports that prisoners at Abu Ghraib have been subjected to hooding, extended handcuffing, beatings with hard objects, slapping, punching, kicking, sleep deprivation, sexual humiliation, including forced masturbation in front of female guards and forced participation in human pyramids composed of naked men, and a variety of forms of persistent psychological abuse.[136]

The 171 page report issued by an Army panel chaired by US Major General George Fay further detailed brutal incidents in which prisoners were sodomized, subjected to extreme temperatures, lead around on a leash while naked and subjected to shocks administered to their genitals via electrical wires. Reading through these hundreds of pages of documentation of beatings and humiliation, it is impossible for the fair-minded reader not to conclude that a *system* of brutality and a *logic* of torture are at work, in which prisoners are subjected to powerful sensations of isolation and helplessness (a key function of blindfolds and hoods). Military interrogators and guards assert their utter control over all the rudimentary aspects of life – food, clothing, sleep, urination, defecation, light, temperature, human contact, dignity – in an effort to "break" prisoners.

Far from being exceptional, or the actions of a few "bad apples," these tactics are part of systematic policy laid out in the CIA's manual, *KUBARK Counterintelligence Interrogation*, first published in 1963. That text, which has been the handbook for US military interrogators for over 40 years, provides the template for the human rights violations committed at Abu Ghraib. And Abu Ghraib is part of a wider pattern involving prisons and secret detention centres in Afghanistan, at Guantanamo Bay, Cuba, and in parts of Eastern Europe. In early 2006, for instance, five United Nations' envoys reported treatment "amounting to torture" at Guantanamo. It comes as little surprise, then, when the American Civil Liberties Union reveals that illegal interrogation methods were approved by the top US military official in Iraq.[137]

The systematic use of torture is just part of an armoury of tactics refined by American military officers and the CIA for decades, particularly in Latin America. It is useful to look at the case of El Salvador in this regard, as there are connections to Iraq in terms of both personnel and policy. After all, a number of high-ranking American military advisers to the Iraqi government's war against insurgents honed their skills in the Salvadoran counter-insurgency of 1980 to 1991, when the US backed a brutal right-wing government in its civil war against leftist rebels. James Steele, the US Military Group commander during the counterinsurgency in El Salvador, is now involved in assisting the battle against insurgents in Iraq.[138] Operating from a mission in El Salvador, Steele directed US Special Forces which trained and advised government troops and paramilitary death squads. And, as so often in Latin America, torture, grotesque human rights violations and massacres of civilians were run-of-the-mill tactics for these US-backed forces. As Amnesty International reports,

> Between 1980 and 1991 El Salvador experienced an armed conflict which led to gross and extensive human rights violations, including extrajudicial executions, other unlawful killings, "disappearances" and torture. Among the victims were human rights defenders, trade unionists, lawyers, journalists, opponents of the government (whether real or presumed) and, for the most part, innocent civilians who had no direct involvement in the conflict. Whole villages were targeted by the armed forces and their inhabitants massacred. Children were direct victims of extrajudicial executions (EJEs) or "disappearance."[139]

Overall, Amnesty estimates that 75,000 civilians were tortured and executed in the conflict. The *United Nations Truth Commission Report* (1983) found that US-trained soldiers were responsible for the vast majority of these massacres and civilian deaths, including the murders of Archbishop Romero, four US churchwomen and six Jesuit priests. The UN also determined that more than two-thirds of the 60 military officers guilty of the worst atrocities were trained at the School of the Americas (SOA), located at Fort Benning, Georgia. Ten graduates of the SOA participated in the appalling massacre of one thousand civilians in the Salvadoran village of El Mozote.[140]

Yet, none of this prevented the US government from anteing up $6 billion in aid to Salvadoran governments and their troops during the civil war. Indeed, Washington appears to have been encouraged by these brutal tactics, many of which were learned at the SOA, from CIA manuals and from US military advisers on the ground. US advisers even worked directly with Dr. Hector Antonio Regalado, the infamous San Salvador dentist dubbed "Dr. Death" for his use of pliers to extract teeth from those he tortured, before they were summarily executed.

And El Salvador was no isolated case. As two reporters for the *Baltimore Sun* reported in 1995, the US government was also intimately involved with torturers and death squads in Honduras, particularly Battalion 316, a secret military unit that housed death squads. Here we find another link to Iraq and the "war on terror," since the US ambassador to Honduras at the time, John Negroponte, has played a central role recently in Iraq and was appointed in 2005 as Bush's director of national intelligence. This despite the fact that, as the *Baltimore Sun* journalists pointed out, Negroponte tried to conceal US involvement in "stalking, kidnapping, torturing, and killing suspected subversives" in Honduras. Describing Honduran-US practices, they further report:

> The intelligence unit, known as Battalion 316, used shock and suffocation devices in interrogations. Prisoners were often kept naked and, when no longer useful, killed and buried in unmarked graves. Newly declassified documents and other sources show that the CIA and the U.S. Embassy knew of numerous crimes, including murder and torture, yet continued to support Battalion 316 and collaborate with its leaders.[141]

What happened at Abu Ghraib, then, was no aberration. It was simply part of a set of brutal, sometimes murderous, practices developed and refined by the American state for decades. Thanks to the brazen arrogance of a photo-shooting soldier, Abu Ghraib exposed the true face of American empire.

A Rogue Superpower

One of the ultimate ironies in the West's "war on terrorism" is the way Bush and his predecessors denounce regimes that ostensibly refuse to respect the rule of law. In a December 2001 speech, for Instance, Bush attacked "rogue states" that, among other things, "harbour, finance, train or equip the agents of terror."[142]

Yet, the U.S. has a curious notion of what respect for international law and human rights amounts to. In recent years, after all, Washington has:

- Refused to sign an international ban on land mines;
- Opposed a world ban on children under eighteen serving in combat – the only nation-state to do so;
- Voted against the creation of an international court to try war criminals;
- Unilaterally scrapped the Anti-Ballistic Missile Treaty designed to contain the arms race.[143]

Under international law, America's wars in Afghanistan and Iraq are also clearly illegal. As Michael Mandel of Lawyers Against the War points out, the Charter of the United Nations stipulates that war as a means of settling international disputes is legal only if authorized by the UN Security Council. The only exception is action in self-defense, and that is legal only until the Security Council has met. Yet, at no time has the Council passed a resolution authorizing military force or mentioning either Afghanistan or Iraq in these regards.[144] Of course, none of this bothers Washington. During the 1991 Gulf War, Madeleine Albright, then the UN Ambassador, instructed the Security Council that America will act "multilaterally when we can, and unilaterally when we must."[145] If multilateral bodies can provide a cover for US aggression, all to the better; if not, the US will act according to the principle of might is right. Washington's doctrine of permanent war involves a brazen self-authorization to use military force wherever and whenever it chooses. If a rogue state is one that refuses to respect international law by taking law into its own hands, then the US clearly fits the definition. And in the age of US-driven globalization, no one is going to stop it. After all, the American government spends more on weapons and military hardware than does the rest of the world combined. And it is more prepared than any other major power to use that weaponry at the drop of a hat – whatever the consequences in human suffering.

* * *

At the end of the day, unending war waged by a rogue super-power is what the peoples of the world get for enduring neoliberal globalization. With each decade of capitalist domination of our planet, the achievement of a world of peace and justice recedes further and further beyond the horizon. And the terrible oppressions and inequalities generated by world capitalism mean that peace and justice are not attainable without a radical transformation of the global order. As one hundred Nobel prize winners recently wrote, "The most profound danger to world peace in the coming years will not stem from the irrational acts of states or individuals but from the legitimate demands of the world's dispossessed … Their situation will be desperate and manifestly unjust."[146] As we have seen, the United States has a plan for dealing with them – the use of permanent war to "keep the violent peace."

Elaborating on the plight of the world's dispossessed, the Nobel laureates continue, "It cannot be expected … that in all cases they will await the beneficence of the rich." Nor have they. And in their global revolt against the rule of capital lies the hope for a different world.

Notes

1 Thomas Friedman, "A Manifesto for the Fast World," *New York Times Magazine*, March 28, 1999.
2 Plato, *The Republic*, trans. Francis MacDonald Cornford (London: Oxford University Press, 1981-2), pp. 18-29. While I reject Plato's own account of justice, his attack on the might-is-right doctrine remains a powerful one.
3 Elisabeth Bumiller, "All Must Join Fight Against Terror, Bush tells U. N.," *New York Times*, November 11, 2001; John Ibbitson, "Bush says U.S. winning 'war to save civilization,'" *Globe and Mail*, November 9, 2001.
4 R. Kabbani, *Europe's Myth of Orient: Devise and Rule* (London: Macmillan, 1986), p. 5.
5 "In his own words," *Globe and Mail*, November 9, 2001.
6 John Pilger, "War on Terror: False Victory," *The Mirror* (London), November 16, 2001.

7 George Bush, September 16, 2001 remarks to reporters at the Pentagon.

8 Ed Vulliamy, "The countdown to war," *The Observer* (London), September 30, 2001.

9 "The myths about globalization (1)," *Globe and Mail*, April 12, 2001.

10 E. J. Hobsbawm, *The Age of Empire 1875-1914* (London: Sphere Books, 1989), p. 59.

11 Nikolai Bukharin, *Imperialism and World Economy* (New York: Monthly Review Press, 1973), p. 87.

12 Marc Ferro, *The Great War 1914-1918* (London: Routledge, 1987), p. 127.

13 Irving M. Zeitlin, *Capitalism and Imperialism* (Chicago: Markham Publishing, 1972), p. 87.

14 See, for instance, Merle Fainsod, *International Socialism and the World War* (New York: Anchor Books, 1969).

15 Eric Hobsbawm, *The Age of Extremes: The Short Twentieth Century* (London: Abacus, 1995), pp. 43, 49.

16 As quoted by Noam Chomsky, *Rethinking Camelot: JFK, the Vietnam War and US Political Culture* (Montreal: Black Rose Books, 1993), p. 20.

17 Philip Amrstrong, Andrew Glyn and John Harrison, *Capitalism Since World War II* (London: Fontana, 1984), p. 26.

18 As quoted by Joyce Kolko and Gabriel Kolko, *The Limits of Power: The World and US Foreign Policy* (New York: Harper and Row, 1972), p. 338.

19 Robert Biel, *The New Imperialism: Crisis and Contradiction in North/South Relations* (London: Zed Books, 2000), p. 59; Armstrong, Glyn and Harrison, p. 59.

20 For the history of this period see Dee Brown's classic, *Bury My Heart at Wounded Knee: An Indian History of the American West* (1970; New York: Henry Holt, 2000). See also Ward Churchill, *Struggle for the Land: Native North American Resistance to Genocide, Ecocide and Colonization*, revised edn. (Winnipeg: Arbeiter Ring Publishing, 1999). It is also worth consulting V. G. Kiernan, *America: The New Imperialism, From White Settlement to World Hegemony* (1978; London: Verso Books, 2005), Part 1, ch. 3; Part 2, ch. 3; and Part 3, ch. 1.

21 As quoted by Kolko and Kolko, p. 13.

22 Harry Magdoff, *The Age of Imperialism: The Economics of U.S. Foreign Policy* (New York: Monthly Review Press, 1969), pp. 176-83.

23 As quoted by Gabriel Kolko, *The Politics of War: The World and United States Foreign Policy, 1943-45* (New York: Vintage Books, 1968), p. 367.

24 As quoted by George M. McCune, "Occupation Politics in Korea," *Far Eastern Survey* 15 (1946), p. 36.

25 Kolko and Kolko, p. 567. My account of the Korean events is heavily indebted to this important study.

26 As quoted by Kolko and Kolko, p. 571.

27 Michael Kidron, *Western Capitalism Since the War* (Harmondsworth: Penguin Books, 1968), p. 49.

28 As quoted by Chomsky, *Rethinking Camelot*, p. 14.

29 Eduardo Galeano, *Open Veins of Latin America: Five Centuries of the Pillage of a Continent* (New York: Monthly Review Press, 1973), p. 128.

30 As quoted by Leo Huberman, *Man's Worldly Goods* (New York: Monthly Review Press, 1952), p. 265.
31 Michael Laslett, "A Bitter Taste," *NACLA Report on the Americas* 34, 6 (May/June 2001), p. 10.
32 Galeano, *Open Veins*, p. 128.
33 Galeano, *Open Veins*, p. 129.
34 Eduardo Galeano, "The Theatre of Good and Evil," *La Jornada*, September 21, 2001, translated by Justin Podur.
35 Laslett, p. 9.
36 Galeanao, *Open Veins*, pp. 85-6.
37 Richard J. Walton, *Cold War and Counter-Revolution: The Foreign Policy of John F. Kennedy* (New York: Viking Press, 1972. Page references to this work are given in the text.
38 Noam Chomsky, *Rogue States: The Rule of Force in World Affairs* (Cambridge, Mass.: South End Press, 2000), p.82.
39 In fact, there are valid criticisms to be made of the Castro regime in the areas of civil and human rights, suppression of legitimate dissent and so on. But such criticisms are nothing less than hypocritical if they are not framed in the context of opposition to American aggression against that island state.
40 As quoted by Chomsky, *Rogue States*, p. 89.
41 See Dan La Botz, *Made in Indonesia: Indonesian Workers Since Suharto* (Cambridge, Mass.: South End Press, 2001), pp. 103-9.
42 As quoted by Gabriel Kolko, *Confronting the Third World: United States Foreign Policy, 1945-1980* (New York: Pantheon Books, 1988), p.181.
43 As quoted by La Botz, p. 114.
44 Thomas Friedman, "A Manifesto for the Fast World."
45 As quoted by Chomsky, *Rethinking Camelot*, p.41, his emphasis.
46 Chomsky, *Rethinking Camelot*, pp. 49, 43.
47 Frances Fitzgerald, *Fire in the Lake: The Vietnamese and the Americans in Vietnam* (New York: Vintage Books, 1989), pp. 491-2.
48 Fitzgerald, pp. 537. Fitzgerald provides the figures that account for 1.4 million killed by 1970. The figure of two million by war's end comes from Gabriel Kolko, personal communication, December 1991. For the estimate of 600,000 killed in Cambodia, see John Pilger, "A War in the American Tradition," *The Independent* (London), October 15, 2001.
49 Fitzgerald, p. 537.
50 John Ibbitson, "Nixon told Kissinger to 'think big' on using A-bomb in Vietnam," *Globe and Mail*, March 11, 2002.
51 Cited by Chomsky, *Rogue States*, p. 169.
52 Eric Toussaint, *Your Money or Your Life: The Tyranny of Global Finance*, trans. Raghu Krishnan (London: Pluto Press, 1999), p. 81.
53 Toussaint, p. 89.
54 Quoted by *Morris Miller, Debt and the Environment: Converging Crises* (New York: United Nations Publications, 1991), p. 215.

55 Bade Onimode, *A Political Economy of the African Crisis* (London: Zed Books, 1988), p. 280.

56 Onimode, Ch. 12.

57 IMF Survey (Washington: International Monetary Fund, 1987), p. 50.

58 Michel Chossoduvsky, *The Globalisation of Poverty: Impacts of IMF and World Bank Reforms* (London: Zed Books, 1997), pp. 34-5.

59 Toussaint, p. 94.

60 Miller, p. 64. I have corrected the spelling of conquistadors in the original.

61 Robert Wood, "The International Monetary Fund and the World Bank in a Changing World Economy" in *Instability and Change in the World Economy*, eds. Arthur MacEwan and William K. Tabb (New York: Monthly Review Press, 1989), p. 313.

62 Toussaint, p. 79.

63 Chossoduvsky, pp. 191, 202.

64 Reuters News Agency, "Raw Desire For Power Fed Rwandan Genocide: Study," *Toronto Star*, April 1, 1999.

65 See the excellent, but chilling discussion in Toussaint, pp. 212-17.

66 Henry Rempel, "Bankrupting the Lower Income Classes in Sub-Saharan Africa" in *Perspectives on Economic Development in Africa*, eds. Fidelis Ezeala-Harrison and Senyo B-S.K. Adjibolosoo (Westport, Conn.: Prager Publishers, 1994), pp. 191-96.

67 Onimode, pp. 152-53.

68 Rempel, p. 200.

69 "Kantor Says US to Fight Farm Trade Barriers," *USIS*, February 23, 1996.

70 Waldon Bello with Shea Cunningham and Bill Rau, *Dark Victory: The United States and Global Poverty*, 2nd edn. (London: Pluto Press, 1999), p. 77.

71 Friedman.

72 Jacques Attali, *Millenium: Winners and Losers in the Coming World Order* (New York: Times Books, 1991), pp. 73, 15.

73 Commission on Integrated Long-Term Strategy, *Discriminate Deterrence* (Washington: U.S. Government Printing Office, 1988), p. 13.

74 *Discriminate Deterrence*, pp. 14-15.

75 Strategic Advisory Group of the Joint Strategic Target Planning Staff, US Strategic Air Command, "The Role of Nuclear Weapons in the New World Order," as quoted in *Navy News and Underseas Technology*, January 13, 1992.

76 Paul Rogers, "A Jungle Full of Snakes? Power, Poverty and International Security" in *A World Divided: Militarism and Development After the Cold War*, eds. Geoff Tansey and others (London: Earthscan Publications, 1994), p. 18.

77 US Department of Defense, *Report on the Quadrennial Defense Review* (Washington: U.S. Government Printing Office, 1997).

78 Rogers, p. 17.

79 Donald Rumsfeld, Pentagon briefing, September 27, 2001.

80 As quoted by Stephen Shalom, "The Continuity of U.S. Imperialism," *New Politics* 7, 2 (Winter 1999), p. 37.

81 Friedman, "Manifesto."

82 Ellen Meiksins Wood, "Kosovo and the New Imperialism" in *Masters of the Universe? NATOs Balkan Crusade*, ed. Tariq Ali (London: Verso Books, 2000), pp., 192, 193. Wood has developd this argument at more length in *Empire of Capital* (London: Verso Books, 2003).

83 Elen Meiksins Wood, "War Without Boundaries," *Canadian Dimension*, November/December 2001, p. 16.

84 Aijaz Ahmad, " 'A Task That Never Ends': Bush Proposes Perpetual War," *Canadian Dimension*, November/December 2001, p. 34.

85 Tony Blair, "Doctrine of International Community," a speech given to the Economic Club of Chicago, April 22, 1999.

86 Both passages quoted by Peter Gowan, "The Euro-Atlantic Origins of NATO's Attack on Yugoslavia" in *Masters of the Universe?*, p. 3.

87 Paul Knox, "Musharraf big loser in Afghan end game," *Globe and Mail*, December 10, 2001.

88 Professor Amila Buturovic, as quoted by Ingrid Peritz, "Letter to hijack suspects exalts joy of death," *Globe and Mail*, September 29, 2001.

89 See *Crisis, Cultures and Colombia* (Toronto: Canadians for Peace in Colombia, 2001), p. 10.

90 As quoted by Noam Chomsky, *Rogue States*, p. 65.

91 Jenny Pearce, *Colombia: Inside the Labyrinth* (London: Latin American Bureau, 1990), p. 57.

92 Ricardo Vargas Meza, *The Revolutionary Armed Forces of Colombia (FARC) and the Illicit Drug Trade* (Washington: WOLA, 1999), as quoted by Chomsky, *Rogue States*, p. 74. The main guerilla group, The Revolutionary Armed Forces of Colombia (FARC) is also guilty of displacing poor and indigenous peoples; perhaps 20 per cent of human rights violations are attributable to the FARC. See Mario A. Murillo, *Colombia and the united States: War, Unrest and Destabilization* (New York: Seven Stories Press, 2004), pp. 73-76.

93 Karl Marx, *Capital*, v. 1, trans. Ben Fowkes (Harmondsworth: Penguin Books, 1976), p. 875.

94 Pearce, pp. 65, 48.

95 James Petras, "The Geopolitics of Plan Colombia," *Monthly Review*, May 2001, p. 35.

96 *Crisis, Cultures and Colombia*, p. 4.

97 "Colombia's conflicts – Guerrillas or terrorists?" *The Economist*, December 8-14, 2001.

98 Reports from Colombia Peace Association, November 9, 12, 20, 2001. For background on the atrocities in Barrancabermeja, see Ana Carrigan, "An Invasion Foretold: Terror triumphs in Colombia," *In These Times*, May 14, 2001, pp. 10-13.

99 Petras, pp. 36-37.

100 See John Ryan, "Afghanistan: A Forgotten Chapter," *Canadian Dimension*, November/December 2001. I disagree with Ryan's characterization of the 1979-92 governments as "Marxist," however.

101 See Diana Johnstone, "Humanitarian War: Making the Crime Fit the Punishment" in *Masters of the Universe?*, p. 153.

102 Ahmed Rashid, *Taliban: Militant Islam, Oil and Fundamentalism in Central Asia* (Princeton: Yale University Press, 2001), pp. 129-31.

103 As quoted by Eduardo Galeano, "The Theatre of Good and Evil."

104 See Rashid, chapters 12-13.

105 As quoted by Rashid, pp. 178, 166.

106 Rashid, p. 174.

107 See "US efforts to make peace summed up by 'oil,'" *Irish Times*, November 19, 2001.

108 The most important of these exceptions are the outstanding journalists John Pilger and Robert Fisk whose writings regularly appear in the British media.

109 Murray Campbell, "Bombing of farming village undermines U.S. credibility," *Globe and Mail*, November 3, 2001.

110 Alan Freeman, "Afghans flee rain of bombs," *Globe and Mail*, November 19, 2001.

111 Peter Cheny, "'I have nothing to go back to,'" *Globe and Mail*, November 29, 2001.

112 Tim Weiner, "U.S. Bombs Strike 3 Villages And Reportedly Kill Scores," *New York Times*, December 2, 2001.

113 Barry Bearak with Eric Schmitt and Craig S. Smith, "Unknown Toll in the Fog of War: Civilian Deaths in Afghanistan," *New York Times*, February 10, 2002.

114 Marc W. Herold, "A Dossier on Civilian Victims of United States' Aerial Bombing of Afghanistan: A Comprehensive Accounting (revised),' March 2002, available at www.cursor.org/stories/civilian_deaths.htm.

115 See Nicholas Watt, Richard Norton Taylor and Luke Harding, "Allies justify mass killing of Taliban prisoners in fort," *Guardian* (London), November 29, 2001 and Robert Fisk, "Now, who are the war criminals?," *Globe and Mail*, November 30, 2001.

116 John Pilger, "War on Terror: False Victory," *The Mirror* (London), November 16, 2001.

117 Tim Golden, "In U.S. Report, Brutal Details of 2 Afghan Inmates' Deaths," *New York Times*, May 20, 2005.

118 Eduardo Galeano, Brecha (Uruguay), September 21, 2001, as quoted in "The Americas React to Terror," *NACLA Report on the Americas* 35, 3 (November/December 2001), p. 9.

119 *National Catholic Register*, May 1999.

120 Chomsky, *Rogue States*, pp. 25-26.

121 As reported in the *Guardian* (London), September 12, 1990.

122 As quoted by Chomsky, *Rogue States*, p. 23.

123 Gregory Elich, "Iraq: A Flight Against the Blockade," *Canadian Dimension*, September/October 2001, p. 26.

124 "Ask the Globe," *Globe and Mail*, September 29, 2001.

125 Elich, p. 25.

126 The first three quotations come from Jeff Lindemyer, "Iraqi Sanctions: Myth and Fact," *Z Magazine*, November 2001, pp. 37-38.

127 Madeleine Albright to Lesley Stahl, 60 Minutes interview, May 12, 1996.

128 As quote by Elich, p. 40.

129 Scott Ritter, "Don't blame Saddam for this one," *Guardian* (London), October 19, 2001.

130 As quoted by John Pilger, "The truths they never tell us," *New Statesman*, November 26, 2001.

131 CBS News, "Plans for Iraq Attack Began on 9/11," September 4, 2002.

132 For just one example of doctored US government intelligence and the culpability of major American media in presenting it as truth see David E. Sanger and David Barstow, "Report Leaked by Cheney Aide Was in Dispute," *New York Times*, April 9, 2006.

133 See www.iraqbodycount.org.

134 See "Mortality before and after the 2003 invasion of Iraq: cluster sample survey," published online October 29, 2004 at http://image.thelancet.com/extras/04art10342web.pdf.

135 Sabrina Tavernise, "U.S. Quietly Issues Estimate of Iraqi Civilian Casualties," *New York Times*, Oct. 30, 2005.

136 Mark Danner, "The Logic of Torture," in *Abu Ghraib: The Politics of Torture* (Berkeley: North Atlantic Books, 2004), p. 27.

137 Michael Gawenda, "US rejects claims of torture," *The Age* (Melbourne), February 18, 2006; : "Top soldier in Iraq okayed illegal methods, ACLU says," *Globe and Mail* (Toronto), March 30, 2005 A newer US inquiry has also documented widespread abuse at American prison camps at Guantanamo Bay. See Neil A. Lewis and Eric Schmitt, "Inquiry Finds Abuses at Guantanamo Bay," *New York Times*, May 1, 2005.

138 See Peter Maass, "The Way of the Commandos," *New York Times Magazine*, May 1, 2005.

139 Amnesty International, *El Salvador: Peace Can Only Be Achieved With Justice* (2001).

140 See Jack Nelson-Pallmeyer, *School of Assassins: Guns, Greed and Globalization* (New York: Orbis Books, 2001), pp. 27, 11; and Leslie Gill, *The School of the Americas: Military Training and Political Violence in the Americas* (Durham: Duke University Press, 2004), p. 137. In the face of mounting opposition, the SOA has recently changed its name to the Western Hemispheric Institute for Security Cooperation.

141 Gary Cohn and Ginger Thompson, "Unearthed: Fatal Secrets," *Baltimore Sun*, June 11, 1995, available online at www.geocities.com/ravencrazy/Baltimore-Sun.html.

142 John Ibbitson, "U.S. to scrap ABM treaty, sources say," *Globe and Mail*, December 12, 2001.

143 See Shalom, p. 38; Pilger, "War on Terror;" Ibbitson.

144 Michael Mandel, "This war is illegal and immoral, and it won't prevent terrorism," speech delivered to a Science for Peace conference, Toronto, December 9, 2001, available on the world wide web at www.scienceforpeace.sa.utoronto.ca/Special_Activities/Dec9_Forum.html.

145 As quoted by Chomsky, *Rogue States*, p. 13.

146 "Our best point the way," *Globe and Mail*, December 10, 2001.

6. DEMOCRACY AGAINST CAPITALISM: THE REVOLT OF THE DISPOSSESSED

> Life is growing ever more precarious for elected South American leaders who advocate market liberalization, privatization and other measures ... Bolivia's Carlos Mesa is the latest victim of a populist uprising ...
>
> Mr. Mesa joins seven other presidents across the continent who have hastily departed office in recent years without being able to finish their terms.
>
> – Editorial, *Globe and Mail* (Toronto), June 11, 2005

Popular rebellions against neoliberalism have been sweeping Latin America in recent years, toppling presidents and inspiring social movements around the world. Spearheaded by indigenous peoples, the unemployed, poor farmers and trade unionists, mass upheavals have punched huge holes in the neoliberal agenda. As I write these lines, hundreds of landless workers have just invaded the Brazilian Parliament building, demanding land reform.[1] That an event like this should occur the very day I started this chapter is not some odd coincidence. As you read these words, similar events are transpiring somewhere else on our planet. That, too, is an inevitable feature of the age of globalization. Every time neoliberalism tears another hole in the fabric of people's lives, rebellion ensues. The elites know it and have coined a term for such events: "the IMF riot."

267

Our rulers have a pat response to these rebellions. Troops and riot police are called out to crack heads, hundreds of pro-testers are arrested, a state of emergency is declared, and basic civil rights are shelved. Then, as if reading from the same script, our governors declare they do it all to defend democracy. In the midst of the mass struggles of 2005 in Bolivia that brought down President Mesa, for instance, Canada's foreign minister called on protesters to end their rebellions and resolve things through "democratic means."[2] Of course, the protesters refuse this self-serving notion of "democracy." After all, Carlos Mesa was toppled by the largest mass protests in Bolivia's history; on a single day at least half a million people demonstrated through the streets of the capital city, La Paz – in a country of nine million. In fact, by imposing their will, the will of the people, the Bolivian insurgents were reclaiming the very meaning of democracy.

In *Global Showdown*, Barlow and Clarke remind us that in ancient Greece the term democracy was derived from the words "demos," meaning people and "kratos" meaning power. In its classical definition, they point out, democracy thus meant people-power.[3] Even this formulation may not be radical enough. For in ancient Greece, the concept of democracy had a deeper meaning: it referred to the power of a specific social class, that is, to the rule of the poor.

This meaning is clearly laid out in one of the great texts of ancient political thought, Aristotle's *Politics*. At various points throughout that work, Aristotle claims that democracy means more than rule of the majority; more precisely, it refers to "a con-stitution under which the poor rule."[4] Aristotle's definition was anything but peculiar at the time. In fact, it corresponded to what everybody knew: having emerged as the product of rebellions by the poor, democracy was a movement of the oppressed majority to impress its collective will on political life.

The Origins of Democracy: Rule of the Poor

Early in the sixth century B.C. the struggle for democracy erupted in ancient Greece with rebellions by the poor against intensified social and economic inequalities. Suffering under crushing debt loads which often forced them to relinquish their lands, the poor resisted, agitated and mobilized. In an effort to restore stability, the ruling class decided in 594 B.C. to implement a sweeping set of reforms: debts were abolished; debt bondage was eliminated along with all use of people as security on a debt; new, democratically elected courts were created in opposition to the old courts run by the aristocracy. Alongside these reforms was one that gave all male citizens the right to attend and vote in the Assembly (the law-making body), thus breaking the control of the rich over political life.[5] For the first time in recorded history, poor men (but not women) were empowered to make the laws by which they were governed.[6]

Until this moment, rulers and law-makers had always been privileged non-labourers, those who enjoyed a life of leisure by living off the labour of others. So unequal were social relations between aristocracy and poor that one poem of the age urged that the best way to treat the *demos* was "to kick them hard."[7] The democratic revolution in ancient Athens turned this world upside down. Now, the poor – the *demos* – having done some kicking of their own, acquired the power to make the laws by which they were governed. The idea of the self-governing people had entered the human vocabulary, albeit with gender limitations. Arguably the most radical and unprecedented thing about this development, as Ellen Meiksins Wood suggests, is that it represented a "union of labour and citizenship," the idea of the labourer as citizen.[8] For the first time since class society emerged, men who worked with their hands – farmers, carpenters, ship-builders and others – claimed equal rights with the rich. And given that the labouring poor were the overwhelming majority, this meant proclaiming the sovereignty of the men of their class – as Aristotle knew when he designated democracy as rule of the poor.

Over the next 130 years, the poor continued to push for reforms that reduced the powers of the aristocrats. Because democracy was something they had struggled for, and because it made such a palpable impact on their lives (particularly for having abolished debts and debt bondage), they were vigilant both in defending and exercising it. Indeed, the system of direct democracy they practiced made it exceptionally difficult for the wealthy to manipulate political life. One historian describes how it worked:

> Direct participation was the key to Athenian democracy: there was neither representation nor a civil service or bureaucracy in any significant sense. In the sovereign Assembly, whose authority was total, every citizen was not only entitled to attend as often as he pleased but he also had the right to enter the debate, offer amendments and vote on the proposals on war and peace, taxation, cult regulation, army levies, war finance, public works, treaties and diplomatic negotiations, and anything else, major or minor, which required governmental decision. Much of the preparatory work for these meeting was done by the boule, a Council of 500 chosen by lot for one year – and again everyone was eligible, save that no man could be a member more than twice in his lifetime ... There was no hierarchy among the offices; regardless of the significance or insignificance of any post, every holder was responsible directly and solely to the demos itself ...[9]

Ancient democracy, for all its limits, was thus much more active, meaningful and participatory than what goes by the name of representative democracy today. As the same scholar points out in another work:

> A considerable portion of the male citizens of Athens ... had some direct experience in government beyond anything we know, almost beyond anything we can imagine. It was literally true that at birth every

Athenian boy had better than a gambler's chance to
be president of the Assembly, a rotating post held for
a single day and, as always, filled by the drawing of
lots. He might be a market commissioner for a year or
two (though not in succession), a juryman repeatedly,
a voting member of the Assembly as frequently as he
liked.[10]

In addition to being immensely more direct and participatory, ancient democracy was also more extensive in scope. No
sphere of public policy was off limits to it. Particularly offensive
to the rich was the fact that the Assembly could interfere with
property rights – by abolishing debts or redistributing land – and
impose limits on their ability to exploit peasants. Rule of the *demos*
meant the sovereignty of the citizens over all aspects of social and
political life. Because they found it exceptionally difficult to manipulate, the wealthy engaged in an enduring conspiracy against
Greek democracy, toppling it several times – frequently with the
assistance of foreign invasions – and occasionally massacring its
leaders. When, after more than two hundred years, Athenian democracy was finally defeated for good the most dramatic effect,
writes one noted scholar, "was the removal from the poor ... of
all protection against exploitation and oppression by the powerful."[11]

Capitalism and the Dilution of Democracy

Although we use the term "democracy" to describe western
political systems today, what we are in fact doing, as Wood points
out, is conflating democracy with liberalism. In modern society,
the rights of the individual – particularly rights to the private
ownership of the means of producing social wealth – have become
the ultimate touchstone of a "democratic society." In practice, this
involves the protection of wealthy individuals against the majority. Rather than resting on the power of the people, therefore,
liberal democracy is founded on a radical attempt to curtail the
rights of the *demos*.

The liberal transformation in the meaning of democracy began with the rise of capitalism, when private property rights became the new religion. Prior to capitalism, as we have seen, individuals did not have absolute rights to property. The feudal lord held land and the right to exploit peasants only as a trust acquired in exchange for a pledge of military, economic and political services to the monarch. Property rights were enmeshed with political office and its duties – and could be revoked.

The rise of capitalism changed all this. As capitalists battled to protect their wealth from incursions by monarchs and governments, they sought to turn private property into something absolute and inviolable, guaranteed and protected by constitutions, and defined as sacred, like life itself.[12] This historical process involved a dramatic privatization of the elements of economic life: rather than part of the public realm, land-holdings in particular (including the former common lands) now became private goods. The economy was thus detached from politics and communal rights and obligations, redefined as a private sphere that ought to be protected from the public.[13] Enormous areas of social life – relating to land, production, prices, profits, incomes and so on – were enclosed, fenced off from the public, demarcated by virtual "No Trespassing" signs known as property laws.

Still, wherever possible, capitalist elites resisted granting even the universal right to vote. Two hundred years after the English Revolution of the 1640s, for instance, British working men were still denied the vote – a denial which in part spurred the Chartist movement of that period. As late as 1860, for instance, of 27.5 million inhabitants of the United Kingdom, only one million had the vote. In the 1866 debates that led to the formation of Canada, the soon-to-be first prime minister of the country bluntly outlined the view of Canada's ruling class. Summarizing the positions taken in a conference on creating a Canadian state, he reported, "not a single one of the representatives ... was in favour of universal suffrage. Everyone felt that in this respect the principle of the British constitution should be carried out, and that classes and property should be represented as well as numbers."[14] As in Britain, owner-ship of an "appropriate" amount of property was made a require-ment of possessing the vote and a non-elected upper house based on wealth was created – all in order that "classes and property should be represented" as a buttress against the *demos*.

After hundreds of years of conflict, capitalist classes finally relented (in most cases somewhere between about 1890 and 1940) and allowed the vote to be extended to the poor – first men, then women. But they did so secure in the knowledge that, however much they didn't like the involvement of the rabble in politics, at least the *demos* couldn't take their property from them, sheltered as it now was behind a barricade of laws that declared it off limits to all but its private owners. The poor could be reluctantly admitted to political life, in other words, once democracy was prohibited from interfering with private economic power. This is the secret of capitalist "democracy": it involves a dramatic contraction in the public sphere and the range of public powers. Major questions related to the distribution of property, the ownership of resources, and the allocation of wealth are now defined as issues of private economic life, best left to the market (where private individuals pursue their self-interest, free of public interference). With the "expulsion of politics" from these spheres, the ambit of democracy has been radically reduced. More than this, democracy has been emptied of its original content – which referred to the absolute sovereignty of the people – and refilled with liberal doctrines of individual (property-based) rights.

Two dramatic shifts in the meaning of democracy are associ-ated with its dilution by capitalism. First, the notion of an actively self-governing people (who make the laws according to which they live) is replaced by the passive doctrine of representation. In the representative system, which was largely an innovation of Ameri-can elites after the Revolution of 1776, people are entitled merely to vote occasionally for those who will make the laws – at the same time surrendering all control over the representatives they elect. Between elections, these representatives assume virtually

273

total power over the ostensibly sovereign people. Representative democracy is thus based upon the ideal of a de-mobilized and de-politicized _demos_ who, because they are not governing themselves, become detached and alienated from the political process. In tune with this arrangement, capitalists construct well-funded political parties with enormous advertising budgets in order to dominate and manipulate public discourse about politics (which is greatly assisted by the fact that the mass media are owned by a handful of capitalist monopolies).

Secondly, the "expulsion of politics" from the economic sphere, as part of the privatization of economic power, means that some of the most important events in peoples' lives – the closing of a factory, difficulties paying the rent, the decline of working class living standards, the lack of affordable housing and so on – are treated as problems of the market and thus outside the purview of politics. This further contributes to the passivity and disengagement of large numbers of people who frequently relate to politics as an obscure and distasteful business utterly remote to their everyday lives. Detached from the issues of daily life, democracy becomes something purely formal – occasional votes in elections dominated by money and influence - lacking any substance as a means by which the people might govern themselves. The "contraction of democracy to liberalism," as Wood describes it, represents its domestication, its containment by capitalist property rights that prevent the people from affecting the real sources of power (and suffering) in society.[15] Capitalism has thus de-clawed democracy, reducing it to a largely formal process, so that the powerful can get on with the real business of enriching themselves at the expense of the majority.

Nevertheless, radical social movements – particularly anti-globalization movements in Latin America at the moment – regularly challenge these limits to democracy. When protesters refuse to accept that issues like health care, jobs, provision of water, access to education and housing should be left to private actors in the market (and their global representatives, like the IMF and

the World Bank), they are implicitly challenging the privatization of economic power that lies at the heart of capitalism. These
movements rightly suggest that it is anti-democratic for powerful
private interests to dictate what happens to the quality of life of
millions of people. Often without realizing it, these critics mobilize an older meaning of democracy as rule of the oppressed
majority against the capitalist reduction of democracy to liberal
individualism (the right of each individual to vote, to participate
in the market economy and to have her property protected).

Implicitly, then, these struggles for radical democracy are
anti-capitalist. By calling for the people – which in modern society ultimately means the working class, urban and rural – to have
control over economic and social policy, they raise a challenge to
the sanctity of capitalist property; they suggest that the overall
direction of socio-economic life and the distribution of wealth and
resources ought to be freely determined by the people as a whole,
not monopolized by those who have property and power.

The ruling class recognizes this. That's why, despite the lip
service they pay to it, they've always been squeamish about democracy. Toward the end of the last major period of social and
political upheaval – the mass strikes, civil rights struggles, anti-
war mobilizations, feminist and gay liberation upsurges of the late
1960s and early 1970s – a ruling class consortium know as the
Trilateral Commission argued that modern society suffered from
"an excess of democracy."[16] It meant two things by this. First,
that people were mobilizing for themselves to change society (not
passively leaving things to elected representatives). And in the
course of doing so they were challenging the capitalist monopoly
over economic decision-making. The claim that society suffers
from "too much democracy," in other words, really means that
the *demos* are starting to interfere with the business of controlling
property and structures of power, and appropriating profit.

Recognizing that during the 1980s and 1990s they had rolled
back many of the gains of the previous period of struggle, the ruling class now wants both to extend and lock in the gains it has

made. This is why the WTO agreements create mechanisms by which private corporations can punish governments that give in to public pressure to reverse privatization, defend public services and so on. It is also why more and more of the global commons – seeds, water, life-forms, human DNA and so on – are being commodified: once they enter the private sphere, they are protected by a vast array of incredibly punitive laws against violators. At the heart of these "trade" agreements, in other words, are laws designed to prevent the people of any nation from democratically making inroads against the immense and unaccountable powers of capital.

In fact, the globalizers are trying to design an "economic" model that is immune to democratic politics. Neoliberal cheerleader Thomas Friedman puts this bluntly when he describes contemporary economic orthodoxy as involving a "Golden Straitjacket." Once a country cuts taxes and social spending and sets out to privatize and deregulate business and finance, its politics effectively die, he argues:

> Two things tend to happen: your economy grows and your politics shrinks ... The Golden Straitjacket narrows the political and economic choices of those in power to relatively tight parameters. That is why it is increasingly difficult these days to find any real difference between ruling and opposition parties in those countries that have put on the Golden Straitjacket. Once your country puts on the Golden Straitjacket, its political choices get reduced to Pepsi or Coke – to slight nuances of policy ... but never any deviation from the core golden rules.[17]

For all these reasons, contemporary anti-globalization struggles raise the fundamental contradiction between (real) democracy and capitalism – and pose the need for anti-capitalist political movements.

Civil Society or Revolt from Below?

As we have seen, the global justice movement is far from agreed about anti-capitalism. While there are critics who simply want to give globalization "a human face," there are also "those who champion the dispossessed," aspiring "not to reform" capitalism "but to stop it."[18] This has given rise to talk of there being "two lefts" in the world at the moment – one responsible, pragmatic and parliamentarist; the other militant, radical and disruptive. The first seeks a place at the table of power alongside the elites; the other seeks to overturn that table and to build new kinds of popular power. As a recent article in *Newsweek* observed, "there are two different lefts" in Latin America today. While one accepts "an essentially orthodox macroeconomic framework" – i.e. neoliberalism – the other challenges it.[19] The difference between these perspectives was for many years apparent at global justice protests, manifesting itself frequently as a clash between the cautious approaches of NGOs and labour leaders in the North and the more confrontational tactics of generally younger "direct action" militants and activists from the South, who organize street protests at trade meetings. In truth, the issue is much larger, transcending what happens at trade meetings, and going to the heart of how we achieve radical social change.

Forbes magazine, a major US business publication, broached this divergence within the global justice movement in several articles in its November 2000 issue. Criticizing the grassroots rebellions in India that pressured the country's Supreme Court to order a halt to Monsanto's field experiments with genetically-engineered cotton, which the magazine blamed for having "wrecked" Monsanto, Forbes lauded such NGOs as Oxfam International for their responsible and cooperative approach. In particular, the magazine commended the group's British campaign manager's claim that "Oxfam's point of view isn't that globalization is bad per se. We don't want to get rid of the World Bank or IMF, because if you didn't have them the situation would be a heck of a lot worse." Operating as a polite, respectable opposition that "would rather duke it out in the conference room than on the streets," the writers pointed out, Oxfam was rewarded with an invitation to contribute to the World Bank's report on international development.[20]

Rather than genuinely transforming policy, NGOs like Oxfam "are in fact helping the WTO out of its crisis of legitimacy," says labour researcher Gerard Greenfield.[21] Having suffered huge public relations disasters, the World Bank and WTO have both undertaken major facelifts designed to give them friendly, more humane images. They care, really care, about poverty, they insist. In fact, the Bank's website now bears the slogan, "Our dream is a world free of poverty." Another prominent box on the web page intones, "Globalization must work for the poor." Slogans come cheap, however. What better way to change image than bringing the critics inside and letting them write policy papers and background documents? Sadly, many NGOs have been all too happy to help these agencies spruce up their appearance. Heavily reliant on donors, particularly governments, most NGOs crave a basic level of respectability in elite circles. Frequently, they are prepared to offer the globalizers a human face by entering a "dialogue" with them and taking some of their funds for charitable operations in the South.

To do so is to engage in a polite version of elite politics, meeting as representatives of "civil society" with world officials behind closed doors. The editors of the *Globe and Mail* captured the strategic choices confronting movements against neoliberalism in the following terms:

> The social democrats of Europe and North America ... argue that globalization must be given a human face. Outside, in the streets of Seattle or Prague or Montreal ... are those who champion the dispossessed. They discern no benefit in capitalism's march across the continents. They seek not to reform it but to stop it.[22]

And between the two strategies – elite accommodation or popular resistance – lie fundamental differences about how genuine social change is to be achieved.

Take the term "civil society," for instance. Many anti-globalization critics embrace it as a category for describing their movement.[23] Yet, the concept is fraught with difficulties. The idea of "civil society" emerged during the rise of capitalism in order to characterize the new spaces of bourgeois social life – the stock exchange, trade fair, coffeehouse, and university – that had developed as alternatives to the institutional space of the court, where monarch and aristocrats had traditionally mingled.[24] The sphere of civil society was constructed as a "polite" space of cultural refinement, commercial exchange, political organizing and intellectual discussion.[25] While the meaning of the term has shifted over time, it is difficult not to see its use today as an attempt to invite mainstream respectability, to avoid being seen as part of the rabble or mob.[26] Hoping to be admitted into the inner sanctums of elite discussion and negotiation, many NGO and labour leaderships have sought to prove their respectability by denouncing those who engage in less polite forms of protest. Oxfam's global advocacy director, for instance, condemned street protesters in Prague for their "brute force."[27] The use of the term "brute" is highly instructive, particularly for its contrast with "civil." After all, brutes are uncivilized, uncultured – and usually non-white. We, these reformers seem to suggest, are polite, educated, refined – in a word, civil.

Others are less concerned about civility when it comes to fighting for human rights and livelihoods. These people – who seize land for the poor, wage general strikes against structural adjustment, loot supermarkets in order to feed their children, build barricades to block giant dams, throw rocks at riot police trying to break up their demonstrations – will never be invited behind closed doors. Organizing movements of peasants, indigenous peoples, workers and the urban poor, their priority is the building of militant mass organizations that serve as creative laboratories for popular strategies and tactics.

Writing about the Latin American left, and echoing *Newsweek*, but from a considerably more congenial political outlook, James Petras perceptively observes that "To talk about 'the Left' ... is misleading because there is more than one, and the older sort remains, like a withering vine, blocking from view the emergence of the new socio-political movements."[28] This observation should be extended beyond the confines of a single continent. Across the international Left today there is a global parting of the ways, particularly in the South, where increasingly militant protests and rebellions against neoliberalism pursue a radically different strategy from the reform-minded lobbying efforts of mainstream NGOs and bureaucratic labour leaders. The divisions that have come into focus during the protests at world trade meetings in fact reflect wider and more enduring strategic differences between an institutionalized left and insurgent socio-political movements.

Because these radical struggles are waged from below, by masses of peasants, workers and marginalized people, and because they are largely fought out in the South, they rarely register on the radar screens in the North. They ought to, however, for they embody the dream of a better world.

Struggles over Land in India: Fighting the New Colonialism

The December 31, 2001 issue of *Outlook India*, a major newsmagazine, presented an interesting study in contrasts. A feature story under the heading "The New Left" documents a stunning transformation in the Left Front, which governs Bengal. The author reports that under the Left Front, "illegal encroachers have been cleared from the Tolly's nullah (canal) area, while squatters have been evicted from at least four government hospitals and suburban railway tracks." The Front's chairman tells the reporter, "Restraint and consolidation are as important, if not more so, as militancy," while its chief minister pronounces, "We will not tolerate labour indiscipline or violence."[29]

Elsewhere in the same issue is a heart-breaking story about the town of Tehri in the state of Uttaranchal. The two hundred-year-old town is slowly being drowned by rising river waters caused by construction of one of the world's highest dams. The struggle against the Tehri dam was more than three decades old at the time. It was also on its last legs, as the last families were fleeing the rising waters. Gazing on the glistening water around him, the town's crusading environmentalist remarks, "This is our water, being used to kill us, then being looted to grow cane in Meerut and flush Delhi's toilets."[30]

Throughout large parts of India, similar battles are being fought, especially in villages and towns along the banks of the giant River Narmada which slices across the middle of the country. Of the more than four thousand large dams in India, three-quarters of them are found in the three large states across which the Narmada cuts. Perhaps fifty million people have been displaced by giant dams in the last half-century. That's three times the population of Australia brutally dispossessed. And of these displaced people, 40 per cent are *adivasis*, indigenous tribal peoples. Across India, at least half of those displaced by large "development" projects are pauperized. Not surprisingly, in recent years, huge numbers of these people have been fighting back, many of them organized by the Narmada Bachao Andolan (Save Narmada Movement – NBA).[31]

Largely marginalized by the political establishment, people facing displacement have resorted to direct actions both desperate and powerfully effective. Since the late 1980s, the NBA has organized sit-ins, court challenges, marches, fasts and occupations in efforts to halt dam construction at Sardar Sarovar, Mashewar, Maan and many other locations. In the case of the Mashewar dam, where sixty-one villages face full or partial submersion, thousands of local people have rallied in the face of baton-wielding riot police and the arrests of hundreds of activists. The women of the area have been in the forefront of the resistance, taking shifts lying on the access roads for months on end in order to block the arrival of construction materials. Against enormous odds – including the typical denunciations of the poor for using "violence and subterfuge" in the face of the destructive projects of capital – a growing movement has been built which has thrown up considerable obstacles to the mania for giant dams, forcing the World Bank to withdraw from at least one major project.[32]

The NBA has also played an important role in the development of grassroots movements against globalization. On November 30, 1999, the Global Day of Resistance against Capitalism and the WTO, the Joint Action Forum of Indian People Against the WTO and Anti-Human Policies, and the All-India Peoples' Resistance Forum organized a series of large protests in various parts of India. Among these actions was the launch of a 3,000-kilometer march of indigenous peoples through 1,500 villages – organized as a wave of rolling land occupations to demand land reform. Also on the Global Day of Resistance, thousands of farmers rallied in Bangalore to issue a notice to Monsanto to "Quit India" or face a campaign of direct action against its installations, the very campaign that *Forbes* magazine blames for "wrecking" the company. Some days earlier, as part of the build-up to November 30, more than three hundred *adavisis* jumped over the fence of the World Bank building in Delhi, blockading it and covering it with posters, graffiti, cow dung and mud. In a poignant open letter to the president of the World Bank, the tribal peoples proclaimed their unending opposition to the new imperialism. Fingering the Madhya Pradesh Forestry Project funded by the Bank, they declared,

> For the World Bank and the WTO, our forests are a marketable commodity. But for us, the forests are a home, our source of livelihood, the dwelling of our gods, the burial grounds of our ancestors, the inspiration of our culture … We will not let you sell our forests.

Notwithstanding the incredible courage and persistence it has displayed, the movement is up against extreme difficulties. In early 2006, India's Supreme Court effectively approved plans to raise the height of the Sardar Sarovar dam in the Narmada Valley – plans which will see an additional 220 villages flooded and 35,000 families forced to flee. As novelist Arundhati Roy writes in *The Greater Common Good*, the majority of these people will be "eventually absorbed into slums on the periphery of our great cities, where it coalesces into an immense pool of cheap construction labour." This is the inevitable result, she continues, of a ruling class that uses the state to appropriate India's resources, "its land its water, its forests, its fish, its meat, its eggs, its air" for the benefit of "a favoured few." Not surprisingly, the indigenous peoples of the Narmada Valley see in this sort of postcolonial capitalism a continuity with colonialism. And they pledge to continue their struggle against all such forms of domination:

> The Madhya Pradesh Forestry Project and other such projects only intensify the colonial takeover of our forests that began with British rule in our country. We fought the British and we will fight the new form of colonialism that you represent with all our strength.[33]

"The Occupation is the Movement": Revolt of the Landless in Latin America

Halfway around the world from India, a struggle against a giant dam played a major role in the emergence of the most powerful and dynamic rural workers movement in the world: Brazil's Landless Workers Movement (MST). At the very end of the 1970s, some 10,000 families were displaced from their land along the Parana River to make way for a giant hydroelectric dam. A few years later, the region became the site of a land occupation movement that figured centrally in the emergence of the MST.

It has rightly been observed that one of the most significant aspects of the growth of radical movements in Latin America is the emergence of struggles in the countryside as a "stronghold for the resurgence of the Left."[34] And this is the case not only in Brazil.

In Bolivia, for instance, rural movements took the forefront after the tin miners' union, long the vanguard of the left, was decimated by an IMF/World Bank restructuring in the mid-1980s, during which 50,000 miners were fired. Having returned to the land in order to survive, tens of thousands of these miners now play active roles in radical peasant movements, particularly as *cocaleros* (coca growers), imbuing these movements with a unique anti-capitalist consciousness. Their struggles converge with those of highly organized indigenous peoples who constitute at least two-thirds of Bolivia's population.

So effective have these peasant and indigenous movements become that, during the year 2000, two major indigenous rebellions shook the Bolivian government. In the second of these revolts, the Aymara people blocked seventy main roads for weeks, paralyzing much of the economy, until the government gave in to their demands for control over their land and water, and better pay for teachers.[35] The Aymara campaigns draw upon an old myth of "war of the six stones:" native peoples fill the roads with thousands of stones, making them impassable. After the army has cleared them, the roads are refilled.[36] These tactics, involving coordinated action among thousands of people, have opened up new spaces of militant resistance. As we shall see below, in recent years major struggles in Bolivia – particularly the "Water Wars" and the "Gas Wars" – involving semi-insurrectionary upheavals of indigenous peoples, urban workers, and rural labourers have posed some of the world's most powerful challenges to neoliberalism.

But it is the Landless Workers' Movement in Brazil which has built the most powerful and mass organization of rural workers, though one which has not yet had the political impact of the mass upheavals in Bolivia. With a membership of one million, the MST is challenging the most unequal pattern of land ownership on the continent, where just over 1 per cent of the country's landowners possess nearly half the land. In addition, struggles for land have been met with extraordinary brutality from wealthy landowners and the army: according to the Pastoral Land Commission of the Catholic Church, at least 1,684 rural workers were assassinated between 1964 and 1991.[37] MST activists have also been regularly murdered by soldiers and military police.

Formed in 1984, the MST has spearheaded a massive challenge to Brazil's ruling class. The organization has initiated more than 1200 land occupations, expropriating more than 50,000 square kilometres of land and settling over 100,000 families on them.[38] And from occupation, the movement moves to production and community building: "Occupy, Resist, Produce" is one of its prominent slogans. Equally significant as its methods of struggle – highway blockades, land invasions and sit-ins at the Agrarian Reform Institutes (responsible for government land reform) – are the MST's forms of organization. Rather than simply promote individual proprietorship of the land, it fosters rural cooperatives of agricultural producers and has developed cooperatively owned factories for meat storage, milk packing and coffee roasting. Once land is occupied, an MST encampment is set up and organized democratically. Decisions are made collectively with a general assembly constituting the highest decision-making body. The movement also carries on important work of public education: it has established 1,200 schools and operates thirty radio stations. Finding that mainstream teachers are not adequate to the task of building a culture of liberation, the MST has developed its own teacher training programs. "We have three fences to cut down," explains one of the movement's organizers: "the fence of the big estate, the fence of ignorance and the fence of capital."[39] In short, rather than just win land, the Landless Workers Movement aims at a radical social transformation. "Our struggle is not only to win the land," explains another organizer. "We are building a new way of life."[40]

As part of this campaign for a new way of life, the movement has struggled to address gender inequalities and to promote women into activist leadership roles. It urges its communities to elect equal numbers of women at all levels, and in 2000 half of the leaders chosen for the national leadership were indeed female. And in an effort to cultivate internationalism, the MST organizes across national borders, linking with peasant movements in Paraguay, Argentina and Uruguay. The movement has also built links with radical labour in the urban centers, and it has begun to innovate in developing sustainable and organic agriculture.[41]

Of course, like all real mass social movements, the MST struggles with the pressures of the existing social order. As much as it positions itself against capitalism, its members are also forced to operate within the framework of a market society. Yet, to its credit, MST practices, education and forms of organization remain powerfully radical. In addition to promoting internationalism, cooperativism and democracy, the MST stresses direct action as the key method for developing militancy and class consciousness. Not only are land occupations effective, they are uniquely empowering and politicizing. "Rural workers learn more on the day of the occupation than during a whole lifetime," claims one activist. Another movement coordinator elaborates:

> The occupation has a symbolic significance for the landless. It is an action that opens a space for political socialization, for struggle and resistance. This space, built by the workers, is the place of experience and training for the movement. The occupation is the movement.[42]

This emphasis on direct action has had a galvanizing effect on labour and student radicals in the cities, helping to counter trends toward a passive, electoral approach, which has become dominant in the Workers Party (PT), whose leaders have, as we shall see, abandoned radicalism for accommodation with capitalism. By stressing militancy, resistance, direct action and anti-capitalism, the MST has played a crucial role in fostering militancy within important sections of the working class movement in Brazil. In fact, the MST has inspired a movement of urban homeless people that models itself on its direct action strategy. In all these ways, the MST has demonstrated the importance of alliances among the poor and the oppressed in both rural and urban settings.

Building Solidarity: Dilemmas of Resistance in Chiapas

The difficulties confronting the heroic struggles in Chiapas underline the strategic importance of building a movement that links together the rural and urban working classes. These issues were thrown into sharp relief for the Zapatista Army of National Liberation (EZLN) shortly after its January 1994 uprising. As commentators have noted, the EZLN offensive was anything but a military success – the movement was quickly forced to abandon all its captured territory – but it was an unexpected political coup. The Zapatista rebellion struck a chord of sympathy across wide sections of the Mexican population. A ferocious response from the Mexican army was halted in large part by an outpouring of solidarity from workers, peasants and students throughout the country.

As the army unleashed its terror in the immediate aftermath of January 1, 1994, more than seventy Zapatistas and up to 275 civilians were killed (along with thirteen government soldiers). The government was thrown into reverse, however, by the hundreds of thousands of ordinary Mexicans who took to the streets to support the Zapatistas' demands and oppose the army's murderous response. Then, when EZLN representatives arrived in San Cristobal in February 1994 for negotiations with the government, tens of thousands of cheering people turned out, forming a "peace cordon" to protect them. The effect was electrifying, not least on the Zapatistas themselves. As EZLN Subcommandte Marcos told interviewers,

... that absurd and marvelous "cordon of peace" ... took us completely by surprise. Remember, when we'd left San Cristobal [after seizing it on January 1] we were going to our death; we were sure we were going to get killed somewhere along the way. Then, see, we came back to San Cristobal and people were waiting for us, applauding us, jostling each other to see us. They'd even organized themselves to make that cordon in the cold, under the rain. People of no party or organization, who weren't obeying any orders, any line, who got no advantage from being there. They were hungry, taking risks, getting photographed there, they could lose their job. All that just because they believed in it. It was our first contact with them; we didn't expect this encounter.[43]

The response of militant workers' organizations in the cities was particularly inspiring: within twelve days of the initial uprising, mass meetings of power workers, teachers, auto workers, health care workers and others demanded an end to the government offensive. Over the course of several days, hundreds of thousands of workers mobilized in the streets in solidarity with the EZLN. So powerful were the expressions of support that in Puruaran, Michoacan, sugar mill workers voted to unite with the Zapatistas.[44] Sensing that its future hinged significantly on alliances with movements outside the indigenous communities of Chiapas, the EZLN high command began developing a wider political strategy. In June 1994, it floated a proposal for a National Democratic Convention. By January of the next year, it was calling for the construction of a Movement for National Liberation as a means of moving beyond the military struggle against the Mexican state. A year later, Marcos urged the formation of a Zapatista Front for National Liberation (FZLN) in addition to the Zapatista Army. At the same time, the EZLN also developed its worldwide connections by sponsoring two International Encounters for Humanity and Against Neoliberalism.[45]

As Marcos acknowledges, the Zapatista leadership was "improvising," searching for a political strategy that could break their isolation by building a national political front for "liberty, democracy and justice." Thus far, for all of its inspiring militancy, the Zapatistas have not succeeded in galvanizing a substantial organized movement, despite the massive sympathy in Mexican society for their cause – manifest also in the hundreds of thousands of cheering people who greeted them in Mexico City in September 1997.[46] Given the absence of a powerful, unified movement, the government has been able to launch repeated military attacks. A brutal campaign beginning in December 1997 saw forty-five native people slaughtered in Acteal, eight in El Bosque and eleven in El Charco – all Zapatista communities.[47] Tens of thousands of Mexican troops continue to operate In Chiapas, periodically arresting, raping and killing suspected Zapatista rebels.

Then, in a blatant betrayal, the Mexican Congress voted in the spring of 2001 to gut the Indian Rights bill agreed to by the previous government in negotiations with the EZLN. By removing key sections of the bill that would have granted autonomy to Mexico's fifty-seven distinct indigenous peoples, the Congress proposed legislation that has been overwhelmingly rejected by both the Zapatistas and the National Indigenous Congress.[48]

In 2006, the Zapatista leadership launched "The Other Campaign," timed to coincide with Mexico's presidential elections. The campaign involved a nationwide tour designed to unite left-wing groups into an anti-capitalist alliance. Subcommandante Marcos declared of the campaign, "Together, we're going to shake up this country from below, lift it up, and stand it on its head." However commendable these sentiments, The Other Campaign failed to generate a meaningful mass movement, underlining the need for the EZLN to find ways to engage in long term alliance building, rather than one-shot campaigns.

The Zapatista movement is thus at something of a crossroads. Twelve years of mobilization and periodic negotiations with government have yet to produce meaningful gains. In the face of military repression and its own uncertainties, the EZLN continues to search for a political strategy that might mobilize "Indians, peasants, laborers, housewives, people in the shantytowns, union members, students, teachers" and others in a common struggle.[49]

Popular Revolts and General Strikes: Ecuador, Puerto Rico and Bolivia

The most significant anti-neoliberal successes in Latin America have come from popular uprisings involving the mobilization of common fronts of peasants, indigenous peoples and workers in united struggle. Young women are playing an increasingly prominent role as leaders of these movements and indigenous activists are often the principal spokespeople.[50] Frequently assuming near-insurrectionary proportions, these movements are light years away from the tame and gradualist approach of the reformist left. A particularly dramatic example occurred in Ecuador in January 2001, when indigenous movements and radical soldiers briefly seized control of the government.

Since 1997, Ecuador has been staggering through a deepening economic and social crisis. Popular resistance blocked government efforts to implement a harsh neoliberal program: two such attempts were defeated in 1999 by massive social protest. As the economic crisis worsened that year — with 150,000 people losing their jobs and the price of water jumping 400 per cent — the Confederation of Indigenous Nations of Ecuador (CONAIE) and the Coordination of Social Movements (CMS) demanded the government's resignation. However, in January 2000, the government managed to unite most sections of big business behind it. It won bourgeois support for "dollarization" of the economy (tying the economy to the US dollar) and began to repress the popular movements — occupying the universities, arresting worker and peasant leaders, sending the army into indigenous communities.

At this point, an indigenous-led uprising shattered the government. Roads and highways were blocked and native peoples

290

surrounded the Congress, drawing out tens of thousands of supporters who took to the streets across the country. On January 21, the leader of the CONAIE joined with radical soldiers to seize the Congress and proclaim a new government. Uncertain as to how to proceed, however, and lacking sufficient support from urban labour movements, the insurrectionists were outmaneuvered by the ruling class.[51]

Still, the popular movement in Ecuador won important gains. In February 2001, a new wave of social mobilization involving indigenous peoples, trade unionists and students blocked roads, organized strikes, occupied universities and confronted police.[52] As a result, the government has been forced to abandon plans for dollarization of the economy and to reject involvement in Washington's Plan Colombia. Then, in April 2005, another popular upheaval – in which 30,000 people battled riot police throughout the night and 1,000,000 descended on the presidential palace the next day – ousted president Lucio Guiterrez from office over his neoliberal and anti-democratic policies. A year later, indigenous protests against moves toward a Free Trade agreement with the US (coming at the same time as strikes and protests in the oil regions of the Amazon) threw Guiterrez's successor into crisis.

But if urban labour movements have been passive and timid in Ecuador, this is not everywhere the case. During the summer of 1998, for instance, hundreds of thousands of workers in Puerto Rico struck against privatization of the US colony's telephone service. The struggle began with a walkout by phone workers on June 18. When riot police were mobilized to beat the strikers – images of which filled TV news broadcasts – thousands of workers and students poured out to bolster picket lines. Electrical, water and transport workers quickly joined the strike.

Then, on June 28, more than 5,000 delegates from unions and community organizations attended an assembly of the Greater Committee of Labour Organizations, comprising unions and student, environmental and community groups, and voted in favour of a nationwide general strike. For two days in early July,

200,000 workers struck against privatization, closing the international airport, the banks, government offices and all campuses of the university – and dramatically reviving a labour movement that had for years been dormant.[53]

The mass strike in Puerto Rico provided a glimpse of a new form of radical labour organizing. Rather than operate according to sector and occupation – as teachers, telephone workers, or transport workers – the Greater Committee of Labour Organizations put the principle of working class solidarity to the fore. It brought activists from women's, student and environmental groups into its assemblies, thereby launching an action that was widely referred to as *La huelga del pueblo* – the people's strike. This approach has been most successfully developed in Bolivia, which has seen one of the most extraordinary uprisings against neoliberalism.

Bolivia is an especially important case because, as the *Financial Times* notes, "the World Bank and the IMF saw [it] as something of a model."[54] The country's government adopted the IMF/World Bank mania for privatization, selling off electrical utilities, the airline and the national train service. Then, in 1999, it added the water system in Bolivia's second largest city, Cochabamba, to its sell-off list. Soon it found a buyer, a newly formed subsidiary of the San Francisco-based Bechtel Enterprises. So sweet was the Bechtel deal that the lease gave the company control of Cochabamaba's water for forty years, guaranteeing it an average rate of return of 16 per cent, and ensuring that its contract would override all future changes to Bolivian law. Immediately after the contract was signed in January, residents of Cochabamba were hit with water rate hikes of 100 per cent or more.[55]

So overwhelming was the public uproar that a mid-January general strike paralyzed the city for four days. A new mass coalition known as *La Coordinadora* emerged to coordinate the struggle against water privatization. On February 4 , an awesome display of people's power erupted in strikes and street protests. Two Bolivian journalists recount the events:

The first cordons of police who try to block the bridges leading to the town center are broken through around 10 a.m. The multitude who reach the main square don't let the forces of order stop them, despite the gas and the bullets, the blows and truncheons.

The resolute pressure of the crowd, fired by the justice of its demands, throws back the police ... The entire rest of the town is now in the hands of the people. A great spirit of solidarity arises, fear conquered, hesitations swept away ...

The people of Cochabamba have recovered their dignity, unleashed their anger, constructed a new solidarity, bearer of hope, victory and elation.

On February 5th, Cochabamba woke in total uncertainty ... Again the streets fill up, the crossroads are blocked and the crowd returns to occupy the central square. Solidarity is organized. The doors open to welcome the wounded; fires are lit at the crossroads; people talk, organize, share vinegar to counter the effects of the gas; entire families fill the street; parents want their children to learn how to defend a just demand; canteens are improvised to feed the demonstrators.

The entire population joins the mobilization.[56]

These protests involved a vast coalition of popular forces: peasant organizations and indigenous movements figured centrally. But so did the Federation of Workers of Cochabamba, led by Oscar Olivera, who grasps something which has typically eluded Bolivia's national labour movement (the COB): that the old style of workplace-centered organization is inadequate to the tasks of the moment. So, the workers' movement of Cochabamba spearheads *La Coordinadora*, building a movement "where the peasant is as welcome as the worker trades unionist, the inhabitant of a popular neighbourhood, the organizer of an association of cultivators, the 'young activist' or again the citizen who feels concerned."[57]

The "water war" becomes a radical popular movement, mobilizing all the exploited and oppressed. Five times a week, citywide assemblies are held with crowds ranging from 5,000 to 100,000. Ancient democracy – a participatory democracy based on rule of the poor – is reborn without exclusions in the streets of Cochabamba. Here, in the mass assemblies, all the decisions are made, decisions to which the movement's leaders are fully accountable. "These people," note two observers, "wish to represent and rule themselves. They block the streets, bar the roads, go to the square with their children, armed with batons and slings, debate in assemblies and then carry out the decisions taken."[58]

Having set April 4 as the date by which the government must cancel the Bechtel contract, the workers organize a general strike and the people again fill the city square. On April 8, the government hits back, declaring a state of emergency and arresting Olivera and other leaders of the movement (all of whom are flown to a remote jail in the jungle). Five protesters are shot dead in the streets. Still, the people do not waver. On April 10, with the general strike entering its seventh day, the popular uprising intensifies. Highway blockades are extended, thousands of people jam the central square, women go door-to-door collecting food for the street protesters. As evening falls, the news breaks: the government has canceled the water contract.

This momentous victory represented more than the defeat of a privatization policy and a consortium of multinational corporations. More importantly, it represented the emergence of a new form of popular power. For one week, writes Oscar Olivera, the insurgent forces of the poor and the oppressed

> briefly replaced... the state itself with a new type of popular government based on assemblies and town meetings held at the regional and state levels. For one week, the state had been demolished. In its place stood the self-government of the poor based on their local and regional organizational structures.[59]

But this inspiring form of popular power could not be sustained in merely one city or region. Recognizing that a battle has been won but that the struggle continues, Oscar Olivera boards a flight to Washington to join protests against the World Bank and IMF. He and his Bolivian comrades are denounced by World Bank President James Wolfensohn as "rioters." It is a label they wear with pride.

From Water Wars to Gas Wars: Bolivia's Cycle of Revolt

Even if popular power in a single town could not replace the old order, Cochabamba's water wars set off a cycle of revolt that, six years later, is far from over. Overlapping with the struggles over water, the month of August, 2001 saw mass actions of indigenous peoples over land and social security – in a country in which two-thirds of the population identify themselves as aboriginal. A year later, the hugely popular Coca Wars broke out, as coca growers, many of them former tin miners, staged potent protests. Fuelled by the energy of these struggles, Evo Morales, representing the Movement Toward Socialism (MAS), received 21 per cent of the vote in the presidential elections that year, just one per cent shy of the winning candidate. Even larger upheavals were yet to come.

In 2003 the largest protests in Bolivian history erupted, products of an intersecting set of revolts. Widespread road blockages early in the year signaled that the Coca Wars were far from over. Anti-IMF protests in February saw huge crowds torch City Hall, the Customs Office and a Coca Cola plant in El Alto, the capital city. Then, in October, the Gas Wars took center stage, in a momentous campaign to de-privatize natural gas and oil and return them to public ownership. When half a million people descended from the *altiplano* (the huge, mountain-side neighbourhoods of the poor above La Paz) in one of the largest mass actions in Latin American history, it was clear that the presidency of Sanchez de Lozada (Goni) was at an end.

Yet, while Goni's resignation represented a major victory, the insurgent movement did not confuse defeat of a president with defeat of neoliberalism. The Gas Wars continued throughout 2004, and the demand for public ownership grew into an ear-shattering roar. Then, in early 2005, the Second Water Wars broke out, this time against privatization of the water and sewer system in El Alto. A general strike called by the neighbourhood movement (FEJUVE- El Alto) paralyzed the capital city and soon spread to other parts of the country. Road blocks and barricades paralyzed the economy. Extraordinarily large and militant actions culminated in early June when, again, up to half a million protestors took over El Alto. Once again, the mass movement toppled a president – this time Carlos Mesa. Before the year was out, Evo Morales and the Movement Toward Socialism would win the general elections.[60]

After Mesa's resignation, one major newspaper observed,

> Life is growing ever more precarious for elected South American leaders who advocate market liberalization, privatization and other measures ... Bolivia's Carlos Mesa is the latest victim of a populist uprising. . .

> Mr. Mesa joins seven other presidents across the continent who have hastily departed office in recent years without being able to finish their terms.

And the editors knew who to blame: "a politicized indigenous population led by militant leftists and supported by coca growers who are angry about U.S. intervention... The protesters have taken to the streets, occupied plants, blockaded highways and threatened to cut off gas shipments."[61]

Of course, many problems remain. As we shall see below, popular forces in Bolivia now confront a crucial tension: between reliance on mass self-activity and self-organization to change society, on the one hand, and reliance on electoral politics on the other. It is a situation fraught with dangers. But for the moment, popular movements in Bolivia have driven a huge hole through the heart of neoliberalism in Latin America. And they have given enormous inspiration to popular movements throughout the region. Nowhere is this more true, perhaps, than in Venezuela.

Venezuela and the "Socialism of the 21st Century"

It is widely recognized today that Venezuela is in the midst of hugely important social struggles. Too many commentators, however, focus excessively on the country's fiery president, Hugo Chavez. To be sure, Chavez is a key part of the story. However, the "Bolivarian Revolution" underway in Venezuela (which derives its name from the great 19th century liberator, Simon Bolivar, who defeated colonial armies in a bid to unify South America on democratic lines) is a much larger story, one with roots that pre-date the December 1998 election of Chavez to the presidency.

In an important sense, 1989 stands out as a crucial year. It was then that the Venezuelan government adopted wholesale an IMF program that dismantled social welfare, price subsidies and wage regulations. With poverty levels already soaring, these cuts were certain to spark opposition. The moment of contestation came, following hikes in gas prices and public transit fares, when university students occupied a bus terminal and quickly attracted the support of workers and street vendors. Highway blockages and looting of food trucks and stores soon followed. As the insurgency rolled into its third day, Venezuela's rulers turned to violence. The army invaded working class districts, shooting hundreds. The final death toll may have topped one thousand.

While repression had stopped the revolt, it only further angered and alienated the poor. And it did not stop radical organizing in the poor communities, or *barrios*. Similar discontent affected rank and file soldiers, some of whom backed a failed coup attempt by the then-unknown Hugo Chavez, an army officer. In the presidential elections the next year, support for the mainstream parties collapsed. Seething popular anger and a crisis of the ruling parties set the stage for Chavez's election in late 1998.

At first, Chavez governed cautiously. He disavowed socialism and courted business support. At the same time, he promoted a new constitution of a left-populist flavour and promised to tackle poverty and social exclusion. Still, his radicalism often seemed more verbal than substantive. Then a series of attacks from the right were met by popular mobilizations that saved Chavez's presidency. And the Bolivarian Revolution tilted decidedly to the left.

The first attack came in the form of a military coup, backed by the US government, in April 2002. The plotters seized Chavez and transported him to an offshore military base. One hundred of his supporters were also arrested. Then the people of the *barrios* went into motion. Sending out the call by word of mouth and community radio stations, thousands poured down the hills above Caracas to surround the presidential palace and demand that Chavez be returned. At the same time, discontent shook the army, as rank and file soldiers, hostile to Venezuela's elites, began declaring their loyalty to Chavez. In the face of this mounting opposition, the coup collapsed and Chavez was restored to the presidency. Emboldened, working class organizations began to press Chavez to proceed more radically.

Seven months later, in December 2002, the right moved again. This time, the privileged management of the state oil company, PDVSA, hostile to Chavez's efforts to increase government control over the company and over oil revenues, called a "strike" (really a management lockout) designed to deprive the government of oil taxes. As anti-Chavez forces took to the streets to demand that the president resign, popular movements again struck back, out-organizing and out-mobilizing the forces of the Right. Unable to win the battle in the streets, the anti-Chavez forces retreated. Once again, movements of the oppressed had defeated the elites.

The third effort to displace Chavez came with a recall referendum held in August 2004. The right had agitated for the referendum, calling on Venezuelans to vote for recall of Chavez. But neighbourhood organizations, progressive unions and left-wing parties again seized the initiative. Mobilizing in workplaces and *barrios*, they produced the largest vote in Venezuela's history. With 70 per cent of eligible voters turning out, fully 58 per cent voted to back Chavez. For the third time, popular movements had saved the leftist president and inflicted a crippling blow on the elites.[62]

In the course of all these events, Hugo Chavez has shifted to the left. Understanding that Venezuela's ruling class will oppose all moves to tackle poverty and social inequality, he has pushed forward his reform program. In recent years, Chavez has moved more decisively to establish public control of the oil industry; he has launched important new social programs, particularly in the areas of health and education; he has more aggressively opposed the economic and military policies of Washington. Equally significant, he has come to define the Bolivarian Revolution as a socialist one.

The term he uses here is "the socialism of the 21st century," to indicate that Venezuela's socialist project does not adhere to any earlier models. While there is much to applaud here – particularly the idea that there are socialisms radically different from the bureaucratic and authoritarian models that dominated Eastern Europe and China – there are also many ambiguities. In particular, Chavez and his supporters rarely have clear answers to questions concerning radical democracy, social ownership and self-management.

In Chapter Seven, I will take up these issues at greater length. But, in essence, what is at stake here is whether this socialist perspective envisages new forms of popular power in which the exploited masses uproot the old structures of power and establish democratic control of economic and political life through grassroots institutions based in neighbourhoods and places of work. For that to occur, new forms of popular power must be developed as a central part of the revolutionary project. Thus far, the record in Venezuela is highly uneven.

Certainly there have been moves to create new mass organizations in Venezuela in recent years. Both "Bolivarian Circles" and "Patriotic Circles" have been launched. Yet, the initiative to create these circles has largely come from above, as efforts to institutionalize support for President Chavez. A revolution that aspires to completely remake the social order, however, needs forms of mass popular self-organization, spaces in which the oppressed begin to take control of more and more aspects of their own lives as part of establishing a participatory democracy and forms of *self-government.* Yet, as left-wing journalist Jonah Gindin, one of the most astute commentators on Venezuela events, observes, thus far In Venezuela "the transition from representative to participatory democracy has been painfully slow."[63]

In the *barrios* of Caracas and other locales there are militant community organizations with heroic records of fighting the police and establishing enhanced community control over local affairs. But, thus far, they are highly localized, and lack the means and resources with which to link into regional and national networks that could begin to establish enduring forms of popular power at larger levels.

Where the greatest progress has taken place, has been in the unions. Here, militant activists, supportive of Chavez but often unwilling to simply rely on presidential initiatives, have fought to create new radical labour organizations. In May 2003, for instance, the National Union of Venezuelan Workers (UNT) was formed, bringing together unions that seek to further the Bolivarian Revolution and create a radical presence for organized labour in the process. Filled with energy and enthusiasm, the UNT appears to be establishing itself as the largest labour movement in Venezuela. And while some UNT activists see themselves simply as *Chavistas* loyal to the president, many argue for an autonomous and radical labour movement that seeks to deepen and extend the revolutionary process by building mass pressure for sweeping change. In fact, these tensions occasionally paralyze the UNT, as they did in June 2006 when its second national congress was suspended because the *Chavista* element opposed electing national coordinators (and other positions) for the UNT on the bizarre grounds that all efforts should focus on the re-election of Chavez to the presidency later that year. While the more independent currents support re-election of Chavez, they insist that building and developing the UNT should not be subordinated to pro-Chavez maneuvers. Nevertheless, despite these internal tensions, the UNT continues to provide the framework for more radical labour politics.

Indeed, a UNT sponsored workshop in April 2005 on worker/government co-management of workplaces called for decisive moves to increase the participation of both workers and communities in the production and distribution of goods and services. Thus far, there is a tiny but important movement in Venezuela through which workers are taking control (or at least partial control) of workplaces. While it is still small, this movement may be a harbinger of things to come. As one left-wing leader in the UNT explains, "We are working a lot on these experiences of workers' control. Giving power to ordinary people, that can be the leap forward for the pursuit of the revolutionary process."[64]

"We must go beyond surface changes," explains Carlos Gomez, national coordinator of Venezuela's American Solidarity Collective. "This is still capitalism."[65] True, the Bolivarian Revolution associated with Hugo Chavez has created important spaces in which momentous social struggles are being waged – and these spaces must be defended against both internal and external attack. Moreover, millions of Venezuelans are embracing the cause of a new socialism that would eradicate poverty and social exclusion. But the structures of capitalist ownership and power are still intact. If a genuinely anti-capitalist revolution is to succeed, new forms of popular power and radical democracy will be required through which the formerly oppressed begin to take control of economic, social and political life. The future of Venezuela's inspiring experiment depends on it.

The Two Souls of Trade Unionism

The mass struggles in Puerto Rico, Cochabamba and Venezuela illustrate the possibilities for a new model of labour action, one that breaks sharply with the bureaucratic, compromising trade unionism dominant in most countries. In fact, the contrast between these two approaches is as old as trade unionism itself.

The heart of the issue is a contradiction inherent to unions in capitalist society. On the one hand, unions are a form of collective organization of workers against capital. By fostering cooperative organization and action, they play a tremendously progressive role in countering fragmentation and building bonds of solidarity. On the other hand, a principal function of unions is to negotiate better terms for the sale of labour to capital – in short, to improve workers' position within capitalism. This produces a conservative tendency within unions, an inclination to accept capitalism and disavow radical change. The result is a contradictory situation in which "trade unions are dialectically both in opposition to capitalism and a component of it."[66]

Once capitalist classes learn to live with unions – which they generally do reluctantly, only after efforts to crush them have failed – they then attempt to co-opt organized labour. They do so by courting a "special relationship" with union leaders who, as their organizations become larger and more complex, typically assume the role of full-time union functionaries. Almost invariably, capitalists offer recognition of unions and a promise to negotiate with them in return for a "responsible" and "business-like" trade unionism that disavows anti-capitalist radicalism. Wages and working conditions are regularized and collective bargaining accepted on condition that union leaders will discipline their own ranks, preventing unauthorized strikes, slowdowns and sabotage. Under these circumstances, there is massive pressure for unions to become bureaucratic bargaining machines, dominated by professional negotiators and their staffs, and disconnected from their rank-and-file members. Seeing members as "uninformed" types who have to be "sold" a contract agreement, union bureaucracies frequently take on the role of managers of discontent, a labour elite that works with management to "smooth over" problems that arise.[67]

Instead of organizations dedicated to the emancipation of all the poor and the oppressed, bureaucratic business unions – the form that is dominant particularly in North America and Europe – assume the role of special agencies for the betterment of the conditions of a small section of workers. They abandon their potential as organizations for radical change and become a loyal opposition, a part of the status quo. To take one recent example, the *New York Times* ran a story in June 2001 entitled "White House and Unions Look for Common Ground," which revealed that American labour leaders were making substantial donations to Republican lawmakers and that a dozen union presidents had recently held a dinner with seventeen Republican politicians.[68] Rather than forming a radical opposition movement, the bulk of America's labour leaders have become minor partners of the US ruling class, publicly supporting Bush's "war against terrorism." The positions of labour leaders in Europe, Canada, Australia or Japan are scarcely better.[69]

Unions that function this way give up any claim to being leading forces for radical social change. Instead, they take up the role of "special interest groups" unconcerned with the plight of the marginalized and unorganized at home and abroad. As long ago as 1865, Marx warned British workers about this danger, urging that they fight for human liberation across the board by demonstrating "that their efforts are far from narrow and egoistic, but, on the contrary, are directed towards the emancipation of the down-trodden masses."[70]

But the position of moderate business unions is far from stable. In periods like the present, capital will take advantage of their passivity and lethargy to slash jobs, reduce wages and even bust unions through the use of scabs during strikes and lockouts (a tactic that has been frighteningly effective in the US). As a result, unions have been in retreat in most of the major capitalist nations, largely incapable of holding their own in the face of the neoliberal offensive against workers.[71] Yet failures of business unionism can create openings for a more militant sort of class struggle unionism to emerge. Indeed, this is precisely what happened in North America in the 1930s and 1940s when the conservative craft unionism of the American Federation of Labour (AFL) was blown out of the water by a wave of militant sit-down strikes that generated a new brand of radical industrial unionism.

The AFL unions had been utterly ineffective in the face of fifteen years of union-busting (1919-34). Moreover, because they concentrated on the skilled crafts where white men predominated, these unions offered almost nothing to women, black and immigrant workers. Beginning in 1934, however, a wave of strikes led by such groups transformed the labour scene and new mass unions emerged, associated with the Congress of Industrial Organizations (CIO). By 1937, the sit-down strike – where workers evicted management, occupied the place of work and transformed it into a living space in which they slept, ate together, and organized entertainment – had become radical labour's new tactic of choice. At America's largest manufacturing company, General Motors, 170 sit-downs took place between March and June of that year; in a two-week period in March, Chicago workers organized nearly sixty sit-down actions. Every kind of oppressed group imaginable sat down: women workers at Woolworth's stores in New York; black and white kitchen and laundry workers at that city's Hospital for Joint Diseases; inmates at the state prison in Joliet, Illinois; high school students in Mineville, New York supporting their teachers' contract dispute; children in a Pittsburgh movie theater (when the owner stopped showing "shorts" before the main feature).[72] The result was the creation of a new culture of class solidarity that broke the anti-union resistance of America's manufacturing tycoons and generated militant forms of working class consciousness and activism.

In the end, however, American capitalism was able to defeat the labour militants who saw the CIO as an instrument of social transformation. The Cold War at home, where radicals of all types were purged, fired and persecuted, combined with the economic expansion of the post-war boom to create conditions in which the new unions could be tamed and domesticated.

The history of trade unionism demonstrates, therefore, an inherent tension within working class organizations in capitalist society. While unions have the capacity to become mass, democratic organizations that mobilize workers to challenge the rule of capital, they also have a tendency to compromise, curry acceptance and lower their sights to piecemeal alterations of the structure of exploitation. For workers smarting under intense oppression, business unionism is often of little value at all. Under such circumstances, militant forms of working class struggle and organization can erupt, as they did in North America in the 1930s. This is true in the North, as the great French strikes of the last decade or so illustrate. But perhaps nowhere has militant unionism been so impressive in recent years as in many of the newly globalized countries, particularly in much of East Asia.

East Asia's New Workers' Movements

It should come as no surprise that East Asia has been the site of new radical workers' movements, as it is the one region outside the core capitalist countries where, over the past quarter-century, a number of nations have emerged as significant industrial producers and exporters. Between 1980 and 1991, for instance, the share of world trade accounted for by Asia (excluding Japan) increased from 9 to 15 per cent – at the same time that virtually every other region of the South dramatically lost ground. By 1994, more than half of all foreign investment in "developing countries" was flowing into East Asian nations such as South Korea, Indonesia, Thailand, Malaysia and Taiwan.[73] Garment and footwear sweatshops, electronics factories, steel mills and auto plants grew up, alongside international airports, luxury hotels and modern telecommunications systems. In the process, new working classes emerged which are making a major impact on social life.

The late 1980s saw an impressive growth in trade union membership throughout much of the region. Between just 1987 and 1989, for example, union membership rose by 27 per cent in Bangladesh, 38 per cent in the Philippines and 100 per cent in Korea.[74] In many of these cases, militant new union movements emerged. While these have faced a number of problems – police repression, anti-union laws, and their own tendencies toward business unionism – they have also, in a number of cases, provided hopeful examples of a more genuinely class struggle unionism. In this regard, the emergence of the new workers' movement in Korea deserves special attention, as do developments in Indonesia.

Indonesia: Bringing Down Suharto and Organizing for Workers' Rights

While militant students played a crucial role in toppling the Suharto dictatorship in May 1998, it would be a mistake to ignore the role of working class activism in destabilizing the regime. In the face of brutal military and state repression, grassroots union organizing and strikes since the late-1980s had created a small but important space for social activism.

The keys to Indonesia's economic growth during the Suharto period (1965-98) were the opening of the country to foreign investment, exploitation of oil and mineral resources, and the development of sweatshop industries catering to the likes of Nike, the Gap and Banana Republic. Young people drawn from the countryside became a new urban proletariat, while in the sweatshops young women constituted a majority of the workforce. At the end of the 1980s, "a new era of workers' resistance began" that involved strikes by hundreds of thousands of workers in the industrial suburbs around the capital city, Jakarta.[75] A high point was reached in April 1994 when the illegal Indonesian Prosperity

Workers' Union (SBSI) organized month-long demonstrations at two hundred factories and a rally of 25,000 workers at government offices.

Meanwhile, left-wing student radicals had launched a workers' organization of their own, the Center for Indonesian Labour Struggle (PPBI). In July 1995, the Center organized a strike of 13,000 garment workers in Bogor; shortly after the fall of Suharto it brought out 20,000 workers in a combined strike and community protest in Surabaya. Among the activists involved in building the PPBI was the charismatic Dita Sari, then in her early twenties. A founder of the People's Democratic Party (PRD), Sari helped organize rallies of 10,000 workers prior to her arrest in July 1996.

Union organization in Indonesia is much more community-based than in the West, since open political activism at the workplaces is often unsafe. Typically, unions are built through secret meetings in working class neighbourhoods, out of sight of the employers and the police. Neighbourhood organizing has given unions a unique resilience, rooting them in the localities where working class activists live. During the upheaval that brought down Suharto in 1998, small groups of radical workers joined students in the streets for the confrontations with riot police that eventually cracked the dictatorship. Since then, workers have gained more legal and political space for organization and unions have grown considerably.

Today, the Indonesian Prosperity Labor Union has developed to probably a few hundred thousand organized members, while the more radical National Front for Indonesian Labor Struggle (FNPBI, successor of the PPBI) has managed to bring together some tens of thousands and has staged successful May Day marches.[76] These new unions often suffer, however, from domination by radical students and professionals and from weak structures of membership democracy. In a promising development, at the FNPBI's second congress, held in July 2000, more workers were brought onto the executive board, a majority of whose members are now women.[77]

The independent workers' movement in Indonesia is especially impressive for what it achieved – and continues to achieve – in the face of state and employer violence. A poor sweatshop proletariat has managed to organize itself, wage militant strikes, engage in political action and force the government to withdraw its most anti-union laws. This is not to underestimate the difficulties the movement faces, particularly from right-wing religious organizations that have been used to attack picket lines and union offices. The government too continues to obstruct independent unionism. In November 2001, for instance, police attacked 1,000 striking department store workers and arrested eight FNPBI leaders, including Dita Sari, who had only been released from her Suharto-era imprisonment in July 1999.

Despite such repression, union activism has continued – and scored important victories. Worker militancy forced the Indonesian government to pass a Manpower Act in 2003 that legally protects the right to organize unions and to strike. Then, in 2006, the government tried to effectively undo the Act, introducing a package of labour "reforms" that would have made it much easier for employers to fire workers; would have encouraged contracting out of union jobs; and would have gutted employer obligations for health benefits and severance pay. Yet, as the *Asia Times* noted (April 25, 2006), these government proposals ran smack into "an increasingly emboldened and sometimes militant workforce." Through the Workers Challenge Alliance, a coalition of dozens of unions and progressive organizations, a campaign of mass action was launched which included plans for a general strike. In the face of mounting working class opposition, the government withdrew the legislation. In defeating a neoliberal assault on labour rights, Indonesia's new labour movements accomplished something many larger, wealthier (but extremely timid and bureaucratic) union movements in the West have failed to achieve. In so doing, they continue to raise a banner of hope for all the exploited and oppressed.

Korea: Laboratory of Class Struggle Unionism

Without a doubt, the most electrifying developments of the past twenty years have occurred in Korea, where mass strikes have created one of the more powerful labour movements in the world.

Korea's industrial transformation has been staggering. After the terrible damage of Japanese occupation followed by war on Korean soil between the United States and Russia, the country began an accelerated process of industrialization. By the early 1990s, more than three-quarters of the population lived in urban areas (unheard of in most of the South) and the country boasted major steel, auto, shipbuilding and electronics industries. Women became an integral component of the industrial working class, comprising 40 per cent of the workforce. And they were the spark plugs of the great labour uprising that has built the new unions.

The democratic union movement in Korea traces itself back to the heroic six-year struggle (1972-78) of women at Dongil Textile to win union rights. Despite beatings, arrests and firings, the women elected the country's first female union president and refused to surrender. Then, in May 1979, when police assaults on women workers resulted in a death, riots broke out in a number of cities. A year later, following the death of dictator Park, 40,000 troops were sent in to Kwangju City to put down a popular uprising. Martial law was imposed, labour rights suspended, and the Garment Workers Union outlawed.[78]

Still, Korean workers refused to buckle. Another strike wave, spearheaded by women workers in the Kurodong industrial estate on the edges of Seoul, galvanized tens of thousands of workers. Then came the explosion of 1987 when the Korean Women Workers Association (KWWA) managed to unite large numbers of sweatshop workers. When employers sent in thugs to beat up

309

women strikers in Masan and Changwon, thousands of workers and students took to the streets. Thirty new unions were formed in Masan-Changwan in the course of the struggle. Meanwhile, the labour explosion had gone national, as hundreds of thousands of workers joined strikes and street battles with riot police. Roughly 1.3 million workers took part in 3,600 strikes in Korea in 1987, organizing 1,200 new unions in the process.[79] Even larger strikes swept Masan-Changwon the following year, leading some to refer to the area as a "liberated zone." By 1990, union membership in Korea had doubled from one to two million in the space of just over three years.

All of this labour organizing was illegal, as were the new unions. To protest this state of affairs, the (illegal) Korean Confederation of Trade Unions (KCTU) waged a million-strong general strike in December 1996. The following year, a catastrophic economic meltdown hit East Asia and unions were thrown onto the defensive; in Korea, 10,000 workers received layoff notices every day at the peak of the crisis.[80] The Asian crisis has had a demoralizing and disorienting affect on workers throughout the region. The KCTU was thrown into crisis, some of its leaders agreeing to accept layoffs of union workers before a rank and file upheaval forced them from office. Nevertheless, a planned general strike was aborted when it became clear that the effects of mass layoffs had shaken workers' confidence.[81] KCTU unions have been unable to prevent layoffs at Hyundai Motors, Mando Machinery, Daewoo Motors and many other workplaces. Severe state repression has also made activism difficult: thousands of Daewoo workers protesting layoffs were attacked by riot police on numerous occasions throughout 2000 and 2001, as were 1,000 striking workers at the Lotte Hotel in Seoul. Altogether, 218 trade unionists were imprisoned in Korea in 2001, including Dan Byuong-ho, KCTU president.

Despite this level of repression, and strategic difficulties that have yet to be sorted through, Korean labour has continued to organize with a militancy and determination that puts unions in the West to shame. August 1999 saw the inauguration of the first nationwide, multi-industry union of women workers, the Korean Women's Trade Union (KWTU), which is now organizing contingent labourers such as women working in restaurants and cafeterias, freelance writers for TV, and golf caddies.[82] In the face of government crackdowns on unions, the KCTU also staged a general strike on July 5, 2001 to protest the arrest and incarceration of trade unionists.

While the KCTU continues to struggle with tendencies toward compromise and bureaucratization, it has not entirely succumbed. Particularly noteworthy is its launch of the Migrant Workers Trade Union (MTU) in 2005. The MTU, with a membership of 400,000, represents a hugely important initiative to organize and defend the most vulnerable and oppressed section of the Korean working class. Under Korean law, migrant workers can work for only three years and for only one employer. As the KCTU points out, "these workers are bound to the employer like slaves." Moreover, the government regularly deports as "terrorists" migrant workers who protest their oppressive conditions. Nevertheless, since 2002, a wave of demonstrations, sit-ins and hunger strikes by migrant workers has thrust their plight and their demands onto the political stage. And the KCTU has distinguished itself, especially by comparison with most unions in the West, as a proud and determined champion of migrant workers and their union.

At the same time, the KCTU has tried to hold to a radical stance on the crucial issues of world politics. After September 11, 2001, the organization came out in powerful opposition to America's "war against terrorism," and has hosted a conference of workers from the South on the theme "another world, another future is possible." Whatever their failings, the courageous struggles of Korean workers are proof that this is so.[83]

New Workers' Movements throughout the South

While the Korean case is the most powerful, as the following instances suggest, there are many other inspiring examples of grassroots union organizing and mass strikes throughout the South.

- In Nigeria, the four million-strong Nigeria Labour Congress (NLC) has launched its own struggles against neoliberalism, including repeated general strikes against increases in fuel prices. While the NLC is plagued by compromises with the government, it has also organized mass protests, albeit bureaucratically controlled. In June 2000, the union federation organized a national strike after the government hiked oil and gas prices by 50 per cent – a hike that triggered immediate rises in bus fares and food prices. Nigeria is the world's sixth largest producer of crude oil, yet the people have seen none of its benefits. In fact, fully seventy per cent of the population lives on less than $1 a day. The idea that should be further impoverished by having to pay more for a commodity that their country produces in huge supplies provokes widespread opposition. Moreover, the gas and oil price increases were seen as IMF-inspired in a country where, as a result of numerous Structural Adjustment Programs, SAP is effectively a swear word. As the NLC's June 2000 general strike got underway, banks, post offices, hospitals and public services all ground to a halt. Strikers and jobless youth threw up barricades on major roads throughout Lagos and other towns. On the first day, the government offered to reduce the price hike, but the unions refused to budge, insisting that the entire increase be rolled back. After five days, the price hikes were reduced from 50 to 10 per cent – a major victory for the unions and popular movements.[84] Still, the government took the offensive again a year and a half later, announcing new increases on January 1, 2002. Once again, the NLC called a general strike, and this one too had massive support. One Lagos newspaper reported that "Alausa was a ghost town as the workers did not turn up for work... In Kaduna, activities were paralyzed as union activists took over the major streets in the metropolis, mounted barricades and prevented vehicular movement."[85] Yet another general strike, this time against a 25 per cent hike in fuel prices, broke out in October 2004, resulting in multiple deaths at the hands of police. Even the repeated arrests of NLC president, Adams Oshiomhole, on January 16, 2002 and again on October 9, 2004, were unable to break the militancy and determination of the strikers whose defiance has inspired workers across Africa.

• In Bangladesh, the National Garment Workers Union (NGWU), organizing a sweatshop proletariat composed largely of young women, has brought 20,000 workers in Dhaka into its ranks. While these are modest achievements in a workforce of 1.2 million garment workers, they are also tremendously important in an industry where life is cheap – witness the rash of factory fires – and where workers earn as little as $42 (US) a month for eighty to one hundred hours of work each week producing goods for Tommy Hilfiger, Gap and J.C. Penney, among others. In a sign of growing strength, the NGWU was able to organize a solid strike in July 2001. Following another horrific fire in February 2006, in which hundreds were killed or maimed, over 18,000 garment workers waged a half-day protest strike. Protests like these are testimony to the courage and determination of its activists in building a fighting union of sweatshop workers.[86]

• While workers, peasants and the poor of India have been reeling under the combined assault of the IMF, World Bank and WTO, on the one hand, and a right-wing Hindu fundamentalist government on the other, major resistance struggles have occurred. In January 2000, a strike by 90,000 power workers in Uttar Pradesh won a twelve-month delay in plans to privatize electricity. Then, in May of that year, one million workers joined a one-day general strike against price increases, privatization, cuts to fertilizer subsidies, attacks on Muslims and other minority groups, and against the IMF, World Bank and WTO. The year ended with December strikes by one million bank workers against privatization, and by 600,000 postal workers demanding pensions for part-time workers. Mass strikes continued in parts of the country throughout 2001, including one in the state of Maharashtra to protest "the onslaught of globalization, privatization and liberalization." Alongside the big, public protest events, there have also been interesting developments at the level of tiny workplaces. While most unions ignore homeworkers, the Navayuga Beedi Karmika Sangam union in Hyderabad, Andhra Pradesh has managed to organize thousands of homeworkers producing beedis (Indian cigarettes). Until the 1970s, beedis were largely produced in factories, but most of these were shut down as manufacturers shifted production to women labouring in the home. In the late 1980s, the union began a house-to-house organizing campaign, bringing 5,000 homeworkers into the union by 1994. While the union has waged strikes, its most effective actions have been citywide demonstrations that overcome isolation and bring the issues to a wider public. In addition to organizing the sorts of workers most labour organizations neglect, the beedi workers' union has won improved wages and entitlements to maternity benefits, paid holidays and weekly days off.[87]

• In recent years, Taiwan has witnessed the rise of a new unionism, much of it associated with the Federation of Independent Unions formed in 1988. Taiwan is a classic case of a "newly industrializing" nation which has witnessed growing restiveness among workers. While there were 485 strikes in the country in 1975, a decade later the number had more than tripled to 1,600; by 1994 the number of labour disputes surpassed 2,000. In November of the latter year, the first ever nationwide strike was organized against government attempts to raise workers' national health payments, with 30,000 workers from more than two hundred unions joining the action. This action was followed in 1995 by mass demonstrations against the privatization of fourteen government-owned firms, including the national telecommunications company.[88] On May Day 2000, a mass rally of 20,000 in the streets of Tapei celebrated the launch of the Taiwan Confederation of Trade Unions.[89]

• Since 1985, when the inspiring September 19 Garment Workers Union was launched after an earthquake hit Mexico City, an upsurge of independent unionism has begun transforming the Mexican labour movement. Especially encouraging was the formation of the May First *Intersindical*, which initially came together to build a militant and independent May Day march in 1995. Up to half a million workers filled the streets of Mexico City on that day; even more came out a year later. The movement has also regularly mobilized in support of the Zapatistas. Like many radical labour movements, the *Intersindical* includes members from community organizations, rank-and-file opposition groups in the "official" unions (tied to the historic ruling party, the PRI) and leftist parties.[90] Even in the *maquiladora* zones, in the face of terrific repression from police and thugs, workers have started to form independent unions. A huge step forward came in 2002 when independent unions, peasants groups and urban social movements came together to create the Union, Peasant, Social, Indigenous and popular Front (FSCISP). By 2004, this radical working class coalition was launching significant mass protests and opening up potential space for new radical politics. [91]

• Perhaps few developments are more inspiring than the series of general strikes waged by unions in Colombia against neoliberalism. In a country where assassinations of union leaders are commonplace, workers have found the courage and conviction to defy the government. Since its signing of an IMF bailout agreement in 1999, the government of President Pastrana has been rocked three times by general strikes. On

June 7, 2001, close to one million workers brought large parts of the country to a standstill. Roughly 300,000 teachers and 125,000 healthcare workers were joined by hundreds of thousands of others, including oil workers in Barrancabermeja. Protesters also set up roadblocks in many parts of the country. As teachers' federation president Gloria Ramirez explained, the general strike was directed not only against recent budget cuts, but against the entire "neoliberal model" imposed by the IMF.[92]

• After years of quiescence, the Congress of South African Trade Unions (COSATU) staged a three-day general strike against privatization in late August 2001 and followed this up in May 2006 with another mass strike. One of the most radical labour movements in the world throughout the 1980s, COSATU had surrendered its militancy once the African National Congress assumed office (first under Nelson Mandela, then Thabo M'Beki). Yet, despite the end of racial apartheid, life has gotten worse for black workers throughout South Africa: half a million jobs have been lost since 1993, leaving one-third of the labour force unemployed. Living standards for the poor have dropped by more than 20 per cent at the same time as water costs have jumped 55 per cent and electricity bills 400 per cent. Eight million people are homeless. "Apartheid based on race has been replaced with apartheid based on class," proclaims former ANC activist Trevor Ngwane. COSATU's general strikes, first launched and then extended only because of enormous pressure from below, could signal the beginning of a new period of mobilization for social justice by Africa's largest working class.[93]

While unions in the North have generally been in retreat and decline for a quarter-century, new workers' movements in the South are demonstrating powerfully that there is a future for working class politics North and South – at least for militant, democratic, grassroots class struggle politics.

Workers of Colour and Social Movement Unionism in the United States

While the South has been the focal point for the most exciting experiments in militant, grassroots unionism, even in the very heartland of world capitalism, the United States, workers of colour have been forging new weapons of struggle. Despite lack of support, and in some cases outright hostility, from bureaucratic business unions that have been in retreat for nearly thirty years, black, Latino and Asian-American workers have given notice that there is a future for radical working class movements in the United States.

Not surprisingly, one of the centers of these developments is California, the most multi-ethnic state in the US. Latinos, most of them from Mexico and Central America, make up one-third of California's population, while Asian-Americans comprise 12 per cent. Traditional "Anglos" account for half the people in the state. Latinos and Asian-Americans comprise the bulk of the proletariat in sweatshops, hotels and janitorial services. In fact, over 70 per cent of immigrant manual workers in California are Latino.[94] While these groups are the most oppressed workers in California – toiling long hours for sub-standard wages and, in the case of "illegals," without labour code protections – they are also the leaders of a growing fight back movement.

Ironically, this resistance began during the anti-union heydays of the Reagan and Bush Sr. administrations. The courageous 1980 strike of San Francisco hotel workers, who had toppled the former leadership of Hotel and Restaurant Employees (HERE) Local 2 and turned it into a militant, grassroots union, was the harbinger of things to come. With Filipina and Latina hotel maids comprising 95 per cent of all picketers, Local 2 won major improvements to wages and working conditions, and has gone on to organize 80 per cent of the large hotels in the city.[95]

In the early 1990s, one of the largest successful organizing drives among Latino immigrants shook the southern California construction industry. In the course of a well-prepared and militant five-month strike – in which hundreds of strikers were arrested, and many of them threatened with deportation – thousands of workers won higher wages and union recognition.[96]

But perhaps no struggle has so clearly blazed a trail for a different kind of unionism than the Justice for Janitors campaign in Los Angeles, associated with the Service Employees International Union (SEIU). For years, SEIU Local 399 had been a declining force in LA's cleaning service industry. While massive amounts of new office space went up in the 1980s and 1990s, the union did nothing to organize the thousands of new janitorial workers from Mexico and Central America, many of whom are women. Then, Justice for Janitors (JfJ) was kick-started in southern California in 1988. After some modest but important organizing successes, JfJ/Local 399 took strike action in late spring 1990. When police brutally attacked a peaceful JfJ march on June 15, the janitors' struggle became the cause celebre of social justice activism in LA. Under massive public pressure, International Service Systems, a multinational building services firm, signed a contract. Seeing the writing on the wall, American Building Maintenance soon also signed a contract with the union – a move that saw between 5,000 and 6,000 immigrant workers win union protection and improved wages.[97] In a tremendous about-turn, worker unionization in cleaning services in LA soared from 10 per cent in 1987 to 90 per cent by 1995.[98]

Offering dramatic proof that their initial successes were no flash in the pan, 8,500 office janitors waged a militant three-week strike in April 2000 – featuring mass rallies, marches and pickets – winning a 25 per cent pay raise over three years. As important as the improved living standards for workers making poverty wages is the boost JfJ has given to immigrant workers' struggles for human rights and social justice. In fact, 1999 saw the largest successful union organizing drive since the 1930s when 74,000 home-care workers in Los Angeles County, most of them Latino, voted to join the SEIU after an eleven-year campaign to organize workers in the industry.[99] As a result of campaigns like these, the labour movement in LA, a traditionally anti-union city, has become the most dynamic in North America. As one observer notes,

> By focusing its organizing on immigrant workers, the city's labor movement is adding workers faster than unions anywhere else in the country. In recent years, unions have organized 6,000 part-time school aides, 2,000 food service workers and retail workers at the international airport and 2,000 Los Angeles park and recreation workers.[100]

But organized labour's breakthroughs in LA have entailed more than just "focusing" on immigrant workers; they have also involved new strategies and forms of organizing. Central to the new strategic approach is a community-based orientation that makes organizing for the civil and human rights of immigrants as important as the fight to improve wages and working conditions. All of this involves a shift toward what has been called social movement unionism, a brand of labour activism in which unions are not merely collective bargaining agents, but also social movements fighting for progressive change on all fronts. In this area, union organizers have been able to draw upon the innovative approaches used by workers' centers that run storefront offices where immigrant workers can meet, learn about their legal rights, discuss union and community organizing campaigns – all away from the eyes of employers and government agencies.

In cities with large immigrant labour forces, workers' centers create openings for new forms of working class organizing. In these spaces, workers of colour have designed consumer boycotts, hunger strikes, union drives, pickets, court challenges and labour strikes to pressure employers, defend immigrants, oppose police racism, win improved wages and conditions of work, campaign for better housing and public services, and defeat anti-immigrant laws. Groups such as *La Mujer Obrera* (The Woman Worker) in El Paso Texas; the Asian Immigrant Women Advocates in Oakland, California (which launched the Garment Workers Justice Campaign); the Center for Third World Organizing; Korean Immigrant Workers Advocate in LA; *Mujeres Unidas y Activas* (which organizes Latina domestic workers in San Francisco); *Fuerza Unida* (United Force) in San Antonio, Texas; People Organized to Win Employment Rights (a union of workfare workers in San Francisco); and the Labor/Community Strategy Center in LA have created workers' organizations based in local communities which frequently operate in several languages. Collaboration between several of these groups in LA also led to the launch of the multi-ethnic Garment Workers Center.[101]

Despite overt hostility from some business unions, these centers have been launching pads for unionizing drives. In 1991, for example, *La Mujera Obrera* unionized three factories and one laundry in Texas.[102] But unlike mainstream North American unionism, which largely limits its focus to contract negotiations, the workers' centers treat all the issues facing poor and immigrant communities – from housing problems and police racism to union rights and the danger of toxic substances dumped in communities of colour – as the terrain of working class organizing. Unlike union leaderships that appear every few years when it's time to negotiate a new contract, the centers aspire to become living organisms, thoroughly integrated into the daily life of poor, working class communities. As Saladin Muhammad, an activist with Black Workers for Justice in North Carolina and Local 150 of the United Electrical Workers put it, the task is to create "a culture of protest" that links civil rights and social justice activism with worker education and labour action.[103]

The effect of organizing thousands of militant immigrant workers of colour has been to radicalize the whole of the labour movement in California. As David Bacon points out, rank-and-file activists have overturned conservative leaderships in several important union locals, and California's labour federation was the first in the US to call "for abolishing employer sanctions against undocumented workers." A number of other unions in the state

are going through significant upheavals as workers of colour remake them as fighting instruments for workers' rights.[104]

But it is not just California where militant, grassroots, community-based union activism is at work. In New York City, the
Chinese Workers and Staff Association (CWSA) has been active
since 1979 organizing restaurant and garment workers. In recent
years, CWSA has worked closely with the Latino Workers Center,
creating a multicultural workers alliance that has produced important gains. Only miles away, the Workplace Project on Long
Island has also developed innovative strategies for organizing Latino workers, many from Central America, who work in restaurants and sweatshop factories and as cleaners.[105]

Sometimes, effective working class activism can be focussed
on social-economic issues entirely outside the workplace. This
has largely been the approach of the Labor/Community Strategy Center in LA and its main offshoot, the Bus Riders' Union
(BRU). Beginning in the mid-1990s, the BRU identified the racial
and class biases of the transit system in LA: while bus riders constitute 94 per cent of all transit passengers, only 30 per cent of the
system's spending goes into bus service. Meanwhile, 70 per cent of
public transit funds are devoted to a rail system that serves a small,
wealthier and predominantly white clientele in the suburbs.[106]
Under the slogan "Billions for Buses, Fight Transit Racism," the
BRU initiated a militant campaign, built a multiracial organization and has won significant battles to improve bus service.

The BRU uses on-the-bus organizing to build its base. Teams
of activists board buses, all of them wearing colourful BRU T-
shirts, to deliver speeches and pass out literature. The union also
mobilizes protests at transit commission and city council meetings
and holds rallies and demonstrations. At the heart of BRU strategy is the recognition of public transit as a working class issue:

> The bus is what we call a factory on wheels, carrying
> the Korean restaurant worker, the Thai woman gar-
> ment workers, the Latino hotel worker, the black de-
> partment store worker, the black and Latino domestic

> workers, high school kids with their boom boxes, the
> black and Latino parolees ... the bus system creates
> one of the multi-racial contexts in which an appeal
> to a common destiny and a common enemy can be
> made ...[107]

The BRU reaches 50,000 transit passengers every month, holds sizable monthly meetings of its multiracial membership, and publishes a bilingual (Spanish/English) newspaper called *Ahora Now*.[108] While it is not clear how it has handled the development of a democratic, multiracial leadership, the BRU has developd a number of effective organizing tactics. In addition, during the 2000 strike of LA transit drivers, the BRU did impressive work building solidarity between predominantly African-American bus drivers (whose union leadership has been hostile to the BRU) and riders, who are predominantly Latino. The BRU organized large rallies to support the drivers' strike and, in an unprecedented development, got 850 drivers to sign letters demanding no cuts in bus service – a demand which their union leaders have traditionally refused to support. The result is an opening toward "a new alliance" of drivers and riders against the LA transit authority.[109]

Black Workers for Justice (BWFJ), which emerged in North Carolina in the 1980s, is another important grassroots, community-based workers' organization. In a notoriously anti-union state, BWFJ managed to wage stunningly successful community actions against both Kmart and the Shoney's restaurant chain for their racist treatment of black employees. Using civil rights tactics – from petitions, to church rallies, to marches and sit-ins – BWFJ has spearheaded militant, community-based working class activism. The group also later waged a successful battle for union rights at Kmart. Linking working class politics to community struggles, the organization has also worked actively around tenants' rights, environmental racism, and anti-war campaigns. In the late 1990s, BWFJ helped to organize 19,000 housekeeping staff at the University of North Carolina's fifteen campuses. Linking with the United Electrical Workers, the group built a mass action campaign that has won significant gains for poor workers. Given this record, it is not surprising that by the mid-1990s, BWFJ had moved beyond North Carolina to establish active chapters in Virginia, South Carolina and Georgia.[110]

BWFJ, Justice for Janitors, the workers' centers and similar movements are all expressions of a new form of working class politics in which issues of race and gender are made central to community-based organizing. California, New York and North Carolina are not the only areas of the US where such strategies are being developed, of course: *La Mujer Obrera* and *Mujeres Unidas y Activas* are based in Texas, and some impressive labour/community campaigns centrally involving African-American workers have been built in cities like Hartford, Connecticut.[111] Similarly, in Canada's largest city, Toronto, the Ontario Coalition Against Poverty (OCAP), the country's most militant and flamboyant anti-poverty organization, has worked to organize taxi drivers, overwhelmingly immigrant men, and street vendors in the city's Chinatown. OCAP also does militant work around immigrant rights, including occupations of Immigration Canada offices to force officials to grant hearings. As a result of this spirited work, individuals and families from Afghanistan, Somalia and elsewhere have won legal status in Canada. Wherever possible, OCAP has made it a habit to mobilize left-wing union activists as part of these campaigns to defend immigrants and refugees.[112]

The latter – winning union support for militant, community-based activism – has, however, often proved difficult. Even some of the most successful campaigns have run into bureaucratic hostility from business union leaders. For instance, Local 399 of the Service Employees International Union (SEIU) in LA, which was built out of the Justice for Janitors campaign, found itself placed in trusteeship – an arrangement in which the national union strips local union members of powers to elect their own representatives and run their own affairs – as a result of their 1995 rank and file campaign to elect a new, more militant local leadership. Since that time, forty more SEIU locals have been placed in trusteeship in an effort to squelch rank and file initiatives.[113]

Still, despite government repression, hostile employers and bureaucratic union leaders, immigrant workers and workers of colour continue to mobilize with great audacity and courage. In October 2004, at least 100,000 people rallied in New York City to support a three-week long Immigrant Workers Freedom Ride. Then, on May Day 2006, perhaps a million and a half immigrant workers revived the real meaning of international workers' day in the US. Pouring into the streets in over 200 cities and towns across the country to demand full legalization and dignity for undocumented immigrant worker, these workers responded to the national call for *Un dia sin immigrante* –- "a day without im- migrants." Skipping work and school, immigrant labourers closed factories and shops to attend the marches and rallies, including a huge rally of perhaps half a million in Chicago. For that one day, in the midst the biggest multi-national civil rights/social move- ment in US history, immigrant workers flexed their muscles and proudly and courageously displayed the potential future of orga- nized labour in North America.

Anti-Racist, Feminist Class Politics

What all the organizations described in this chapter point to is a new kind of working class politics: a class struggle politics, to be sure, but also an anti-racist, feminist class politics. When we look at the central role of women organizers in the Save Narmada Movement in India, the Landless Workers Movement in Brazil, or the new labour movement in Korea, the leading role played by indigenous peoples in popular uprisings in Ecuador and Bo- livia, the powerful agency of immigrants and workers of colour in movements like Justice for Janitors or the workers' centers, we see the outlines of a form of labour organizing that is based upon the self-activity of the most oppressed sections of the global working class.

And here we find the seeds of a radically different form of class politics. After all, mainstream trade unionism, particularly in the North, has frequently been dominated by organizations of white male workers. Immigrants, contingent workers, women of colour in homes and sweatshops have only rarely found a place in these institutions. Seeking respectability, privileged labour leaders have created a movement that typically excludes the "rabble" and the marginalized, and disavows their "in your face" style of activism. Rather than leading a struggle for universal emancipation, one that challenges all structures of privilege and oppression, too often mainstream unionism has been, in Marx's words, "narrow and egoistic." Instead of seeing racism and sexism as problems that must be addressed by the whole labour movement, mainstream union officials have repeatedly dismissed struggles around these issues as "divisive," as threats to the "unity" of workers around economic goals. The result has often been a politics of labour "unity" that refuses to embrace the struggles of the most oppressed workers.

From the start, as we have seen in chapter 4, capitalism has been a system of racial and gender domination, one in which class exploitation is always constituted in and through forms of gender and racial subordination. Writing about Canada, Himani Bannerji reminds us that "Forms of property and labour enshrined in Canada, from the first land grabbing occupation to now, have been wholly organized by and inscribed with the difference of 'race' and ethnicity. There is no 'class' here without 'race.'"[114] Without the theft of aboriginal lands and the destruction of native ways of life, without enslavement of Africans, without colonization and imperial domination of most of the peoples of the globe, the actual capitalism we face today would not exist. To organize in any meaningful sense against the historical reality of capitalism is impossible without organizing against racism, the oppression of women, and imperialism.

To be sure, effective organization against the system requires a class politics, one dedicated to ending the exploitation of all who sell their labour. But since the sellers of labour are organized in terms of systems of racial and gender domination, capitalism cannot be attacked at its roots unless racial and gender oppression are fundamentally and centrally challenged. Class politics is not an abstraction, not a program for social change transported from the skies. Class politics are the politics of resistance, opposition and transformation that grow out of the concrete experience of oppressed peoples. As a result, they are as complex and multi-dimensional as real human beings.

People organized into social classes have experiences framed simultaneously by gender, sexual and ethno-racial relations; they live in actual communities where issues of housing, schools, safety for women on the streets, police harassment and public transportation impinge upon their lives; and they fight back around some or all of these issues in different ways at different moments in their lives. What they resist and how they resist it depends upon their perception of the horizons of social possibility. As Robin Kelley, historian of the black working class in America, puts it, "Politics is not separate from lived experience or the imaginary world of what is possible; to the contrary, politics is about these things. Politics comprises the many battles to roll back constraints and exercise some power over, or create some space within, the institutions and social relationships that dominate our lives."[115]

Authentic working class politics are about overcoming alienation by winning new dimensions of control over work, play, life, leisure and culture. And in a class-divided society based upon white supremacy, patriarchy and (hetero)sexual regulation, this can only mean overcoming all these forms of oppression and exclusion.[116] Real human emancipation — which requires liberation from alienated labour and life — must be just that: emancipation from all forms of subordination and oppression. Anything less is not radical politics. And the only radical politics equal to the task is an anti-racist feminist politics of working class struggle.

To be sure, the movements discussed in this chapter merely carry the "seeds" of such a politics, to use the term I've employed above. Like all real movements, they negotiate tensions between resistance and accommodation, revolt and compromise, and they struggle internally with gender and racial hierarchies. Nevertheless, by creating new forms of militant struggle and organization in which workers of colour, indigenous peoples, and women in sweatshops play leadership roles, they are living proof of the concrete possibility of an anti-racist, feminist class politics. It is the job of radical anti-capitalists to help nurture those seeds by fostering a political climate in which they might develop and thrive.

Radical Democracy and the Search for Alternatives

An anti-racist, feminist class politics is also the only meaningful politics of radical democracy today. As we saw at the outset of this chapter, the impulse for democracy has always come from below, from the struggles of the poor and the exploited to improve their lives. Capitalism has, of course, endeavoured to tame and control democracy by excluding it from the sphere of social-economic relations. But all the movements we've described trespass beyond the signs that cordon off private property. By occupying lands in Brazil, blocking roads leading to giant dam projects in India, taking over a city square in Bolivia to break a water privatization contract, or boarding buses in Los Angeles as part of a "no fare" campaign, these movements refuse to accept that a tiny fraction of the world's population ought to control all decisions related to the use, distribution and ownership of the world's economic resources. And they also refuse to accept that democracy ends where "economics" begins, that the people have no right to affect the ownership and distribution of society's wealth. Instead, these movements insist that there can be no just society without the right of people to control those relations that affect their livelihood and their survival. In so doing, whether fully aware of it or not, they mobilize a radical democracy against capitalism.

And yet, thus far, these movements have been much more effective at resisting than at overturning; while capable of stopping something regressive, they rarely venture toward the beginning of something entirely new. As the late Daniel Singer explained in a perceptive analysis of the French strikes and demonstrations of 1995, the great accomplishment of the movement was that it had shattered "the fatalistic acceptance" of neoliberal dogma by showing that people could stop a government in its tracks. Yet, as Singer warned, winning a single battle is not enough:

> The rulers give up individual proposals but not their strategy. The protesters win a battle and, then, lacking objectives, are unable to launch a counteroffensive ... It is ... the idea that there can be no alternative that the French protesters have now battered ... They did not, however, substitute an alternative of their own ... they did not offer an alternative project, the vision of a different society.

Radical movements cannot change societies without such a vision, however. It is possible to resist, to engage in the powerfully negative act of saying No, without a clear vision of an alternative. But that accomplishment, while immensely important in terms of building confidence and capacities for struggle, only postpones the next battle. For capitalism is unrelenting; give it a chance to try again and it will, often with devastating consequences. What Singer goes on to say about the French events, might be said about any of the struggles we've examined, even one as powerful as the uprising in Cochabamba:

> After twenty years or so of total ideological domination, the very refusal, rejection and resistance were vital... It is a crucial beginning. But is only a beginning. On the basis of this negative achievement, the genuine search for a radically different society must begin.[117]

Notes

1 This protest was organized by the Movement for the Liberation of the Land-less (MLST), a much smaller organization than the Landless Workers Movement (MST) which I discuss below.

2 See "Bolivia's turmoil has its roots in inequity," *Globe and Mail*, June 11, 2005.

3 Maude Barlow and Tony Clarke, *Global Showdown: How the New Activists are Fighting Global Corporate Rule* (Toronto: Stoddart, 2001), pp. 207, 168.

4 Aristotle, *Politics*, trans. Ernest Barker (London: Oxford University Press, 1958), Book III, Ch. 8, p. 116; see also pp. 115, 162-64.

5 For a good summary see W. G. Forrest, *The Emergence of Greek Democracy 800-400 BC* (New York: McGraw-Hill, 1966), Ch. 6.

6 Slaves too were excluded from political life. It is important to emphasize, how-ever, that, in contrast to slavery in the "New World," there was no ethno-racial basis to Greek slavery. Slaves were generally other Greeks, captured as prisoners during wars. Moreover, they sometimes had a relatively high social status (as bank managers, for instance) and were frequently freed from servitude after a number of years of service. I say this not to justify the institution, but to contrast it with later forms.

7 G. E. M de Ste. Croix, *The Class Struggle in the Ancient Greek World* (London: Duckworth, 1983), p. 279.

8 Ellen Meiksins Wood, *Democracy Against Capitalism: Renewing Historical Mate-rialism* (Cambridge: Cambridge University Press, 1995), p. 188. See also, Meiksins Wood, *Peasant-Citizen and Slave: The Foundations of Athenian Democ-racy* (London: Verso Books, 1988).

9 M. I. Finley, *The Ancient Greeks* (Harmondsworth: Penguin Books, 1977), p. 75.

10 M. I. Finley, *Democracy Ancient and Modern* (London: Hogarth Press, 1985), p. 20.

11 De Ste. Croix, p. 317.

12 See especially, Wood, Ch. 7. I have tried to trace part of this process in English political thought in McNally, "Locke, Levellers and Liberty: Prop-erty and Democracy in the Thought of the First Whigs," *History of Political Thought* 10, 1 (Spring 1989), pp. 17-40.

13 For a particularly illuminating discussion of this see Dennis Soron, "Eco-nomic Fatalism and Popular-Democratic Struggle," Ph.D. dissertation in Social and Political Thought, York University, Toronto, December 2001.

14 On Britain see Eric Hobsbawm, *The Age of Capital, 1848-1875* (New York: Mentor Books, 1975), p. 111; John A. Macdonald, "Speech on the Québec Resolutions" in *Canadian Political Thought*, ed. H. D. Forbes (Toronto: Ox-ford University Press, 1985), p. 85.

15 Wood, p. 229. Wood uses the expression "expulsion of politics" with respect to economic life on p. 44.

16 See Michel Crozier, Samuel P. Huntington and Joji Watanuki, *The Crisis of Democracy: Report on the Governability of Democracies to the Trilateral Commission* (New York: New York University Press, 1975).

17 Thomas Friedman, *The Lexus and the Olive Tree*, as quoted in "Globalisation and its critics," *The Economist*, September 29, 2001.

18 "Capitalism, its critics and its global challenge," *Globe and Mail* editorial, October 28, 2000.

19 Jorge Castaneda, "Latin America's Two Left Wings," *Newsweek*, January 9, 2006.

20 Tomas Kellner, "Power Without Firebombs," *Forbes*, November 27, 2000.

21 Gerard Greenfield, "The Success of Being Dangerous: Resisting Free Trade and Investment Regimes," *Studies in Political Economy* 64 (Spring 2001), p. 86.

22 *Globe and Mail* editorial, October 28, 2000.

23 See, for instance, Barlow and Clarke, pp. 2, 5, 92, 125, 164-7, 169, 172, 180, 186-7, 191, 194, 204-5, 220. To their credit, toward the end of their book (p. 207), Barlow and Clarke do suggest that "To simply call it a civil society movement is not quite enough."

24 See, for instance, Jurgen Habermas, *The Structural Transformation of the Public Sphere*, trans. Thomas Burger (Cambridge, MA: MIT Press, 1991). For some interesting criticisms of the class, gender and racial exclusions characteristic of bourgeois civil society, see essays by Nancy Fraser, Mary P. Ryan and Geoff Eley in *Habermas and the Public Sphere*, ed. Craig Calhoun (Cambridge, MA: MIT Press, 1992).

25 For a discussion of how politeness and refinement became central concerns of the Scottish middle classes in the eighteenth century see David McNally, *Political Economy and the Rise of Capitalism* (Berkeley: University of California Press, 1988), pp. 154-74, 192-208.

26 Some commentators trace their use of "civil society" back to the Italian Marxist, Antonio Gramsci. In so doing, they tend to forget that Gramsci analyzed the institutions of civil society as a key terrain upon which the capitalist class secured its "hegemony" over subordinate classes.

27 Kellner.

28 James Petras, "Latin America: The Resurgence of the Left," *New Left Review* 223 (1997), p. 17.

29 Ashis K. Biswas, "The New Left?" *Outlook India*, December 31, 2001.

30 Soma Wadhwa, "Drown Town," *Outlook India*, December 31, 2001.

31 For detail on the NBA and its struggles see the extensive coverage by Maggie Black in *New Internationalist* 336 (July 2001) or visit the website in solidarity with the movement at www.narmada.org. The novelist Arundhati Roy has published a major essay "The Greater Common Good", in solidarity with the people of the Narmada, included in *The Cost of Living* (New York: Modern Library, 1999).

32 This particular denunciation comes from B. G. Verghese, "A Poetic Licence," *Outlook India*, July 5, 1999. For continuing resistance, see NBA press releases of December 13 and December 25, 2001, available at www.narmada.org.

33 "Open Letter to the President of the World Bank," November 1999.

34 Petras, p. 18.

35 See Jimmy Langman, "Bolivian natives draw hope from the past," *Globe and Mail*, September 4, 2001. For background see Petras, pp. 26-28.

36 Natalia Vinelli, "Interview with Felipe Quispe Huanca, 'We want to govern ourselves,'" *International Viewpoint* 331 (May 2001), p. 27.

37 Alexander Norris, "Patroes and pistoleiros: Brazil's land barons refine tactics," *New Internationalist* 236 (October 1992).

38 See Sue Branford and Jan Rocha, *Cutting the Wire: The Story of the Landless Movement in Brazil* (London: Latin American Bureau, 2002), , p. xii. See also Anders Corr, *No Trespassing: Squatting, Rent Strikes and Land Struggles Worldwide* (Cambridge, MA: South End Press, 1999), p. 146; Petras, p. 24.

39 As quoted in Branford and Rocha, p. 67.

40 Kinnto Lucas, "Here we are all leaders," *International Viewpoint* 333 (July 2001), p. 34.

41 On women in the MST see Branford and Rocha, pp. 258-62. On regional links see Petras, p. 21. And on agricultural practices see Angus Wright and Wendy Wolford, *To Inherit the Earth: The Landless Movement and the Struggle for a New Brazil* (Oakland: Food First Books, 2003), pp. 293–300, and Branford and Rocha, pp. 218-27.

42 Quoted by Branford and Rocha, p. 65; quoted by Lucas, p. 33.

43 "Marcos's Reflections: Just Another Organization or Something Truly New? La Realidad, August, 1996" in *Rebellion in Chiapas: An Historical Reader*, ed. John Womack, Jr. (New York: New Press, 1999), p. 320.

44 Richard Roman and Edur Velasco Arregui, "Worker Insurgency, Rural Revolt, and the Crisis of the Mexican Regime" in *Rising from the Ashes? Labor in the Age of "Global" Capitalism*, eds. Ellen Meiksins Wood, Peter Meiksins and Michael Yates (New York: Monthly Review Press, 1998), p. 132.

45 For details see Womack Jr., pp. 278-339. Some of the relevant documents are available on the Internet at www.ezln.org.

46 Figures on the size of this rally tend to vary from about 80,000 (Womack Jr., p. 332) to 500,000 (Roman and Velasco Arregui, p. 132).

47 Paul Hill and Karen Last, "Masks and Silences: the return of the subcommmandante," *New Socialist*, August/September 1998, p. 12.

48 John Ross, "Rebel Silence," *Now*, July 5-11, 2001. For background see Womack Jr., 304-15.

49 "Marcos and the Ark on the Mountain: San Cristobal, July 15-16, 1998" in Womack Jr., p. 359. On The Other Campaign, see Greg Brosnan, "Rebel leader touring Mexico," Reuters, January 2, 2006, and "Sixth Declaration of the Lacandon Jungle," available at www.narconews.org.

50 See James Petras, "The New Revolutionary Peasantry," *Z Magazine*, October 1998; and Petras, "Latin America," pp. 27, 43.

51 I am drawing heavily upon the excellent account by Juan Adolfo Montenegro, "No road but the struggle," *International Viewpoint* 320 (April 2000), pp. 17-19.

52 Ernesto Herrera, "Ecuador: indigenous mobilization defeats neoliberalism," *International Viewpoint* 329 (March 2001), p. 10.

53 Cesar Ayala, "National Strike in Puerto Rico, *New Socialist*, August/September 1998, pp. 14-15 (reprinted from Green Left Weekly).

54 Richard Lapper, "Anger in the Andes," *Financial Times*, April 26, 2000.

55 Jim Shultz, "Just add water," *This Magazine*, July/August 2000, p. 13.

56 Raquel Gutierrez and Alvaro Garcia Linera, "The rebirth of the multitude," *International Viewpoint* 323 (July-August 2000), pp. 12-13.

57 Gutierrez and Garcia Linera, pp. 13-14.

58 Gutierrez and Garcia Linera, p. 14.

59 Oscar Olivera, *Cochabamba! Water War in Bolivia (Cambridge: South End Press, 2004), p. 125.*

60 In addition to the marvelous book by Oscar Olivera, for excellent analysis of Bolivian events see the ongoing coverage by Jeffrey Webber, including the following: "Left Indigenous Struggles in Bolivia, *Monthly Review*, September 2005; "Bolivia, the Second Gas War: The hopes and limitations of popular forces," *New Socialist* 52, July-August 2005; and "We're not crazy: The days of May and June in Bolivia," *New Socialist* 53, Sept/Oct. 2005.

61 "Bolivia's turmoil has its roots in inequity," *Globe and Mail*, June 11, 2006. In the course of these struggles, they have built some of the most powerful movements of the oppressed – indigenous peoples, the unemployed, poor farmers and urban workers – anywhere in the world.

62 For an excellent treatment of all these events, as well as a balanced assessment of Chavez, see Michael McCaughan, *The Battle of Venezuela* (New York: Seven Stories Press, 2005). See also Carlos Torres and others, *The Unexpected Revolution: The Venezuelan People Confront Neoliberalism* (Toronto: Socialist Project, 2005).

63 Jonah Gindin, " Possible Face of Venezuelan Democracy" in Torres, p. 34.

64 "Venezuela: The Party of Revolution and Socialism – Interview with Stalin Perez Borges," *IV Online magazine: IV 371*, October 2005. On Venezuelan labour today, see Jonah Gindin, "Made in Venezuela: The Struggle to Reinvent Venezuelan Labor," *Monthly Review*, June 2005, pp. 73-87.

65 As quoted by Zachary Lown, "Life in a Stronghold of the 'Bolivarian Revolution'," *Znet*, March 8, 2006. Available at www.zmag.org.

66 Perry Anderson, "The Limits and Possibilities of Trade Union Action," in *The Incompatibles*, eds. Robin Blackburn and Alexander Cockburn (Harmondsworth: Penguin Books, 1967), p. 264.

67 See Richard Hyman, *Industrial Relations: A Marxist Introduction* (London: MacMillan, 1975), p. 195.

68 Steven Greenhouse, "White House and Unions Look for Common Ground," *New York Times,* June 3, 2001.

69 As of this moment (December 2001), the Canadian Labour Congress has not come out against Bush's war, although delegates to the Ontario Federation of Labour Convention in November 2001 did pass an anti-war resolution.

70 As quoted by Richard Hyman, *Marxism and the Sociology of Trade Unionism* (London: Pluto Press, 1971), p. 10.

71 For a good analysis of the origins of the present retreat of American labour see Kim Moody, *An Injury to All: The Decline of American Unionism* (London: Verso Books, 1988). On the Canadian case see Bryan Palmer, *Working Class Experience: Rethinking the History of Canadian Labour, 1880-1991,* 2nd. edn. (Toronto: McClelland and Stewart) Ch. 7.

72 Jeremy Brecher, *Strike!* (San Francisco: Straight Arrow Books, 1972), pp. 206, 208, 209, 211.

73 See David McNally, "Globalization on Trial: Crisis and Class Struggle in East Asia" in *Rising from the Ashes?*, p. 143.

74 Kim Moody, *Workers in a Lean World: Unions in the International Economy* (London: Verso Books, 1997), p. 202.

75 Dan La Botz, *Made in Indonesia: Indonesian Workers since Suharto* (Cambridge, MA: South End Press, 2001), p. 125.

76 La Botz, pp. 214, 237-40.

77 La Botz, p. 245. Gerard Greenfield is quite right to point out the problem of middle-class activists dominating these new unions and to insist upon the necessity of rank and file membership control of these workers' organizations (Greenfield, "Organizing, Protest and Working Class Self-Activity: Reflections on East Asia" in *Socialist Register 2001,* eds. Leo Panitch and Colin Leys [London: Merlin Press, 2000] pp. 241-42). Should these unions be able to make such a transition, the student radicals who initiated them will deserve real credit for their role in helping to build an independent workers' movement. Undoubtedly the biggest problem of internal democracy exists in the SBSI whose president, Muchtar Pakpahan, despite important accomplishments, exerts a monolithic control (see La Botz, pp. 222-23).

78 Miriam Ching Yoon Louie, *Sweatshop Warriors: Immigrant Women Workers Take on the Global Factory* (Cambridge, MA: South End Press, 2001), p. 130.

79 Moody, p. 214; Louie, p. 131.

80 McNally, "Globalization on Trial," p. 142.

81 McNally, p. 151.

82 Louie, p. 135.

83 For the KCTU's anti-war statement (and other documents), see www.kctu.org.

84 See Joel Olatunde Agoi, "Business paralysed as strike in Nigeria continues," *Daily Mail and Guardian* (Johannesburg, South Africa), June 9, 2000;

and "Nigeria – General Strike," anonymous account at www.x21.org/s26/struggles/nigeria.

85 Gabriel Orok and others, "Lagos, Abuja, Kaduna Shut Down," *P. M. News* (Lagos), January 16, 2002; Funmi Komolafe and others, "Fuel: NLC defies FG, Begins Strike Nationwide," *Vanguard* (Lagos), January 16, 2002.

86 For background see Jeremy Seabrook, *In the Cities of the South: Scenes from a Developing World* (London: Verso Books, 1996), pp. 115-26, and reports on the July 2001 strike actions at www.antiimperiallista.com. See also Barry Bearka, "Lives Held Cheap in Bangladesh Sweatshops," *New York Times*, April 15, 2001. On the 2006 strike see "Bangladesh: Garment Workers Unite for Struggle," April 5, 2006 in the online journal *Political Affairs*.

87 Rohini Hensman, "Organizing Against The Odds: Women in India's Informal Sector," *Socialist Register 2001*, pp. 250-51.

88 Moody, pp. 217-18.

89 Trina Leung, "Taming the Tigers," *New Internationalist*, December 2001, p. 17.

90 See Moody, p. 219 and Roman and Velasco Arregui, p. 137.

91 On job losses in the maquiladora zones see Ginger Thompson, "Fallout of U.S. Recession Drifts South Into Mexico," *New York Times*, December 26, 2001. For background on one successful maquiladora union drive see "Kuk Dong Workers Form Union," *Against the Current* 92 (May/June 2001), p. 19. On FSCISP and radical labour in Mexico see Dan La Botz, "Mexico's Labor Movement in Transition," *Monthly Review*, June 2005.

92 Krishna Lalbiharie, "General Strike Rocks Colombia," *Canadian Dimension*, July/August 2001, p. 10.

93 Jon Jeter, "For South Africa's poor, a new power struggle," *Washington Post*, November 6, 2001; Naomi Klein, "It's not enough to bring Soweto to Rosedale," *Globe and Mail*, November 21, 2001; Mark MacKinnon, "Massive protests splinter Mandela's grand coalition," *Globe and Mail*, August 30, 2001. For a sweeping analysis of neoliberalism in post-apartheid South Africa see John Saul, "Cry for the Beloved Country," *Monthly Review*, January 2001.

94 David Lopez and Cynthia Feliciano, "Who Does What? California's Emerging Plural Workforce" in *Organizing Immigrants: The Challenge for Unions in Contemporary California*, ed. Ruth Milkman (Ithaca: Cornell University Press, 2000), pp. 28, 25, 26.

95 See Miriam J. Wells, "Immigration and Unionization in the San Francisco Hotel Industry" in *Organizing Immigrants*, pp. 109-29; and Louie, p. 205.

96 Ruth Milkman and Kent Wong, "Organizing the Wicked City: The 1992 Southern California Drywall Strike" in *Organizing Immigrants*, pp. 169-98.

97 Catherine L. Fisk, Daniel J. B. Mitchell and Christopher L. Erickson, "Union Representation of Immigrant Janitors in Southern California: Economic and Legal Challenges" in *Organizing Immigrants*, pp. 202-6.

98 Robin D. G. Kelley, *YO' mama's disFUNKtional* (Boston: Beacon Press, 1997), p. 131.

99 Steven Greenhouse, "Los Angeles Warms to Labor Unions as Immigrants Look to Escape Poverty," *New York Times*, April 9, 2001.

100 Greenhouse.

101 For background on these centers, see Louie, chs. 5-6; Kelley, pp. 149-50; and John Anner, ed., *Beyond Identity Politics: Emerging Social Justice Movements in Communities of Color* (Cambridge, MA: South End Press, 1996).

102 Louie, p. 203.

103 As quoted in Vanessa Tait, *Poor Workers Unions: Rebuilding Labor from Below* (Cambridge: South End Press, 2005), p. 150.

104 David Bacon, "Unions and the Fight for Multi-Racial Democracy," paper presented to the California Studies Conference, University of California at Berkeley, February 6, 1999.

105 See Tait, Ch. 4 and Sarumathi Jayaraman and Immanuel Ness, eds., *The New Urban Immigrant Workforce: Innovative Models for Labor Organizing* (Armonk, NY: M. E. Sharpe, 2005, Ch. 6.

106 Eric Mann, "Class, Community and Empire: Toward an Anti-Imperialist Strategy for Labor" in *Rising from the Ashes?*, p. 105.

107 Eric Mann, " 'A Race Struggle, A Class Struggle, A Women's Struggle All At Once:' Organizing On the Buses of LA," *Socialist Register 2001*, p. 267.

108 Ahora Now is available by subscription from Labor/Community Strategy Center, The Wiltern Center, 3780 Wiltshire Blvd., Suite 1200, Los Angeles, California 90010.

109 David Bacon, "Bus Strike Ends in Victory for Driver-Rider Alliance," *Labor Notes*, December 2000.

110 See Tait, pp. 145-51.

111 See Louise B. Simmons, *Organizing in Hard Times: Labor and Neighbourhoods in Hartford* (Philadelphia: Temple University Press, 1994; and Kelley, pp. 135-37.

112 See www.ocap.ca.

113 Tait, pp. 199-200]. The resort to stripping union members of their democratic rights is a reminder of just how powerful is the threat that grassroots, multiracial organizing poses to bureaucratic business unionism.

114 Himani Bannerji, *Thinking Through: Essays on Feminism, Marxism, and Anti-Racism* (Toronto: Women's Press, 1995), p. 33.

115 Robin D. G. Kelley, *Race Rebels: Culture, Politics and the Black Working Class* (New York: The Free Press, 1996), pp. 9-10.

116 I have not been able to do any justice to the complex issues of sexual regulation and capitalism in this book. Important studies for making sense of these issues are Gary Kinsman, *The Regulation of Desire: Homo and Hetero Sexualities*, rev. edn. (Montreal: Black Rose Books, 1996); Donald Morton, ed., *The Material Queer: A LesBiGay Cultural Studies Reader* (Boulder: Westview Press, 1996); and Rosemary Hennessy, *Profit and Pleasure: Sexual Identities in Late Capitalism* (New York: Routledge, 2000).

117 Daniel Singer, *Whose Millennium? Theirs or Ours?* (New York: Monthly Review Press, 1999), pp. 148-49.

7. Freedom Song: Liberation and Anti-Capitalism

> Capitalism is a system where the robbers are free and they are admired and used as examples.
>
> – Zapatista Army of National Liberation, "Sixth Declaration of the Selva Lacandona"

> Overthrow capitalism – and replace it with something nicer!
>
> – Slogan on May Day 2001 banner, London, England

After several decades of having been regularly pronounced dead, anti-capitalism is back. Nowhere is this more true than in Latin America, the site of the most momentous struggles against neoliberalism. In Bolivia and Venezuela in particular, social movements are explicitly formulating their struggles in opposition to capitalism. And in Mexico, the Zapatista movement, which had avoided naming capitalism as the problem in its early declarations, devoted pages of its 2005 manifesto to criticizing capitalism as a social system. Even in the Global North, anti-capitalism has come out of the closet. *The Economist* magazine, a major journal of ruling class opinion, repeatedly describes global justice activists as "anti-capitalists," a term that has found its way into other areas of the mainstream media.[1] Recognizing the growing popularity of anti-capitalist attitudes and radical protest politics, even corporations have rushed to cash in.

A year and a half after the Seattle protests, Gap stores un-
veiled a new promotional display that featured faded black jeans
hanging in front of a red banner with the words "independence,"
"freedom" and "we the people" scrawled across the display
window in fake black spray paint. A few months later, Rockstar
Games released a video game for Sony PlayStation 2 called "State
of Emergency." Players of this game can march down a city street
and hurl a rocket or brick into a storefront window or punch a
riot cop – all to a music beat.[2] Even more outlandish, Volkswa-
gen ran a newspaper ad that pictured its 1999 Passat beneath the
headline, "Defies the laws of capitalism." Wall Street brokerage
houses also got in on the action. One ran a TV ad depicting common people smashing their way into the stock exchange, shatter-
ing windows whose shards of glass rained down on the traders,
while a worldbeat tune played in the background. The audience
was then invited to buy stocks through Datek, an online trading
company.[3]

Clearly, the moment has arrived when we need to clarify the
meaning of authentic anti-capitalism. We now confront the risk
that, rather than a meaningful political alternative for large numbers of people, anti-capitalism, particularly in the North, might
be turned into a set of attractive images, a sort of radical chic, for
the promotion of commodities.

In Search of Alternatives

The challenge, therefore, is to explore the meaning of anti-
capitalism not as image or slogan, but as a meaningful political
alternative. That challenge arises directly out of the upsurge of
movements against neoliberalism. After all, the creativity and dynamism displayed thus far by the mass social justice movements
is nothing short of breathtaking. In the course of a few years, the
movement has shattered the silence imposed by the "neoliberal
consensus," won significant victories in countries like Bolivia and
Ecuador, and proclaimed publicly that another world is possible.

337

For the first time in a quarter century, it is possible to seriously envision a global movement intent on a post-capitalist future for humankind.

Success inevitably creates new challenges, however, especially for radical mass movements. Not only does the ruling class learn from its setbacks but, in addition, the movement's supporters expand their hopes and expectations. Consequently, the question of how to shift from the defensive - simply trying to block what the other side is doing - to the offensive - where we organize to construct a different kind of future - cannot be avoided. Moreover, these two stances, the defensive and the offensive, are integrally connected: where we would like to go decisively shapes the sort of movement-building strategies we ought to employ.

As the examples of Bolivia, Venezuela and Nigeria show, the ruling class does not give up at its first setback. It regroups, marshals its forces, attempts to weaken the opposition, and relaunches its offensive. Yet, social movements cannot keep trying to fight the same battle over and over. At some point, they must be capable of mobilizing for larger goals. Failing that, to cite Daniel Singer, there is a danger that "The protesters win a battle and, then, lacking objectives, are unable to launch a counteroffensive."[4] In the longer term, that is a formula for demoralization and sapped energies – exactly what the other side seeks, if it can't get repression to do the job.

That is what makes Singer's reminder of the need to develop "an alternative project, the vision of a different society" so crucial.[5] Of course, addressing that question will necessarily bring debates to the fore. And this is as it should be. Without extended discussion and debate, social movements cannot develop into radical mass movements. There can be no real transformation from below unless huge numbers of people work together, reflect on their successes and failures, and debate how to move forward together. As in the life of individuals, social movement growth comes through active discovery, not passive reception. Genuine growth is always dialogical – it requires engagement in a dynamic, developing, and open-ended dialogue. Some who feel "owner-ship" over the movements may perceive this as a threat. But real democracy comes from below, or not at all. It requires opening up the political space for a multiplicity of voices to be heard and to shape the movement.

Among other things, this means promoting the discussion on alternatives to capitalism. As I argue below, this requires exploring socialism from below, radical democracy and the de-commodification of life and labour. Much of the literature of the movement evades these topics, particularly in the North. The authors of an important analysis of the anti-globalization move-ment, for instance, skirt just such issues when, without clarification or elaboration, they recommend "struggle to restrain or replace capitalism."[6] Yet, there is literally a world of difference between the two options: if the best we can do is to restrain capitalism, then another world, a world organized to satisfy human needs not corporate profit, is clearly not possible.

If another world is to be possible, we will need an analysis and a strategy informed by anti-capitalism. To say this is not to invite abstract speculation divorced from the actual struggles of real people. Certainly, anti-capitalism has sometimes had those characteristics, subsisting as the esoteric belief system of marginal leftist groups who appear to share nothing in common with the vast majority of people. But today, anti-capitalism has started to move away from the margins, today it has the potential to become a living social cause. This is especially true in parts of the South, where mass movements are raising powerful challenges to world capitalism, but it is also true within the social justice movements in parts of the North, as mass struggles in France, or movements of immigrant workers in the US remind us. A meaningful anti-capitalism must start from the terrain of these very real and de-termined movements. Indeed, starting here is the best antidote to any tendencies for anti-capitalism to become an abstract dogma detached from real movements.

In this regard, the approach outlined by the young Karl Marx is highly instructive. Taking issue with the propensity of his philosophical colleagues to concoct purely intellectual recipes for social reform, Marx countered, "we do not anticipate the world with our dogmas but instead attempt to discover the new world through the critique of the old." Indeed, insisted Marx, this is the only way to avoid elitism. "Hitherto philosophers have left the keys to all riddles lying in their desks, and the stupid uninitiated world had only to wait around for the roasted pigeons of absolute science to fly into its open mouth." But, he continued, "I am ... not in favour of our hoisting a dogmatic banner." However, the avoidance of dogmatic banners does not prevent one from engaging in political activity and criticism. It means that, in doing so, one should not "confront the world with new doctrinaire principles and proclaim: Here is the truth, on your knees before it!" A critical, non-dogmatic approach proceeds with the following injunction:

> ... we shall develop for the world new principles from the existing principles of the world. We shall not say: Abandon your struggles, they are mere folly; let us provide you with the true campaign-slogans. Instead we shall simply show the world why it is struggling ... The reform of consciousness consists entirely in making the world aware of its own consciousness ...[7]

Authentic anti-capitalism thus finds the principles of a new world in the actual movements of the present, it assists those in struggle in clarifying the nature of the system they resist and the alternatives they seek. To "show the world why it is struggling" requires that anti-capitalists be part of the radical struggles of the day (not armchair commentators) while making it a priority to contribute to the movement's self-clarification of goals and objectives.

De-Commodifying Human Life

If there is one thing that links together the wide range of social justice struggles occurring around the globe, it is opposition to commodification. When the landless in Brazil seize land, the urban poor in LA demand better bus service, indigenous people in India block roads to stop a giant dam, workers in Bolivia rally to prevent privatization of water, the unemployed in Argentina block highways and demand public spending to create jobs – in all these struggles and more, people are affirming that the economy should be oriented to satisfying human needs, not governed by private profit-making.

Underlying such demands is a promising critique of commodification that is developing within the anti-globalization movement. In *Global Showdown*, for instance, Barlow and Clarke argue that "There are certain goods and services that should not be traded, commodified, patented, or privatized in the global economy."[8] These include: pernicious goods, such as toxic waste; life building blocks, such as air, water and genes; inheritance goods like animals, plants and seeds; and democratic rights, including food, health care and education. This is an impressive list, identifying significant areas of social-economic life that should be treated as parts of the global commons and protected from commodification. There is, however, a glaring absence here, one whose social implications are enormous: human labour.[9]

As we have seen, a society that commodifies human labour – turning it into a good that can be bought and sold like any other – reduces our creative energies and capacities to mere factors of production. Alienation, disempowerment and dilution of democracy are inherent in such an arrangement. Moreover, by depriving workers of ownership and control of the means of work, a capitalist market system allows the owning class to exploit the alienated labour of wage earners.

For all these reasons, a society that seeks to overcome commodification must be committed to *de-commodifying* human labour, to eliminating its status as an article for purchase and sale. But this entails a revolution in the nature of work and the relations of ownership and control, a radical overturning of class relationships. It means overcoming the separation of producers from the means of labour – by establishing workers' control of the work process and communal ownership of the instruments of work. And this requires that social production – the production of the goods and services desired by the community – be carried out, in Marx's words, by "an association of free people, working with the means of production in common, and expending their many different forms of labour-power in full self-awareness as one single social labour force."[10] Three principles are enunciated here: workers' self-management ("free association"), communal ownership, and social coordination of production. Let us spend a moment on each.

The principle of workers' self-management – democratic control by workers over the organization of work and the conditions in which they produce – is central to any genuine anti-capitalism. Without this element of workplace democracy, labour cannot be dis-alienated and restored to its status as a form of creative human activity. Workers' self-management requires that workers regularly assemble, debate and discuss the organization of the production process (be it of goods or services) and elect delegates (who can be recalled or removed by the majority at a moment's notice) to coordinate specialized tasks.

Workers' self-management is impossible, of course, in a system of privatized ownership of the instruments and places of work. So long as work is organized on the basis of maximizing profits for private owners, the labourers will not be able to direct the work process according to their own needs and priorities. The pre-capitalist principle of the commons – of economic resources that belong to the community as a whole – thus needs to be revived in a post-capitalist context. Just as vast expanses of lands, rivers and forests once belonged to communities, who collectively regulated their use, the same ought to be true of ownership of lands, natural resources, utilities, factories, offices and the like. It is only on a foundation of communal ownership that workers, freed from the imperatives of profit maximization, will have the genuine liberty to manage their working lives.

We come, finally, to the principle of social coordination of economic life, or what is sometimes referred to as democratic social planning. The central idea here is that, rather than being geared to maximizing private profit, production should begin with a democratic and participatory exercise designed to establish the priority needs of people – for food, housing, electricity, water, health care education, leisure, cultural goods (such as books, music, theatre), child care, public transportation and so on. On the basis of this sort of participatory planning exercise, social-economic information would be gathered to guide and inform decisions about the kinds of work to be done and the distribution of social resources. The flow of goods and services between workplaces and communities would thus be coordinated by means of an economic framework that had been arrived at democratically. We should note here that this kind of participatory social planning has nothing in common with the "command economy" approach pioneered in the former Soviet Union, where state bureaucrats attempted to centrally direct production without the slightest pretense of worker and citizen involvement. Rather than overcoming alienated labour, the Russian model recreated it.[11]

De-commodifying economic life can only mean democratizing it. It means breaking down the fences that prohibit the will of the majority from intruding upon economic-property arrangements. A society that has moved beyond commodification is one that has embraced the most thoroughgoing radical democracy in all spheres of social life.

"Socialism for the 21st Century"? Marxism, Anarchism and Socialism from Below

Historically, the sort of alternative to capitalism I have been describing has gone by the name of socialism. The word itself first emerged in Britain and France in the late 1820s to denote the movement dedicated to solving the "social problem" of mass poverty. By the 1840s, socialism was becoming the term for a future society based on social principles of human cooperation.[12]

The rise of Stalin's dictatorship in Russia in the 1920s, on the ashes of the hopeful revolution of 1917, did inestimable damage to the idea of socialism (and its companion, communism). For many people, socialism came to mean a bureaucratic one-party state that trampled on basic civil rights. With a dictatorial, militarized, police-state society masquerading as "socialism," it is little wonder that anti-capitalist alternatives fell on hard times.

While there were always alternative socialist traditions vehemently opposed to Stalinism, they too were damaged by the association of the Russian model with socialism. This was especially true when the Stalinist system collapsed in Eastern Europe at the end of the 1980s, widely cited as evidence socialism was dead. As *The Economist* magazine perceptively noted, "However much the left in the West disavowed or even despised Soviet communism," it "was humiliated by association, found its values deeply suspect, and suffered a monumental crisis of confidence."[13]

Salivating at the opportunity to impose its will while the left seemed down for the count, western capitalism unleashed its complete agenda – the global commodification model promoted by the WTO, IMF and World Bank. And the realities of that agenda – structural adjustment for the South, accelerated degradation of the environment, dismantling of social programs, and escalating poverty – produced the backlash that put anti-capitalism back on the political agenda.

Yet, as we have seen, many leftists, wary of an association with anti-capitalism, have chosen to restrict themselves to criticizing neoliberalism. Others, like the designer of the banner whose slogan introduces this chapter, have humourously called for replacing capitalism with "something nicer" – without any attempt to name what that might be. That "something nicer" needs a name. Social movements will not develop if they refuse to name and define alternative possibilities. For that reason, it is vitally important to recover and renew the socialist traditions that are farthest from Stalinism, those socialisms that have made human liberty, freedom, self-government and radical democracy their defining values. If socialism is to have a future, it will be because these variants have been able to popularize their vision of a democratic, cooperative and non-oppressive alternative to capitalism.

In much of North America and parts of Europe, although less typically in the South, many young activists searching for a radical alternative have turned to anarchism.[14] To some extent, the attractions of anarchism have to do with the obvious failings of the traditional lefts that have made their peace with the system. More than this, some anarchist groups have brought a dynamism, energy and creativity that have been sorely lacking in protest politics. Yet, defining anarchism itself is no easy matter. When *Newsweek* magazine attempted to map "the new anarchism" after the 1999 Seattle protests, its list ranged from a major social critic like Noam Chomsky to the technophobic Unabomber, Ted Kaczynski.[15] It is certainly the case that anarchism contains a wide number of strains and variants – from left-wing social anarchism which, as Chomsky notes, overlaps with "radical Marxism," to right-wing versions of anarcho-capitalism which are really extreme forms of liberal individualism.[16] Like socialism, to which I return in a moment, anarchism might be said to have two main traditions. Murray Bookchin, perhaps the most widely-read American writer associated with anarchism, after Chomsky, puts it this way:

> At one extreme of anarchism is a liberal ideology that focuses overwhelmingly on the abstract individual (often drawing on bourgeois ideologies) ... This anarchism celebrates the notion of liberty from rather

> than a fleshed out notion of freedom for. At the other
> end of the anarchist spectrum is a revolutionary lib-
> ertarian socialism that seeks to create a free society,
> in which humanity as a whole – and hence the indi-
> vidual as well – enjoys the advantages of free political
> and economic institutions.[17]

Anarchism is not unique in this regard. Hal Draper pointed out in a pioneering essay thirty-five years ago that socialism also has "two souls." One, which he called *socialism from above*, is elitist to the core, looking to a state bureaucracy to reengineer society from the top. The other strain, *socialism from below*, holds that "socialism can only be achieved through the self-emancipation of activized masses in motion, reaching out for freedom with their own hands, mobilized 'from below' in a struggle to take charge of their own destiny as actors (not merely subjects) on the stage of history."[18]

This conception of socialism from below can serve as a useful touchstone for anti-capitalists today. Too often, past conflicts between various Marxist and anarchist currents have become obstacles in the here-and-now to sorting out real areas of agreement and divergence and to devising ways of working together in radical movements. Simple labels do not help in these regards, since each current is so heterogeneous. It is certainly true that some self-styled "Marxists" have been state-worshipping elitists, just as it is true that there have been hopelessly individualistic "anarchists" hostile to socialism and collective action and organization. But it is equally true that important Marxist figures and groups have been dedicated to an emancipatory socialism from below, just as significant anarchist movements have rejected bourgeois individualism in favour of socialist forms of liberty and action. While it is easy to construct caricatures of each position, this does little to enhance political understanding, solidarity, or social activism. Moreover, anarchists and Marxists have frequently found themselves on the same side of important struggles, working together in the same movements.[19]

For all these reasons, it may be more helpful to try to define a common political vision – such as socialism from below or libertarian socialism – as a point of reference, rather than starting from un-helpfully loose labels such as "anarchist" or "Marxist." Given its emphasis on promoting the self-emancipation of the majority and the establishment of radically democratic control over society, economy and political life, the use of socialism from below as a reference point may enable activists from disparate traditions to explore their common ground.[20]

While Draper locates the essence of socialism from below in Marx's famous statement that "the emancipation of the working classes must be conquered by the working classes themselves," it is instructive that in his *ABC of Anarchism*, Alexander Berkman also defines the "emancipation of the workers ... by the workers themselves" as a central principle.[21] Furthermore, in an admirable spirit of solidarity and fair-mindedness, Berkman proclaims the shared commitments of Marxism and anarchism to a society without classes or a state: "The greatest teachers of socialism – Karl Marx and Friedrich Engels – had taught ... that anarchism would come from socialism," he writes.[22] Along similar lines, Daniel Guerin, author of several major works on anarchism, proposes that "the constructive ideas of anarchism ... may ... contribute to enriching Marxism."[23] In the same spirit, Murray Bookchin has recently heaped praise on Marx's *Communist Manifesto* and *Capital* while urging that Marxists and social anarchists "incorporate the insights of both forms of socialism and go beyond them."[24]

In so doing, Bookchin was implicitly acknowledging what many anarchists recognize: that it is theorists working in the Marxist tradition who have done most to map the political economy of capitalism and to develop a systematic account of imperialism. These are indispensable assets for any movement that seeks to radically change the world. Moreover, activists of the Marxist left often have a greater depth of experience when it comes to building progressive currents in the trade unions or creating mass organizations that oppose imperialist war or fight for women's right to choose. At the same time, many Marxists need to heed the anarchist caution about the dangers of bureaucratic and anti-democratic forms of organization within the Left.

After Marx's death in 1883, the strongest and clearest commitments to revolutionary democracy and socialism from below within the Marxist tradition are found in the life and works of Rosa Luxemburg, who left Poland as a teenager to become the outstanding leader of the radical left in the German socialist movement during the first two decades of the twentieth century.[25] In a series of writings and speeches, particularly those penned during the revolutionary events of 1918-19 in Germany (in the course of which she was murdered), Luxemburg beautifully summarized the commitments of socialism from below:

> The socialist revolution is the first which is in the interests of the great majority and can be brought to victory only by the great majority of the working people themselves.

> The mass of the working class must … personally, by its own activity bring socialism step by step to life.

> The essence of socialist society consists in the fact that the great laboring mass ceases to be a dominated mass, but rather, makes the entire economic and political life its own life and gives that life a conscious, free and autonomous direction.[26]

Elsewhere, she explicitly rejected the idea that a government could create socialism from the top, insisting on the necessity for socialism to be created from below, by the masses:

> Socialism will not and cannot be created by decrees; nor can it be created by any government, however socialistic. Socialism must be created by the masses, by every proletarian. Where the chains of capitalism are forged, there they must be broken. Only that is socialism, and only thus can socialism be created.[27]

Consistent with this, Luxemburg stressed that democracy must always, at every moment, be the lifeblood of the socialist project. While strongly supporting the revolution in Russia in 1917, she worried that the leaders of the Bolshevik Party were prepared to override socialist democracy, warning that,

> socialist democracy is not something which begins only in the promised land only after the foundations of the socialist economy are created; it does not come as some sort of Christmas present for the worthy people who, in the interim, have loyally supported a handful of socialist dictators. Socialist democracy begins simultaneously with the beginnings of the destruction of class rule and the construction of socialism.[28]

Socialism from Below: Radical Democracy for the Age of Globalization

Of course, the radical traditions of socialism from below would be of merely historical interest were they incapable of being revived and developed as part of living movements in the present and the future. Fortunately, there is every reason to think that, in addition to offering a sharp contrast with bureaucratic and authoritarian socialist traditions, socialism from below speaks directly to the forms of self-organization that many radical movements against globalization are devising today.

In the case of the Landless Workers Movement (MST) in Brazil, for instance, groups that seize lands are democratically self-organized. In each locale, a network of between five and twenty families forms a self-governing base community that elects delegates who cooperate with other base communities on issues ranging from firewood to education. As a rule, a general assembly is convened among all the communities in an area every two or three months, and this constitutes the highest decision-making body. Every individual takes some kind of larger social-political responsibility according to the principle that "here we are all leaders."[29]

Something quite similar happened in poor, working class communities in parts of Argentina in 2001. The upsurge of popular struggles at the time was spearheaded by the Unemployed Workers Movement (MTD), a grassroots movement independent of the unions and political parties. While these movements, known as *piqueteros*, or picketers, have fractured in the last few years, with some becoming hooked into the state, at their height many of them practiced inspiring forms of radical democracy. As James Petras explained:

> The MTD is organized with a very decentralized structure. Each municipality has its own organization based on the barrios [neighbourhoods] within its frontiers. Within a barrio, multi-block areas have their informal leaders and activists. Each municipality is organized by its general assembly where all members participate. Policy is decided in the assembly; the demands and organization of the blockades are decided collectively in assembly... Hundreds and even thousands of women, men, and children participate in the blockage, setting up tents and soup kitchens at the side of the road... If the government decides to negotiate, the movement demands that negotiations take place with all the piqueteros [picketers] at the blockage. Decisions are made at the site of the action by the collective assembly.[30]

During the high points of struggle in 2001-2, the MTD was sometimes able to extend participatory democracy beyond mass actions into the day-to-day life of communities. Indeed, in some working class communities at the time, the movement helped create "quasi-liberated zones, where the power of mobilization neutralizes or is superior to that of local officials." New forms of popular democracy – radical, participatory and direct – were thus generated in the course of the struggle against neoliberalism. While the movement was unable to sustain these levels of popular mobilization, the most militant have continued to practice innovative forms of mass politics.

What these examples show is that the most effective movements against globalization are those that practice radical democracy. When the people of Cochabamba, Bolivia were in the thick of the water wars, they held as many as five municipal assemblies in the course of a week, one of them bringing out 100,000 people, in order to decide the direction and methods of the struggle.[31] What we witness in these cases is the development of new forms of direct democracy as the means of waging struggle and organizing communities of the oppressed against global capital. The commitments of socialism from below to self-emancipation and radical democracy converge powerfully with these exciting developments, indicating that, far from a relic of the past, radical socialist democracy may become a driving force in the struggle for another world.

Ten Guiding Principles for Anti-Capitalist Politics

Let us now try to enunciate some of the guiding principles for twenty-first century anti-capitalism that can be derived from the struggles of the past and the present. Ten principles stand out as particularly important:

1. Opposition to gender, sexual and racial oppression as well as economic exploitation

As we have seen, not only is capitalist domination organized through patterns of gender and racial domination, but women workers, indigenous peoples and people of colour have been playing leading roles in struggles for global justice. Genuine liberation cannot be provided by a narrow "class" politics that evades these issues; it requires the self-emancipation of women, sexual minorities, and racially-oppressed peoples. Yet, class politics are crucial if capitalism is to be challenged. Consequently, we need an anti-racist, feminist class politics, i.e., one that makes feminism and anti-racism central building blocks of its struggle for full human emancipation.

2. Radical democracy and popular power

Anti-capitalism requires the extension of democracy into the economic sphere and the overcoming of passive, representative "democracy" by activist, direct democracy. Radical democracy – one that goes to and grows from the roots of social life – will once again rest upon rule of the poor. And this means all of the world's poor, organized by means of new forms of self-government in workplaces and communities. A liberated society will promote the replacement of bureaucratic administration by forms of "free association" of self-governing peoples.

3. Opposition to imperialism and war, support of self-determination for oppressed peoples

If we are to have a just and peaceful world, this will entail an end to the domination of most of the world's peoples by elites from a handful of imperialist nations. This will necessarily require cancellation of international debts and the construction of cooperative programs for world social development. It will also mean disarmament and support for the rights of all oppressed peoples – indigenous peoples and dominated nations – to self-determination, to choosing for themselves the forms of self-government that address their needs.

4. Communal ownership of social-economic resources

Since there can be no movement beyond capitalism so long as we have private ownership of the world's economic resources, human liberation will entail new forms of communal ownership. Common ownership refers, of course, not to items for personal use, but to social control over the land, water, resources, technologies, infrastructure and collective knowledge of human kind. These should be utilized for the good of the human community, not private capitalists.

5. Production for need based on workers' control and democratic social coordination

The dis-alienation of labour requires workers' control and self-management of the work process. At the same time, the satisfaction of human needs necessitates a democratic and participatory process by which social priorities can be established and coordination organized across workplaces and communities. Democracy at work and in creating a coordinating framework for social production are essential elements of an improved form of social life.

6. Social ecology

A rationally organized society will treat the natural environment as a vital and integral part of the bio-cultural lifeworld. Forms of production should be compatible with biodiversity (maintaining the diversity of forms of life) and sustainability. A rational agriculture which does not deplete and degrade the soil and water, the development of environmentally sound sources of energy, and a commitment to safe, environment-friendly technologies ought to be fundamental social goals.[32]

7. Internationalism

An emancipatory society can only exist if people have overcome the horizons of nationalism and embraced their common humanity. Localism and nationalism cannot be the ethos of liberated peoples. Radical movements ought to promote an internationalist consciousness and practical programs designed to eliminate global inequalities and move toward an egalitarian world order. At the same time, unlike contemporary globalization, genuine internationalism will celebrate the rich diversity of cultural experiences that comprise the global human struggle for freedom and provide space for their self-expression.[33]

8. A culture of freedom

Some past radical theories and movements have seen human liberation in narrowly economic terms. As crucial as it is to ensure the satisfaction of all basic human needs, human life also involves imagination, play, culture, sexuality, art, music, architecture, and so on. A culture of liberation must be devoted to the free development and free expression of human creative energies, it must see emancipation as involving new forms of non-authoritarian relations in all spheres.[34]

9. Constructive involvement in all genuine struggles against oppression

To be a meaningful and living movement, anti-capitalism cannot be a dogma preached by esoteric groups. Instead, it must be a dynamic and developing current within real movements. Anti-capitalists have a responsibility to show the relevance of radical democracy, opposition to all forms of oppression and self-organization from below as principles that can make current struggles against neoliberalism and capitalism more powerful and effective. This means demonstrating the power of direct action, mass mobilization and participatory democracy, and it requires a commitment to constructive involvement in all genuine movements against oppression.

10. Self-emancipation and democratic mass movements

Since a liberated society can only be achieved through the self-emancipation of the oppressed and exploited, the struggle for a new society will require the creation of democratically organized mass movements in which people develop their capacities to change and remake the world. Liberation cannot be achieved *for* people by military or political elites; it can only be conquered from below, by people claiming their freedom for themselves.

Building Movements for Global Liberation

It follows from everything above that truly emancipatory social movements need to be based upon politics of direct action, mass mobilization and participatory democracy. All three of these elements are indispensable and interrelated.

Direct action

At the heart of the concept of direct action is the notion that, in order to radically change the world, oppressed people need to change themselves too. From being dominated masses who feel powerless to affect the world, they need to begin experiencing themselves as makers of history, as people capable of understanding and changing the world. For the young Marx, "this coincidence of the changing of circumstances and ... self-changing" is the very essence of "revolutionary practice."[35] This sort of self-transformation is no purely intellectual process but, rather, a fundamentally experiential one. It requires that oppressed people begin to *feel* the difference they can make – by being part of a militant strike, a highway blockade, a land occupation, actions that make a real impact on events.

The direct action approach is based upon a politics of *self-activity*. Steering away from appeals to politicians, bureaucrats or other elites to "help" the downtrodden by doing something for them, it demands and mobilizes, encouraging working people and the poor to act for themselves. While it may occasionally involve electoral participation, it sees this form of politics as radically inferior to and subordinate to building militant direct actions – rallies, pickets, demonstration, strikes, occupations.[36]

Mass mobilization

Some who profess direct action nonetheless fall into elitist politics that do little to build mass action. Believing that the struggle to change the world is reliant on the heroic resistance of tiny minorities in conflict with police and the state, these groups tend toward *substitutionism* – the idea that the action of an elite few can substitute for struggles by masses of people to change the world.

Change in the direction of radical democracy, in the direction of active and effective rule of the majority, requires that people begin to sense their *collective* power to change the world. And this is not possible if the majority are mere spectators observing the actions of a radical elite. Without mass action and mobilizations in which thousands, even millions, of people participate, revolutionary change from below cannot occur, nor can the illusion that change only comes from above be shattered. Mass mobilization and collective self-activity are indispensable to the self-transformations that make a new society possible. Only under such circumstances can people truly begin to see, as a radical motto from the French Revolution of 1789 put it, that

> The great seem great to us
>
> Only because we are on our knees
>
> – Let us rise![37]

The forms of direct action that are truly emancipatory, therefore, are mass direct actions. Only in these can we discern the germs of a new form of democracy.

Participatory democracy

If they are to create the preconditions for another world, mass social movements must be laboratories of direct democracy. It is not enough that they should mobilize masses of people, though this is vital. Equally crucial, they need to be controlled from below, through democratic structures that enable grassroots activists to become strategists and tacticians of the movement.

The approach used by the *piqueteros* in Argentina in 2001-2 offers a model. Not only was the group organized democratically in working class communities, but participants made all key decisions openly and democratically in the heat of the action. If the government wanted to negotiate in response to a highway block-ade, the movement's decisions were made by the participants. While some activists will have more experience or training in certain areas of the movement's work, democratic mass organizations need to operate on the principle that, as members of the Landless Workers Movement put it, "here we are all leaders."[38]

* * *

Where mass movements succeed at developing all three of these components of radical organizing, we can say with confidence that the germs of a new world are taking shape within the struggle against the old.

Changing the World: The Problems of Elections, the State and "Taking Power"

Once we set out to radically change the world, a number of strategic issues arise that have bedeviled progressive movements for 150 years. Is society to be transformed through elections? By seizing the state? Or by creating a sort of "anti-power," to use the term popularized by John Holloway in his book *Change the World Without Taking Power?* The left's experiences with electoral politics provide a good point of entry into these problems.

Recent developments in Latin America have generated a renewed interest in electoral politics, as a series of governments that pledge opposition to neoliberalism have been voted into office. In 2002, former metalworker, Ignacio (Lula) Da Silva was elected president of Brazil on the Workers' Party (PT) ticket. The following year, Nestor Kirchner won Argentina's presidency and Lucio Guiterrez, backed by indigenous movements, became Ecuador's head of state. Then in late 2005, Evo Morales of the Movement Toward Socialism (MAS) swept the Bolivian elections to become the first indigenous president in the history of Latin America. And through this period, Hugo Chavez won elections and a referendum to consolidate his hold on the presidency of Venezuela.

All these developments have created a renewed excitement about electoral politics in much of Latin America, producing much higher voter turnouts in a number of countries. Yet, these electoral developments are highly ambiguous. While electoral support for Chavez in Venezuela and Morales in Bolivia has, for the moment at least, opened important spaces for social struggle, the elections of Lula in Brazil and Guiterez in Ecuador have been disastrous for radical movements, as we shall see. To make sense of these developments, we need first to look at electoral politics and the modern state.

The most important point to grasp is one made by Rosa Luxemburg roughly one hundred years ago: whoever wins an election in capitalist society attains political *office, not power*. After all, power in modern society is embedded in property – in the ownership of the means of production, distribution and exchange – and the authority it confers. This power, represented by money, involves control over others, specifically over the labour and life-activity of those who comprise the working class.

Because capitalism hives off the economy as a private sphere outside the public realm of government and politics, elections to political office leave the structure of wealth and social power intact. This is why we need to distinguish office from power. Furthermore, should a government of the left try to significantly change that structure, it will be overthrown or economically crippled. The first was the fate of Socialist Party President Salvador Allende of Chile, when a 1973 coup organized by the Chilean military and the American CIA resulted in his death and the murder of about 20,000 others. Alternatively, big business can go on an "investment strike" in the face of government policies they dislike, resulting in layoffs, mounting unemployment and reduced government revenues. This was the treatment that French President Francois Mitterand received in the early 1980s for merely trying to introduce a modest package of social and economic reforms. As the economy reeled, Mitterand did a quick U-turn and never again challenged the designs of the capitalist class; indeed he simply adopted the basic economic program of the right. Capital had shown him where true power lies in this society: in control of the economy, not political office.

Fortunately for ruling classes, the *reformist* or social democratic parties of the world – like Labour in Britain, the New Democrats in Canada, the Socialist Party in France – do not need a lot of pressure to do capital's bidding. These professional, bureaucratic political parties long ago made their peace with capitalism. While many of the rank and file members aspire to real change, their professionalized leaderships (MPs, labour leaders, lawyers and political consultants) form part of the political elites of late capitalism, even if they do not wield the same sort of power as bankers and industrialists. These people identify with the state structures of capitalism and consider a challenge to those structures to be frightening anarchy. When striking rail workers invaded Canada's parliament buildings in 1973, for instance, it was the leader of Canada's social democrats, David Lewis of the NDP, who was dispatched to scold them and ask them to leave. In fact, whenever capitalism confronts a real challenge, such as a mass strike movement of millions that paralyzes the economy and begins to reorder social relations, social democrats invariably rush to defend and protect capitalism and its state. The classic case was the murder of Rosa Luxemburg and her comrade Karl Liebknecht by the social democrats in Germany in 1919, when that country was in the throes of a popular revolution. So frightened by the specter of a real workers' revolution were the social democrats, that they became the guard dogs of the old order. Indeed, the reformist parties of social democracy are so integrated into capitalism that it truly comes easy for British Labour's Tony Blair to line up with George Bush and his war machine, as it does for social democratic governments everywhere to cut spending on health, education, or welfare.[39]

The great flaw of reformism is its belief that society can be radically transformed by changing governments while leaving the basic institutions and property relations of capitalism intact. The reality, however, is that rather than capturing power when they are elected, reformist parties are instead *captured by* power. They are integrated into a bureaucratic and anti-democratic system of ruling that obeys the imperatives of capital. This machinery of capitalist power remakes them in its own image. Whatever their original intent, reformist politicians quickly become servants of capital. "Instead of taking a stand for the establishment of a new society," wrote Rosa Luxemburg, the reformist takes " a stand for the surface modification of the old society."[40]

Once we understand reformism in these terms, then the outlandishly right-wing character of Lula's government in Brazil comes as less of a surprise. Still, it is not hard to see why many were shocked. After all, the Workers Party (PT) of Brazil emerged out of heroic struggles of factory workers against a military dictatorship. Lula himself was a metalworker who had faced repression by employers and the state. The PT also declared itself for socialism and allied with the dynamic Landless Workers Movement (MST). Yet, since forming the government with Lula as President in 2002, the PT's record has been appalling. Consider the following:

- Lula appointed a past president of a major US investment bank as had of Brazil's central bank;
- He made the millionaire chairman of an agricultural company the head of the Trade and Development Ministry;
- He hugged US President George W. Bush during the 2005 Summit of the Americas and has publicly criticized Venezuelan leader Hugo Chavez for his anti-US policies;
- He cut the minimum wage and slashed funding to food, education and social security programs;
- He pursued a privatization policy that included selling off four state banks;

- Rather than create 10 million new jobs, as he promised, Lula oversaw the loss of one million jobs;
- His government also cut corporate taxes and introduced new tax breaks for foreign investors;
- At the same time, it cut pensions for public employees;
- Lula also eliminated price controls on thousands of medicines and pharmaceutical products.[41]

While these policies have bewildered many, they obey *the logic of electoralism* at work in capitalist society. To succeed in the electoral arena, parties generally need favourable coverage from mass media controlled by wealthy members of the capitalist class. And such coverage is obtained by behaving "responsibly," by showing that one's party is no threat to the status quo. Similarly, reformist parties seek to raise millions of dollars for their advertising campaigns, just as they hope not to alienate the elites and the military. As a result, the logic of electoralism requires that they dilute their policies – the PT, for instance, dropped all talk of socialism and anti-imperialism during the 2002 campaign. The same logic also pressures them to offer public reassurance that they will not be a threat to the capitalist class. In the Brazilian case, Lula did this by signing a pact with the IMF promising to cut public spending, preserve privatization and so on.[42] As the PT became more and more a tool of the Brazilian ruling class, it began to ape all the corrupt habits of its traditional capitalist parties. A huge scandal erupted shortly after Lula's election in which PT functionaries were shown to have built illegal slush funds, laundered through foreign banks, in order to finance its election campaign. Almost the entire PT leadership has had to resign in disgrace and thousands upon thousands of disaffected members have left the party.[43]

It is crucial to emphasize that there is nothing abnormal at work here. The transformation of the PT fits a pattern that has been observed with reformist parties everywhere – from the German Social Democrats to British Labour to Canada's New Democratic Party. At root, the error of electoral reformism consists in the idea that the institutions of the modern state are neutral, that they can be adapted to progressive, anti-capitalist causes. Yet, as the young Marx showed, the state in capitalist society embodies a unique kind of political alienation.[44] Organized on hierarchical and bureaucratic lines, it smothers and appropriates the initiatives of citizens, rendering them passive entities to be governed by bureaucratic power. State power is thus alienated from citizens and concentrated in obscure ministries and government departments. And these constitute a network of strange, bewildering and intimidating rules and regulations of the sort depicted in Kafka's famous novel, *The Trial*. So, when a reformist government takes control of elected office, it does not transform the relations between citizens and the state. Instead, it simply becomes the face of an alienating, impersonal, anti-democratic state. It proceeds to govern in the old way – one that disempowers the majority while allowing capitalists to dominate economic and social life.

Once a party sets its sights on becoming the government, rather than fighting for a project of radical self-government of the oppressed, it has tied itself to the status quo. In so doing, it comes to treat people as passive instruments capable, at most, of voting, but certainly not of governing themselves. But a passive people do not make up the human material of radical democracy. They are susceptible to all the advertising pitches and ideological deceptions coming from government, traditional parties, the mass media and the ruling class. As a result, the reformist search for votes increasingly conforms to the dominant biases and assumptions of the ruling institutions: patriotism, respect for bureaucratic authority, and so on. Subordinating everything else to short-run electoral calculations, the reformist leaders stop talking of capitalism as the problem. They drop the word socialism from their vocabularies. They sound and act more and more like any of the elite parties. And, once in office, that's exactly how they behave.

Of course, the experiences of Venezuela and Bolivia could be said to constitute exceptions to this rule. But the reality is not so simple. After all, Venezuela's Hugo Chavez made repeated efforts to woo big business.[45] Not only did the elites rebuff him, they tried to overthrow him. In fact, as we have seen, Chavez was largely saved by the people of the *barrios*. Their pressure, in conjunction with the maneuvers of the right, has prevented Chavez from following the traditional electoralist path. Even so, Venezuela's Bolivarian Revolution has largely confined itself to using oil revenues for laudable social programs. It has not made any real moves against the wealth and power of Venezuela's capitalist class. As much as that revolution needs to be defended, it is still a long way from any genuinely socialist project.

As for Bolivia, the MAS government led by Evo Morales has proceeded quite cautiously. Vice-President Alvaro Garcia Linera, for instance, argues that his government intends merely to create a sort of "Andean-Amazonian capitalism." Socialism, if it is to be pursued, will have to wait 50 to 100 years, he adds.[46] Still, it will be difficult for Evo Morales to do the mad dash to the right that Lula has executed in Brazil. But the reason for this lies in the strength of Bolivia's popular movements, the most powerful in Latin America, which simply won't allow Morales to "do a Lula." Left to their own devices, Morales and Garcia Linera would soon be compromising with multinational capital in ways that would make observers dizzy – and sick. Rather than exceptions to the rule, then, the Venezuelan and Bolivian cases simply demonstrate that radical mass movements are the only significant counter-pressure to betrayal by electoralist politicians.

The miserable record of electoral reformism has pushed many social activists toward a kind of *anti-politics*. The task of radicals, such activists argue, is not to build movements to take power in society, but simply to try to disrupt and dissolve power. Such a perspective has been put forward most influentially by John Holloway.[47] Holloway's argument has a number of strengths. In particular, it makes clear that genuinely revolutionary movements defeat themselves if they set out to take over the existing institutions of power, whether by electoral or insurrectionary means. Holloway understands that the forms of the modern state are alienating, bureaucratic and disempowering. Where his argument fails, however, is in its advocacy of building an abstract sort of *anti-power*. After all, radical, participatory democracy is itself a form of power – but one controlled and organized from below, by the majority.

We need to keep in mind here that one of the oldest meanings of the word power is *to be able*. And radical socialists fight for a state of affairs in which the formerly oppressed majority fight *to be able* to govern themselves collectively and democratically, control their social-economic interrelations, and regulate their communal life. To make things happen, to exercise freedom, is to use power, to exercise the capacity to make things happen. This is what it means to *empower* people or, better, for people to empower themselves. Of course, we are talking here of a very different kind of power from that which prevails in class divided societies. We are talking about power organized and exercised from below, by active human subjects engaged in a project of participatory self-government. But to call this anti-power is misleading, as it fails to clarify the kinds of counter-power radical movements must build if they are to genuinely change society.

Let us take one of the most important popular struggles of recent years, the Water Wars in Cochabamba, to illustrate this point. Describing what happened at the height of the struggle in April 2000, when mass assemblies became the locus of popular decision-making, Oscar Olivera writes that the networks of the mass struggle

> Transformed themselves into a type of social organization that recognized no source of authority other than itself. That is, they became a government based on a structure of assembly-style, deliberative and representative practices of democracy …. this dense web of plebeian democratic practices … replaced the state as the mechanism of government. [48]

A number of formulations here are crucial. First, Olivera points out that the mass assemblies became a government, a locus of decision-making. In this respect, they became a new form of social power, of popular power. At the same time, they were radically democratic, growing out of mass assemblies of the people. But it is important to emphasize that these were not a mere anti-power. They were not just dissolving the old relations of power; they were also building new ones. The poor and the oppressed were instead constructing a counter-power, one designed ultimately to replace bureaucratic rule with rule of the people – which in class society, as Aristotle recognized in a different context, can only mean rule of the poor.

When mass popular protest reaches latently revolutionary forms, a situation of dual power tends to emerge. Opposite to and in conflict with the old older, there emerges a rival center of popular power.[49] Ultimately, one or the other must prevail. In a full-fledged revolutionary situation, the new forms of power start to displace and replace the old elitist ones. Again, Oscar Olivera's analysis of the Water Wars is relevant here. "For one week," he writes about Cochabamba in 2000, "the state had been demolished. In its place stood the *self-government* of the poor based on their local and regional organizational structures."[50] In short, as they approach their heights, mass upheavals begin to challenge the old order with new forms of self-government and popular power. And this involves a struggle for power. But it is also to struggle to remake and *transform power* – a point that eludes Holloway and others. These writers tend to imagine power in monolithic terms, as if there is only one possible way of acting upon the world to make things happen. But what the experience of radical and revolutionary movements show is that there are alternative forms of power. And the most revolutionary of these is radical, participatory, assembly-style democracy. That is a form of power – popular power – well worth fighting for.

Movement-Building, Reform and Revolution

How, then, is popular power to be built? Mass movements for revolutionary change do not seem to just spring into existence after all. So, what is it that generates them?

Here, again, we need to turn to the historical experience of actual mass movements. Let us, once more, start with Bolivia. What we discover is deeply instructive: mass movements in Bolivia were built around issues that are not in and of themselves revolutionary – for de-privatization of water, for indigenous rights, for public ownership of natural gas. True, these demands are strongly anti-neoliberal. But capitalism could in principle survive by granting any or all of these demands, as much as capitalists might be deeply reluctant to do so.

In short, the people engaged in these struggles started by fighting for specific social, economic and political reforms. But the *ways* in which they fought for them – mass direct action, mass strikes, popular assemblies – began to pose a fundamental challenge to one of the great pillars on which capitalist power rests: the passivity of the oppressed. Once the oppressed began to organize and mobilize themselves on a mass scale, then the foundations of the old order began to shake. The same thing tends to happen during all great revolutionary upheavals in society. During the Russian Revolution of 1917 – which ended the dictatorship of the Tsars, led to Russia's disengagement from the slaughter of the First World War and raised up hopes for a government of workers and peasants – the poor and the downtrodden mobilized around three demands: Land, Bread and Peace. Again, each of these represents a reform. But the way in which the oppressed fought for these demands – by creating a network of workers, soldiers and peasants councils capable of displacing the old state – was revolutionary. And for a short time, an inspiring revolutionary experiment took place in Russia.[51] Similar dynamics, though not on the same scale, took place in Spain in 1936-37, when the working class fought capital, the Church and the fascists.

It seems clear, therefore, that mass movements emerge around specific social reforms – like land for the landless in the case of the MST in Brazil.[52] But such movements, if they are organized democratically from below, have the potential to create new forms of organization that prefigure, even if ever so slightly, a new way of organizing society. And once we think about movement-building in these terms, much of the traditional debate about reform and revolution appears differently.

Most of the time, the objectives of reform and revolution simply appear as polar opposites. On the one hand, mass trade unions and social-democratic parties tend to demand limited social reforms, but never challenge capitalism as a system. On the other hand, we encounter radical left-wing organizations that oppose capitalism and advocate revolution but essentially constitute fringe groups without any significant base of support. As a result, a politics of reform crystallizes around large organizations and a politics of revolution around small ones.

This often produces a choreographed debate between reform and revolution. The reformists, who oppose all efforts to displace capitalism, denounce those committed to anti-capitalism as "un-realistic" and "impractical." Meanwhile, those who promote anti-capitalism too easily fall into a knee-jerk denunciation of all struggles for social reforms, be they for homes for the homeless or lower bus fares. During the Québec City protests against the Summit of the Americas (April 2001), for instance, one anarchist group distributed a tabloid that claimed, "reforms are like chloroform, they put us to sleep."[53]

The key problem with such formulations is that they address reforms in the abstract rather than discussing how we organize and fight for them. The emphasis is put on the object (reform) but not on the process (the struggle) that produces it. This approach results in cavalier dismissals of important mass struggles as "reformist," which is a terrible mistake if we are serious about mass social transformation from below. After all, every meaningful social movement – be it a radical union in Korea, the Landless

Workers Movement in Brazil, or the Save Narmada Movement in India – fights for social reforms such as union rights or land to live on. None of these things on its own constitutes a revolution. But what distinguishes these movements from passive and elitist politics are the *methods* of struggle they employ. Rather than engaging in lobbying politicians, imploring them to "help" the lower orders, or simply turning out to vote for some candidate, they mobilize the collective self-activity of oppressed people. As Rosa Luxemburg argued, the difference between reformists and revolutionaries does not have to do with which group supports social reforms (since both groups ought to do so). Rather, it has to do with how they build reform struggles, whether they use them as a means to enhance the confidence and self-organization of oppressed peoples.

Disavowing radical change, the classic reformist prefers polite negotiations among elites to the mobilization of loud and angry masses who are seizing land or blockading highways. Committed to militant anti-capitalism, on the other hand, the revolutionary seeks to build struggles in which masses of people win reforms for themselves, through their own efforts and actions, as part of building the revolutionary capacities for even more profound social change. Equally important, anti-capitalists ought to promote struggles which transgress capitalist property rights, such as land and factory occupations, or which refuse to respect capitalist profitability, as in demands for jobs and provision of social services irrespective of whether they can be organized for profit.

People committed to socialism from below cannot afford to turn their backs on any genuine struggles for reforms that might improve the lives of the poor and the oppressed. Recognizing that the vast majority of people desperately want improvements in their conditions of life, and rightly so, radical anti-capitalists ought to help build mass direct action struggles that develop people's sense of their own capacities while clarifying the nature of the system they resist. By promoting revolutionary (from below) methods of struggling for reforms, it is possible to build mass-based movements – like many of those analyzed in chapter 6 – in which struggles for reform are linked with larger revolutionary objectives.

While revolutionary socialist movements and organizations have generally had a stronger record of working in this sort of way, some important anarchist movements have also employed this approach with great imagination and creativity. A good example is the rent strike of tens of thousands of working class families organized by the CNT, an anarcho-syndicalist union, in Barcelona in 1931.[54] As Nick Rider points out, the radicals of the CNT were able "to identify and express widely felt needs and feelings" and formulate concrete demands for rent reductions that mobilized large numbers of the poor. Analyzing the political strategy used by CNT activists, he concludes: "Faced with the conventional opposition between reformism and revolution, they appear, in effect, to have put forward a third alternative, seeking to obtain practical improvements through the actual development, in practice, of autonomous, libertarian forms of self-organization, in such a way that they would, it was hoped, be beyond the power of the State to recuperate them."[55]

Indeed, according to Luxemburg, this is the only genuinely revolutionary approach since it works with mass movements on their actual terrain of struggle while utilizing methods of action that, by building popular self-organization, point toward a different social order. For movements for socialism from below, in Luxemburg's words, "the struggle for reforms is its means; the social revolution its *goal*."[56]

Workplaces, Streets, Communities and Mass Movements

The task, therefore, is to build large, democratic anti-capitalist movements and organizations rooted in workplaces and communities. To talk of a movement that links workplace and community organizing flies in the face of the dominant perspectives within the broad Left, however, in which there tends to be a sharp division between unions, which concentrate on workplace issues while neglecting wider social and community problems, and community organizations, which frequently concentrate on their own backyard without venturing into the world of workplace struggles and union politics. Yet, as we shall see, this division undermines the sort of militant activism that is necessary for radical change.

To complicate things further, a current of opinion has emerged that focuses neither on the community nor the workplace, but on the streets. Often associated with youth movements and some brands of anarchism, this current sees militant street actions as a powerful alternative to workplace and community organizing which, it must be conceded, have often been done in boring and bureaucratic fashions. Spirited street protests – from Reclaim the Streets actions to the battles in the streets of Seattle, Melbourne, Québec City, or Genoa – can easily seem the most festive and empowering form of political action.[57] In the midst of the protests in Québec City, for instance, one twenty-two-year-old university student told a journalist, "If we create a revolution we can change the system. When the power of money is defeated by the power of the street, it must be not just in Canada, but around the world."[58]

There is much to commend in these sentiments, particularly their radicalism and internationalism. But there is a fundamental strategic problem with the suggestion that "the power of the street" can defeat "the power of money." As important as street protests are, all the historical evidence indicates that capitalism cannot be brought down by rebellions in the streets alone. Eventually, the forces of law and order can smash street-based movements that are disconnected from struggles at work and in communities. Moreover, exclusively street politics evade a crucial question as to where power resides in capitalist society. After all, in the workplaces – the auto factories, burger sweatshops, banks, offices, steel mills, mega-farms, hospitals, coffee bars, mines, schools, oil fields and so on – lies the power to stop the flow of capitalist production, profits, finance and services. When the machinery of exploitation shuts down and the flow of profits dries up, capital is thrown into a profound crisis. This is especially true when workplace struggles take the form of worker occupations.

Moreover, because of the nature of exploitation and alienated labour, the workplaces are crucial sites of struggle and resistance. A movement that does not build upon resistance there, and that fails to mobilize the counter-power to capital that mass strikes and workplace occupations represent, cannot possibly succeed. As a historian of the wave of worldwide rebellions in 1968 has argued, great leaps in political radicalism are intimately connected with mass strikes: "In the modern world, the essential indication of these leaps, the signal for a whole epoch of class struggles, is the general strike. Such strikes ... involve the spontaneous and conscious action of millions of people."[59]

We have seen in chapter 6 the absolutely central role of mass strikes in some of the most important and powerful struggles against globalization – be it France in 1995, Korea since the late 1980s, Nigeria, Colombia, Puerto Rico and Bolivia in recent years, or COSATU's general strikes in South Africa in August 2001 and 2006. Because of their mass, collective character and their enormous social-economic impact, mass strikes must be central to any perspective for revolutionary social change.

Here, however, we need to distinguish mass strikes from bureaucratically controlled general strikes that lack grassroots militancy and self-organization. In some situations, trade union officials will use general strikes, completely orchestrated from above, as a ritual pressure tactic to force the government to negotiate. This has often been the case in both Brazil and Argentina in recent years.[60] Authentic mass strikes, in contrast, involve an outpouring of spontaneous protest and action that create new forms of self-organization. As Rosa Luxemburg, the finest theorist of the mass strike argued, "the mass strike is not artificially 'made,' not 'decided' at random, not 'propagated.'" Moreover, a real mass strike is not "one act, one isolated action," such as a one-day stayaway from work. [61] Instead, it is a wave of protests – strikes, street battles, workplace occupations, mass demonstrations – in which all these forms of struggle "run through one another, run side by side, cross one another, flow in and over one another."[62] In a genuine mass strike, in other words, workplace-based struggles flow out into the communities and the streets, inspiring actions there that, in turn, re-invigorate the struggle in the workplace. Authentic mass strikes thus break down the barriers between workplace, community and street, uniting protests in all these spaces into one common movement. Indeed, only in this way, argued Luxemburg, can a mass strike "become a real people's movement," one that draws in the unemployed, women in the home and others into a concerted assault on power.[63] We get a glimpse of how this can happen in the 1998 general strike in Puerto Rico which became known as *La huelga del pueblo* – the people's strike.

It is crucial to emphasize here that the overflowing of the workplace struggle into the community is crucial. Some of the most oppressed people frequently lack a paying job, and a truly participatory mass movement must provide space for their self-activity and organization. In addition to having their own specific grievances, which the mass movement needs to take up, the unemployed and women in the home have a powerful determination and unique talents that any mass movement desperately needs. In Argentina, the unemployed have frequently spearheaded struggles – and "housewives" have had a leading position in this regard.[64] Non-workplace based militancy frequently plays an inspirational role in radicalizing employed and unionized workers, as it has in Argentina. On a smaller scale, rank and file trade unionists who joined the predominantly youth-led street actions in Seattle and Québec City were generally effusive in their praise for the energy, courage and determination of the protesters. As a staff person with the Canadian Auto Workers union reported, "A lot of our members who came to Québec are now telling me they want to take part in the fight-back that takes place in the streets. A lot want training in direct action. Our activists are becoming more radical."[65] Finally, while street mobilizations cannot succeed on their own, as part of a multi-faceted movement they provide a common arena for working class and oppressed people to come together – in their hundreds of thousands, even millions – to glimpse their potential power, develop new bonds of solidarity, and experience the empowering thrill of taking public space away from control by the authorities.

Genuine mass strikes also tend to generate new forms of popular self-organization. During the Winnipeg general strike of 1919, for instance, the city's strike committee organized distribution of bread and milk so the poor and the working class would not suffer, while denying control of a profitable operation to the business class. Only trucks bearing the sign, "Permitted by authority of the strike committee" could freely travel the streets.[66] In a similar vein, the workers leading a mass strike in Minneapolis in 1934 organized a union-controlled farmers' market which enabled farmers to sell their goods and people to find fresh food. Not only did this allow the strikers to continue shutting down the operations of local capitalists, but farmers organizations joined the mass pickets.[67] More recently, during the mass struggles in Chile (1970-73), workplace-based committees, called *cordones*, began to establish elements of workers' control, a phenomenon developed to a higher level by city-wide workers' councils during the revolutionary events in Portugal in 1974-75 following the overthrow of fascism. Workers' councils such as these establish alternative forms of power that embody the potential for a radically different form of society. Moreover, as I discuss in the next section, popular organizations of this sort create the framework in which people can undergo the self-transformations necessary to remake society.

Rather than a one-sided emphasis on the streets, the communities or the workplaces alone, socialism from below looks to mass strikes that paralyze the flow of capitalist profits, turn workplaces into centers of working class self-management, mobilize oppressed groups in their communities, foster local structures of democratic self-government, and take to the streets in demonstrations of popular power, celebration and opposition to the authorities, local and global. Anything less, any perspective that ignores the strategic power of the workplaces, the mobilizing capacities of people in their communities, and the tremendous power of street mobilizations will certainly falter.

Can it Happen? Revolution and Self-Transformation

Perhaps the most common objection to the view of social transformation from below I've outlined is the claim that working class, poor and oppressed people will never rise to the task. Many commentators point to apathy, competition, the controlling influence of the mass media, and the dominance of the ruling ideas as evidence that ordinary people will simply never come to awareness of their common interests, forge powerful bonds of solidarity, and develop a shared vision of a new society for which they are prepared to fight.

Clearly, it would be foolhardy to dismiss the power of these objections. Modern capitalist societies have developed extensive mechanisms of ideological domination, and the experience of constant subordination can create profound feelings of inferiority and passivity among oppressed and exploited people. For about a century and a half, capitalism has survived all manner of revolts and resistance – often by means of sheer barbarism. In the midst of imperial war, ecological destruction, the banalization of daily life, and grinding poverty for billions, it would be utterly naïve to imagine that a socialist future is in any way guaranteed.

Yet, hope remains. It announces itself in every refusal to go along with repression and domination, with every resistance to exploitation and oppression. And nurturing that hope, building it, enabling it to become the fuel of real movements to change the world is crucial. If hope dies, so does any prospect for a future beyond capitalism.

Fortunately, resistance movements have not disappeared. And in some parts of the world they could be said to have grown considerably stronger in recent years. This is crucial. For, so long as resistance to capital is alive, so are prospects for truly revolutionary change.

The reason has to do with the self-transforming powers of mass struggle. Most discussion of prospects for radical social change lack this insight, which was central to Marx's view of revolution. The Marxian commitment to revolution is often misunderstood as having to do with the necessity of violence to anti-capitalist transformation. In fact, Marx's attitude to social revolution can be summed up in the slogan of the first mass workers' movement, the British Chartists of the 1830s and 1840s: "peaceably if we can, forcibly if we must." While holding out slim hopes for some relatively peaceful transitions to working class self-government, Marx generally expected ruling classes to violently resist mass democratic change – by staging "a slave-holders' revolt," as he put it. And he believed a "movement of the immense majority" had every right to use force to put down minority violence.[68] But Marx's notion of revolution involved much more than a commitment to the right of the majority to forcibly constrain the exploiting class. Most fundamental to Marx's idea of revolution was the insistence that meaningful change can come only through a mass movement from below. Only by winning radical democracy for themselves, by conquering their own freedom, could the oppressed remake themselves as people capable of free self-government.

In one crucial passage, as we have seen, Marx described revolutionary practice as the "coincidence" of "the changing of circumstances" and "self-changing."[69] Revolution thus has two interrelated components: changing of social rules and regulations (ownership, property, forms of government) and self-transformation. Elsewhere, Marx explained that for anti-capitalist revolution to be possible, "the alteration of people on a mass scale is necessary, an alteration that can only take place in a practical movement, a revolution." A revolution is necessary not only to overthrow the rule of the dominant class, he continued, "but also because the class overthrowing it can only in a revolution succeed in ridding itself of all the muck of ages and become fitted to found society anew."[70] In short, the process of revolution – mass mobilization, participation in new forms of democracy, overturning old forms of domination, taking control of workplaces and communities – transforms the participants themselves. Novelist George Orwell captured a sense of this in describing Barcelona in December 1936, at the height of the Spanish revolution:

> It was the first time I had ever been in a town where the working class was in the saddle. Practically every building of any size had been seized by the workers … Every shop and café had an inscription saying it had been collectivized … Waiters and shop-walkers looked you in the face and treated you as an equal. Servile and even ceremonial forms of speech had temporarily disappeared. Nobody said 'Senor' or 'Don' or even 'Usted'; everyone called everyone else 'Comrade' and 'Thou' … Above all, there was a belief in the revolution and the future, a feeling of suddenly having emerged into an era of equality and freedom. Human beings were trying to behave as human beings and not as cogs in the capitalist machine.[71]

The experience of acting as human beings, not cogs, as members of a society of equals, is both exhilarating and transforming. Possibilities that previously seemed unreal, open up. Getting rid of "the muck of ages" becomes conceivable because the individual's behaviour and sense of self is shifting, changing and developing so rapidly. Social upheaval involves immense learning processes – not abstract book learning (although books, pamphlets and leaflets are read voraciously) but practical, deeply experiential learning.[72] Because they open the space for new forms of popular self-organization, radical social upheavals provide a framework in which oppressed people can remake themselves so that they might be capable of authentically remaking society. Drawing on the evidence of five major popular revolts between 1968 and 1981, British socialist Colin Barker maintains that in such circumstances:

> New hopes emerge. Previous habits of subordination and deference collapse. A new sense of personal and collective power develops. The 'common sense' of class society falters. Historic hierarchies – in workplaces, in the state, in schools and colleges, in families – are threatened or actually tumble. Old divisions between different groups of workers, national and ethnic groups, among peasants, between men and women are shattered and re-shaped by the development of new solidarities. Ordinary people find themselves performing tasks and assuming responsibilities from which society previously excluded them. New kinds of competence appear, new divisions of labour, new powers.
>
> Popular confidence and imagination grow by leaps and bounds. With them, practical intelligence also rises: nothing is so mentally numbing as the habit of subordination. Every 'festival of the oppressed' involves a sudden release of collective pleasure. Perspectives alter, the horizons of possibility extend.
>
> ... New languages, symbols, artistic forms are adopted to express the new conditions; the flourishing of posters, symbols, newspapers, leaflets, badges and jokes bear witness to the profound shifts going on in the consciousness of millions ...
>
> Previous property rules are challenged. Premises are occupied. Existing uses of places and things are altered. Land is taken over, workplaces seized ... The workers are in the boardroom, the crowd is in the palace, the confidential files are opened, the workers' commission is inspecting the warehouses. What was closed is open ...[73]

Having expanded the social horizons of everyday life – by entering formerly forbidden environs like the boardroom, the bank and the government office, which they now bring under their collective control – insurgent masses also expand their intellectual and cultural horizons. As they change institutions and social arrangements, they remake themselves. While huge social upheavals and popular revolutions give us the most dramatic examples, we can also see germs of this process today in the democratically organized mass gatherings of tens of thousands in Cochabamba, or the assemblies of the Landless Workers Movement in Brazil where "everyone is a leader."

And this is why the hope of truly revolutionary change, a radical democracy from below, is not a pipe dream. To be sure, it is by no means guaranteed. Indeed, it faces very considerable odds. But in every great wave of social protest and upheaval, we can discern the faint outline of another world. The seeds of a new society of freedom and equality are planted on the streets and the picket lines. Hope resides there, fragile though it often seems.

"Hope is On the Side of the Movement"

Thus far, one great accomplishment of global justice struggles, particularly in Latin America, is to have punctured the Washington consensus, to have challenged the legitimacy of major institutions of the ruling class, like the IMF and the WTO, and to have overturned parts of the neoliberal global agenda.[74] Most important, however, is the way they have created a new sense of hope and possibility for popular movements. After decades of defeats for labour and social movements, after a vicious offensive by capital against social programs and living standards, mass protests have reemerged.

To be sure, things are still quite difficult, even grim, for activists in many parts of the world. Since the cynical manipulation of the 9/11 attacks by western governments to engineer a nasty clamp down on civil rights and dissent, resistance movements have fallen off in much of the North. The anti-war movement, despite American troubles in Iraq and Afghanistan, has been unable to stop the US war machine. Israel continues to encroach on land in Palestine and oppress its people; paramilitaries continue to slaughter activists in Colombia.

Yet, amidst misery and suffering – which must be named, remembered and mourned – something else stirs. It is, as commentators on Cochabamba tell us, the spirit of solidarity and the conquest of fear. Everywhere that movements of resistance converge, something of this potent combination is at work. Consider the personal account of involvement in the April 2001 Québec City protests by a self-described "dull normal," who "mainly came along to see what the big ruckus was all about." Summarizing the lessons of her experiences in the streets, she begins: "I came away with all my limbs and belongings intact, but any faith I had in my so-called democratic government was yanked out by the roots. It wasn't just the tear gas. It was the whole idea of the fence, the rows upon rows of riot cops, the preemptive arrests of well-known protesters ..." But there is something more. "The second thing I learned," she writes, "was that tear gas and rubber bullets are no match for the wit and imagination I saw among the protesters. Their creativity took me by surprise...."[75]

Three months later, on July 21, 2001, at least a quarter of a million people filled the street of Genoa. Three days later, having witnessed police violence and the murder of a protester, Carlo Giuliani, up to half a million people took to the streets in dozens of Italian cities and towns. One analyst, summing up the experience, wrote that:

> The political-ideological climate is changing: a new period of reconstruction of the movement of the exploited and the oppressed has opened ... Hope is on the side of the movement.[76]

This new period was disrupted by the wave of repression that followed less than two months later, in the aftermath of September 11, 2001. But, while the political terrain worsened for movements in the North, hope was not extinguished. It continues to shout its name, from the streets of Paris to the hills surrounding La Paz.

Looking Forward from 1968: Opportunities and Challenges

This reawakening of hope is of inestimable value. Yet, hope and inspiration are not enough. They need to be fused with analysis and organization. And this requires an honest assessment of strengths and weaknesses. The development of an authentic world-transforming movement proceeds, to again quote Rosa Luxemburg, "not by the creation of a revolutionary hurrah-spirit, but quite the contrary: only by an insight into all the fearful seriousness, all the complexity of the tasks involved."[77]

Looked at in this spirit, one major shortcoming of the current political conjuncture stands out in sharp relief: the passivity of working class organizations in the North despite the upsurge in global justice struggles. Even during the heady days of 1999-2001, when tens of thousands of trade unionists turned out to the protests in Seattle and Québec City, for instance, bureaucratic labour leaderships directed their members away from the sites of the militant direct actions – the area of the Convention Center in Seattle and the "Wall of Shame" in Québec City. While the labour marches were large, colourful and festive in character, they remained highly controlled affairs that avoided tactics designed to disrupt the gatherings of global elites. As a result, trade unionists did not experience the sort of radicalization undergone by many who found themselves in the thick of the struggle. One trade union member who joined the protests at the wall in Québec City described the experience: "At the front we are all just people asserting our rights and protesting our injuries. No other affiliations matter. People trade water, bandannas, food and other supplies freely. The solidarity is incredible... People are speaking openly about 'the revolution'."[78] However, few union members underwent the radicalization that exposure to naked police violence produces. Nor did they experience the qualitative leap in solidarity – with colourful punks, feminists, young environmentalists, queer activists, militant anarchists and socialists, among others – that common action in the face of state violence can produce.

On balance, the organized labour movements in the North have not been dramatically affected by the upsurge of global justice activism. Many of them have continued to focus on economic protectionism – limiting "foreign imports" into their countries' markets, as if an American or Canadian job is more valuable than that of a Korean or Mexican worker – rather than international solidarity and global justice as their response to globalization.[79] Militant actions by rank and file workers have remained few and far between. Even one of the most upbeat assessments of the Genoa protests acknowledges that there were no strikes as part of the mobilizations.[80] Consequently, radicals in the North have their work cut out for them. The building of a real labour left – consisting of rank and file opposition movements in the mainstream unions, activists from workers' centers, and militants from grassroots union locals, anti-poverty groups and so on – will have to become a crucial long-term political priority. The importance of such work, and the consequence of not doing it, are thrown into sharp relief when we study the last great period of global radicalism and its high point, the student protests and mass strikes in France in 1968.

Since the rise of capitalism, there have been a handful of years when revolution was contagious, when mass upheavals in one place triggered popular explosions in country after country, when the revolution literally hopped borders as if they did not exist. 1848 was such a year. Revolution overthrew the monarchy in France in February. Throughout March it swept southwest Germany, Bavaria, Berlin and moved on to Austria, Hungary and Italy. "Within a matter of weeks no government was left standing in an area which is today occupied by all or part of ten states." Nor was the upheaval confined to Europe. The contagion spread to Brazil and Colombia too. "In a sense it was the paradigm of the 'world revolution' of which rebels were henceforth to dream."[81]

The spectre of world revolution returned in 1919. Under the impact of the late months of World War I and the upheaval in Russia, workers, soldiers and sailors overturned governments in Germany, Austria, Hungary; insurrections occurred in Italy and Spain; unrest swept much of Mexico; general strikes rocked Belfast, Glasgow, Seattle, Winnipeg; and militant workers' movements made their mark in South Africa, China, Argentina, Chile, and many more countries.[82] While Marx's "old mole" of revolution, who burrows under the ground only to emerge into the light of day, poked its head up again in 1936 (especially in France and Spain), it was 1968 when it once more shook the ruling powers on a massive scale.

The dimensions of what happened in 1968 have all too easily been forgotten and suppressed. Yet they were truly extraordinary.[83] Just a quick month-by-month overview records the following:

- January: Huge anti-nuclear demonstrations in Japan, one of which leads to an occupation of the US embassy; a stunning offensive against the US army by national liberation forces in Vietnam captures cities in the US-occupied South and seizes the American embassy compound in Saigon.
- February: The International Congress on Vietnam sponsored by the Socialist Students Movement of Germany opens at the Free University of West Berlin with 10,000 participants from more than ten countries. Meanwhile student protests against the fascist regime break out at the university in Madrid, Spain.
- March: A dynamic and growing movement for democracy and "socialism with a human face" begins to openly defy the Stalinist regime in Czechoslovakia; a wave of student sit-ins and street-fights with police sweeps Italy; 10,000 students and supporters take to the streets for democracy and human rights in Poland; and 25,000 anti-Vietnam war demonstrators chant "Victory to the NLF" in Trafalgar Square, London.

- April: Student protests against the military dictatorship in Brazil become bolder. When troops kill a demonstrator, further protests erupt, and 15,000 metal workers join the students. In Memphis, Tennessee, the murder of Martin Luther King leads to riots by outraged African-Americans in forty cities, including New York, Chicago, Washington and Baltimore.
- May: France, France and again France: Student protests against police repression and the Vietnam War lead to nights of street-fighting with riot police. Barricades go up, student strikes spread and then the workers enter the fray. At the movement's peak, ten million workers are on strike, a million people pour through the streets, and a million workers occupy their workplaces. French President Charles De Gaulle flees to Germany, looking for assistance in the event the insurgents seize power.
- June: An immensely popular student protest movement shakes the government of Yugoslavia; Japanese railworkers call on students to help block trains taking ammunition to the US army in Vietnam; the opposition movement surges forward again in Czechoslovakia.
- July: Events in Czechoslovakia reach fever pitch. The leaders of the Soviet Union issue ominous threats against the dissident movement. The rebels against Stalinism release a manifesto declaring, "Everything we fight for could be summed up in four words. Socialism. Alliance. Sovereignty. Freedom."
- August: Tanks sweep through the streets of Prague as Russia invades Czechoslovakia in order to crush the protest movement. Meanwhile, student and anti-war protesters flock to Chicago to organize protests against the Vietnam War at the Democratic National Convention. The Chicago mayor unleashes riot police, troops and the National Guard, and four nights of pitched battles ensue as thirty million Americans watch gas mask-clad TV reporters try to cover the events through clouds of tear gas. Ironically, the barbarism of both superpowers is exposed simultaneously.

- **September:** The women's liberation movement disrupts the Miss America contest in Atlantic City, New Jersey, publicly announcing the birth of second wave feminism. Mexican students use the occasion of the Summer Olympics in Mexico City to demonstrate for democracy. As hundreds of thousands take to the streets, the students occupy the university.
- **October:** Mexican police massacre three hundred students, but the spirit of revolt will not die. During the medal ceremonies at the Olympics, 200-metre gold medalist Tommie Smith and bronze medalist John Carlos raise their fists in Black Power salutes. The two athletes are expelled from the US Olympic team. In England, anti-war students occupy the London School of Economics, running seminars on The Sociology of Revolution, Combating Bourgeois Culture, and Colonial Revolution, among others. A few days earlier, Black Panther leader Eldridge Cleaver gives a lecture to students at the Berkeley campus of the University of California.
- **November:** Student demonstrations kick start a mass movement against the US-backed military dictatorship in Pakistan. The government shuts down the schools and universities, but the workers enter the fray, paralyzing the railway system, closing factories. So widespread and so powerful is the movement that the dictatorship of Field Marshal Ayub Khan will collapse within four months.
- **December:** Europe's best-organized working class movement awakens in Italy with huge strikes, prelude to an even larger upheaval that will sweep the country in the "hot autumn" of 1969. The Brazilian government declares a "state of siege" and shuts down the Congress. But as the year draws to a close, the same slogan appears again and again on walls throughout Paris: "continuons le combat" – the struggle continues.

This summary does not do full justice to the magnitude of 1968, nor to the scope of the struggles. Nevertheless, it ought to illustrate just how widely the spirit of revolt was in the air – and how quickly it spread. It also indicates the extent to which student movements could elicit powerful responses from workers, as occurred particularly in Brazil, Czechoslovakia, France, Italy and Pakistan.

Yet, if we take the most explosive case – France in May 1968 – it is also clear that the lack of an organized movement capable of cementing the alliance between militant workers and student radicals had debilitating effects. In the absence of a sustained, organized alliance, the Communist Party (CP) – which had long ago abandoned revolution and had become a party of polite reform from above – was able to demobilize the struggle. In the mass demonstrations, CP marshals physically prevented students from mingling with workers. Then, in a series of behind-the-scenes maneuvers, the CP negotiated an agreement with the government to end the strikes in exchange for wage increases.[84] While it would be naïve to argue that the French events represented an immediately revolutionary situation, an interim resolution that established elements of workers' control in the factories and offices, forced major social and political concessions from the state, and kept the ruling class on the defensive (rather than enabling it to retake the offensive) could have established time and space for the continued growth of the radical movement. Moreover, given that popular upheavals would continue for several years – the hot autumn in Italy (1969), the worker-peasant upsurge associated with the election of the Popular Unity government in Chile (1970-73), the overthrow of Portuguese rule in its African colonies, the collapse of Portuguese fascism and the corresponding workers' revolt in Portugal (1974-75) – a more favourable resolution in France might have contributed to and fed off of a sustained international radicalization.

This ought to be a salutary warning for global justice radicals today. We need to be cognizant of the bureaucratic and reform-minded types in union leaderships and NGOs today who, like the French Communist Party in 1968, will attempt to deradicalize mass movements intent on anti-capitalist change. Yet, it will not be possible to challenge these influences unless radicals take to heart the task of long-term consistent work to support rank and file workers and their unions. Too often, radicals have reacted against the bureaucratic conservatism of organized labour by turning their backs on unions. This approach merely perpetuates the disconnection between unionized workers and radical activism. Since unions also contain a capacity for radical self-transformation – witness the upheavals within organized labour in California under the impact of rank and file struggles by workers of colour – anti-capitalists have the opportunity both to learn important lessons about grassroots workplace organizing and to influence the development of militant forms of working class struggle – if they are prepared to commit sustained energies to solidarity with workers and their unions. Such a long-term commitment could be crucial if, somewhere in the future, we are not to see a repetition of the great disappointments of 1968 and after. When the next wave of mass working class struggle breaks, those committed to revolutionary change from below will need to have in place ongoing connections with workers organizations if they are to credibly challenge those who will endeavour to divert and constrain the movement once more.

Thinking Long-Term, Organizing for Change

A glimpse at what has transpired in Argentina in recent years underlines the importance of organizing for socialist change.

During the half-year period December 2001 to July 2002, Argentina experienced the highest level of mass popular mobilization in the world. For three days in late December, fierce and sustained street battles overthrew a president. Then, under the pressure of a mounting wave of demonstrations and street blockades, three successive aspirants to the presidency were forced to resign. About four million people participated directly in these actions in the streets. In working class communities, the unemployed workers' movements, or *piqueteros*, seized and blockaded streets and highways to wring concessions from the authorities.

In the most radicalized neighbourhoods, the *piqueteros* organized sustained popular organizations that took control of key aspects of community life. Meanwhile, a wave of takeovers of bankrupt and idle factories brought at least 100 workplaces under some form of workers' control. [85]

Popular movements in Argentina then confronted a dilemma. They were throwing up embryonic elements of dual power – encroaching on the control of the state over communities and of capitalists over workplaces. But, these forms of popular power had to be extended into a national network of workplace and neighbourhood councils if they were to genuinely undermine the power of the capitalist state. Short of that, the ruling class would be sure to regroup and use a combination of repression and concessions to roll back popular power. National networks of popular power were not going to happen, however, without a sizable and credible revolutionary movement/organization capable of winning support for the *idea* of displacing the old state machinery and fostering forms of *practice* that did effectively that. Argentina lacked such a revolutionary movement, and no group proved capable of creating one in the midst of the struggle. As a result, the police reclaimed control of most of the occupied factories, *piqueteros* movements were repressed, or their leaders bought off. Today, popular movements are massively weaker than they were only a few years ago. And the authority of the state and the ruling class have been significantly restored. While there remain inspiring pockets of proud resistance – the occupied Zanon factory or those *piqueteros* movements that continue to mobilize from below – the movements in Argentina failed to mount a sustained opposition to the state.

Events in Argentina highlight the socialist insight that the world cannot be changed without effective political organization. Ruling classes and reformists all possess powerful networks of organization for disseminating their ideas and mobilizing their supporters. If they are to counter the effect of these, socialists too need such networks, though they must be organized along demo-cratic, not bureaucratic, lines.

Typically, mass social upheavals involve a range of contend-ing political perspectives and approaches. As new senses of self and community develop, there is an intense struggle between old-er worldviews and new perceptions of what might be possible. The reform-from-above types try to reroute explosive militancy into old channels of polite negotiation and bureaucratic adjustments. Meanwhile, the radicals, often lacking coordination across the various struggles, work desperately to offer an alternative vision. As a rule, however, the approach that prevails does so because it is most capable of propagating its perspective and influencing mass organizations, as the CP did in France in 1968. Typically, the bureaucratic and reform-minded groups have the resources and networks to carry the greatest influence. As much as groups of militants and activists may rebel against the top-down approach of bureaucratic reform, without resources and coordination, they will be unable to present a credible alternative to a mass audience. To do that, they need meeting spaces; networks of communication, coordination and democratic decision-making among thousands of activists; and mass publications that allow them to popularize an alternative vision for the movement. In short, they need politi-cal organization that enables them to engage in common projects of education, organization and movement-building.

On my wall hangs a poster with the words, "Organize. Edu-cate. Resist." It comes from a particular moment in the anti-neo-liberal struggle in Toronto during the mid-1990s.[86] Yet, while the product of a particular moment in the struggle, the trio of terms the poster promotes is a useful guide. We need to *organize* anti-cap-italists so that they might share experiences, cooperate, deepen their understanding, *educate* themselves, and work more effectively to build movements that more effectively *resist* capitalism.

Of course, there are models of socialist organization that have failed miserably. Top heavy bureaucratic models have been developed by parliamentary reformists and the old-style Communist parties. Equally unhealthy models, based on the fanaticism of true believers, have contributed to nasty legacies of sectarian infighting among small, isolated grouplets. Much of this is due to the disconnection of the radical left, particularly in the North, from real mass movements, a disconnection that breeds frustration, bitterness and a tendency to magnify small differences. Yet, for all that, we need anti-capitalist organizations and movements if the world is to be genuinely changed. Moreover, if we believe that society can be run democratically, it follows that it ought to be possible to build vibrant, democratic socialist movements.

To talk of effective anti-capitalist organization is, of course, to invite a series of questions: do we mean a coalition, a movement, a party, or something else? Clearly, something more than a coalition has to be intended, since these come together around a specific grievance and a concrete campaign and often cease functioning after the battle has been waged. The project of social transformation has to be built across campaigns and struggles, however, as a long-term objective. So, we come to the ideas of a movement and a party. Yet, terminology can be a problem here. Take, for instance, the notion of a party of the left. In many countries, the very mention of a party suggests a bureaucratic electoral machine whose preoccupation is with parliamentary politics. At points in the past, radical leftists have tried to counterpose the idea of a revolutionary party, or "a party of a new type" to the tired reformist model. Yet, even the notion of a revolutionary party has often been corrupted – not only by undemocratic or sectarian groups that have used the term, but also by mass organizations such as the bizarrely named Institutional Revolutionary Party (PRI) which established a form of authoritarian rule in Mexico for roughly sixty years. In countries such as Korea and Brazil, on the other hand, the idea of a "workers' party" is very much a positive point of reference for working class militants, something they have been widely discussing and trying to build.

The term "movement" can be equally tricky. Take, for instance, the electoral party that won the 2005 elections in Bolivia.

As we have seen, it calls itself the Movement Toward Socialism (MAS), even though it is largely an electoral party-type formation. Yet, in other contexts, a movement often refers to a looser, less durable and less lasting kind of structure.

At this stage of development, it is likely that different political cultures and traditions will shape both the language and the form of serious anti-capitalist organizations. As a result, rather than trying to delineate a single model for anti-capitalist organizing (a dubious proposition at the best of times), or a uniform terminology, it makes more sense to elaborate common goals and objectives that fit a specific context. As one insightful socialist writer put it, "useful argument about the problems of socialist organization is impossible at the level of 'universal' generalizations. Organizations do not exist in a vacuum. They are composed of actual people in specific historical situations, attempting to solve real problems with a limited number of options open to them."[87] Given the level of popular struggle and mass organization, what makes sense for anti-capitalist activists in Venezuela or Bolivia will have little immediate relevance to the tasks that confront the radical left in Britain, Canada, France or the US. And each of these cases presents its own unique challenges and opportunities.

At this stage of the game, the radical anti-capitalist left probably needs to do most of the following. First, build common fronts for joint work and action as part of all the major social justice struggles of the day. Second, bring together anti-capitalist activists from the unions, anti-poverty groups, feminist organizations, anti-racist movements, environmental coalitions, aboriginal groups, sexual rights movements, militant student groups, and radical, non-sectarian political currents who are committed to working together in a spirit of solidarity and joint work. This means developing a creative anti-racist, feminist, green class politics that articulates a common emancipatory project. Third, create spaces – conferences, forums and so on – for political education, debate, and decision-making. Just as the ruling class has its institutions of knowledge for propagating the ruling ideas, anti-capitalist movements need their own forums for developing a pedagogy and a knowledge of the oppressed. Fourth, begin constructing the rudiments of democratically run, participatory, anti-capitalist organizations that hold large, open, social, political, educational and cultural events; produce literature, videos and CDs, and create international networks with similarly minded groups and organizations in other parts of the world. Fifth, do all of this in the spirit of revolutionary pluralism, an ethos that, rather than trying to force adherence to a single revolutionary outlook, welcomes a plurality of radical perspectives, each of which brings different strengths and weaknesses to the common anti-capitalist project. [88]

In some countries, sections of the radical left have begun to create new kinds of anti-capitalist and socialist alliances. It remains to be seen how many of these can chart the path toward larger, more vibrant socialist movements and organizations. Nevertheless, the move to create large, militant and non-sectarian alliances on the socialist left is to be commended and supported. [89]

At one level, all of these proposals are fairly modest. Yet, we need to be able avoid the capitalist propensity to look for the quick fix, the instant solution. It is vital to think about the struggle against capitalism as the work of a lifetime. Equally vital is to begin moving in the right direction, to begin building organizations committed to anti-capitalism, radical democracy and revolution from below. We owe it to ourselves, and to all those struggling for a better world, to do what we can to bring about a movement dedicated to these principles. We have seen the savage effects of rampaging globalization on peoples' lives and the natural environment, after all. More importantly, in the resurgence of radical mass movements against these ravages we see the emergence of what the Zapatistas call "the international of hope." It announces itself from the jungles of Chiapas, the sweatshops of Bangladesh, the factories of Korea, the student and workers demonstrations in France, the encampments of the Landless Workers Movement, and hundreds of other place and spaces.[90] It is our reminder that another world really might be possible.

Notes

1 See "The case for globalisation," *The Economist*, September 23, 2000, p. 19, "Anti Capitalist Protests," *The Economist*, September 23, 2000, pp. 85-87, and "Globalisation and its critics: A survey of globalisation," *The Economist*, September 29, 2001, pp. 3, 20. For the spread of the term see, for example, Alan Rugman and Karl Moore, "Biting the hand that feeds us," *Globe and Mail*, January 4, 2002. For the shift in Zapatista declarations see Zapatista Army of National Liberation, "Sixth Declaration of the Selva Lacandona (2005), Part III.

2 The Gap's display was launched on June 18, 2001. On the video game, scheduled for release in October 2001, see The Associated Press, "Those Seattle WTO Riots? It's just a game now, folks," *Seattle Times*, May 29, 2001.

3 My description of this ad draws on Thomas Frank, *One Market Under God: Extreme Capitalism, Market Populism, and the End of Economic Democracy* (New York: Anchor Books, 2000), p. 90.

4 Daniel Singer, *Whose Millennium? Theirs or Ours?* (New York: Monthly Review Press, 1999), p. 148.

5 Singer, p. 149.

6 Jeremy Brecher, Tim Costello and Brendan Smith, *Globalization from Below: The Power of Solidarity* (Cambridge, MA: South End Press, 2000), p. 17. There are many excellent things about this book, but the articulation of an anti-capitalist perspective is not among them.

7 Karl Marx, "Letters from the Franco-German Yearbooks: Marx to Ruge, September 1843" in Marx, *Early Writings* (Harmondsworth: Penguin Books, 1992), pp. 207, 208, 209.

8 Barlow and Clarke, p. 182.

9 This is also an absence in the perspective set out by Walden Bello and Nicola Bullard, "The Global Conjuncture: Characteristics and Challenges," Keynote speech at the National Convention against Globalization, New Delhi, India, March 21-23, 2001, available at www.focusweb.org. For more on this point see my artticle, "The Commodity Status of Labour: The Secret of Commodified life" in *Not for Sale: Decommodifying Public Life*, eds. Gordon Laxer and Dennis Soron (Toronto: Broadview Press and Garamond Press, 2006), pp. 39-54.

10 Karl Marx, *Capital*, v. 1, trans. Ben Fowkes (Harmondsworth: Penguin Books, 1976), p. 171.

11 For a wonderful description of alienated labour in Stalinist societies (in this case Hungary in the 1960s-70s) see Miklos Haraszti, *A Worker in a Worker's State*, trans. Michael Wright (Harmondsworth: Penguin Books, 1977). I have described some of the mechanisms and processes by which democratic social planning might function in *Against the Market: Political Economy, Market Socialism and the Marxist Critique* (London: Verso Books, 1993), Ch. 6.

12 See George Lichtheim, *The Origins of Socialism* (London: Weidenfeld and Nicolson, 1969). The idea of communism also emerged in the 1840s, often indicating the position of the more militant working class socialists in contrast with the often more gradualist and reformist perspective of middle class socialists. For most purposes, I will treat the two concepts as interchangeable – as referring to a classless society based upon new forms of democratic self-government.

13 "Globalisation and its critics: A survey of globalisation," *The Economist*, September 29, 2001, p. 19.

14 Barbara Epstein, "Anarchism and the Anti-Globalization Movement," *Monthly Review* 53, 4, September 2001.

15 "The New Anarchism," *Newsweek*, December 13, 1999, p. 38. By "technophobe," I am referring to an extreme hostility to technology in principle. As should be clear, it is the social use of technologies which is the key issue, not technology per se, although some specific technologies are clearly incompatible with rational human and environmental purposes. I am personally disinclined to include someone like Kaczynski in the anarchist camp. Unfortunately, there are self-professed anarchists who do not want to disavow him. See, for instance, "Black Bloc Interview" in *The Anarchist Papers*, ed. Dimitrios Roussopoulos (Montreal: Black Rose Books, 2002), p. 188.

16 Noam Chomsky, "Introduction" to Daniel Guerin, *Anarchism* (New York: Monthly Review Press, 1970), p. xv. For a fair-minded analysis of different strains of anarchism see Ulrike Heider, *Anarchism: Left, Right, and Green*, trans. Danny Lewis and Ulrike Bode (San Francisco: City Light Books, 1994).

17 Murray Bookchin, "Whither Anarchism?" in Bookchin, *Anarchism, Marxism and the Future of the Left* (San Francisco: AK Press, 1999), p. 160. Bookchin makes much the same point in his earlier work, *Social Anarchism of Lifestyle Anarchism: An Unbridgeable Chasm* (San Francisco: AK Press, 1995), pp. 4-7.

18 Hal Draper, "The Two Souls of Socialism" in Draper, *Socialism from Below*, ed. E. Harberkern (New Jersey: Humanities Press, 1992), p. 3. As should be clear from what I have to say below, while holding this essay in especially high regard, I dissent from Draper's one-sided critique of anarchism. While much of what he has to say about the individualist and conspiratorial tendencies within anarchism is compelling, Draper is not fair to some of the currents within social anarchism. I also reject my own restatement of Draper's interpretation in the first edition of my booklet, *Socialism from Below* (Toronto: Workers' Action Books, 1980).

19 This is especially true today in anti-poverty and global justice movements. But there are a variety of historical precedents. Indeed, even during the Spanish Revolution, anarchists and the Marxists of the Workers' Party of Marxist Unity (POUM) worked together not only against fascism but also in opposition to the policies and practices of the Spanish Communist Party.

20 While I am using socialism from below here, others may prefer libertarian socialism. My hope is simply to avoid a term in the first instance that commits anti-capitalist radicals to either anarchism or Marxism. As examples of efforts to promote a constructive dialogue along these lines see Todd Gordon and Jerome Klassen, "Anarchism, Marxism and Renewing Socialism from Below," *New Socialist*, October/November 2001, pp. 20-23, and the reprinting of this article along with a friendly response by Wayne Price in *The Northeastern Anarchist*, No. 3, Fall/Winter 2001, pp. 44-46. Too much should not be made of this, perhaps, but at least these examples point to a spirit of open, constructive dialogue.

21 Karl Marx, "Provisional Rules" in Marx, *The First International and After*, ed. David Fernbach (Harmondsworth: Penguin Books, 1974), p. 82; Alexander Berkman, *The ABC of Anarchism* (London: Freedom Press, 1992), p. 44.

22 Berkman, p. 1.

23 Daniel Guerin, "Introduction" to *Ni Dieu ni Maitre* (Lausanne, 1969), as cited by Chomsky, "Introduction" to Guerin, *Anarchism*, p. xvii.

24 Murray Bookchin, *Anarchism, Marxism and the Future of the Left*, pp.290-91 and "The Communist Manifesto: Insights and Problems," *New Politics* 6, 4 (Winter 1998), pp. 69-77. The passage on incorporating the insights of both traditions can be found on p. 77 of the latter article.

25 Born in 1870, Luxemburg was brutally murdered (on orders of the leaders of Germany's social democratic government) in the midst of a revolutionary upheaval in 1919. The most extensive scholarly biography of Luxemburg in English is J. P. Nettl, *Rosa Luxemburg* (London: Oxford University Press, 1966), an abridged edition of which was published in 1969. An excellent left-wing political biography is Paul Frolich, *Rosa Luxemburg: Her Life and Work*, trans. Joanna Hoornweg (New York: Monthly Review Press,1972). More recently, Elzbieta Ettinger has added to our knowledge of Luxemburg's life in *Rosa Luxemburg: A Life* (Boston: Beacon Press, 1986), although the treatment of Luxemburg's politics is often superficial. On the failed revolution in which Luxemburg lost her life see Sebastian Haffner, *Failure of a Revolution: Germany 1918-19*, trans. Georg Rapp (New York: The Library Press, 1973) and Chris Harman, *The Lost Revolution: Germany 1918 to 1923* (London: Bookmarks, 1982), Chs. 3-5.

26 Rosa Luxemburg, "What Does the Spartacus League Want?" in Luxemburg, *Selected Political Writings*, ed. Dick Howard (New York: Monthly Review Press, 1971), p. 368.

27 Rosa Luxemburg, "Our Program and the Political Situation" in *Selected Political Writings*, pp. 396-97.

28 Rosa Luxemburg, "The Russian Revolution" in *Rosa Luxemburg Speaks*, ed. Mary-Alice Waters (New York: Pathfinder Press, 1970), pp. 393-94.

29 Kintto Lucas, "Here we are all leaders," *International Viewpoint* 333 (July 2001), pp. 31-32.

30 James Petras, "The Unemployed Workers Movement in Argentina," *Monthly Review* 53, 8 (January 2002).

31 Raquel Gutierrez and Alvaro Garcia Linera, "The rebirth of the multitude," *International Viewpoint* 323 (July-August, 2000), p. 14.

32 I have chosen to adopt Murray Bookchin's term – social ecology – to describe this outlook. While Bookchin's emphases have shifted across a number of writings (see Heider, Ch. 2), he has done important service in foregrounding these issues. See, for instance, Bookchin, "Ecology and Revolutionary Thought" and "Towards a Liberatory Technology" in his *Post-Scarcity Anarchism* (San Francisco: Ramparts Press, 1971). For Marxist writings that cover similar ground, see John Bellamy Foster, *The Vulnerable Planet: A Short Economic History of the Environment* (New York: Monthly Review Press, 1994) and *Marx's Ecology: Materialism and Nature* (New York: Monthly Review Press, 2000); Elmar Altvater, *The Future of the Market*, trans Patrick Camiller (London: Verso Books, 1993), Ch. 5: "Towards an Ecological Critique of Political Economy;" and Ted Benton, ed., *The Greening of Marxism* (New York: Guilford Press, 1996).

33 Note that with this insistence on freedom, I exclude those aspects of (most) cultures which are reactionary, racist, patriarchal and homophobic.

34 Again, this emphasis on non-authoritarian relations precludes individual expressions of "creativity" based upon forms of oppression.

35 Karl Marx, "Theses on Feuerbach" in Marx, *Early Writings*, p. 422.

36 Some proponents of direct action, especially some anarchist currents, argue against any involvement in electoral politics. Others, however, are prepared to support a limited involvement in electoral work so long as this does not become the overriding focus of movement-building and is clearly subordinated to direct action struggles. This tends to be true of some Marxist currents, and also of "autonomists" such as the Ya Basta! Group in Italy.

37 As quoted by Hal Draper, *Karl Marx's Theory of Revolution*, v. 1 (New York: Monthly Review Press, 1977), p. 225.

38 This does not mean that such movements cannot elect organizers and delegates for special purposes. It is to insist, however, that there should be complete democratic control over any elected officers, who ought to be accountable to mass assemblies or conventions, and that the movement ought to be committed to the continual development of new leaders.

39 On the events of 1919 in Germany see Haffner, *Failure of a Revolution*, and Chris Harman, *The Lost Revolution*. The classic study, focussed on the British Labour Party is Ralph Miliband, *Parliamentary Socialism* (London: Merlin Books, 1964). For the record of social democracy in Western Europe see Ian Birchall, *Bailing Out the System: Reformist Socialism in Western Europe, 1944-1985* (London: Bookmarks, 1986).

40 Rosa Luxemburg, "Reform or Revolution" in *Rosa Luxemburg Speaks*, ed. Mary Alice Waters (New York: Pathfinder Press, 1970), p. 78.

41 James Petras and Henry Veltmeyer, *Social Movements and State Power: Argentina, Brazil, Bolivia, Ecuador* (London: Pluto Press, 2005), pp. 69-81.

42 Ibid., pp. 63-64, 69.

43 See Thomas Maack, "The Workers' Party Self-Destructs," *NACLA Report on the Americas* 39, 3 (Nov-Dec 2005), pp. 4, 41.

44 For a good, though somewhat difficult, treatment of these issues, see Stathis Kouvelakis, *Philosophy and Revolution: From Kant to Marx* (London: Verso, 2003), Ch. 5.

45 See McCaughan, p. 88.

46 See Tom Lewis, "Will Evo Morales end Neoliberalism?" *International Socialist Review* 46 (March-April 2006).

47 See John Holloway, *Change the World Without Taking Power: The Meaning of Revolution Today* (London: Pluto Press, 2002).

48 Oscar Olivera, *Cochabamba! Water War In Bolivia* (Cambridge, MA: South End Press, 2004), p. 81.

49 The idea of dual power is one that has been developed in both the Marxist and anarchist traditions, though sometimes with different inflections.

50 Olivera, p. 125.

51 On Russia's 1917 revolution in the factories see Daniel H. Kaiser, *The Workers' Revolution in Russia, 1917: The View from Below* (New York: Cambridge University Press, 1987) and S. A. Smith, *Red Petrograd: Revolution in the Factories 1917-18* (Cambridge: Cambridge University Press, 1983). Greatly valuable is Victor Serge, *Year One of the Russian Revolution*, trans. Peter Sedgwick (Chicago: Holt, Rinehart and Winston, 1972). Russia's hopeful revolution was utterly destroyed as Josef Stalin built his dictatorship in the mid-1920s. But it is important to emphasize that the revolution was decaying and degenerating before Stalin consolidated his hold on power. This theme is taken up in Samuel Farber, *Before Stalinism: The Rise and Fall of Soviet Democracy* (London: Verso Books, 1990). Among other things, Farber is deeply critical of Bolshevik policy during the Kronstadt rebellion of 1921.

52 For more on this point, see Chapter 6.

53 *Anarchists/Les Anarchistes*, distributed by the Northeastern Federation of Anarcho-Communists (NEFAC).

54 Anarcho-syndicalism refers to the political current that saw the building of mass unions (syndicats in French, hence the word syndicalism) that would launch insurrectionary general strikes as the way to overturn capitalism and usher in an anarchist society. For a brief introduction see Guerin, pp. 77-81.

55 Nick Rider, "The Practice of Direct Action: The Barcelona Rent Strike of 1931," *The Northeastern Anarchist* 3 (Fall/Winter 2001), pp. 42, 43. This article is reprinted from *For Anarchism: History, Theory, and Practice* (London: Routledge, 1989).

56 Rosa Luxemburg, "Social Reform or Revolution" in *Selected Political Writings*, p. 52.

57 On Reclaim the Streets see Naomi Klein, *No Logo: Taking on the Brand Bullies* (Toronto: Vintage Canada, 2000), pp. 311-23.

58 Quoted in Zev Singer, "It's about giving him fear," *Ottawa Citizen*, April 22, 2001.

59 George Katsiaficas, *The Imagination of the New Left: A Global Analysis of 1968* (Boston: South End Press, 1987), p. 9.

60 See James Petras, "Latin America: Resurgence of the Left," *New Left Review* 223 (1997), p. 44; and Petras, "You have to take action from below," *Socialist Worker* (US), January 11, 2002.

61 Rosa Luxemburg, "The Mass Strike, the Political Party, and the Trade Unions" in *Rosa Luxemburg Speaks*, pp. 160-61.

62 Ibid., p. 182.

63 Ibid., p. 197.

64 Petras, "You have to take action from below."

65 CAW director of international affairs, Carol Phillips, as quoted by Thomas Walkom, "Melange of Québec protesters united in rethinking strategy," *Toronto Star*, April 28, 2001.

66 See D. C. Masters, *The Winnipeg General Strike* (Toronto: University of Toronto Press, 1973) and Norman Penner, *Winnipeg 1919: The strikers' own history of the Winnipeg General Strike*, 2nd edn. (Toronto: Lorimer, 1975).

67 Farrell Dobbs, *Teamster Rebellion* (New York: Pathfinder Books, 1972), pp. 108-9.

68 Marx's reference to a "movement of the immense majority" is found in "The Communist Manifesto" in Marx, *The Revolutions of 1848*, p. 78.

69 Marx, "Theses on Feuerbach" in *Early Writings*, p. 422.

70 Karl Marx and Frederick Engels, *The German Ideology* (Moscow: Progress Publishers, 1976), p. 60. I have altered the translation to change the gendered language.

71 George Orwell, *Homage to Catalonia* (Harmondsworth: Penguin Books, 1966), pp. 9-10.

72 I have described this elsewhere as "corporeal knowledge." See David McNally, *Bodies of Meaning: Studies on Language, Labor and Liberation* (Albany: State University of New York Press, 2001), Ch. 5.

73 Colin Barker, "Perspectives" in *Revolutionary Rehearsals*, ed. Colin Barker (London: Bookmarks, 1987), pp. 225-26.

74 A point made by Bello and Bullard.

75 Kaisa Walker, "Radicalizing in Québec – a personal account," *The Varsity* (University of Toronto), May 31, 2001.

76 Vercammen, p. 5.

77 Luxemburg, "The Russian Revolution," p. 369.

78 David McNally, "Mass Protests in Québec City: From Anti-Globalization to Anti-Capitalism," *New Politics* 8, 3 (Summer 2001), pp. 79-80.

79 This is true even of an ostensibly more "left-wing" union such as the Canadian Auto Workers whose president repeatedly calls for limiting auto imports from Korea and Japan as the way to preserve jobs of Canadian

auto workers. See, for instance, Steven Chase and Greg Keenan, "Couldn't stop Ford closing, Ottawa says," *Globe and Mail*, January 12, 2001, and Greg Keenan, "CAW urges Ottawa to act on import controls," *Globe and Mail*, February 23, 2002.

80 Behan, p. 18.

81 Eric Hobsbawm, *The Age of Capital, 1848-1875* (New York: Mentor Books, 1975), p. 4.

82 While the literature on 1919 is voluminous, a good starting point is David Mitchell, *1919: Red Mirage* (New York: MacMillan, 1970).

83 In the chronology that follows, I draw especially on the marvelous volume by Tariq Ali and Susan Watkins, *1968: Marching in the Streets* (New York: The Free Press, 1998). Also useful are Katsiaficas, *The Imagination of the New Left*; Daniel Singer, *Prelude to Revolution: France in May 1968* (New York: Hill and Wang, 1970); Chris Harman, *The Fire Last Time* (London: Bookmarks, 1988); Richard Johnson, *The French Communist Party Versus the Students* (New Haven: Yale University Press, 1972); Barbara and John Ehrenreich, *Long March, Short Spring: The Student Uprising at Home and Abroad* (New York: Monthly Review Press, 1969); Patrick Seale and Maureen McConville, *French Revolution 1968* (Harmondsworth: Penguin Books, 1968).

84 See especially Singer, *Prelude to Revolution*, and Johnson.

85 For an excellent analysis of events in Argentina see James Petras and Henry Veltmeyer, *Social Movements and State Power: Argentina, Brazil, Bolivia, Ecuador* (Lodnon: Pluto Press, 2005), Ch. 2.

86. The context was a series of strikes and mass actions against the Ontario Tory government of Mike Harris. For an analysis of this resistance campaign see David Camfield, "Assessing Resistance in Harris's Ontario, 1995-1999 in *Restructuring and Resistance: Canadian Public Policy in an Age of Global Capitalism*, eds. Mike Burke, Colin Mooers and John Shields (Halifax: Fernwood Publishing, 2000), pp. 306-17

87 Duncan Hallas, "Towards a Revolutionary Party" in Hallas and others, *Party and Class* (London: Pluto Press, 1971), p. 9..

88 I borrow the term revolutionary pluralism from conversations with Gary Kinsman, author of *The Regulation of Desire*, 2nd edition (Montreal: Black Rose Books, 1996). While it emphasizes the importance of a diverse range of revolutionary perspectives, the term is not meant to suggest that anti-capitalists should avoid debating important questions. Instead, the term gestures to an ethos that rejects monolithism while cultivating democratic norms of debate and respect for a diversity of positions on a whole range of "non-fundamental" questions (while holding to agreement on issues of fundamental principle such as opposition to racism).

89 The formation a few years ago of the Scottish Socialist Party is one of the most interesting and promising of these experiments.

90 Zapatistas, *Zapatista Encuentro: Documents from the 1996 Encounter for Humanity and Against Neoliberalism* (New York: Seven Stories Press, 1998), p. 13.

8. Conclusion: A Life Worth Living

> Life is what they owe us: the right to govern and to
> govern ourselves, to think and act with a freedom that
> is not exercised over the slavery of others, the right to
> give and receive what is just.
>
> – Zapatistas, "First Declaration for Humanity and
> Against Neoliberalism"

In the days following the New Year's 1994 seizure of San Cristobal and other towns by the Zapatistas, the Mexican Army launched a vicious counter-attack in which at least seventy people were killed. Many others were captured, among them twenty-four-year-old José Pérez. Interrogated as to his motives, the young fighter replied simply, "I want there to be democracy, no more inequality – I am looking for a life worth living."[1]

No one could have put it more clearly or eloquently. In a world of imperial wars, crushing poverty, gender, racial and sexual oppression, and appalling exploitation, the demand for those two basic things – "democracy, no more inequality" – represents nothing less than a call for revolution.

It may seem startling that this heartfelt plea for a life worth living should be so threatening to the powers that be. Yet, it is the nature of capitalism to degrade, dehumanize, and oppress – to commodify everything and to exploit all but the tiny minority who control the world's wealth. Rather than an accident, a perverse distortion of an otherwise fair system, this drive to commodify and exploit is the very nature of the beast. With its blatant pillage of resources, theft of lands, and sweatshop exploitation, contemporary globalization merely reveals more blatantly the essence of capitalism. And so, the simple, poignant demand for a life worth living constitutes a virtual declaration of war.

A life worth living. Whoever tastes of it is transformed. George Orwell glimpsed it in worker-controlled Barcelona in 1936, where "waiters and shop-walkers looked you in the face and treated you as an equal." Witnessing people "trying to behave as human beings and not as cogs in the capitalist machine," Orwell was forever changed.[2] He never forgot that image. All of us who live in this society of infinite commodification would be wise to hold onto it too. For it is this image – of human beings behaving decently, as equals, as humans, not as cogs in the machine – which allows us to remember that a different world is possible.

As the war planes thunder overhead, as death squads murder peasants and indigenous peoples, as factory fires take the lives of young women workers, as people struggle to make it through one day after another in a lifetime of alienated labour, the world's leaders prattle on about "freedom," "progress" and "civilization." At some level, they know they lie. They know it is their interests, and those of their class, that they protect. Yet, so imbued are they with the elitism of their class that they truly believe their interests, and theirs alone, matter, that the vast majority of humankind are little more than beasts of burden. Meanwhile, they pray that elaborate spectacles of "greatness" – of billionaires and movie stars, of generals and politicians who can order a war machine to reduce a country to rubble – will keep that great mass of humanity mesmerized, that, as the rulers of ancient Rome hoped, circuses will pacify the plebians. Yet memory and imagination resist the victory of forgetting and the death of hope.

Discussing the peculiar obsession of some scientists with measuring and anatomizing Albert Einstein's brain, evolutionary biologist Stephen Jay Gould once wrote, "I am, somehow, less interested in the shape and convolutions of Einstein's brain than in the near certainty that people of equal talent have lived and died in cotton fields and sweatshops."[3] Gould's insight is a refusal to be mesmerized, a refusal to buy into the cult of greatness manufactured by the ruling class. It is a reminder that for eons the majority of people have been deprived of the means of attaining their own unique greatness.

Today, once again, oppressed and exploited peoples are rising. Twenty years of capitalist globalization have resulted in such grotesque inequalities, so many shattered hopes and dreams, so much suffering, that resistance has become inevitable. Twenty years ago, Bolivia was, along with Chile, one of the two countries in Latin America most slavishly adhering to the globalization model. As its economic policies were completely revamped by the World Bank and the International Monetary Fund, its leaders sold off the mines, the gas fields and the water supply to multinational capital. Today, Bolivia's people are in revolt. They have smashed a water privatization contract and thrown successive neoliberal presidents out of office. As Washington's neoliberal model for Bolivia goes up in flames, the oppressed are searching for alternatives. The danger is that they will shortchange themselves, by settling for mere tinkering from above.

Desperate to tip the odds in their own favour, the ruling classes and their hangers-on work overtime to discredit the search for real alternatives. They seek to destroy the utopian idea, the dream of a better world. Yet, as Oscar Wilde once wrote, "A map of the world that does not include Utopia is not even worth glancing at."[4] And that is exactly the map our rulers offer us – one from which Utopia, the place of a better future, has been removed. For the poor and the oppressed, however, that place can never entirely disappear. The suffering inflicted by the present order invariably produces a struggle to overcome it. And Utopia lives in the space of that struggle, just as that struggle gives it both reality and truth.[5] Utopia marks a place yet to be found, a place where unnecessary suffering has been eliminated, where solidarity and happiness live. "When the truth cannot be realized within the established

401

social order," wrote one critical thinker, "it always appears to the latter as mere utopia." Yet, the fact that the ruling class, which has perverted the very meaning of words, argues against Utopia "speaks not against, but for, its truth."[6] It is the present order that is false – just listen to the words that roll from the lips of world leaders. Like freedom, truth resides in that place for which the oppressed continue to struggle.

That place is one of community, freedom and solidarity. It is a place in which people have escaped commodification to live as free beings, as ends in themselves, no longer means for the enrichment of a few. It is a place where nature is no longer degraded and destroyed, where people are celebrated in the richness of their diversity. It is a place where life is worth living, the space of hope.

You won't find that place on any official maps. But if you put those maps aside and listen, you can hear its sounds. Listen to the voices from the barrios and the villages, from the *maquiladora* zones and the guerrilla encampments, from the factory quarters and the coffee fields. They are whispering the word freedom. Listen. Hear the poetry of the future. One day, those whispers may become a roar, declaring to all prepared to listen that another world is possible.

Notes

1 Quoted by John Womack, Jr., ed., *Rebellion in Chiapas: an historical reader* (New York: The New Press, 1999), p. 12.
2 George Orwell, *Homage to Catalonia* (Harmondsworth: Penguin Books, 1966), pp. 9-10.
3 Stephen Jay Gould, "Wide Hats and Narrow Minds" in Gould, *The Panda's Thumb: More Reflections in Natural History* (New York: W. W. Norton, 1982), p. 151.
4 As quoted by David Harvey, *Spaces of Hope* (Berkeley: University of California Press, 2000), p. 133.
5 This is the meaning of utopia within Marxism. When Marx and Engels criticized "utopian socialism," what they meant was a socialism rooted in the mind of a detached theorist, not the real struggles of the oppressed. The Marxian utopia is concrete, since it takes as its starting point "the struggles of the present age." On concrete utopia see Ernst Bloch, *The Principle of*

Hope, v. 3, trans. Neville Plaice, Stephen Plaice and Paul Knight (Cambridge, MA: MIT Press, 1995), p. 1373.

6 Herbert Marcuse, "Philosophy and Critical Theory" in Marcuse, *Negations: Essays in Critical Theory* (Boston: Beacon Press, 1968), p. 143.

INDEX

and Empire, 163-67
and Irish, 146-47
psychological dimensions of, 168-73
and unfree labour, 148-51
See also modern racism
Radical democracy, 327-28
Reclaim the Streets, 370
Revolutionary Armed Forces of
Colombia   (FARC), 243
Revolutionary pluralism, 391
Ritter, Scott, 252-53
Roediger, David, 172
Royal African Company, 143, 152
Rumsfeld, Donald, 236, 253, 254
Rwanda, 229-30

Sari, Dita. 307-08
Save Narmada Movement (NBA), 281-82,   384, 368
Seattle protests, 3-4, 15-18, 27
Self-emancipation, 346, 347, 351, 354
Sex trade, 181-83
Sexual violence, 176, 178
Singer, Daniel, 328, 338
Sit-down strikes, 13, 304
Slave revolts, 154
Slavery, and colonialism, 143-45
        and the Irish, 148
        Marx on, 145
        in world today, 185, 187, 193
Smith, Adam, 84, 86
Social ecology, 353, 395n32
Social movement unionism, 317-19
Socialism, 344-49
Socialism from below, 346-48, 349-51
South Korea, 12-14, 58-59
South Korean labour movement, 13-15
Soviet Union, 217, 220, 221, 232, 246,
        343, 383
Stalin, Josef, 214-15, 344
Structural adjustment loans (SALs),
227-   29
Structural adjustment programs (SAPs),
        189, 228, 312
Sub-Saharan Africa, 50-51, 55-58, 229,
31
        and HIV-AIDS, 110
Substitutionism, 356
Suharto, 13, 223, 306-08

Summit of the Americas, 37, 48, 360,
367
Surplus value, 90, 93, 129
Sweatshops. *See* Global Sweatshops

Taiwan Confederation of Trade Unions,
        315
Taliban, 177, 246-47
Terminator seeds, 112
Thailand, 12-13, 59, 111, 182-83, 186
Third World debt, 99, 228
Torture, 68, 73, 249, 252, 255-58
Trade Related Intellectual Property
Rights   (TRIPs), 109, 232
Trade unions. *See* Unions
Trilateral Commission, 275

Unemployed Workers Movement
        (Argentina), 350
Unions, in East Asia, 305-11
        in the global South, 311-18
        two souls of, 302-05
        See also social movement
unionism
United Fruit Company, 218-19
Utopia, 401-02, 402n5

Veltmeyer, Henry, 108
Vietnam war, 224-226, 239, 383

Wade, Robert, 52
Wage labour, 94-95. *See also* working
        class
Wages of whiteness, 168-73
War, 205
        Cold war, 215-17
        First World War, 29-30, 207
        Korean War, 216
        Second World War, 208-09
        Vietnam War, 224-26, 239, 383
        without boundaries, 237-39
Water, 113-14
        privatization in Bolivia, 21-22
White supremacy, 153-55, 165-66, 169
Wilde, Oscar, 401
Williams, Eric, 148
Women, and domestic labour, 180
        in India, 179
        and informal economy, 180-81
        in sex trade, 181-83